Lecture Notes in Computer Science

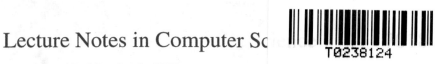

Commenced Publication in 1973
Founding and Former Series Editors:
Gerhard Goos, Juris Hartmanis, and Jan van Leeuwen

Frank Olken Monica Palmirani
Davide Sottara (Eds.)

Rule-Based Modeling and Computing on the Semantic Web

5th International Symposium, RuleML 2011 – America
Ft. Lauderdale, FL, USA, November 3-5, 2011
Proceedings

Springer

Volume Editors

Frank Olken
Frank Olken Consulting
P.O. Box 527, Berkeley, CA, 94701, USA
E-mail: frankolken@gmail.com

Monica Palmirani
University of Bologna
CIRSFID
Via Galliera 3, 40121 Bologna, Italy
E-mail: monica.palmirani@unibo.it

Davide Sottara
University of Bologna
DEIS
Viale Risorgimento 2, 40136 Bologna, Italy
E-mail: davide.sottara@unibo.it

ISSN 0302-9743 e-ISSN 1611-3349
ISBN 978-3-642-24907-5 e-ISBN 978-3-642-24908-2
DOI 10.1007/978-3-642-24908-2
Springer Heidelberg Dordrecht London New York

Library of Congress Control Number: 2011938949

CR Subject Classification (1998): D.2, I.2, C.2.4, H.4, H.3, C.2, I.2.11

LNCS Sublibrary: SL 2 – Programming and Software Engineering

Typesetting: Camera-ready by author, data conversion by Scientific Publishing Services, Chennai, India

Printed on acid-free paper

Springer is part of Springer Science+Business Media (www.springer.com)

Preface

The 5th International Symposium on Rules: Research–Based and Industry–Focused, RuleML–2011@BRF, collocated with the International Business Rules Forum in Fort Lauderdale, Florida, was the second installment of the RuleML Symposium in 2011. The first RuleML-2011 conference was held in conjunction with the 22th International Joint Conference on Artificial Intelligence (IJCAI), in Barcelona, Spain, in July (see *Lecture Notes in Computer Science* 6826, Springer 2011). The second conference was located with the Business Rule Forum, the premier world-wide industry conference on business rules and decisioning, held in Florida, in November of 2011.

RuleML-2011@BRF was a conference created, inspired and supported by the RuleML Initiative. RuleML (`http://www.ruleml.org`) is a non-profit umbrella organization. It includes several Technical Groups, organized by representatives from academia, industry, and government, working on rule technologies and their applications. Its aim is to promote the study, research, and application of rules in heterogeneous, distributed environments such as the Web. The RuleML community has developed the RuleML/XML standard aiming at a complete and modularized XML language for modeling and serializing declarative as well as reactive rules. RuleML maintains effective links with other major international societies. It acts as an intermediary between various "specialized" rule vendors, industrial and academic research groups, as well as standardization bodies such as W3C, OMG, and OASIS. For example, a cooperative arrangement with the NIEM community (National Information Exchange Model, promoted by the US federal government `https://www.niem.gov`), was consolidated with the help of Oracle Corporation.

The International Symposium on Rules, RuleML, has evolved from an annual series of international workshops held since 2002. In 2005 and 2006 it became an international conference. It has become an international symposium since 2007, held jointly with the International Business Rules Forum. For 2011, RuleML envisioned the opportunity to capture the attention of the most advanced AI community with the RuleML-2011@IJCAI conference, and this provided new key actors in the community. For this reason, the Program Committee of RulML-2011@BRF was composed of over 100 experts coming from heterogeneous fields, 16 special Track Chairs, and dedicate Challenge Award Chairs.

Due to its orientation toward the industrial sector, RuleML-2011@BRF included the RuleML Challenge Award which is dedicated to showcasing highlighted demos: this year, the Challenge was dedicated to Rules, Objects and Ontologies. RuleML-2011@BRF intended specifically to create a unique place where academic researchers and industry experts involved in the field of rules and semantic technology could meet and cooperate to go beyond the state of the art and develop applications usable in the market. This cross-fertilization was a focus of RuleML-2011@BRF and, for this reason, particular attention was put on invited presentations and demos coming from universities and companies. RuleML-2011@BRF emphasized the synergy between high-quality research and industry operating in the rule modeling, markup, and reasoning domain, with particular regard to the usability of such rule systems in the Web environment.

The papers in this volume concern the RuleML-2011@BRF conference and include 4 keynote speeches (some in the form of short papers, some as abstracts), 4 invited presentations coming from industry partners and standard organizations, 12 full papers, 5 short papers, 5 invited track and position papers. Sixty authors were involved, coming from 11 different countries from around the world. The contributions covered topics spanning a wide terrain, such as (Web) rules, semantic technology, cross-industry standards, rules and automated reasoning, rule-based distributed/multi-agent systems, rules and norms, rule-based event processing and reaction rules, vocabularies and ontologies, as well as business rules. More and more the rule modeling research needs to be integrated with ontology and semantic techniques [de Sainte Marie; Tang; Gravier et. al.], linguistics aspects [Omrane et. al.], emerging knowledge discovery issues, agent systems and business rule management [Kao; Pitt et. al.; Olivieri et. al.; Feldman; Vanthienen]. It is necessary to learn, in a way that is as much as possible automatic, rules from large volumes of data, from documents available on the Web and from events/actions occurring at specific moments in time [Paschke, Vincent and Springer; Vincent; Skarlatidis et. al.]. On the other hand, it necessary to evolve standards, such as RuleML, to customize rule systems for a multitude of real-world cases [Athan and Boley; Sadnan; Osmun et. al.; Becker and Mackay; Palmirani et. al.] and to permit the development of computable, effective and concrete applications using the new generation of rule-engines [Yahya and Theobald; Zhao et. al.; Grosof]. Finally, databases can be managed using new approaches [Bak et. al; Urban et. al.; Shiva et. al.]; considering the growth of "unstructured data," they need to be normalized and queried using hybrid, rule-based reasoning engines. So, an interesting scenario is emerging from the papers presented in this volume: rules not only support knowledge modeling and reasoning, but also consistency management of large data volumes to get more precise answers to queries [Aasman].

We enriched the RuleML-2011@BRF technical panel with three more specific vertical tracks in emerging fields like cloud computing and rules [Spies; Tabet and Pohlman], NIEM and rules [Webber], as well as clinical semantics and rules [Fry and Sottara; Bragaglia et. al.]. Due to the above efforts, RuleML-2011@BRF, like its predecessors, offered a high-quality, application-oriented program, which was the result of the joint effort of the members of the RuleML-2011@BRF Program Committee.

A special thanks is due to the excellent Program Committee for their hard work in reviewing the submitted papers. Their very useful comments and suggestions were instrumental to achieving a high publication quality. We also thank the symposium authors for submitting good papers, responding to the reviewers' comments, and abiding by our production schedule. We further wish to thank the keynote speakers, industrial partners, and the invited track authors who contributed their interesting talks. We are very grateful to the organizers of the nth14 International Business Rules Forum for enabling this fruitful collocation with RuleML-2011@BRF. We would especially like to thank Rising Media for its support.

The RuleML-2011@BRF Symposium was financially supported by industrial companies, research institutes, and universities, and was technically supported by several professional societies. We wish to thank our sponsors for their financial support, which helped us to offer this event, and for their technical support, which enabled us to attract many high-quality submissions.

August 2011

Frank Olken
Monica Palmirani
Davide Sottara

the keynote speakers, industrial partners and the invited [illegible] who contributed their interesting talks. We are very grateful [illegible] [illegible] business [illegible] [illegible] We would especially like to thank [illegible] its support.

The [illegible] [illegible] [illegible] [illegible] [illegible] [illegible] [illegible] [illegible] [illegible] [illegible]

[illegible]

Conference Organization

General Chairs

Mike Dean	Raytheon BBN Technologies, USA
Said Tabet	RuleML Initiative, USA

Program Chairs

Frank Olken	Frank Olken Consulting, USA
Monica Palmirani	CIRSFID, University of Bologna, Italy
Davide Sottara	DEIS, University of Bologna, Italy

Steering Chairs

Christian de Sainte Marie	IBM ILOG, France
John Hall	Model Systems, UK

Challenge Chairs

Stefano Bragaglia	DEIS, University of Bologna, Italy
Marco Montali	KRDB, Faculty of Computer Science, Italy
Charles Petrie	Stanford University, USA
Mark Proctor	Red Hat, UK

Metadata Chairs and Social Media Chairs

Adrian Paschke	Free University of Berlin, Germany
Nick Bassiliades	Aristotle University of Thessaloniki, Greece
Jie Bao	Rensselaer Polytechnic Institute, USA
Richard Cyganiak	DERI Galway, Ireland
Lina Wolf	HPI Potsdam, Germany

Rule Responder Symposium Planner Chairs

Kalliopi Kravari	Aristotle University of Thessaloniki, Greece
Zhili Zhao	Free University Berlin, Germany

Web Chairs

Luca Cervone	CIRSFID,University of Bologna, Italy
Gkhan Coskun	Free University of Berlin, Germany
Ho-Pun (Brian) Lam	NICTA and University of Queensland, Australia

Track Chairs

Rules, Semantic Technology, and Cross-Industry Standards

Benjamin Grosof	Vulcan Inc., USA

Rules and Automated Reasoning

Eric Jui-Yi Kao	Stanford University, USA

Rule-Based Distributed/Multi-Agent Systems

Nick Bassiliades	Aristotle University of Thessaloniki, Greece

Vocabularies, Ontologies, and Business Rules

Dragan Gasevic	Athabasca University, Canada
Ebrahim Bagheri	Athabasca University, Canada

NIEM and Rules

Devid Webber	Oracle Corporation, USA

Cloud Computing and Rules

Said Tabet	RuleML Initiative, USA

Clinical Semantics and Rules

Emory Fry	Naval Health Research Center San Diego, USA

Fuzzy Rules and Uncertainty

Davide Sottara	DEIS, University of Bologna, Italy

Rules and Norms

Antonino Rotolo	CIRSFID, University of Bologna, Italy
Leon Van Der Torre	University of Luxembourg, Luxembourg
Thomas Gordon	Fraunhofer FOKUS, Germany

Rule-Based Policies, Reputation, and Trust

Pierangela Samarati	University of Milan, Italy

Rule-Based Event Processing and Reaction Rules

Alex Kozlenkov	Betfair Ltd., UK
Adrian Paschke	Free University of Berlin, Germany
Paul Vincent	TIBCO Software, UK

Program Committee

Hassan Ait-Kaci	IBM, Canada
Patrick Albert	IBM ILOG, France
Darko Anicic	FZI Karlsruhe, Germany
Alexander Artikis	NCSR "Demokritos", Greece
Colin Atkinson	University of Mannheim, Germany
Costin Badica	University of Craiova, Romania
Sidney Bailin	Knowledge Evolution, USA
Matteo Baldoni	University of Turin, Italy
Claudio Bartolini	HP Labs, USA
Bernhard Bauer	University of Augsburg, Germany
Moritz Becker	Microsoft Research Cambridge, UK
Mikael Berndtsson	University of Skövde, Sweden
Jonathan Bnayahu	IBM Haifa Research Lab, Israel
Guido Boella	University of Turin, Italy
Peter Bollen	University of Maastricht, The Netherlands
Lars Braubach	University of Hamburg, Germany
Christoph Bussler	Merced Systems, Inc., USA
Jordi Cabot	Universitat Oberta de Catalunya, Spain
Carlos Castro	Universidad Técnica Federico Santa María, Chile
Donald Chapin	Business Semantics Ltd., UK
Federico Chesani	University of Bologna, Italy
Horatiu Cirstea	Loria, France
Kendall Clark	Clark&Parsia, LLC, USA
Matteo Cristani	University of Verona, Italy
Claudia D'Amato	University of Bari, Italy
Celia Da Costa Pereira	Università degli Studi di Milano, Italy
Luiz O. B. Da Silva Santos	University of Twente, The Netherlands
Jens Dietrich	Massey University, New Zealand
Juergen Dix	Technische Universitaet Clausthal, Germany
Weichang Du	University of New Brunswick, Canada
Schahram Dustdar	Vienna University of Technology, Austria
Andreas Eberhart	Fluid Operations, Germany
Jenny Eriksson Lundstrom	Uppsala University, Sweden

Vadim Ermolayev	Zaporozhye National University, Ukraine
Opher Etzion	IBM, Israel
Luis Ferreira Pires	University of Twente, The Netherlands
Michael Fink	TU Wien Austria
Paul Fodor	State University of New York at Stony Brook, USA
Enrico Francesconi	ITTIG-CNR, Italy
Aldo Gangemi	Semantic Technology Lab ISTC-CNR, Italy
Adrian Giurca	Brandenburg University of Technology at Cottbus, Germany
Guido Governatori	NICTA, Australia
Ioannis Hatzilygeroudis	University of Patras, Greece
Stijn Heymans	Technische Universität Wien, Austria
Pascal Hitzler	Wright State University, USA
Chris Hogger	Imperial College, UK
Yuh-Jong Hu	National Chengchi University, Taiwan
Joris Hulstijn	Thauris BV, The Netherlands
Giovambattista Ianni	Università della Calabria, Italy
Minsu Jang	E&T Research Institute, Korea
Mustafa Jarrar	Birzeit University, Palestine
Yiannis Kompatsiaris	Informatics and Telematics Institute, Greece
Manolis Koubarakis	National and Kapodistrian University of Athens, Greece
Wolfgang Laun	Thales Rail Signalling Solutions GesmbH, Austria
Domenico Lembo	La Sapienza Università di Roma, Italy
Francesca Alessandra Lisi	Università di Bari, Italy
Jorge Lobo	IBM Research, USA
Ching Long Yeh	Tatung University, Taiwan
Emiliano Lorini	IRIT, Université Paul Sabatier, France
Thomas Lukasiewicz	University of Oxford, UK
Ian Mackie	Ecole Polytechnique, France
Michael Maher	NICTA, Australia
Christopher Matheus	Vistology, USA
Jing Mei	IBM, China
Zoran Milosevic	Deontik, Australia
Angelo Montanari	University of Udine, Italy
Anamaria Moreira	URFN, Brazil
Leora Morgenstern	IBM, USA
Joerg Mueller	Technische Universität Clausthal, Germany
Chieko Nakabasami	Toyo University, Japan
Grzegorz J. Nalepa	AGH University of Science and Technology, Krakow, Poland
Jose Ignacio Panach	Universidad Politecnica de Valencia, Spain
Adrian Paschke	Free University Berlin, Germany

Fabio Porto	Ecole Polytechnique Fédérale de Lausanne, Switzerland
Alun Preece	Cardiff University, UK
Maher Rahmouni	HP Labs, UK
Dave Reynolds	HP Labs, UK
Graham Rong	MIT Sloan School of Management, USA
Michael Rosemann	Queensland University of Technology, Australia
Giovanni Sartor	University of Bologna, Italy
Marco Seirio	RuleCore, Sweden
Guy Sharon	IBM Haifa, Israel
Silvie Spreeuwenberg	LibRT, The Netherlands
Giorgos Stamou	National Technical University of Athens, Greece
Giorgos Stoilos	National Technical University of Athens, Greece
Nenad Stojanovic	University of Karlsruhe, Germany
Umberto Straccia	ISTI-CNR, Italy
Terrance Swift	XSB Inc.
Jan Vanthienen	Katholieke Universiteit Leuven, Belgium
Wamberto Vasconcelos	University of Aberdeen, UK
George Vouros	University of the Aegean, Greece
Hui Wan	IBM T.J. Watson Research Center, USA
Kewen Wang	Griffith University, Australia
Segev Wasserkrug	IBM, Israel
Shen Yi-Dong	Chongqing University, China

RuleML2011 Sponsors and Parnters

Silver Sponsors

Bronze Sponsors

Model Systems

Partner Organizations

W3C WORLD WIDE WEB consortium

Media Partners

SpringerLink

Table of Contents

Keynotes Speakers (Abstracts and Short Papers)

Invited Presentations (Abstracts)

Rules, Semantic Technology, and Cross-Industry Standards

Rules and Automated Reasoning

Rule-Based Event Processing and Reaction Rules

Vocabularies, Ontologies and Business Rules

Business Executives Sharing Knowledge with Inference Engines: News from the ONTORULE Project

Christian de Sainte Marie

IBM, 9 rue de Verdun, 94253 Gentilly, France
csma@fr.ibm.com

Abstract. The EC-funded ONTORULE project[1] was started with the stated objective of realizing the old promise to give back to the business user the ownership and control over the business knowledge that is put to action in business applications. The project team identified several conditions that must be satisfied to achieve that objective, including: i) the separation of conceptual and operational knowledge at all levels; ii) the separation of the business representation of the knowledge, from its operationalization and from its implementation in business applications; iii) the provision of tooling to handle and manage the mapping between the different representations, the recombination of the different kinds of knowledge, and the inter-dependencies between all of them. This talk will present and discuss the progress made in ONTORULE and the results of the project to this point. All the public deliverables of the project are downloadable from the project web site, as well as technology prototypes, demonstrators, and a list of publications[2].

[1] The ONTORULE project is partially funded by the European Commission under Grant Agreement n° 231875.

[2] www.ontorule-project.eu

F. Olken et al. (Eds.): RuleML 2011 - America, LNCS 7018, p. 1, 2011.

Rule-Enhanced Domain Models for Cloud Security Governance, Risk and Compliance Management

Marcus Spies

Knowledge Management,
LMU University of Munich
marcus.spies@ieee.org

Abstract. As security is essential for the adoption of cloud computing, several standards defining security domains, related threats and controls are being established. The common goal is to enable cloud security specific IT governance for cloud providers and client enterprises alike. The ensuing mandatory control objectives and control processes must cover regulatory compliance and risk management in view of the growing public sector and industry demand for cloud computing services. As of today, most of these standards are represented in textual or semi-structured form. However, the growing adoption of cloud computing calls for tool-supported monitoring and auditing. This paper shows how this can be accomplished based on a domain modelling approach that includes definitions and processing components for rules corresponding to control objectives and various aspects of control processes.

1 Introduction

In July 2011, Microsoft Inc. published a document proving the compliance of the company's Office 365 cloud service with the security requirements from Cloud Controls Matrix (CCM), a standard defined by the Cloud Security Alliance (CSA) [19,34]. The CCM contains requirements for a set of governance and operational domains as defined in the CSA cloud security guidance document [9]. The concept of control as internal regulation and alignment along business goals, IT goals and process goals is in line with current frameworks for IT Governance, most prominently COBIT [36] building on COSO [10]. More specifically, the CSA defined governance domains are

- Governance and Enterprise Risk Management
- Legal and Electronic Discovery
- Compliance and Audit
- Information Lifecycle Management
- Portability and Interoperability.

The operational domains are

F. Olken et al. (Eds.): RuleML 2011 - America, LNCS 7018, pp. 2–9, 2011.

- Traditional Security, Business Continuity and Disaster Recovery
- Data Center Operations
- Incident Response, Notification and Remediation
- Application Security
- Encryption and Key Management
- Identity and Access Management
- Virtualization.

It should be noted that these domains have counterparts in IT governance and IT technical / operational management without reference to cloud computing. However, there are cloud specific issues, risks and requirements that are consequences of the cloud computing service and deployment models with their specific combinations of client vs provider component and data responsibilities, see [4,17]. An prominent example of such a key issue is multi-tenancy – the fact that the same cloud service must be available to multiple clients without resources and / or data sharing or data leakage. In the case of Microsoft Office 365, compliance with this requirement is, among other control activities, demonstrated by the use of organizational units assigned to clients in the Active Directory technology (see [19], p 48).

2 Domain Models and Intelligent Processing in Software Assurance and GRC for Cloud Services

As shown in the introduction, a key use case of CCM is as a requirements matrix against which cloud service providers can document compliance, referring to their technical infrastructure, the operational environment, defined and endorsed business practices etc. In case of [19], additional references to certifications and audits are provided to support the compliance claims even further. This argumentation by reference can be considered as instance of *software assurance* with a particular focus on cloud services.

A further use case of CCM and related requirements frameworks is the provision of registries for compliance or governance related documents, metadata and even operational data, as a recent example (as of summer 2011), CSA is providing a Security, Trust and Assurance Registry (STAR, see the CSA web pages for details). This initiative is related to a more technical set of specifications for IT security related metadata descriptions and exchange by NIST [38].

For simplicity of reference, such registries will be referred to as *GRC-registries* (governance, risk, compliance management) in the sequel. GRC registries with appropriate handling of privacy and benchmarking capabilities are highly important for vendors and clients of software services alike. For a related example of GRC-registries not confined to the software industry, see [20,21].

The industrial and practical impact of both use cases, software assurance and GRC-registries, is, however, limited by the degree to which the assurance or registry data are provided such that at least partly *automated consistency and correctness analyses* are possible. To see this, consider a set of assurance documents by the same vendor – evidently, many arguments will be repeated. Cross references to audit reports or external standards like ISO 27001/2 will appear in a redundant way, as well. Should there be any updates or changes in the arguments needed, they will affect many documents and will require additional checks by service clients, external auditors etc.

In order to enable at least semi-structured representation of assurance and GRC-registry information, an upcoming metadata standard being defined by OCEG (the Open Compliance and Ethics Group) – GRC-XML [35,33]. GRC-XML uses the eXtensible Business Reporting Language XBRL [12]. A key feature of XBRL is the ability to structure data according to multiple connected taxonomies. Taxonomies in XBRL are not limited to generalization / specialization hierarchies, they can contain many additional relationship metadata.

While GRC-XML will enable providers of GRC-registries and software assurance resource collections to eliminate redundancies and simplify the retrieval process of assurance arguments, governance and IT operational practice documentations and the like, there will still be a lot of manual validation work needed in order to check coherence and consistency of assurance profiles and GRC-practices. In addition, a key requirement of compliance management is adaptation to changes in the regulatory environment. Applicable regulations to a software service may be different by industry, country, and the regulations may change in response to detected vulnerabilities, cases of service failures etc. Handling changes and modifications requires adaptation of the data or metadata schemes themselves, not just modifications of the registry entries or the assurance documents. Adaptation of the data or metadata schemes may require renewed validation.

As a consequence, large-scale adaptable GRC-registries and software assurance profile registries require not only a higher degree of data structuring, but also a higher degree of *intelligent processing of the assurance or GRC-controls etc reports and argumentations.*

3 Domain Ontologies and Rules Processing – The State of the Art

The key technologies for intelligent argumentation processing are the logic-based formulation of domain models, often referred to as domain ontologies, together with definition standards and processing components for rules operating on elements of these domain ontologies.

A commonly adopted standard language for domain ontologies is the web ontology language OWL [24] that is subdivided into several sublanguages with increasing levels of expressive power [22]. Domain ontologies are related to UML class diagrams, there even exist partial model transformations defined in a specification by the Object Management Group [25]. However, the logical foundations of a domain ontology have specific advantages w.r.t. to model checking (compare this to the use of OCL in UML modelling, [26,39]). In particular, a reasoner component operating on a domain ontology allows to check –

subsumption of concepts – this allows to work with succinct declarative definitions of object classes, relationships and constraints and to infer a closer description of the permissible individuals.

satisfiability of concepts – this allows to verify consistency with a given system of object classes, relationships and constraints. It can be used in case of an incoming changed rule or regulation for assessing the impact of changes in the regulatory environment on needed adaptations to the domain model.

a state description for missing entities – this allows, e.g., to detect incompleteness in a requirements engineering framework.

In an often used concrete syntax, OWL is based on RDF [15], which is itself a common standard for web content management. Formally, OWL is building on description logic (DL), a subset of first order logic that is decidable [3,11]. Description logic itself has many variants, and the OWL specification is allowing increasingly more of them in order to adapt to industry and user modelling needs. The different sublanguages of OWL allow constructs with different levels of tractability or reasoning complexity. An important OWL 2 profile is the EL profile (EL standing for existential restrictions based language) that is building on recent complexity results for DL with special focus on admissible series of relation compositions (or object property chains, in OWL parlance). While arbitrary relation composition constraints can lead to so-called role-value-maps that are known to be undecidable [3,14], a restriction on the range of the final element of the chain to an existing concept allows for polynomial time satisfiability checks and related reasoning operations [2,1]. A dedicated reasoner for OWL EL is available, see *http://lat.inf.tu-dresden.de/systems/cel/*. Another important OWL 2 profile is RL (for rule language) that lifts some restrictions of OWLs EL for allowing closer proximity to logic programming. A comprehensive recent discussion (including an implementation for the OntoBroker tools suite) can be found in [13]. Some OWL editors allow in addition a dialect OWL full [23] that allows to reify properties and to build higher order classes, which in most cases leads to undecidable class descriptions.

While rules in the OWL RL profile correspond to valid logical inferences in description logic, many practical applications of domain ontologies require additional rule processing. This has been discussed in depth in the specification of RuleML [5] and it has led to a typology of execution contexts and procedural extensions to knowledge representation systems which motivates central rule markup constructs in RuleML [37]. Production rules, event-condition-action (ECA) and reaction rules all are characterized by specific execution contexts – production rules modify knowledge bases (`assert`, `retract`), ECA rules consume events and reaction rules produce events. These functionalities are combined into one layer in [29], it may be extended by an interface description language and process algebras. Finally, a knowlege representation layer adds higher level reasoning capabilities based on temporal and transaction logic to the ReactionRuleML language architecture [29]. In terms of implementation, the constraint handling rules mechanism [14] in combination with a host language and processing system like a sufficiently interoperable Prolog engine (like [7]), can provide many of the required reasoning capabilities, see [14], chapter 6.

4 Basic Architecture of Domain Models for Cloud Security GRC

The goal of the present approach is to set up domain ontologies for cloud security service security governance, risk and compliance management. These ontologies are enriched with business rules addressing various execution contexts related to the assurance and registry use cases. This is important to note since an ontology in the sense of a requirements catalogue would be rather straightforward to set up but not adequate for these use cases. The intended intelligent processing of assurance arguments and data / metadata registries requires to include a generic layer into the ontology architecture. More specifically, the following basic domains should be covered –

Time, time intervals and basic temporal logic for this, we build on the EU FP 6 MUSING project that provided a rich set of ontologies with focus on company and industry data processing related to Basel II assessments, see [16].

IT governance conceptual framework – this currently being built on the basis of [36]. This is a very interesting ontology, since we have very few concept / sub-concept relationships, but a very high amount of object properties and property chains.

IT operational risk and risk management – for this component, we build again on the MUSING results, see [30,16].

IT security management and evaluation essentials – this is being built based on the Common Criteria approach [8], an overview is given in Fig. 1.

Cloud Computing and Cloud Security domain model – this is built based on [4,17], [9] and related documentation.

Structures of argumentation – here, we build on results from the EU ESTRELLA project, specifically the legal knowledge interchange format (LKIF) together with its supporting ontologies [6]. This will be extended to cover the recently published software assurance evidence metamodel and the related argumentation metamodel by the Object Management Group, see [28,27]. For a recent discussion of argumentation structures relevant to cloud services security, see [32].

An important design choice for this work is the level of rule processing needed in various ontology components. In many situations, a model can actually be formulated sufficiently well in description logic such that standard DL reasoners can do the inferencing work. The logical foundation behind this observation is the deduction theorem [18] stating that the antecedent of an implication derivable from an axiomatic theory can be used to extend the theory such that the consequent is now deducible immediately. A short example shall demonstrate where

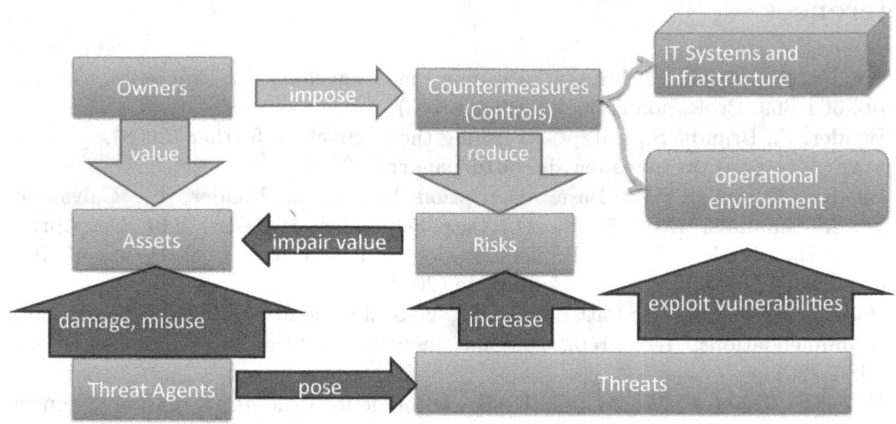

Fig. 1. An overview of the Common Criteria Security scenario model [8], from [31]

the domain model needs enrichment by rules that go beyond logical inferences. Take the following informally stated production rule –

IF *control multi-factor authentication for remote users (CCM, domain security architecture, control SA-07, [34]) is to be implemented,* THEN *set up the system components smartCard authentication* AND *one-time access code generation based on a specific generating keys.*

Note that several choices for multi-factor authentication are possible, therefore, the contrapositive to this rule does not make sense – if some entity chooses not to use smartCards and one-time access code generation devices, it cannot be concluded that this entity fails to implement CCM control SA-07. Therefore, we have a case of needed production rule processing here which should not be artificially integrated into a security domain model.

On the other hand, the following requirement can readily be captured in an appropriate ontologiy domain model – *Policy, process and procedures shall be established to triage security related events and ensure timely and thorough incident management (CCM, domain information security, incident management, control IS-22, [34]).* This control clearly requires a general IT system setup which is needed regardless of specific choices of complex event processing implementations and scoring systems. So, in this case, the recommended approach is conceptual modelling using appropriate constructs in description logic. Building on these, specific ECA rules (see section above) should then be used to model the detailed behaviour of the security event scoring and the entire incident management system.

Acknowledgement. The author is indebted to Marlin Pohlman and Said Tabet, both with EMC and contributing to several of the standards mentioned in this paper, for many insights and fruitful discussions.

References

1. Baader, F., Brandt, S., Lutz, C.: Pushing the el envelope. In: Proceedings IJCAI, pp. 364–369. Professional Book Center (2005)
2. Baader, F., Brandt, S., Lutz, C.: Pushing the el envelope further (2008), http://lat.inf.tu-dresden.de/~clu/papers/
3. Baader, F., Nutt, W.: Basic description logics. In: Baader, F., Calvanese, D., McGuinness, D.L., Nardi, D., Patel-Schneider, P. (eds.) The Description Logic Handbook - Theory, Implementation and Algorithms, ch. 2, pp. 47–100. Cambridge University Press, Cambridge (2004)
4. Badger, L., Grance, T., Patt-Corner, R., Voas, J.: Cloud computing synopsis and recommendations. Tech. rep., National Institute of Standards and Technology, NIST (2011)
5. Boley, H., Tabet, S., Wagner, G.: Design rationale for RuleML: A markup language for semantic web rules (2001)
6. Breuker, J., Hoekstra, R., Boer, A., Berg, K.v.d., Sartot, G., Rubino, R., Wyner, A., Bench-Capon, T., Palmirani, M.: OWL Ontology of Basic Legal Concepts (LKIF-Core) (January 22, 2007), http://www.estrellaproject.org/lkif-core/
7. Carlsson, M.: SICStus prolog users manual. Tech. rep., Swedish Institute of Computer Science (2011)
8. CCRA: Common criteria for information technology security evaluation, parts 1 to 3 (2009)
9. Cloud Security Alliance: Security guidance for critical areas of focus in cloud computing (2010)
10. Committee Of Sponsoring Organizations of the Treadway Commission: Coso erm: Enterprise risk management - integrated framework (2004)
11. Donini, F.: Complexity of reasoning. In: Baader, F., Calvanese, D., McGuinness, D.L., Nardi, D., Patel-Schneider, P. (eds.) The Description Logic Handbook - Theory, Implementation and Algorithms, ch. 3, pp. 101–141. Cambridge University Press, Cambridge (2004)
12. Engel, P., Stanley, M., Hamscher, W., Shuetrim, G., van Kannon, D., Wallis, H.: Extensible Business Reporting Language (XBRL). Recommendation, XBRL International (2003)
13. Feier, C.: Complexity and optimization of combinations of rules and ontologies. Tech. rep., EU-IST Integrated Project (IP) 2009-231875 ONTORULE (2009)
14. Frühwirth, T.: Constraint Handling Rules. Cambridge University Press, Cambridge (2009)
15. Klyne, G., Caroll, J.: Resource description framework (RDF): Concepts and abstract syntax (2009)
16. Leibold, C., Krieger, U., Spies, M.: Ontology based modelling and reasoning in operational risks. In: Kenett, R., Raanan, Y. (eds.) Operational Risk Management: A Practical Approach to Intelligent Data Analysis, pp. 41–60. Wiley, New York (2010)
17. Mell, P., Grance, T.: The NIST definition of cloud computing (2011)
18. Mendelson, E.: Introduction to Mathematical Logic. Chapman Hall, London (1997)
19. Microsoft Inc.: Standard response to request for information security and privay - office365 (2011), http://www.microsoft.com/download/en/details.aspx?id=26647

20. Mitchell, S., Switzer, C.S.: GRC Assessment Tools "Burgundy Book" – Tools for Evaluating Principled Performance 2.0. Open Compliance and Ethics Group, OCEG (2009)
21. Mitchell, S., Switzer, C.S.: GRC Capability Model "Red Book" 2.0. Open Compliance and Ethics Group, OCEG (2009)
22. Motik, B., Grau, B.C., Horrocks, I., Wu, Z., Fokoue, A., Lutz, C.: OWL 2 web ontology language profiles (2009), http://www.w3.org/TR/owl2-profiles/
23. Motik, B., Patel-Schneider, P., Horrocks, I.: OWL 1.1 web ontology language structural specification and functional-style syntax (2006)
24. Motik, B., Patel-Schneider, P., Parsia, B.: OWL 2 web ontology language structural specification and functional-style syntax (2009), http://www.w3.org/TR/owl2-syntax/
25. Object Management Group: Ontology definition metamodel specification (2009)
26. Object Management Group: Object constraint language version 2.2. Tech. rep., Object Management Group (2010)
27. Object Management Group: OMG Argumentation Metamodel (ARM) (2010)
28. Object Management Group: OMG Software Assurance Evidence Metamodel (SAEM) (2010)
29. Paschke, A., Kozlenkov, A., Boley, H., Tabet, S., Kifer, M., Dean, M.: Reaction RuleML – reaction rules for the rule markup language (2007), http://ruleml.org/reaction/
30. Spies, M., Schacher, M., Gubser, R.: Intelligent regulatory compliance. In: Kenett, R., Raanan, Y. (eds.) Operational Risk Management: A Practical Approach to Intelligent Data Analysis, pp. 215–238. Wiley, New York (2010)
31. Spies, M.: Continuous auditing and risk management in cloud computing, http://raw.rutgers.edu/docs/wcars/21wcars/presentations/
32. Spies, M.: A software assurance evidence approach to cloud security. In: Proc. Database and Expert Systems Conference, Toulouse (2011)
33. Spies, M., Tabet, S.: Emerging standards and protocols for governance, risk and compliance management. In: Kajan, E. (ed.) Handbook of Research on E-Business Standards and Protocols: Documents, Data and Advanced Web Technologies. IGI Global, Hershey (in press, 2011)
34. Swain, B., Agcaoili, P., Pohlman, M., Boyle, K.: Cloud controls matrix (2010)
35. Tabet, S., GRC-XML Initiative: GRC-XML Risk and Control Taxonomy Alpha Release (2009)
36. The IT Governance Institute: Control objectives for information and related technology (COBIT®) 4.1. Tech. rep., Information Systems Audit and Control Association (2010)
37. The RuleML Group: Schema specification of RuleML, version 1.0 (2010)
38. Waltermire, D., Quinn, S., Scarfone, K.: The technical specification for the security content automation protocol, SCAP (2010), http://csrc.nist.gov/publications/PubsSPs.html#SP-800-126
39. Warmer, J., Kleppe, A.: The Object Constraint Language – Getting your Models ready for MDA, 2nd edn. Object Technology Series. Addison Wesley, Boston (2003)

Rules, Tables and Decisions: A Family History Tale

Jan Vanthienen

Katholieke Universiteit Leuven
Faculty of Business and Economics
Leuven Institute for Research in Information Systems
Naamsestraat 69
3000 Leuven (Belgium)
jan.vanthienen@econ.kuleuven.be

Abstract. Modeling, managing and implementing complex (business) logic has been a common concern in many approaches, from rule-based systems to declarative process modeling, from complex event processing to decision management, from ontologies to decision model notations, analytics and semantics.

Rules, tables and decisions have a long history and share some common family attributes: independence, consistency, agility and expressive power.

This presentation will show how and why approaches modeling rules, tables and decisions have been successful in the past and what is required for an even more promising future.

F. Olken et al. (Eds.): RuleML 2011 - America, LNCS 7018, p. 10, 2011.

Event-Driven Rules: Experiences in CEP

Paul Vincent

TIBCO Software, London, UK
pvincent@tibco.com

Abstract. Event Driven Architectures (EDA) and Complex Event Processing (CEP) are demonstrating interesting alternatives to the app-server-executing-business-logic approaches that are used in both business and cloud IT deployments today. Applying rules (and rule-based inferences) to events is a natural solution for business event processing, and the benefits of the "event-decision-action" pattern enabled by rules have proved very useful in a number of application cases. Here we introduce how rule-driven CEP is becoming a leading application area for rule technology together with some recent case studies on how declarative rules provide a suitable knowledge representation for event-driven processes in business applications.

F. Olken et al. (Eds.): RuleML 2011 - America, LNCS 7018, p. 11, 2011.

Efficient Rule and Query Execution with CLIF++

Jans Aasman

Franz Inc.
2201 Broadway, Suite 715
Oakland, CA 94612
ja@franz.com

Abstract. CLIF++ is a variant on Common Logic with some interesting extensions. We added aggregates, a query language, and a combination of forward and backward chaining rules. The execution engine for CLIF++ uses our new set based query planner that was developed for efficient SPARQL execution. In our talk we'll show some of these query transformations and show a demo. CLIF++ can be used in all the situations where you need the ability do define first order logic predicates and the ability to active triggers to execute rules when triples are added or deleted.

F. Olken et al. (Eds.): RuleML 2011 - America, LNCS 7018, p. 12, 2011.

Recent Advances in the SILK Knowledge Representation and Its Usage

Benjamin Grosof*

Vulcan Inc.
505 Fifth Ave S
Suite 900
Seattle, WA 98104
BenjaminG@vulcan.com

Abstract. SILK[1] is an expressive Semantic Web rule language and system equipped with scalable reactive higher-order defaults. We present some of its latest novel language features and examples of its usage, including to answer questions about causal processes in college-level biology, e.g., for an e-learning application. A new feature is to permit formulas of more complex form, including quantifiers and disjunction, in prioritized defeasible rules. We also briefly present our progress and lessons to date in interoperating between SILK and ResearchCyc[2]. Part of Vulcan Inc.'s Project Halo[3], SILK integrates and extends recent theoretical and implementation advances in semantic rules and ontologies. It addresses fundamental KR requirements for scaling the Semantic Web to large knowledge bases in science and business that answer questions, proactively supply info, and reason powerfully. SILK radically extends the KR power of W3C OWL RL, SPARQL, and RIF, as well as of SQL and production rules. It includes defaults (cf. Courteous LP), higher-order features (cf. HiLog), frame syntax (cf. F-Logic), external actions (cf. production rules), and sound interchange with the main existing forms of knowledge/data in the Semantic Web and deep Web. These features cope with knowledge quality and context, provide flexible meta-reasoning, and activate knowledge.

* http://www.mit.edu/~bgrosof
[1] http://silk.semwebcentral.org
[2] http://research.cyc.com
[3] http://projecthalo.com

F. Olken et al. (Eds.): RuleML 2011 - America, LNCS 7018, p. 13, 2011.

Rules and OMG Standards

John Hall

Model Systems
17 Melcombe Court
Dorset Square
London MW1 6EP
United Kingdom
john.hall@modelsystems.co.uk

Abstract. The Object Management Group (www.omg.org), founded in 1989, is the largest and longest-standing not-for-profit, open-membership consortium that develops and maintains computer industry specifications. Any organization may join OMG and participate in its standards-setting process. The best-known OMG specifications include the Unified Modeling Language™ (UML®), Model Driven Architecture® (MDA®), Common Object Request Broker Architecture (CORBA®) and Business Process Model and Notation™ (BPMN®). OMG membership includes more than 470 organizations, with half being software end-users in over two dozen vertical markets, and the other half representing almost every large organization in the computer industry and many smaller ones. Most of the organizations that shape enterprise and Internet computing today are represented on OMG's Board of Directors. OMG is an ISO Publicly Available Specification (PAS) submitter, able to submit its specifications directly into ISO's fast-track adoption process. OMG's UML, MetaObject Facility (MOF™) and Interface Definition Language (IDL™) specifications are already ISO standards and ITU-T recommendations. This presentation is focused on OMG specifications that are about rules, including:

- Semantics of Business Vocabulary and Business Rules (SBVR™);
- Production Rule Representation (PRR™);
- Business Motivation Model (BMM™);
- Related work-in-progress and requests for proposals.

It will describe what these specifications contain, and how they are related to other OMG specifications and to the wider realm of rules-related standards.

F. Olken et al. (Eds.): RuleML 2011 - America, LNCS 7018, p. 14, 2011.

Understanding NIEM and Rules Needs

David R.R. Webber

Oracle Corporation
david.webber@oracle.com

1 Introduction

The National Information Exchange Model (NIEM) approach is being adopted for government information sharing applications in the United States, Canada and Mexico. While these XML based message exchanges themselves solve the mechanics of moving data electronically there exists a whole raft of other challenges on both sides of the exchange equation. Senders need help determining when, if and how to distribute information and similarly receivers need to understand how to utilize the information with effective analysis and decision making. Also associated with these information transfers are legal issues of control, privacy, security and auditing. All these are areas where rule agents and rule technologies can be effectively applied to automate aspects of the exchange handling, provide alerts and information checking and then analysis to guide human decision makers. In the arena of healthcare exchanges rule agent participation can alert medical staff to potential life threatening situations and help guide patient care processes to avoid common mistakes and omissions.

These rule areas and needs vary widely from simple scenario checking to complex semantic reasoning about information along with statistical analysis and trend reporting. Similarly case management handling provides challenges in pattern matching, event relating and connecting seemingly disparate information fragments.

Within NIEM the original founding organizations, Department of Homeland Security (DHS) and Department of Justice (DOJ) have now been joined by the Health and Human Services (HHS). As more healthcare related information exchange occurs then additional rule handling needs surface such as medical best practices, patient record management, patient treatment evaluation and drug interaction tracking.

The information exchanges today consist of raw data content in XML formats while associated semantic and ontological information technologies have not been fully applied for NIEM purposes. Given the broad scope of NIEM and the emerging involvement of international partners the technical challenges faced by NIEM implementations are increasing not decreasing. Applying of rules technologies to help solve and ameliorate these can be divided into three categories, short term, medium term planning and long range goals.

2 Short Term Needs

Immediate short term needs revolve around specific application areas and provide the potential for quick wins where rule and agent technology can be applied directly to

F. Olken et al. (Eds.): RuleML 2011 - America, LNCS 7018, pp. 15–16, 2011.

information exchange data points and uses. Most obvious is vocabulary alignment and core component refinement across related domain dictionaries and collections information components. Here inspecting and identifying candidate components and similar and shared components is extremely time consuming and labor intensive when done by hand utilizing spreadsheets and lists of components. Automating comparisons can dramatically reduce the level of effort and enhance communities sharing and reuse through rapid and consistent search and discovery tools. Since effective reuse is critically dependent on selecting the correct components quickly and easily from the overall collections. The OASIS SET Technical Committee work and associated open source tools are instructive in what has already been shown to be possible (OASIS SET TC – http://www.oasis-open.org/committees/set). Similarly the Open II project produced by MITRE Corporation in collaboration with Google, University of California at Irvine, and University of California at Berkeley has tools for comparing sets of domain components (http://www.cs.berkeley.edu/~kuangc/publications/sigmod10-openii.pdf).

A further need is renaming and aligning components to standard Naming and Design Rules (NDR) requirements. Here the open source CAM toolkit (http://www.cameditor.org) has created a set of tools designed to work with ERwin™ data models of components derived from SQL database tables and produce NIEM NDR consistent component sets. The CAM toolkit also includes tools to check the consistency of component names and spellchecking support. Effective analysis of components must be predicated by alignment of names and terms to ensure maximum consistency of the results.

Once such housekeeping has been performed then the next need is to consolidate redundant component collections into their atomic parts for reuse dictionary artifacts. This ensures optimum numbers of components and prevents exponential growth in components as more and more domains are added. For this agent tools need to inspect the actual names of components, separating them into terms and deducing potential similar or equivalent parts. This can use contextual occurrence as well as semantic and linguistic techniques.

The goal of this short term work is to produce core component collections that are optimized for a domain and are rapidly and easily reused when designing and building new information exchanges. NIEM itself has evolved and grown rapidly over the past five years and while manual harmonization of components has occurred.

Design and Implementation of Highly Modular Schemas for XML: Customization of RuleML in Relax NG

Tara Athan[1] and Harold Boley[2]

[1] Athan Services, Ukiah, CA, USA
taraathan@gmail.com

[2] Institute for Information Technology, National Research Council Canada, Fredericton, NB, Canada
harold.boley@nrc.gc.ca

Abstract. We present a re-conceptualization and re-engineering of the non-SWSL portion of the Derivation Rules subfamily of RuleML in the Relax NG Compact (RNC) schema syntax. The benefits arising from RNC schemas include decreased positional sensitivity and greater flexibility in modularization (from fine-grained modular to monolithic), as well as unification of human-readable ("Content Models") and machine-readable (XSD/XML) versions. We introduce a Relax NG schema design pattern, enforced by RNC meta-schemas, that guarantees monotonicity (grammatical extension implies syntactic containment) when any of a large number of small expansion modules are merged. The original fifteen Derivation RuleML sublanguages are thus embedded in a syntactic lattice with hundreds of thousands of languages with semantics inherited from the top language. The original RuleML sublanguages are available through links, and customized languages are available through a GUI web-app. The GUI serves as the front end to a PHP-specified parameterized schema that takes a selection of customization options and returns a schema driver file. These options are encoded to facilitate determination of syntactic containment between any pair of languages. As in earlier (Derivation) RuleML language hierarchies, (logical) expressivity forms the backbone of the language lattice. The (parameterized) RNC schema serves as a pivot format from which XSD schemas, statistically-random XML test instances, monolithic simplified RNC content models, and HTML documentation are automatically generated. The RNC-based re-engineering of Derivation RuleML has already led to the discovery and patching of errata in RuleML versions 0.91 and 1.0, as well as to suggested enhancements of version 1.0 and a newly conceived version 1.1. The specifications of the RNC-based RuleML schemas are maintained at `http://wiki.ruleml.org/index.php/Relax_NG`.

1 Introduction

RuleML is a family of languages for Web rule interchange that was originally specified in Document Type Definitions (DTDs) [W3C98], then switched to XML

F. Olken et al. (Eds.): RuleML 2011 - America, LNCS 7018, pp. 17–32, 2011.

Schema Definition Language (XSD) schemas [TBMM04]. Here we present a re-engineering of the non-SWSL portion of the Derivation Rules subfamily of RuleML in the Relax NG Compact (RNC) schema syntax [ISO08] on the basis of lattice [Nat] and hedge automaton theory (cf. [Mur98]). This novel, RNC schema formalism has already supported the re-conceptualization and transition from RuleML version 0.91 to 1.0, and gave insights for its evolution to version 1.1 and beyond.

Goals. A re-engineering of the RuleML schemas was undertaken to achieve the following:

- **Maximize Alignment with Semantics:** to the extent possible, semantic constraints should be incorporated into the schema.
- **Maximize Customizability:** A fine-grained, highly cohesive, and loosely-coupled modular schema design will allow a user to custom-build a RuleML sublanguage by assembling a selection of modules.
- **Maximize Automation:** The assembly of custom schemas and the production cycle of schema releases should be automated as much as possible.
- **Maximize Reliability:** The new schemas should be exhaustively tested against the existing hand-written XSD schemas and instances, e.g. via automatically-generated testing instances as well as hand-written exemplary instances for 'near-miss' (invalid) and 'corner' (valid) cases.
- **Maximize Extensibility:** The schemas should enable extension by users, as well as RuleML developers.

An Example of Customizable Schema Definition: Equations. In the original RuleML 0.91 family of languages, equations are available from Horn logic languages up, which also include, e.g., negations, disjunction, and quantification. However, equations are also desirable from Hornlog down, e.g. between individual constants in Datalog, even when Datalog is further specialized to only binary relations or to only facts. Hence, in RuleML 1.0, equations should be freely combinable with the other RuleML sublanguages. Similarly, languages with only binary relations in RuleML 0.91 are just allowed for Datalog, but in RuleML 1.0 should be also allowed up the family tree. We thus propose a method to permit free combinations of fine-grained modular features for customizable schema definition.

Of course, it is always possible to author or validate with a more permissive schema, i.e., a schema defining a language that syntactically contains the language of interest. However, a minimal schema improves the efficiency of validation, enhances authoring in a content-completion environment, and improves reliability when a minimal feature set is mandated by specification.

In the previous modularization approach, a significant redefinition of the XSD schema would be required to add equations to a smaller sublanguage, such as `bindatagroundfact`. With the re-engineered Relax NG schema, we may accomplish this task with the following steps:

1. Open the GUI[1] and select only the language features desired. For the smallest language with equations, we select the first options in the radio button sets (Expressivity - Atomic Formulas, Default Attributes - Required to be Absent, and Term Sequences - None) and deselect all checkboxes except Equations.
2. Click the Refresh Schema button to see the corresponding schema driver file and the URL that may be used to perform validation. This long URL has base `http://ruleml.org/1.0/relaxng/schema_rnc.php`, which points to the PHP-specified parameterized schema, and a query string `?backbone=x0&default=x5&...` that encodes the selected language options. Notice the schema driver file contains only nine modules, out of over fifty available.
3. Associate the schema driver file with an xml file using the `xml-model` processing instruction [GK10], where the value of `href` is the URL obtained in step 2 with all ampersands escaped as `&`.
4. Edit the xml file with an xml-model processor, such as oXygen[2], to create equations such as[3]:

```
<?xml-model href=
"http://ruleml.org/1.0/relaxng/schema_rnc.php?backbone=x0&amp;default=x5&amp;termseq=x0&amp;
lng=x1&amp;propo=x0&amp;implies=x0&amp;terms=x10&amp;quant=x0&amp;expr=x0&amp;serial=x0"
type="application/relax-ng-compact-syntax"?>
<RuleML xmlns="..."><Assert><formula>
    <Equal>
      <left><Ind>Lady Gaga</Ind></left>
      <right><Ind>Stefani Joanne Angelina Germanotta</Ind></right>
    </Equal>
</formula></Assert></RuleML>
```

The Original Fifteen Languages as a Lattice. A partially-ordered set (poset) in which every pair of elements has both a greatest lower bound (glb, infimum) and a least upper bound (lub, supremum) in the set is called a lattice. The fifteen languages in the non-SWSL[4] portion of the Derivation RuleML language subfamily satisfies the lattice conditions with respect to the partial ordering imposed by syntactic containment, as shown in Figure 1 and may be embedded in the larger lattice described in Section 2.1. The binary numbers below each named language demonstrate how a code can be used to identify unnamed languages uniquely as well as facilitate the determination of order by bit-wise comparison. These codes were generated from the lattice diagram, starting from the bottom and proceeding through the diagram upward and left-to-right, as shown below. Given a language whose code has not yet been determined:

1. determine the conjunction (i.e. bit-wise maximum) of all of its sublanguages;

[1] GUI: `http://ruleml.org/1.0/gui/`

[2] oXygen: `http://www.oxygenxml.com/`

[3] The RuleML 1.0 namespace is still open; it will appear at `http://ruleml.org/1.0/`

[4] An extension of Hornlog RuleML was developed to serialize SWSL (Semantic Web Services Language) in XML, whose syntax goes significantly beyond the other languages (`http://www.w3.org/Submission/SWSF-SWSL/#sec-markup`), and so cannot be accommodated in the lattice shown in Figure 1.

2. if the conjunction is not equal to any other code assigned so far, it may be selected as the code, but if the language contains features that are not in any of its sublanguages, one may choose to proceed to step 3;
3. otherwise add a 1 at the least-significant 'unused' (i.e. so far not used anywhere else in the lattice) bit to the conjunction from step 1.

The choices made in step 2 of this non-deterministic procedure when applied to generating the 'original fifteen' are seen in Figure 1 (note caption for caveat).

Overview of the Relax NG Language. The Relax NG language was chosen for this re-engineering effort because of its decreased positional sensitivity and its greater flexibility in modularization (from fine-grained modular to monolithic), as well as unification of human-readable ("Content Models") and machine-readable (XSD/XML) versions. These benefits are achieved through unique features of the Relax NG schema language [ISO08], including the `notAllowed` reserved word to create abstract patterns, definitions with `combine` attributes (|=, &= in the compact syntax) to merge definitions that are decomposed across modules, and the interleave operator & (a generalization of the `xsd:all` group) to create order-insensitive content models. Because Relax NG is theoretically grounded in *hedge automaton* theory, modularization is always possible since regular hedge languages are closed under the operations of intersection, union and complement [Mur98].

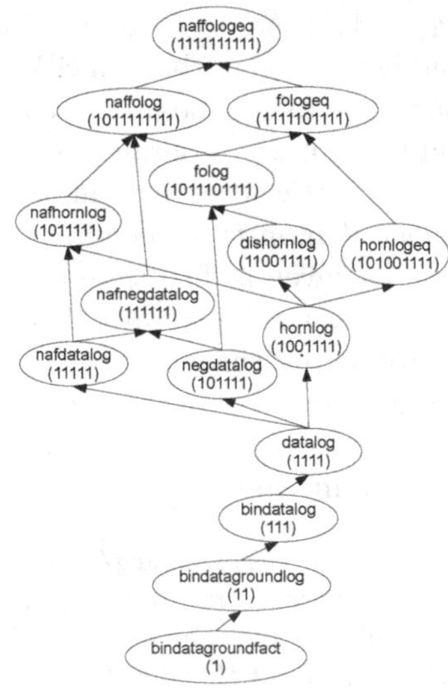

Fig. 1. Hasse diagram of the 'original fifteen' language lattice with arrows, and illustrative binary codes, indicating syntactic containment. The code assignment was generated by the procedure described in Section 1, but is not unique for this poset, as it depends on the way the Hasse diagram has been drawn (as a 2-D projection of a unique Directed-Acyclic Graph), as well as choices made in the implementation of the non-deterministic procedure. When the partial order of post-schema validation infoset (PSVI) containment (see Section A) is considered, the 'original fifteen' violate the lattice conditions due to the use of default attributes. Therefore, the implemented schemas use a different coding that reflects grammatical, syntactic, and PSVI containment, described in Section 2.1.

2 Design of the RuleML Relax NG Schema

The design consists of several components with different levels of abstraction. For the beginning user, URL redirects[5] provide default access to serializations[6] of the original fifteen RuleML sublanguages. For the advanced user, the GUI web-app allows selection among many syntactic options and computes the URL of the dynamically-generated driver file for the customized language. A PHP-specified parameterized schema[7] implements the mapping from the syntactic options to the corresponding subsets of modules.

2.1 GUI Web-App and Language Options Encoding

The GUI web-app consists of an XHTML form that accepts a user's input of language options through radio buttons and check boxes. A URL that points to a PHP script, described in the next section, with a query string of the language options encoded compactly, is generated by the form and may be used directly for validation of instance documents.

The language options are organized into facets of semantically-related dimensions. Each dimension is Boolean, and the dimensions are freely combinable, although some are 'dormant' (produce no syntactic or semantic change) unless an 'activating option' is also selected. For example, the slot cardinality attribute, `card`, is dormant unless slotted arguments are included, because this attribute is only allowed on the `slot` element. In the GUI, each dormant option is disabled unless at least one of its activating options is selected. For each group of options (e.g. backbone, default, ...), the Boolean values are treated as bits of a hexadecimal number. The full selection of options is assembled as a hexadecimal-valued query string[8] e.g.

```
backbone=x3f&termseq=x7&default=x3&serial=xf&propo=x3f}
        &implies=x7&terms=xf3f&quant=x7&expr=xf&lng=x1
```

to form a unique syntactic code for each language. Bit-wise dominance between two codes is equivalent to syntactic containment of the corresponding languages. The option facets are described in the following subsections, with the facet parameter name(s) given parenthetically in the title of each subsection.

Backbone (backbone). The logical connectives of propositional logic and the variables and quantifiers of predicate logic are implemented in independent modules so that a great variety of expressivities may be constructed by 'mixing-in' various schema modules. However, only certain combinations of these modules are accessible from the GUI, corresponding to an unbranched hierarchy from ground atomic formulas to full first-order logic, which we call the "backbone" of the language lattice (see Figure 2).

---

[5] E.g., the URL for Datalog in relaxed-form RNC: `http://ruleml.org/0.91/relaxng/datalog_relaxed.rnc`

[6] See the 'Serialization' subsection of Section 2.1.

[7] PHP: `http://ruleml.org/0.91/relaxng/schema_rnc.php`

[8] When the query string is used in an `href` attribute, `&` should be escaped as `&`.

Positional Arguments (termseq). In Atomic formulas and in Expressions, the sequence of positional arguments (as opposed to the bag of slotted arguments) may be necessarily empty (None), limited to empty or length two (Binary), or allowed to be of arbitrary finite length (Polyadic) (see Figure 3).

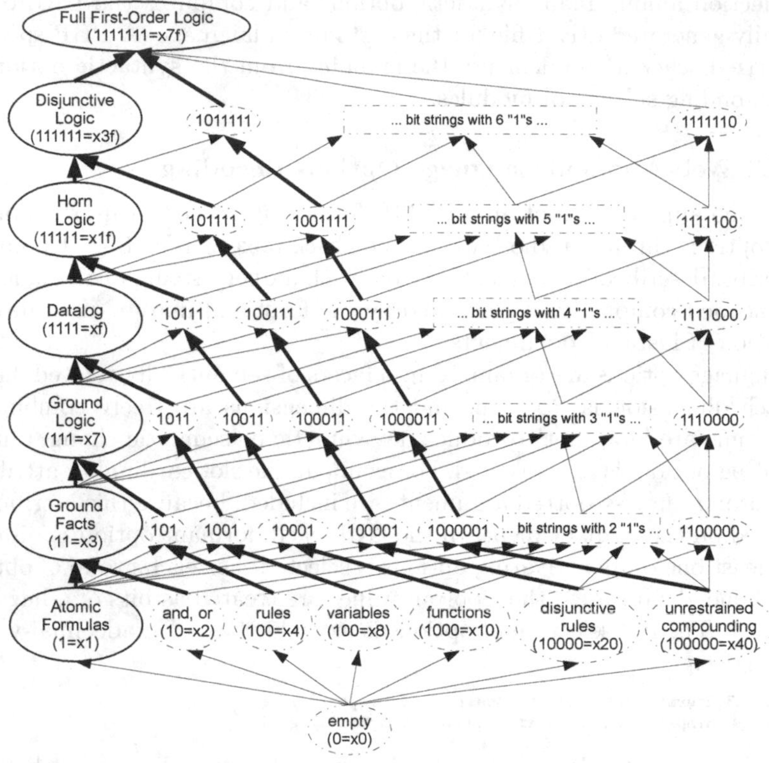

Fig. 2. Hasse diagram of the backbone sublattice with binary and hexadecimal codes. The options within solid ovals are available from the GUI, the others can be accessed through the parameterized schema, as described in Section 2.2.

Attributes with Default Values (default). In the RuleML XSD schemas, certain attributes are defined with default values. In some situations it may be advantageous to eliminate the default values so that the language is more compact; this is the first option, "Required to be Absent". The second option, "Required to be Present", allows the Relax NG schema to emulate the post-schema validation infoset (PSVI) of instances validated against XSD schemas, by requiring attributes having default values to be present. This constraint is necessary for PSVI emulation because Relax NG validation does not allow modification of the info-set, in contrast to XSD validation, which inserts attributes having default values when they are absent in the instance document. The third alternative, "Optional", allows such attributes to be absent or present, and thus is the *join* (w.r.t. lattices, the least upper bound) of the former two languages.

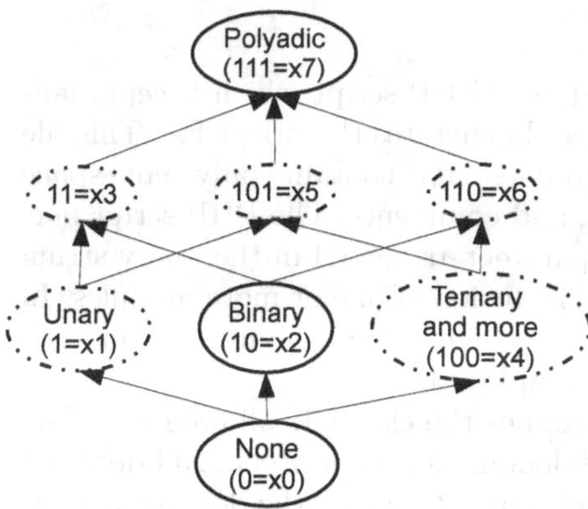

Fig. 3. Hasse diagram for the term sequence facet. Options available from the GUI include polyadic term sequences, binary term sequences, and the absence of term sequences ("None"), the latter corresponding to propositional and frame-like languages. Additional options such as unary term sequences are not yet available, but are accommodated in the parameter encoding for this facet for future implementation.

Serialization (serial). Only three serialization forms are implemented in the URL redirects: the "relaxed-", "normal-" and "mixed- form" serializations. Advanced users have additional options available through the GUI web-app. The *normal-form* serialization, corresponding to all of the serialization options unchecked, realizes canonical ordering of child elements and required 'striping'[9] as well as the "Required to be Present" treatment of attributes with default values described above in Section 2.1. The *relaxed-form* serialization, corresponding to all of the serialization options checked, is maximally insensitive to the order of child elements while still retaining unambiguous semantics, and has optional striping, as well as the "Optional" treatment of attributes with default values.[10] A *mixed-form* schema is also implemented to reproduce the syntax of the original XSD schemas for testing purposes, but is not available from the GUI.

Mix-Ins (propo, implies, terms, quant, expr). Additional syntactic options include equivalence, meta-logic, negations, semantic variants of implications, expressions and equations, slots, rest variables, object identifiers, resource identifiers (IRIs), degree of uncertainty, explicit typing, reification, and skolem constants.

Alternate Names (lng). The default abbreviated English element and attribute names may be replaced by long English names. The modules implementing that replacement serve as a template for other alternate name sets, enabling internationalization. Expansion modules are used to add the alternate names, and contraction modules are required to remove the default names. The language lattice of the alternate name set is isomorphic to that of the default name set.

---

9 *Striping*: the alternation of 'Node' (upper-cased 'Type-tag') elements with 'edge' (lower-cased 'role-tag') elements.

10 Additional options for disabling explicit datatyping and the schema location attribute are necessary for the normal form as a workaround to a bug in the translator from Relax NG to XSD schemas.

2.2 Parameterized Schema

The parameterized schema is implemented as a PHP script which accepts language options encoded in a query string[11] and generates the driver file. This file assembles the grammar by inclusion of modules, and contains only namespace declarations, start and include statements, and comments. The PHP script performs a monotonic transformation of the parameters passed in the query string into Boolean variables, each indicating the inclusion of one or more modules. In a few cases, a pair of modules is replaced by one syntactically equivalent module so that simpler grammar patterns may be employed.

The start pattern of the driver file determines the elements allowed as a document root. In general, the specification of document root in Relax NG does not translate to XSD schemas, where any global element may be the document root. In the RuleML driver files, the start pattern is constructed as a choice among all globally defined elements, in order to maintain equivalence to XSD schemas, and to allow RuleML fragments to validate.

2.3 Design Patterns for Modules

The modularization of the parameterized schema is constrained by the requirement of realizing the original fifteen languages. However, there is still considerable freedom in the design. Certain design decisions influence the nature of the "enriched" lattice by altering the coverage of the new languages that are created. Our design pattern has a number of aspects in common with the XHTML 2.0 Relax NG schema [IG09], but is significantly more constrained in order to maximize both decoupling and monotonicity of the modular system.

Module Decoupling. Like XHTML2.0 and the existing RuleML XSD schemas, the Relax NG schema uses a flat schema design pattern, which declares all the elements globally using named patterns, enhancing extensibility. There are many ways to decouple such patterns in Relax NG, including using abstract patterns, unreachable patterns and 'linking modules'. For example, in RuleML a `Negation` formula (strong negation) is allowed to occur within a `Naf` formula (weak negation, `Negation as failure`), provided both kinds of negation are included in the language. The RNC code that activates this coupling is

```
NafFormula.choice |= Negation-node.choice
```

We call definitions of one pattern as a formula of other named patterns *linking* definitions, to distinguish them from definitions that explicitly define elements or attributes. We can place this linking definition in the `Negation As Failure` module `naf_module.rnc` or the `Negation` module `neg_module.rnc`, or potentially another module.

[11] The query string may be manually edited to obtain some options not directly available from the GUI.

Unreachable Patterns: The linking definition may be placed in the `Negation` module. If a language includes strong but not weak negation, the `NafFormula.choice` pattern is valid but unreachable. This approach is efficient in lines of code, but can be hard to read in modular form, since the definition of some patterns, in this case `NafFormula.choice`, is fragmented across modules.

Abstract Patterns: If the linking definition is not placed in the `Negation As Failure` module, the module where it occurs will be invalid on its own unless we add an additional definition to make the `Negation-node.choice` pattern abstract. In Relax NG Compact (RNC) syntax, an abstract pattern is created with the `notAllowed` reserved word as follows:

```
Negation-node.choice |= notAllowed
```

If we place the linking definition into the `Negation` module, then the abstract pattern is overridden whenever this module is included, and the link is activated if both negation modules are included in the language. Having a large number of `notAllowed` definitions causes the code to look cluttered and to be more difficult to maintain, so these definitions are collected into a single 'initialization' module, which is included in every schema driver file. Similarly, patterns combined with the interleave attribute are initialized `empty`.

Linking Modules: If the linking definition is placed in a third 'linking' module, the greatest flexibility would be attained, allowing the decision to couple the two kinds of negation to be made independent of their inclusion in the language. *Linking* modules contain linking definitions, but no new element or attribute definitions. The patterns on both sides of the link must be defined in the initialization module to ensure that the modules may be combined freely to form a valid grammar.

In RuleML/RNC, we use the Linking Module design whenever feasible, as this provides maximum modularity. In particular, this design pattern is used to implement the transition from the Datalog / Horn logic languages to the full first-order logic languages without resorting to redefinition, by placing linking definitions for unrestricted formula compounding into a *folog* expansion module.

Monotonicity from Segregated Names. In Relax NG schemas, pattern names are the non-terminal symbols used to write production rules. One of the features of our schema design pattern is segregation of pattern names according to the allowed value of the `combine` attribute of their definitions. The segregated naming design pattern has been specified in a set of meta-schemas[12] in the RNC language, that can be used to validate base grammars, and expansion and contraction modules after translation into the XML-based Relax NG syntax. To illustrate the constraints on these categories, we draw examples from several RuleML modules.

An extension point and several abstract patterns for equality are initialized in `init_expansion_module.rnc` as follows:

[12] `http://www.ruleml.org/1.0/designPattern`

```
Equal-node.choice |= notAllowed     # for alternate names of equality element
Equal-datt.choice |= notAllowed     # for required attributes of equality element
reEqual.attlist &= empty            # for optional attributes of equality element
Equal.header &= empty               # for modifying children of equality element
Equal.main |= notAllowed            # for main content of equality element
```

In `equal_expansion_module.rnc`, the above patterns are assembled as follows:

```
Equal-node.choice |= Equal.Node.def
Equal.Node.def =
    element Equal { (Equal-datt.choice & reEqual.attlist), Equal.header, Equal.main }
Equal.header &= SimpleFormula.header?
Equal.main |= leftSide-edge.choice, rightSide-edge.choice
```

Additional definitions provide the patterns for the left- and right-hand sides. In `long_name_expansion_module.rnc` we have

```
Equation-node.choice |= Equation.Node.def
Equation.Node.def =
    element Equation { (Equal-datt.choice & reEqual.attlist), Equal.header, Equal.main }
```

In `short_name_contraction_module.rnc` we have

```
Equal.Node.def &= notAllowed
```

These schema snippets illustrate the full range of definitions permitted in the Relax NG schema design pattern. We utilize three categories of pattern names.

Choice Combine: In base grammars and expansion modules, patterns with names from the choice category must be defined with the choice combine operator `|=`. In the example above, `Equal.choice` and `Equal.main` are names in the choice category. In practice, choice patterns are defined as `notAllowed` in the initialization expansion module, and then overridden in expansion modules, as shown above. Choice combine definitions are not allowed in contraction modules.

No Combine: In base grammars and expansion modules, patterns with names from the no-combine category must be defined, with =. In base grammars and contraction modules, it is permitted to have definitions having names from this category with the combine attribute `interleave`, whose pattern is the notAllowed reserved word. We use this construction in the alternate names modules, as shown above, to remove abbreviated element names when they are replaced with long or internationalized names. Because neither of the definitions

```
Equal.Node.def &= empty
Equal.Node.def |= notAllowed
```

would be permitted in the intialization expansion module, the names in the no-combine category are never initialized. This introduces limitations on how abstract components may be defined. To define abstract elements and attributes, we introduce a more abstract choice pattern, such as `Equal-node.choice`, as shown above. Such choice patterns are extension points that hold alternate name elements or alternate constructions that serve the same role in the grammar, and unify elements that have similar semantics.

Interleave Combine: In base grammars and expansion modules, patterns with names from the interleave combine category must be defined with the interleave combine operator &=. Names from the interleave combine category may not be defined in contraction modules. The interleave combine is used to initialize interleave patterns, such as lists of optional attributes, as empty. Other uses are to add attributes to an attribute list, and, in the order-insensitive syntaxes, to add children to the interleave header patterns, as shown above for the `Equal` element. An additional constraint is required to attain monotonicity. In an expansion module, the right-hand side of a definition with a combine attribute of interleave must be optional (`?`), zero-or-more (`*`), or empty, as shown above for the `reEqual.attlist` pattern.

2.4 Transformation

The RNC parameterized schema serves as a pivot format from which XSD schemas, statistically-random XML test instances, monolithic simplified RNC content models, and HTML documentation are automatically generated.

Auto-generated Normal Form XSD. The Jing/Trang software is used to transform the parameterized schema and included modules into monolithic normal-form or mixed-form XSD schemas as follows:

- Jing[13] with switch `s` is used for simplification of modular RNC schemas into monolithic Relax NG XML syntax (RNG);
- Trang[13] is used for transformation of RNG schemas into XSD.

The XSDs corresponding to the original fifteen RuleML sublanguages are made available for remote validation[14] or download in a zip archive that also includes the PHP script for the parameterized schema and Windows batch scripts for transformation and validation.[15]

Instance Generation. The oXygen software package is used to generate instances from XSD schemas. Instances generated from the original XSD schemas are used to exhaustively test that the RNC relaxed-form languages syntactically contain the corresponding original RuleML language, while instances of the normal- and mixed-form XSD schemas auto-generated from RNC are similarly employed for testing for syntactic containment or equivalence, respectively, relative to the original languages.

Simplified RNC as Content Model. The `jing -s` transformation described in Section 2.4 is also the first step in generating the simplified, monolithic RNC

13 `http://code.google.com/p/jing-trang/`

14 Horn logic in normal-form XSD:
`http://www.ruleml.org/0.91/xsng/hornlog_normal.xsd`

15 Normal-form Zip Archive:
`http://ruleml.org/0.91/relaxng/ruleml0-91_normal_rnc.zip`

schemas that serve as auto-generated content-model documentation, replacing error-prone hand-generated documentation, the second step being transformation by `trang` back into RNC. The `jing -s` simplification is a by-product of the validation process, and so does not provide the ideal documentation, as meaningful pattern names, e.g. `formula-Query.Node.def`, are replaced by simplified names, e.g. `formula_3`, that somewhat obfuscate meaning in the translation. Nevertheless, this is an easy and highly reliable method for condensing the modular grammar into a monolithic, and more human-readable, form.

HTML Documentation of Syntax and Semantics. Absent an application to generate documentation directly from Relax NG schemas, chaining `Trang` transformation into XSD with oXygen documentation tools for XSD schemas provides this capability to some extent. Relax NG annotations, which are preserved under Trang transformation, provide the semantics of components. The documentation need only by prepared for the top language[16], as sublanguages inherit their semantics from the top language.

3 Implementation of the RuleML Schema Design

The RNC-based re-engineering of Derivation RuleML has already led to the discovery and patching of errata in RuleML versions 0.91 and 1.0, as well as to suggested enhancements of version 1.0 and a newly conceived version 1.1.

3.1 Implementation in RuleML 0.91

The RNC implementation for RuleML 0.91 reproduces the previously released RuleML 0.91 sublanguages, with the exception of the following patches, which fix errata[17] discovered during the Relax NG re-engineering:

- Accidental omission of type declarations in the content model of `Rulebase`, unexpectedly allowing arbitrary content in some elements.
- Relaxation of order sensitivity resulted in an overly general content model for atomic formulas, expressions, and some types of generalized lists, allowing semantically-incorrect multiple occurrences of rest variables.

In addition to the fifteen original RuleML 0.91 sublanguages, the language lattice generated by the parameterized RNC schema permits many other languages. A few notable features of the thus enriched language lattice are listed here:

- Equations are made available at all levels of expressivity.
- A short URL (`http://ruleml.org/0.91/rnc`) for the top RuleML language redirects to the parameterized schema of the most inclusive language (except for alternate element names).
- Propositional languages are introduced by allowing an option that requires positional argument sequences to be empty. To realize this, the pattern for

[16] `http://www.ruleml.org/0.91/relaxng/naffologeq_relaxed.rnc`

[17] `http://wiki.ruleml.org/index.php/XSD-Errata0.91#RuleML_0.91_XSD_Errata`

the positional arguments in atomic formulas is initialized as empty, and only extended in optional modules for binary and polyadic term sequences.
- Expansions of the propositional languages with slots and/or object identifiers provide a pure frame-like and/or object-oriented syntax.
- The option to restrict positional argument sequences to zero or two members (as in the RuleML `bin` languages) is made available at all backbone levels. At present, the restriction is applied simultaneously to atomic formulas, expressions and plexes (generalized lists); this may be relaxed later.
- More alternatives are available for stripe-skipping and child order in `Implies` and `Entails`, including skipping the stripe of only one child (`body` or `head` in 0.91, `if` or `then` in 1.0) and simultaneously relaxing the order constraints on these children. Canonical ordering (`body` before `head`) is only imposed when both stripes are skipped. The GUI allows stripe-skipping and order-insensitivity to be selected independently.

3.2 Implementation in RuleML 1.0

The Relax NG schemas for Derivation RuleML 1.0 are a relatively small upgrade from the 0.91 versions. We adopt several name changes already incorporated into the RuleML 1.0 XSD schemas [BPS10]. Beyond Derivation RuleML, we consider Relax NG versions of all of Deliberation RuleML, including higher order logic and modal logic, as well as of Reaction RuleML, including actions and events.

3.3 Preview of Proposed RuleML 1.1

A primary goal of the proposed RuleML 1.1 revision is alignment with semantics, including removal of semantically-invalid constructs that were previously included because of limitations of XSD. Such constructs can be identified through a more formal specification of the semantics, as in PSOA RuleML [Bol11] and the planned Common Logic (CL) RuleML, and a mapping of syntactic sugar to the corresponding traditional first-order logic statements.
- The entire Fuzzy RuleML specification [DPSS06] will be implemented, where all formulas, not only `Atoms`, may have a `degree` (of uncertainty) child.
- Following the recommendations from [Vli03], for all terminal elements except `Data` and also for all attributes with arbitrary values, the `xs:string` datatype will be replaced by `xs:token`, which has the same lexical space as `xs:string`, but its value space consists of lists of tokens separated by single spaces. This is appropriate because RuleML is for the most part a 'data-oriented' application where white space is not significant, other than as a token separator. This will allow users, e.g., to more easily extend the schema to a restricted vocabulary without concern for white-space multiplicity.
- Within `Entails`, elements `if` and `then` will be allowed formulas as children, in addition to formulas wrapped in a `Rulebase` element, increasing module independence.
- The performatives module will be decomposed to separate the definition of the `Query` element from the definitions of `Assert` and `Retract`, allowing the

creation of a knowledge-base language (`Assert` and `Retract` performatives only) and a query language. These languages are already being used in OO jDREW [BBH+05].
- The content model of `Reify` will be restricted to Node elements, to remove the meaningless reification of edge elements.
- The `Data` element will be split into two (namely, `Data` and `Structure`), one having simple content (cf. XML Schema Part 2, Datatypes [BM04]) and the other complex content (cf. XML Schema Part 1 and Relax NG). This will give `Data` back its original 'leaf-level', `Individual`-like meaning and reserve the new `Structure` for 'tree-level', `Expression`-like content. This is necessary to allow the restriction of `Reify` described above while maintaining auto-translation from RNC normal-form to XSD, and is also desirable to avoid a definition for `Data` that mixes simple and complex types.
- Context-sensitive constraints, such as "`Functions` within `Equals` within an `Equivalent` must be either interpreted (`per value`) on both sides or uninterpreted (`per copy`) on both sides", will be realized in RNC schemas, but are not translatable to XSD (without Schematron), as they require non-deteriministic patterns.

4 Conclusions

Through the re-conceptualization and re-engineering of the RuleML schemas, considerable progress has been made towards the goals stated in Section 1:

To increase alignment with the semantics, names were assigned to recurring grammar patterns, e. g. formulas allowed in conclusions, enabling pattern reuse.

In order to increase customizability, a schema design pattern was developed which allowed us to build a system with over fifty freely combinable modules, leading to more than $2^{50} > 10^{15}$ grammars generating an estimated 300,000 different (and meaningful) languages. Further, we used the partial-order relations of containment (of grammars and languages) to organize the resulting grammars and their generated languages into lattices, related by order-preserving mappings, and labeled by codes that facilitate the determination of containment between any pair of grammars or languages.

To increase automation and reliability, we developed a GUI, a PHP-specified parameterized schema, scripts for transformation and validation, and meta-schemas to enforce the schema design.

To increase extensibility, numerous extensions points have been introduced, as named patterns. The use of such extension points has been illustrated by modules that implement an alternate element name set. Further development of the RuleML languages will take advantage of this extensibility to introduce new features in versions 1.1 and beyond.

References

[BBH+05] Ball, M., Boley, H., Hirtle, D., Mei, J., Spencer, B.: The OO jDREW Reference Implementation of RuleML. In: Adi, A., Stoutenburg, S., Tabet, S. (eds.) RuleML 2005. LNCS, vol. 3791, pp. 218–223. Springer, Heidelberg (2005)

[BM04] Biron, P.V., Malhotra, A.: XML Schema Part 2: Datatypes, 2nd edn. W3C Recommendation, W3C (October 2004), http://www.w3.org/TR/xmlschema-2/

[Bol11] Boley, H.: A RIF-Style Semantics for RuleML-Integrated Positional-Slotted, Object-Applicative Rules. In: Pasche, A. (ed.) RuleML 2011 - Europe. LNCS, vol. 6826, pp. 194–211. Springer, Heidelberg (2011)

[BPS10] Boley, H., Paschke, A., Shafiq, O.: RuleML 1.0: The Overarching Specification of Web Rules. In: Dean, M., Hall, J., Rotolo, A., Tabet, S. (eds.) RuleML 2010. LNCS, vol. 6403, pp. 162–178. Springer, Heidelberg (2010)

[DPSS06] Damasio, C.V., Pan, J.Z., Stoilos, G., Straccia, U.: An approach to representing uncertainty rules in ruleml. In: Proc. of the 2nd International Conference of Rules and Rule Markup Languages for the Semantic Web, RuleML 2006 (2006)

[GK10] Grosso, P., Kosek, J.: Associating schemas with xml documents 1.0, 1st edn. (2010), http://www.w3.org/TR/xml-model

[IG09] Ishikawa, M., Gylling, M.: XHTML 2.0 RELAX NG Definition (2009), http://www.w3.org/TR/xhtml2/xhtml20_relax.html#a_xhtml20_relaxng

[ISO08] ISO. ISO/IEC 19757-2: Document Schema Definition Language (DSDL) Part 2: Regular-grammar-based validation - RELAX NG (2008), http://standards.iso.org/ittf/PubliclyAvailableStandards/c052348_ISO_IEC_19757-2_2008E.zip

[Mur98] Murata, M.: Hedge automata: a formal model for xml schemata (1998), http://www.horobi.com/Projects/RELAX/Archive/hedge_nice.html

[Mur11] Murata, M.: Re: Theory question: sub-grammars and sub-languages (2011), http://tech.groups.yahoo.com/group/rng-users/message/1345

[Nat] Nation, J.B.: Notes on lattice theory, http://www.math.hawaii.edu/~jb/lat1-6.pdf

[TBMM04] Thompson, H.S., Beech, D., Maloney, M., Mendelsohn, N.: XML Schema Part 1: Structures. World Wide Web Consortium (2004), http://www.w3.org/TR/2004/REC-xmlschema-1-20041028/

[Vli03] van der Vlist, E.: Relax Ng. O'Reilly (2003)

[W3C98] W3C. Guide to the W3C XML Specification ("XMLspec") DTD, Version 2.1. World Wide Web Consortium (1998), http://www.w3.org/XML/1998/06/xmlspec-report.htm

A Language Lattices

Informal Definitions of Containment. There is a variety of levels at which we may define a partial ordering on a family of XML markup languages and their grammars (schemas). We list here informal definitions of three of the containment-based partial orderings that are relevant to the RuleML language lattices. Formal definitions of these and other orderings and their mathematical consequences are provided on the RuleML Language Lattice Wiki Page[18]

[18] http://wiki.ruleml.org/index.php/Language_Lattice.

- **PSVI Containment:** A language L_1 is a PSVI sublanguage of another language L_2 if every valid document in L_1 can be mapped to a valid document in L_2 with the same post-schema-validation infoset.
- **Syntactic Containment:** A language L_1 is a syntactic sublanguage of another language L_2 if every grammatically-valid document of L_1 is also a grammatically-valid document of L_2.
- **Grammar Containment:** A language L_1 is a grammatical sublanguage of another language L_2 if the grammar of L_2 is an extension of the grammar of L_1 created by adding new production rules and/or new terminal symbols.

Monotonicity from Schema Design Pattern. In general, these partial-order relations are not equivalent. We introduced above a schema design pattern that guarantees syntactic containment given grammar containment.

We consider the operation of merging two grammars as modules that are both included, without overrides, by a driver file. According to [Mur11], if the Relax NG syntax did not include the interleave combine attribute, the merger operation would be monotonic; that is, any valid instance of one of the modules would also be a valid instance of the merged grammar. Such monotonicity is very powerful, but at a high price – the fine-grained modularization we seek would be impossible without the interleave combine.

Our objective can be met with a compromise – we aim for a weaker monotonicity and allow a restricted usage of the interleave combine. Consider the operation of merging two grammars, one being the base grammar and the other we call an expansion module. If any valid instance of the base grammar is also a valid instance of the merged grammar, then we have a one-sided monotonicity that is sufficient to establish the correspondence between the subset of included modules and the lattice of languages generated by syntactic containment partial order. This monotonicity also provides modular extensibility with backward compatibility, i.e., a grammar may be extended by including an expansion module without invalidating previously valid instance documents.

The segregated names schema design pattern described in Section 2.3 provides the desired monotonicity property. The use of an interleave combine with an optional child in an expansion module can be shown to preserve monotonicity by transforming the base grammar and expansion module pair to a pair of modules without interleave combine whose merger is equivalent to the merger of the first pair. For example, the two interleave combine definitions

```
x.interleave &= a
x.interleave &= y?
```

are equivalent to the following choice combine definitions:

```
x.choice |= a
x.choice |= a & y
```

Towards RIF-OWL Combination: An Effective Reasoning Technique in Integrating OWL and Negation-Free Rules

Mohammad Sadnan Al Manir*

sadnan.almanir@unb.ca

Abstract. In this paper we focus on the combination of Description Logics (DLs) and negation-free rules, both expressed in the standard First-Order logic semantics. We propose an algorithm that is sound for every such combination but not complete. Our algorithm uses existing standard reasoning tools for retrieving facts from the DL Knowledge Base with which rules are put together to form a logic program. Rule reasoner is then used for answering queries in this program. We identify the reasons behind the incompleteness and chose a subset which combines restricted DL and rules. This subset consists of DL Horn-$\mathcal{SHIQ}$ language and rules such that DL predicates are allowed only in the rule bodies and all the rules are DL-safe. A prototype implementation of the reasoning process is also presented. The combination chosen here can express strictly more information in the DL component compared to the well known combination DLP extended using rules.

Keywords: Description Logics, rules, integration, reasoning, combination.

1 Introduction

Description Logics (DLs) [16] - a family of Knowledge Representation (KR) formalisms, subset of function-free First-Order Logic (FOL) with equality have gained enough maturity and is the basis for Web Ontology Language OWL 2 [5,6]. DLs can model information using constructors and complex expressions can be built. Moreover, ontology modeling is close to having a tree structure and concepts and roles in the language correspond to unary and binary predicate respectively. Negation-free rules are based on Horn logic fragment of FOL and on the contrary to DLs, can model information in a non-tree structure and is able to express queries with arbitrary arity.

Bringing these two KR formalisms in a common framework could enhance the expressive capability of information because knowledge that cannot be modeled

* This work was done as part of a Master degree program in Vienna University of Technology, Austria and Free University of Bozen-Bolzano, Italy. Special thanks to Jos de Bruijn and Thomas Eiter in Knowledge Based Systems Group, Institute of Information Systems, Vienna University of Technology, Austria for their valuable suggestions.

F. Olken et al. (Eds.): RuleML 2011 - America, LNCS 7018, pp. 33–48, 2011.

in either DLs or rules, can be modeled in their integration. The interoperability between the rules and ontologies is a necessity as these building blocks are side by side in the semantic web stack [2]. Thus our RIF-OWL combination [4] reflects a strong focus in the development of Semantic Web stack formation. RIF [3] is proposed by the Rule Interchange Format (RIF) Working Group as rules.

A new reasoning algorithm is proposed in this paper for such integration. In this algorithm, the DL reasoner takes a DL Knowledge Base (KB) $\mathcal{O}$ as input and retrieves the entailed facts $\mathcal{F}$ from the ontology. Then a set of rules, more specifically RIF rules in $\mathcal{P}$ is put together with these facts forming a logic program $\mathcal{P}' = \mathcal{F} \cup \mathcal{P}$. Now answering conjunctive queries in this program is possible using a rule reasoner. Our algorithm is sound and easily implementable with existing reasoning tools. But the algorithm is not complete for all such integrations. To regain completeness, we choose a particular subset of such combinations where the components DL and rules are restricted. In this subset, the DL is chosen as Horn-$\mathcal{SHIQ}$ and rules are DL-safe and DL-atoms are allowed to occur only in rule bodies, not in heads. The implementation uses standard DL reasoner Pellet [1] and XSB [20,22] rule reasoner.

Over the years a number of integration approaches and reasoning in such integrations have been investigated. Among these $\mathcal{AL}$-log [9], CARIN [7], SWRL [10,11,12], DLP [13] extension using rules, DL-safe SWRL rules [14] are notable and precede this work. It is interesting to notice how restrictions on DLs and rule components introduce trade-off between expressiveness of these components and decidability of reasoning.

In CARIN, It was found that certain combinations of DL constructors were responsible for undecidability of reasoning and hence these constructors are disallowed in the combination. DLP which is a fragment of DL $\mathcal{SHIQ}$, falls essentially in Horn fragment of FOL. Here the DL is restricted by mainly disallowing disjunction and existential information in the consequents of the DL axioms. The transformation of DLP is then straightforward and they can be easily extended with rules resulting the combination of DLs and rules enabling decidable reasoning. DLP is different in nature from the DLs in $\mathcal{AL}$-log, CARIN and SWRL because of its correspondence to Horn fragment. While DLP falls essentially in Horn fragment from the very beginning requiring no more restrictions on its DL, each of the DLs in $\mathcal{AL}$-log, CARIN and SWRL needs further restrictions for decidable reasoning in their rule integration.

Different reasoning techniques mentioned above use rule restrictions in syntactic forms. Except for DLP, all three of $\mathcal{AL}$-log, CARIN and DL-safe SWRL use rule restrictions for decidable reasoning. All of the restrictions on rules are on the variables that belong to DL-atoms and are based on the idea of typical rule safeness. While $\mathcal{AL}$-log and DL-safe SWRL use DL-safety restriction, CARIN uses role-safety. The difference is twofold: First, while DL-safety considers both concept ($\mathcal{AL}$-log rules allow only concepts) and role atoms, role-safety only considers roles. Second, in role-safety restriction, only one variable in role is required to appear in non-DL-atom unless it already appears so. The DL-safety restriction requires all the variables instead.

All these restrictions put limitations on the expressive power of the combined language. Our intension is to find RIF-OWL combination where the DL component is strictly more expressive than DLP ontologies [13] and sound and complete reasoning is possible using existing reasoning tools.

We organize this paper starting with the definition of our combination in the next section. We discuss our algorithmic properties along with soundness and completeness in detail. Then we move on to identify the reasons behind incompleteness and propose a specific combination for which the algorithm is complete. Finally we compare our approach with existing similar approaches and conclude with the scope for improvement in future.

2 Preliminaries

Due to space constraints FOL and Description Logics syntax and semantics have been avoided here. The standard semantics of FOL and expressive DL $\mathcal{SHOIQ}$ which is a logical counterpart of OWL DL are described in details in preliminaries of [23]. The symbols used in the following sections follow these preliminaries.

2.1 Combination of DLs and Rules

Here we define the syntax and semantics of combinations of DLs and rules in terms of standard FOL.

Syntax. To define the combined KB, we need to fix the alphabets for predicate symbols.

Definition 1(Alphabets of predicates). Let $\mathcal{A} = \mathcal{A}_{\mathcal{O}} \cup \mathcal{A}_{\mathcal{P}}$ be a set of alphabets such that

- $\mathcal{A}_{\mathcal{O}}$ and $\mathcal{A}_{\mathcal{P}}$ are disjoint $\mathcal{A}_{\mathcal{O}} \cap \mathcal{A}_{\mathcal{P}} = \emptyset$
- $\mathcal{A}_{\mathcal{O}}$ consists of only unary and binary predicate symbols from DLs known as DL-predicates and
- $\mathcal{A}_{\mathcal{P}}$ contains n-ary predicate symbols that are not DL-predicates

Definition 2(Combined Knowledge Base). A Combined Knowledge Base $\mathcal{C}$ is a pair written as $(\mathcal{O}, \mathcal{P})$ where

- $\mathcal{O}$ is a DL KB
- $\mathcal{P}$ is a program with rules over the predicate alphabets $\mathcal{A}$ and the constants C, i.e., a set of rules where each rule r in $\mathcal{P}$ is of the form

$$p(X) \leftarrow q_1(Y_1), \ldots, q_l(Y_l), s_1(Z_1), \ldots, s_m(Z_m) \tag{1}$$

such that $l \geq 0, m \geq 0$, $p(X)$, *and* $p \in \mathcal{A}$, *each* $q_i(Y_i)$, $s_j(Z_j)$ for $0 \leq i \leq l$, $0 \leq j \leq m$ is an atom where each $q_i \in \mathcal{A}_{\mathcal{P}}$ and each $s_j \in \mathcal{A}_{\mathcal{O}}$.

Semantics. Our proposed combination semantics relies on the standard First-Order interpretation of both the DLs and the rule component of the combined KB $\mathcal{C}$ over predicates in $\mathcal{A}$ and constants in C.

The First-Order representation of a rule in (1) is as follows

$$\forall \bar{x}, \bar{y}_1, \ldots, \bar{y}_l, \bar{z}_1, \ldots, \bar{z}_m . q_1(\bar{y}_1) \wedge \ldots \wedge q_l(\bar{y}_l) \wedge s_1(\bar{z}_1) \wedge \ldots \wedge s_m(\bar{z}_m) \rightarrow p(\bar{x})$$

Definition 3(Model and Satisfiability). A *model* of a combined KB $\mathcal{C} = \langle \mathcal{O}, \mathcal{P} \rangle$ is an interpretation $\mathcal{N}$ such that $\mathcal{N}$ satisfies $\pi(\mathcal{O}) \cup \mathcal{P}$. $\mathcal{C}$ is called *satisfiable* if it has at least a model. A sentence α is called satisfiable in $\mathcal{C}$ iff $\alpha \models \mathcal{C}$ i.e. $\alpha \models \pi(\mathcal{O}) \cup \mathcal{P}$.

Definition 4(Entailment). A sentence α is *entailed* by $\mathcal{C}$ denoted as $\mathcal{C} \models \alpha$ iff for each model $\mathcal{N}$ of $\mathcal{C}$, $\mathcal{N}$ satisfies α.

3 Reasoning in Combined Knowledge Base

Query answering is a reasoning problem in the integration of DLs and rules. As conjunctive queries are known to be useful in various practical applications, hence it is practical to use them as an expressive formalism for querying our combined KB.

Definition 5(Conjunctive Query). A *Conjunctive Query* (CQ) q is an expression of the form $q(\bar{x}) \leftarrow \exists \bar{y} \varphi(\bar{x}, \bar{y})$ where φ is a formula built from the alphabets of atoms in $\mathcal{A}$ using the conjunction ($\wedge$) connective with *free* variables $\bar{x}$ and $\bar{y}$. We call the variables in $\bar{x}$ the *distinguished* variables and those in $\bar{y}$ the *non-distinguished* variables. A CQ q is *boolean* if the arity of q is 0.

The *answer* to a CQ q over a KB $\mathcal{C} = \langle \mathcal{O}, \mathcal{P} \rangle$ is a tuple of constants $\bar{c}$ as a result of the substitution of the distinguished variables $\bar{x}$ with the set of constants in C.

The answer $ans(q, \mathcal{C})$ to a CQ q over $\mathcal{C}$ is represented as follows:

$$ans(q, \mathcal{C}) = \{\bar{c} \mid \exists \bar{y} \varphi(\bar{c}, \bar{y})\}$$

4 Our Approach

We get all kinds of facts $\mathcal{F}$ from the DL KB $\mathcal{O}$ using a standard DL reasoner (e.g., Pellet). We then form a new logic program $\mathcal{P}' = \mathcal{P} \cup \mathcal{F}$ where $\mathcal{P}$ contains a set of rules. To answer the query q over the logic program $\mathcal{P}'$ we use a rule reasoner (e.g. XSB). The algorithm returns "YES" if the query q is entailed by the logic program $\mathcal{P}'$, otherwise it says "Unknown".

The pseudocode of the algorithm is given in the following page.

Algorithm 1. CombinedKBEntails $(q, \mathcal{C}, \bar{c})$

Require: Combined KB $\mathcal{C} = \langle \mathcal{O}, \mathcal{P} \rangle$
Conjunctive Query q as $q(\bar{x}) \leftarrow \exists y \varphi(\bar{x}, \bar{y})$
Answer tuple $\bar{c}$ as a tuple of constants

Ensure: CombinedKBEntails $(q, \mathcal{C}, \bar{c})$ says YES if modified logic program entails $q(\bar{c})$, otherwise says Unknown

```
Begin
Derive the set F of all facts from Ontology O such that
    F = ⋃_{C∈A_O} {C(a) | π(O) ⊨ C(a)} ∪ ⋃_{R∈A_O} {R(b,c) | π(O) ⊨ R(b,c)}
Form a logic program P' such that
    P' = P ∪ F
if P' ⊨ q(c̄) then
    return YES
else
    return Unknown
end if
End
```

4.1 Properties of the Algorithm

Our algorithm is modular: DL reasoner is used in first step and then rule reasoner in the logic program.

The algorithm is sound. This intuition is, we replace the ontology with all the facts. A set of these facts are entailed by the ontology which means they are true in the ontology model(s). From the property of monotonicity it is immediate that if more rules or axioms are added to these facts, there will be more entailments. So whenever we take an entailment of the part of the KB, this is also an entailment of the whole KB.

The soundness can be formally expressed as a theorem as follows:

Theorem 1: *Given a Knowledge Base* $\mathcal{C} = \langle \mathcal{O}, \mathcal{P} \rangle$ *with ontology* $\mathcal{O}$ *and logic program* P*, a conjunctive query* q *and a tuple of constants* $\bar{c}$*, if CombinedKBEntails(q,* $\mathcal{C}, \bar{c}$*) returns "YES" then* $\mathcal{C} \models q(\bar{c})$.

Proof : To prove that the algorithm is *sound* we have to prove that if $\mathcal{P}' \models q(\bar{c})$ then $\mathcal{C} \models q(\bar{c})$. It will be enough to show that for function $\mathcal{M}$ that returns a set of models, $\mathcal{M}(\mathcal{C}) \subseteq \mathcal{M}(\mathcal{P}')$.

The model $\mathcal{M}$ for the KB $\mathcal{C} = \langle \mathcal{O}, \mathcal{P} \rangle$ is the model of its components

$$\mathcal{M}(\mathcal{C}) = \mathcal{M}(\mathcal{O}) \cap \mathcal{M}(\mathcal{P}) \tag{2}$$

We have the set of facts $\mathcal{F}$ that are retrieved from the ontology. Naturally this $\mathcal{F}$ is entailed by the ontology $\mathcal{O}$. So we can write

$$\mathcal{M}(\mathcal{O}) \subseteq \mathcal{M}(\mathcal{F}) \tag{3}$$

Again the model $\mathcal{M}$ for the modified logic program $\mathcal{P}'$ is the intersection of the models of logic program $\mathcal{P}$ and $\mathcal{F}$. Using (2) and (3) we get

$$\mathcal{M}(\mathcal{P}') = \mathcal{M}(\mathcal{F}) \cap \mathcal{M}(\mathcal{P})$$

As the algorithm answers "YES", we can write

$$\mathcal{M}(\mathcal{P}') \subseteq q(\bar{c}) \tag{4}$$

Clearly the model in $\mathcal{C}$ lies also in the model in $\mathcal{P}'$

$$\mathcal{M}(\mathcal{C}) \subseteq \mathcal{M}(\mathcal{P}') \tag{5}$$

As the two inclusions in (4) and (5) hold, the following inclusion also holds

$$\mathcal{M}(\mathcal{C}) \subseteq \mathcal{M}(q(\bar{c}))$$

and from the definition of entailment

$$\mathcal{C} \models q(\bar{c})$$

Thus, soundness states that we can use any kind of Ontologies and rules in our combination and any decision we get from the procedure is supported by the semantics of the combinations.

The algorithm is not *complete* and to show that we look at the example below:

Example 1. Let an ontology in DL KB $\mathcal{O}$ contains $B \sqsubseteq C$ and a program $\mathcal{P}$ contains a fact $B(a)$.

Here B subsumes C in $\mathcal{O}$ and a is a member of B in $\mathcal{P}$. If we combine this $\mathcal{O}$ and $\mathcal{P}$, because of the axiom in $\mathcal{O}$, a should as well be a member of C. So, according to the semantics it is the case that $\mathcal{C} \models C(a)$.

Now for the KB $\mathcal{C} = \langle \mathcal{O}, \mathcal{P} \rangle$ using the procedure we retrieve the facts as follows:

$$\mathcal{F} = fact(\mathcal{O}) = \{\alpha \text{ is a fact} \mid \mathcal{O} \models \alpha\} = \emptyset$$

The new logic program $\mathcal{P}'$ is formed as follows: $\mathcal{P}' = \mathcal{F} \cup \mathcal{P} = \{B(a)\}$

Clearly $\mathcal{P}' \not\models C(a)$

hence the decision procedure $CombinedKBEntails(q, \mathcal{C}, (a))$ returns "Unknown" even though $\mathcal{C} \models C(a)$.

Hence we can conclude that even though the combination semantics says $\mathcal{C} \models q$, the algorithm says "Unknown". Therefore the algorithm is not complete. From this it is clear that to achieve completeness of our algorithm, we cannot use any kind of ontologies and rules in our combination. There should be some kind of restrictions on these components.

4.2 Computational Complexity of the Algorithm

The first step of our algorithm states that we retrieve all the entailed facts from the ontology. Although the size of the set of facts is polynomial in the size of the whole ontology, retrieving does not depend only on this data. Because we also retrieve the inferred facts, it also depends on the TBox as TBox is no more static during this process. Hence it makes sense to talk about the whole ontology. Thus, the set of inferred facts $\mathcal{F}$ is polynomial in the ontology (both ABox and TBox). In DL Horn-$\mathcal{SHIQ}$ these entailments of instances is exponential because of non-static TBox even if we have polynomial number of facts. Hence deriving polynomial number of facts is still exponential.

Then rule reasoning is performed. In general, if the rules contain function symbols then reasoning is undecidable. In the absence of functions in rules, the complexity of rule reasoning is exponential.

Therefore, the complexity of our algorithm is exponential in the size of the combined KB.

5 Restrictions on Knowledge Base Components

From example above it is found that for every ontologies and rules in the combinations, the algorithm is sound but not complete. We analyze every case for which the algorithm results incompleteness. Based on the analysis we propose a combination subset by putting restrictions on DLs and rules component to regain completeness. We also discuss the immediate effects of these restrictions.

5.1 Disjunction

Incompleteness due to Disjunct Construct. Disjunction in $\mathcal{O}$ shows a proof of incompleteness of our algorithm. An example is as follows:

Example 2. Let an ontology in DL KB $\mathcal{O}$ contains

$$A \sqsubseteq B \sqcup C$$

$$A(a)$$

and a logic program $\mathcal{P}$ contains a set of rules $\begin{cases} r(x) \leftarrow B(x) \\ r(x) \leftarrow C(x) \end{cases}$

Here A subsumes B or C and a is a member of A in $\mathcal{O}$, on the other hand in $\mathcal{P}$, all the elements under B and C are also elements under r.

For the combination of $\mathcal{O}$ and $\mathcal{P}$ and for axiom in $\mathcal{O}$, a should as well be a member of either B or C and hence a must be a member of r as well. So, according to the semantics it is the case that $\mathcal{C} \models r(a)$.

Now for the KB $\mathcal{C} = \langle \mathcal{O}, \mathcal{P} \rangle$, $\mathcal{F} = \{A(a)\}$

The new logic program $\mathcal{P}'$: $\mathcal{P}' = \mathcal{F} \cup \mathcal{P} = \begin{cases} A(a) \\ r(x) \leftarrow B(x) \\ r(x) \leftarrow C(x) \end{cases}$

Clearly $\mathcal{P}' \not\models r(a)$

Hence the algorithm $CombinedKBEntails(q, \mathcal{C}, (a))$ returns "Unknown" even though $\mathcal{C} \models r(a)$.

So, we disallow all situations that are equivalent to disjunction. We consider the class of ontologies in $\mathcal{O}$ which is essentially disjunction free. Such an expressive ontology language is Horn-$\mathcal{SHIQ}$.

Disallowing Disjunction. The DL Horn-$\mathcal{SHIQ}$ was introduced in [15] as a fragment of $\mathcal{SHIQ}$. The basic idea is not to allow disjunction ($\sqcup$) in their expressions by putting syntactic restrictions on $\mathcal{SHIQ}$. This way, there is a correspondence of Horn-$\mathcal{SHIQ}$ expressions and Horn fragment of FOL with equality. Following [17] without loss of generality, the normal form of Horn-$\mathcal{SHIQ}$ is rewritten in [18] and described here.

Definition 6(Horn-$\mathcal{SHIQ}$). A (normal) Horn-$\mathcal{SHIQ}$ KB contains General Inclusion axioms (GCI) of the forms

$$A \sqcap B \sqsubseteq C \qquad A \sqsubseteq \forall R.B \qquad A \sqsubseteq \geq nS.B$$
$$\exists R.A \sqsubseteq B \qquad A \sqsubseteq \exists R.B \qquad A \sqsubseteq \leq 1S.B$$

where A, B, C are concept names including special concepts $\top$ and $\bot$ and R is a role, S is a simple role and $n \geq 1$.

5.2 Modular Reasoning

Incompleteness due to Modular Reasoning. The modular property of our algorithm states that reasoning is done in two stages. For retrieving facts we use DL reasoner and query answering uses rule reasoner. As these two reasonings are separate, there is no interaction. Therefore, in rule reasoning if we use DL atoms in the head of the rules of the logic program, there are certain inferences we don't get from this algorithm that agree with the combination semantics. The fact is we don't have any feedback from the program back to the ontology as DL reasoner is no longer part of rule reasoning process any more.

DL Predicates only in Rule Body. To avoid this problem the restriction on rules is defined such that DL (ontology) predicates can only be used in the rule bodies. This means our combination does not allow *concepts* and *roles* to appear in the heads of the rules.

As a result, the flow of inferred information in only in one direction, i.e. from DLs to rules.

5.3 Named/Unnamed Objects

Incompleteness due to Unnamed Objects. From the concept of open-domain we know that unnamed objects are expressed using existential quantification in DL KB $\mathcal{O}$. On the other hand, logic program $\mathcal{P}$ only deals with objects that are explicitly mentioned in their KB. So in their combination, while reasoning, the logic program cannot handle those unnamed objects introduced in $\mathcal{O}$ thus resulting the incompleteness of our algorithm.

Example 3. Let $\mathcal{O}$ contains $C \sqsubseteq \exists R.\top$
$C(a)$

and $\mathcal{P}$ contains a rule $r(x) \leftarrow R(x,y)$

Here $C \sqsubseteq \exists R.\top$ and a is a member of C in $\mathcal{O}$. And in $\mathcal{P}$, x is a member of predicate r if x is also a member of a relation R. If we combine this $\mathcal{O}$ and $\mathcal{P}$, according to the semantics it is the case that $\mathcal{C} \models r(a)$.

Now for the KB $\mathcal{C} = \langle \mathcal{O}, \mathcal{P} \rangle$, $\mathcal{F} = \{C(a)\}$

The new logic program $\mathcal{P}'$ stands: $\mathcal{P}' = \mathcal{F} \cup \mathcal{P} = \begin{cases} C(a) \\ r(x) \leftarrow R(x,y) \end{cases}$

Clearly $\mathcal{P}' \not\models r(a)$

Hence the algorithm $CombinedKBEntails(q, \mathcal{C}, (a))$ returns "Unknown" even though $\mathcal{C} \models r(a)$.

To remedy this problem, we make sure that only named objects are considered during the evaluation in logic program. This is done by restricting the rules such that they only consider named objects. A syntactic restriction on the variables called *DL-safeness* is introduced for this purpose.

Only named objects are considered

Definition 7(DL-safe rule). A rule r is *DL-safe* if each variable occurring in r also occurs in a non-DL atom in the body of r. A logic program is DL-safe if all of its rules are DL-safe.

Hence, DL-safety ensures that each variable is bound only to individuals explicitly mentioned in the DL KB. For example, *Student, livesAt* and *eatsAt* are concepts and roles from $\mathcal{O}$, the following rule is not DL-safe, because both x, y and z occur in DL-atom, but not in an atom with a predicate outside $\mathcal{O}$.

$$Lazystudent(x) \leftarrow Student(x), livesAt(x,y), eatsAt(x,z)$$

The previous rule can be made DL-safe by adding special non-DL atoms $\widetilde{\mathcal{O}}(x)$, $\widetilde{\mathcal{O}}(y)$ and $\widetilde{\mathcal{O}}(z)$ to the body of the rule and by adding a *fact* $\widetilde{\mathcal{O}}(a)$ for each individual a occurring in $\mathcal{O}$ or $\mathcal{P}$. Thus the above rule can be made DL-safe as follows:

$$Lazystudent(x) \leftarrow Student(x), livesAt(x,y), eatsAt(x,z), \widetilde{\mathcal{O}}(x), \widetilde{\mathcal{O}}(y), \widetilde{\mathcal{O}}(z)$$

Limited Expressiveness of DL-safe Conjunctive Query

Definition 8(DL-safe Conjunctive Query). A Conjunctive Query is called DL-safe Conjunctive Query if after the (syntactic) transformation it acts as if it were a DL-safe rule.

DL-safe rules are less expressive than conjunctive queries. Let us consider an example $\mathcal{O} = \{(\exists hasChild.Person)(Peter)\}$. Here the ontology states that Peter has a child but does not disclose who it is i.e. the child is not explicitly present in the ABox.

Now for the conjunctive query retrieving all objects having a child is written as $q(x,y) = \exists hasChild(x,y)$. Clearly $\mathcal{O} \models \exists hasChild(Peter, y)$ giving an answer $Peter$ to the CQ $q(x,y)$ for the KB $\mathcal{O}$.

When we transform CQ to a rule that is DL-safe, this results in a DL-safe rule $q(x) \leftarrow hasChild(x,y), \widetilde{\mathcal{O}}(x), \widetilde{\mathcal{O}}(y)$ where $\widetilde{\mathcal{O}}(x), \widetilde{\mathcal{O}}(y)$ are introduced for DL-safeness making sure the explicit existence of object y in the KB.

The logic program $\mathcal{P}' \not\models Q(Peter)$ because the child object is unknown and $\widetilde{\mathcal{O}}(y)$ cannot find anything to substitute with y. So, it is clear that the presence of non-distinguished variables poses problems for the CQ when DL-safety restriction is applied.

To avoid this problem, rolling-up technique introduced in [19] can be used. The intuition is that the queries which have a tree structure with non-distinguished variables can be transformed into queries without non-distinguished variables. For example, we can add an axiom $\exists R.C \sqsubseteq D$ to the ontology $\mathcal{O}$. As a result, the CQ stands $q(x) \leftarrow D(x), \widetilde{\mathcal{O}}(x)$.

5.4 Equality (Inequality)

Incompleteness due to Equality (Inequality). The DL KB $\mathcal{O}$ contains equality/inequality. Due to the presence of this property the algorithm shows incompleteness as it does not agree with the combination semantics. The following example shows how this happens:

Example 4. Let $\mathcal{O}$ contains $a = b$ and $\mathcal{P}$ contains a fact $p(a)$

If we combine this $\mathcal{O}$ and $\mathcal{P}$, according to the semantics it is the case that $\mathcal{C} \models p(b)$.

Now for the KB $\mathcal{C} = \langle \mathcal{O}, \mathcal{P} \rangle$, $\mathcal{F} = \emptyset$

The new logic program $\mathcal{P}'$ stands: $\mathcal{P}' = \mathcal{F} \cup \mathcal{P} = \{p(a)\}$

Clearly $\mathcal{P}' \not\models p(b)$

Hence the algorithm $CombinedKBEntails(q, \mathcal{C}, (b))$ returns "Unknown" even though $\mathcal{C} \models p(b)$.

Thus (in)equality acts also as a reason for incompleteness of our algorithm.

Constants are not allowed in logic program. To avoid incompleteness it is required that the program in general to be partially constant-free. The logic program is not entirely constant-free as facts of the form $\widetilde{\mathcal{O}}(a)$ can be present for a a named individual. But if we would have only equality-free DL KB which also does not have functionality and cardinality restriction in that case we could use constants in the program.

In short, the restrictions state that DL KB $\mathcal{O}$ contains only the classes of ontologies called Horn-$\mathcal{SHIQ}$ and for the rules, DL (ontology) predicates can only be used in the rule bodies and all the rules be DL-safe. In addition, the logic program should be partially constant-free.

Theorem 2. *Given a Knowledge Base $\mathcal{C} = \langle \mathcal{O}, \mathcal{P} \rangle$ with DL KB $\mathcal{O}$ and partially constant-free logic program P containing facts of the form $\widetilde{\mathcal{O}}(a)$ where a is a named individual, a conjunctive query q and a tuple of constants $\bar{c}$. If $\mathcal{O}$ is Horn-$\mathcal{SHIQ}$ and P, q are DL-safe and P has no DL-predicates in the head, then it is the case that if $\mathcal{C} \models q(\bar{c})$ then* CombinedKBEntails(q, $\mathcal{C}, \bar{c}$) *returns* "YES".

Proof: We start by recalling the required definitions to formulate the proof.

Definition 9(Homomorphism). A *homomorphism* $h : \mathcal{I} \rightarrow \mathcal{J}$ between two interpretations $\mathcal{I}$ and $\mathcal{J}$ is a mapping h from the domain $\Delta^{\mathcal{I}}$ to the domain $\Delta^{\mathcal{J}}$ such that for every constant c, $h(c^{\mathcal{I}}) = c^{\mathcal{J}}$ and for every predicate symbol p and every $\bar{a} \in \Delta^{\mathcal{I}}$, if $\bar{a} \in p^{\mathcal{I}}$, then $h(\bar{a}) \in p^{\mathcal{J}}$.

Definition 10(Canonical Model). An interpretation $\mathcal{I}$ is a canonical model of a theory φ if $\mathcal{I} \models \varphi$ and for every interpretation $\mathcal{I}' \in Mod(\varphi)$, there exists a homomorphism $h : \mathcal{I} \rightarrow \mathcal{I}'$.

Definition 11(Canonical Model Property). A theory φ has the canonical model property if it holds that whenever φ is satisfiable, it has a canonical model.

Definition 12(Minimal Model). Let $\mathcal{P}$ be a positive logic program. A Herbrand interpretation M of $\mathcal{P}$ is a model of $\mathcal{P}$ if for every rule $r \in gr(\mathcal{P})$, $B^{+}(r) \subseteq M$ implies $H(r) \cap M \neq \emptyset$. A Herbrand model M of a logic program $\mathcal{P}$ is *minimal* iff for every model M' such that $M' \subset M$, $M' = M$.

Every positive normal logic program has a single minimal Herbrand model, which is the intersection of all Herbrand models.

(**Proposition 1**). The DL Horn-$\mathcal{SHIQ}$ has a canonical model property. It follows from the above proposition that Horn-$\mathcal{SHIQ}$ ontology $\mathcal{O}$ has a canonical model $\mathcal{I}$.

An interpretation $\mathcal{I}' = (\Delta^{\mathcal{I}'}, \cdot^{\mathcal{I}'})$ extends an interpretation $\mathcal{I} = (\Delta^{\mathcal{I}}, \cdot^{\mathcal{I}})$ of signature $\mathcal{C} = \langle \mathcal{O}, \mathcal{P} \rangle$ if $\Delta^{\mathcal{I}} \subseteq \Delta^{\mathcal{I}'}$, for every constant symbol $c \in C$, $c^{\mathcal{I}} \subseteq c^{\mathcal{I}'}$, and for every predicate symbol $p \in \mathcal{A}$, $p^{\mathcal{I}} \subseteq p^{\mathcal{I}'}$

We take canonical model and extend it using the rules using a fixpoint computation. As ontology predicates don't occur in rule heads, fixpoint computations does not add anything to the extension of the ontology predicates. This is obvious from the construction of fixpoint computation.

During fixpoint computation, in first step we add named elements to $\widetilde{\mathcal{O}}$. After that, in each next step, for every tuple of elements in rules we assign only named elements such that rule body is going to be satisfied. Thus we add these tuple to the head predicate extension. Obviously the fixpoint operator is monotonic and this fixpoint is going to result in in interpretation $\mathcal{I}'$ which is necessarily a canonical model of $\mathcal{C}$.

Thus we derive an extended interpretation $\mathcal{I}'$ that is a model of the combination such that $\mathcal{I}' \models \mathcal{C}$. We observe that this $\mathcal{I}'$ is a canonical model of $\mathcal{C}$. It follows that whenever the ontology is satisfiable the combination is also satisfiable.

Because $\mathcal{I}'$ is a canonical model we can take the named part of this interpretation over the alphabet $\mathcal{A}_\mathcal{O}$, let's call this $\mathcal{I}\mid_{named}$ which is defined as follows:

(**Definition 13**). The interpretation of the named part of the extended canonical model is defined as $\mathcal{I}'\mid_{named}= (\Delta^{\mathcal{I}'}, \cdot^{\mathcal{I}'\mid_{named}})$ where

$$a^{\mathcal{I}'\mid_{named}} = a^{\mathcal{I}'} \text{ for each term } a \text{ and}$$
$$p^{\mathcal{I}'\mid_{named}} = \{\bar{u} \mid \bar{u} \in p^{\mathcal{I}'} \textit{ and } \exists a_1, \ldots, a_n \textit{ such that } a_1^{\mathcal{I}'} = u_1, \ldots, a_n^{\mathcal{I}'} = u_n\}$$

The set of entailed ontology facts are denoted as $\mathcal{F}_\mathcal{O}$ which contains the named part of the ontology the predicate p of which are such that $p \in \mathcal{A}_\mathcal{O}$

Clearly for a named entailed fact $p(\bar{a}) \in \mathcal{F}_\mathcal{O}$ it is the case that

$$\mathcal{I}\mid_{named} \models p(\bar{a}) \text{ iff } \mathcal{C} \models p(\bar{a}) \text{ iff } \mathcal{O} \models p(\bar{a})$$

On the other hand, the rule parts of the extended interpretation $\mathcal{I}'$ over the alphabets $\mathcal{A}_\mathcal{P}$, lets call this $\mathcal{I}\mid_{Rule}$ satisfy the rules

$$\mathcal{I}\mid_{Rule} \models \mathcal{F}_\mathcal{P}$$

where $\mathcal{F}_\mathcal{P}$ is the set of entailed rule facts for which the predicate are over the set of alphabets $\mathcal{A}_\mathcal{P}$.

Hence after the extension using fixpoint computation the extended interpretation $\mathcal{I}'$ consisting of named part and rule part over the predicate alphabets $\mathcal{A}$ is a model of the modified logic program $\mathcal{P}'$

$$\mathcal{I}' \models \mathcal{F} \cup \mathcal{P}$$
$$\mathcal{I}' \models \mathcal{P}'$$

The *Herbrand Universe* U_H is the set of all ground terms over function and predicates. The *Herbrand Base* B_H is the set of all atomic formulas which can be formed using the predicate symbols of $\mathcal{A}$ and the terms in U_H. A *Herbrand Interpretation* M is a subset of B_H.

We define Herbrand Interpretation M as a set of ground atomic formulas satisfied by $\mathcal{I}'\mid_{named}$ and by $\mathcal{I}'\mid_{Rule}$.

The Herbrand Interpretation M is a model for $\mathcal{P}'$. $\mathcal{I}'\mid_{Rule}$ contains only named objects because the rules are DL-safe and $\mathcal{F}$ is simply represented by named part from ontology as $\mathcal{I}'\mid_{named}$.

Finally, to prove our theorem we have to show that this Herbrand model is the minimal Herbrand model.

The grounding of logic program P, denoted as $gr(\mathcal{P})$ is the union of all possible ground instantiations of P, obtained by replacing each variable in r with a term in U_H, for each rule $r \in P$.

Let us suppose that M is not minimal model of $\mathcal{P}'$. Then M satisfies some ground atomic formula that is not entailed.

So, M is not MM of $\mathcal{P}'$ iff $\exists \alpha \in M.\mathcal{P}' \not\models \alpha$.

As α was satisfied in the canonical model then either it is represented in the named DL part in which case it is obviously entailed by $\mathcal{P}'$ or it is in rule part which is just an extension of the DL part by fixpoint procedure.

Therefore, no such α exists and we can conclude that M is indeed the minimal model $\mathcal{P}'$.

6 Implementation and Experiments

We use Java API to access the functionalities of Pellet DL reasoner. We use this API to retrieve all facts from the ontology. RIF rules are rewritten into XSB compatible format using a syntactic translator. The facts and rules are then put together to form the logic program. Rule reasoning is then performed using XSB.

The input of DL ontology is written in human readable syntax and rules are written in RIF format. A short description of RIF syntax is added with examples for this purpose. The architecture of the reasoning process is described in details. We have added two examples of the whole reasoning process based on our algorithm one of which shows the success and one shows the failure to answer query.

Due to space constraints the details of our implementation is avoided in this paper. However a full chapter is dedicated for this purpose and interested reader is requested to take a look at the EMCL Masters Thesis [23].

7 Relationship with Other Combination Approaches

Our research is a step followed from the previous contributions e.g., $\mathcal{AL}$-log, CARIN, DL-safe SWRL and DLP extended with rules.

At first, we start with restrictions on DLs. The combinations of DL constructors are among the well known sources for undecidable reasoning. Just like our approach, in CARIN and DLP extension with rules the DL component is restricted to disallow certain constructors in their axioms. For example, DLP does not allow existential restriction and disjunctive constructors in their axiom consequents while Horn-$\mathcal{SHIQ}$ in our case does allow existential restriction.

Unlike DLP extended with rules approach all the previous approaches including our combination use rule restrictions. These restrictions are syntactically imposed on the variables occurring in rules and can vary. For example, CARIN uses role-safety which apply to only one variable in roles while (strong) DL-safety restriction used in $\mathcal{AL}$-log and DL-safe SWRL apply to all the variables in concepts and roles. We also use DL-safety restriction here. This restrictions on rules, in turn, poses problems for using arbitrary conjunctive query.

Both $\mathcal{AL}$-log and CARIN uses modular reasoning approach where DL reasoning and rule reasoning is performed in isolation and there is no feedback from one reasoner to the other. As our reasoning adopts the same technique of modular reasoning, as a result just like $\mathcal{AL}$-log and CARIN approach DL-atoms are allowed to occur only in rule bodies, not in heads. This is not the case for DLP extension with rules and SWRL approach as they use only one reasoner, namely rule reasoner. Therefore, while SWRL and DLP extension with rules support the interoperability of DLs and rules in semantic web stack, our method including $\mathcal{AL}$-log and CARIN approach don't.

From the discussion above based on restriction on rules, it is clear that our combination is not as expressive as DLP extension with rules in terms of interoperability. But in terms of restriction on DL component, we are able to express more knowledge from syntactic point of view. As DLP is based on Horn framework, it cannot express existential restriction on the right hand side of the inclusion axioms. Horn-$\mathcal{SHIQ}$ on the other hand, is able to express such axioms. Hence, we can still have a reasonably expressive ontology language which can capture some practical needs. Although modular reasoning approach used in CARIN and $\mathcal{AL}$-log limits us to express DL-atoms in rules bodies only, we have significant advantage over these two approaches. The algorithm used in this research enables us to use any existing standard reasoning tools which by the way is not possible in $\mathcal{AL}$-log and CARIN. Because of the algorithms used in $\mathcal{AL}$-log and CARIN, new reasoning tools are required to implement in those cases.

8 Conclusion

We have discussed a combination of DLs and rules corresponding towards the integration of RIF-OWL and development of next generation Semantic Web architecture. We have proposed a simple algorithm for reasoning in this combination which is sound but not complete for all such combinations. To regain completeness we investigate one subset of such combination by imposing required restrictions on DLs and rules. We implemented one prototype of the reasoning approach and showed that our algorithm is capable of using existing reasoning tools. Compared to the well known combination DLP extended using rules, our combination is strictly more expressive with respect to the ontology information.

We also have seen the tradeoff in expressiveness due to putting restrictions. We would like to work on some of those in future as there are scopes for both DLs and rules component. For example, in DLs, Horn-$\mathcal{SROIQ}$ could be an interesting choice as part of expressive DL language $\mathcal{SROIQ}$ [21].

On the other hand, use of (strong) DL-safe rules hinders the full expressiveness of arbitrary conjunctive query. There might be a possibility of using weak DL-safety [8] instead. The modular approach also known as hybrid approach lets us use DL predicates only in rule bodies which directs information flow only from DLs to rules not the other way around. An improved algorithmic solution would be worth investigating for interoperability between DLs and rules.

References

1. Sirin, E., Parsia, B., Grau, B.C., Kalyanpur, A., Katz, Y.: Pellet: A practical OWL-DL reasoner. Journal of Web Semantics 5(2), 51–53 (2007)
2. W3c semantic web activity, November 2 (2001)
3. Kifer, M., Boley, H. (eds.): Rif basic logic dialect, w3c editor's draft, December 18 (2008)
4. de Bruijn, J. (ed.): Rif rdf and owl compatibility, w3c editor's draft, September 22 (2008)
5. Grau, B.C., Horrocks, I., Motik, B., Parsia, B., Patel-Schneider, P., Sattler, U.: OWL 2: The next step for OWL. Journal of Web Semantics: Science, Services and Agents on the World Wide Web 6(4), 309–322 (2008)
6. W3C OWL Working Group (eds.): Owl 2 web ontology language, document overview, September 22 (2008)
7. Levy, A.Y., Rousset, M.-C.: Combining horn rules and description logics in carin. Artif. Intell. 104(1-2), 165–209 (1998)
8. Rosati, R.: DL+log: Tight integration of description logics and disjunctive datalog, pp. 68–78 (2006)
9. Donini, F.M., Lenzerini, M., Nardi, D., Schaerf, A.: Al-log: Integrating datalog and description logics. J. Intell. Inf. Syst. 10(3), 227–252 (1998)
10. Sattler, U., Baader, F.: Number restrictions on complex roles in description logics, a preliminary report. In: Proceedings of the 5th International Conference on the Principles of Knowledge Representation and Reasoning (KR 1996), pp. 328–338 (1996)
11. Tobies, S., Horrocks, I., Sattler, U.: Practical reasoning for expressive description logics. In: Ganzinger, H., McAllester, D., Voronkov, A. (eds.) LPAR 1999. LNCS, vol. 1705, pp. 161–180. Springer, Heidelberg (1999)
12. Horrocks, I., Patel-Schneider, P.F., Boley, H., Tabet, S., Grosof, B., Dean, M.: Swrl: A semantic web rule language combining owl and ruleml. W3c member submission, World Wide Web Consortium (2004)
13. Grosof, B.N., Horrocks, I., Volz, R., Decker, S.: Description logic programs: combining logic programs with description logic. In: WWW, pp. 48–57 (2003)
14. Motik, B., Sattler, U., Studer, R.: Query answering for owl-dl with rules. J. Web Sem. 3(1), 41–60 (2005)
15. Hustadt, U., Motik, B., Sattler, U.: Data complexity of reasoning in very expressive description logics. In: Kaelbling, L.P., Saffiotti, A. (eds.) IJCAI, pp. 466–471. Professional Book Center (2005)
16. Baader, F., Calvanese, D., McGuinness, D.L., Nardi, D., Patel-Schneider, P.F. (eds.): The Description Logic Handbook: Theory, Implementation, and Applications. Cambridge University Press (2003)
17. Krtözsch, M., Rudolph, S., Hitzler, P.: Complexity boundaries for horn description logics. In: AAAI, pp. 452–457. AAAI Press (2007)
18. Eiter, T., Gottlob, G., Ortiz, M., Šimkus, M.: Query answering in the description logic horn-. In: Hölldobler, S., Lutz, C., Wansing, H. (eds.) JELIA 2008. LNCS (LNAI), vol. 5293, pp. 166–179. Springer, Heidelberg (2008)
19. Tessaris, S.: Questions and answers: reasoning and querying in Description Logic. PhD thesis, University of Manchester (2001)

20. Sagonas, K., Swift, T., Warren, D.S.: Xsb as an efficient deductive database engine. SIGMOD Rec. 23(2), 442–453 (1994)
21. Horrocks, I., Kutz, O., Sattler, U.: The even more irresistible sroiq. In: Doherty, P., Mylopoulos, J., Welty, C.A. (eds.) KR, pp. 57–67. AAAI Press (2006)
22. The XSB System, `http://xsb.sourceforge.net/xsbsystem.html`
23. EMCL Master Thesis 2008-09, `http://www.emcl-study.eu/fileadmin/master_theses/thesis_al.pdf`

Relaxed Safeness in Datalog-Based Policies

Moritz Y. Becker and Jason Mackay

Microsoft Research, Redmond, USA
{moritzb,jmackay}@microsoft.com

Abstract. This paper presents a safeness condition that is more liberal than the one commonly imposed on Datalog, based on classifying predicate arguments into input and output arguments, thereby extending the expressiveness of Datalog-based policy languages. It is also shown that the relaxed safeness condition is a powerful tool for adding important features to such languages.

1 Introduction

Datalog is the basis of many rule languages for the Semantic Web (e.g. [5,17,8,11]) as well as of many policy languages related to trust and access control (e.g. [14,13,10,15,3,2]). However, Datalog on its own is not expressive enough for many real-world policy scenarios, which commonly require features such as negation, functions, constraints, or updates. Extending Datalog with such features is not trivial, however, as it may require complex changes to the evaluation engine, which is expensive and in many cases infeasible. Furthermore, ad hoc extensions can easily break Datalog's complexity and termination properties; for example, just adding a single function symbol leads to undecidability. In this paper, we propose to replace a commonly used syntactic restriction on Datalog clauses called *safeness* (essentially, variables in the head must occur also in the body; see Section 2) by a slightly more complex, but more liberal, condition that we call *I/O-safeness* (Section 3). Informally, predicate argument positions first need to be classified as input or as output arguments, and the syntactic restrictions ensure that the arguments are always used in accordance with their input/output specification. I/O-safeness guarantees finiteness of query results.

Input/output modes have been considered before for logic programming [9,18,19], where the focus has been on extending the class of Prolog programs which can be evaluated correctly using SLDNF resolution. In contrast, the current paper focusses on using input/output modes to safely add features to Datalog that are required in common policy scenarios. We show in Section 4 that our definition of I/O-safeness not only itself increases a policy language's expressiveness, but also facilitates powerful extensions of the language that are particularly useful in a policy setting; moreover, they preserve Datalog's nice properties and do not require changes to the evaluation engine. In particular, we present,

1. a heuristic method for preventing intractable policies (Section 4.1);
2. a safe method for extending a language with arbitrary constraints and external functions (Section 4.2);
3. and a method for extending a policy language to support implicitly hierarchical predicates (Section 4.3).

F. Olken et al. (Eds.): RuleML 2011 - America, LNCS 7018, pp. 49–57, 2011.

2 Datalog and Safeness: Background

This section briefly recalls Datalog and its standard syntactic safeness condition. For a more thorough introduction, see e.g. [6].

An *expression* e is either a variable or a constant. *Predicate symbols* p are associated with an *arity* $\mathbf{ar}(p) \geq 0$. An *atom* P is of the form $p(e_1,...,e_n)$, where $n = \mathbf{ar}(p)$. A *rule* ρ is of the form $P:-P_1,...,P_k$, where $k \geq 0$ and the P_i are atoms. P is the *head*, and $\vec{P} = P_1,...,P_k$ is the *body* of ρ. If $k = 0$, the rule is called a *fact*, and we omit the ":–". A *policy* $\mathcal{P}$ is a finite set of rules.

We write $\mathbf{vars}(\varphi)$ to denote the set of variables occurring in a phrase of syntax φ. We say that φ is *ground* if $\mathbf{vars}(\varphi) = \emptyset$. A phrase of syntax φ' is an *instance* of φ iff $\varphi' = \varphi\sigma$ for some variable substitution σ.

A ground atom P is *derivable* from a policy $\mathcal{P}$ (we write $\mathcal{P} \vdash P$) if P is a ground instance of a fact in $\mathcal{P}$, or $P:-P_1,...,P_n$ is a ground instance of a rule in $\mathcal{P}$ such that $\mathcal{P} \vdash P_i$ for all $i \in \{1,...,n\}$. A *query* Q is an atom, and the *answers* to the query (with respect to a policy $\mathcal{P}$) is the set of all ground instances P of Q such that $\mathcal{P} \vdash P$.

Definition 1 (Safeness). A rule $P:-\vec{P}$ is *safe* if $\mathbf{vars}(P) \subseteq \mathbf{vars}(\vec{P})$. A policy is *safe* if all its rules are safe. □

Proposition 2. Let $\mathcal{P}$ be a policy, and Q be a query. If $\mathcal{P}$ is safe, then there are only finitely many answers to Q with respect to $\mathcal{P}$. □

3 I/O-Safeness

In this section, we present an alternative safeness condition on Datalog rules, called I/O-safeness, that is more lenient than the standard one from Def. 1 and yet preserves the finiteness property from Prop. 2. In Section 4, we present several applications facilitated by this safeness condition.

Consider again the standard safeness condition. The intuition behind it is that all variables in a body atom of a rule will be ground *after* the atom has been evaluated, because they will eventually be grounded by some ground fact. Variables thus have the function of *output* arguments. The main idea in I/O-safeness is that we also allow for *input* arguments: here we guarantee that the input arguments of an atom are ground *before* the atom is evaluated. These guarantees are enforced via syntactic restrictions.

Output variables in the head of a rule must be ground after the rule body has been evaluated, so they are required to be equal to some input variable in the same head, or to also occur as an output variable in the body. This implies that all output arguments e_i in a fact $p(e_1,...,e_n)$ must either occur also as an input variable e_j or be ground.

Input variables in the body, on the other hand, must be ground before the atom they occur in is evaluated, so they are required to occur also as an input variable in the head of the same rule, or as an output variable in a preceding body atom (throughout, we are assuming a left-to-right evaluation strategy for body atoms). Finally, we also need to ensure that all input arguments in queries are ground – in other words, a query must not have any input variables.

Formally, we associate each predicate symbol p with a non-empty set $\mathbf{mode}(p)$ of *modes* from the set $\{\text{IN}, \text{OUT}\}^{\mathbf{ar}(p)}$. We extend the mode function to atoms in a natural way, i.e., $\mathbf{mode}(p(e)) = \mathbf{mode}(p)$. This definition allows more than one mode for a given predicate symbol. We can thus have multiple *calling patterns* in which the predicate can be used.

Definition 3 (Input/Output variables). Let $P = p(e_1,...,e_n)$ be an atom, $\mu = (m_1,...,m_n) \in \mathbf{mode}(p)$, and $i \in \{1,...,n\}$. We say that e_i is an *input variable* (*output variable*, respectively) *in P with respect to* μ, if

1. e_i is a variable, and
2. $m_i = \text{IN}$ ($\mu_i = \text{OUT}$, respectively).

We write $\text{IN}_\mu(P)$ and $\text{OUT}_\mu(P)$ to denote the sets of all input variables and output variables in P with respect to μ. □

Definition 4 (I/O-Safeness). A rule $P{:-}P_1,..,P_n$ is *I/O-safe* if for all $\mu \in \mathbf{mode}(P)$ there exist $\mu_1,...,\mu_n$ such that $\mu_i \in \mathbf{mode}(P_i)$ (for all $i \in \{1,...,n\}$) and

1. $\text{OUT}_\mu(P) \subseteq \text{IN}_\mu(P) \cup \bigcup_{j=1}^{n} \text{OUT}_{\mu_j}(P_j)$, and
2. $\forall k \in \{1,...,n\}.\ \text{IN}_\mu(P_k) \subseteq \text{IN}_\mu(P) \cup \bigcup_{j=1}^{k-1} \text{OUT}_{\mu_j}(P_j)$.

A policy is *I/O-safe* if all of its rules are I/O-safe. A query Q is *I/O-safe* if there exists $\mu \in \mathbf{mode}(Q)$ such that $\text{IN}_\mu(Q) = \emptyset$. □

Proposition 5. Let $\mathcal{P}$ be a policy, and Q be a query. If $\mathcal{P}$ and Q are I/O-safe, then there are only finitely many answers to Q with respect to $\mathcal{P}$. □

Example 1. Policies often deal with access to resources, and typically define predicates such as canAccess(*User*,*Operation*,*File*). Under the standard safeness conditions, we can then write rules such as canAccess(u,`Read`,f):−canAccess(u,`Write`,f) and canAccess(`A`,`Write`,`//foo/bar.txt`). But the arguably legitimate rule

$$\text{canAccess}(u,\texttt{Write},f){:-}\text{admin}(u) \tag{1}$$

is deemed unsafe. However, this rule can be made I/O-safe with the mode assignment $\mathbf{mode}(\text{canAccess}) = \{(\text{OUT}, \text{OUT}, \text{IN})\}$. The previous two rules are also I/O-safe. But allowing a rule such as (1) comes with a tradeoff: queries such as canAccess(`A`,`Write`,f) ('which files can `A` write to?') are now I/O-unsafe; since the file argument is an input argument, it cannot be enumerated, and must be ground in queries. But this is reasonable, as rules such as (1) may give users permissions to access a large set of files. In the presence of Rule (1), a legitimate query would be e.g. canAccess(`A`,`Write`,`/foo.txt`). □

4 Advanced Applications of I/O-Safeness

4.1 Preventing Intractable Policies

The time complexity of Datalog evaluation is polynomial in the number of facts in the policy (i.e., assuming that the rules with non-empty bodies are fixed) [7]. The degree of the polynomial is bounded by the maximum number of distinct variables in a single rule. Even though this number is usually small, policy evaluation can be intractable in practice. In policy applications, the number of rules is typically small, whereas the number of facts in the policy may go into the billions. Therefore, even a linear search over a single predicate may already be prohibitively expensive.

In Example 1 in the previous section, we saw that the mode of canAccess could be set to (OUT, OUT, OUT) in the absence of rules like (1), allowing I/O-safe queries or body conditions such as canAccess(x, Write, y). But in any realistic file system with a large number of files, such a query would be very expensive. Clearly, requiring the third parameter to be instantiated at runtime is highly advisable, corresponding to the mode (OUT, OUT, IN). If the number of users that can access a single file may be large, it may be even better to use the more restrictive (IN, OUT, IN), as the first and the third parameters jointly almost determine the second parameter (the access mode).

We can generalize this observation: predicates often have subsets of arguments that determine, or nearly determine, the other arguments in the predicate. If the predicate is expected to be large, it is advisable to make sure that one of those subsets of arguments is ground at runtime, i.e., when the corresponding atom is evaluated. The general rule is thus to set the mode of all such groups of arguments to IN.

This provides a heuristics for controlling the complexity of a policy. It is still possible to write intractable policies, but much harder, and it is much less likely to happen inadvertently. If a policy or a query fails the I/O-safeness check, the system could either reject the policy or just issue a warning. The latter case is useful because there are situations where I/O-safeness can be legitimately ignored, e.g. if an administrator needs to enumerate all files that a user can access and the time that this takes is not crucial.

4.2 Constraints and Functions

Datalog on its own is not expressive enough for many real-world policies. For example, it cannot express constraints such as inequality or regular expressions as a predicate, nor functions that perform arithmetic operations or that access the environmental state. It is tempting to add constraints and functions to Datalog, in order to be able to write policies such as

$$\mathsf{adult}(x) :- \mathsf{dob}(x,d), \mathtt{CurTime}() - d \geq 18\ \mathtt{yrs}. \qquad (2)$$

It is impossible to express the example above in Datalog without constraints and functions. But there is a good reason why Datalog does not support arbitrary functions and constraints by default. Even just adding one function symbol to the language turns it into a Turing-complete language, which is undesirable for most policy applications. Similarly, as the name suggests, Constraint Logic Programming (CLP) [12] adds constraints to logic programming, which also renders the resulting language Turing-complete for many constraint classes. Moreover, it requires an execution strategy that is by far more complex than Datalog's.

We show that I/O-safeness allows Datalog-based policy languages to be extended with constraints and functions, without sacrificing Datalog's simplicity and efficiency, and more liberally than in existing languages. More concretely, our solution supports arbitrary types of constraints, and allows constraints to be placed at arbitrary positions within the rule body as long as the I/O-safeness condition is satisfied. Moreover, it also supports pure functions.

As a first step, we observe that constraints and functions can be viewed as syntactic sugar for predicates that are evaluated outside the Datalog engine. In particular, functions can be represented as relations with an extra argument for the output (or several extra arguments, if the output is a tuple). For example, Rule (2) could be rewritten internally without syntactic sugar as

$$\mathsf{adult}(x) :- \mathsf{dob}(x,d), \mathsf{curTime}(t), \mathsf{subtr}(t,d,r), \mathsf{gte}(r, 18\ \mathtt{yrs}),$$

where curTime, subtr and gte are defined *externally*: when these predicates are to be evaluated as subgoals at runtime, the answers to them are provided by external modules that need not be written in a rule-based language. Therefore, the only required change to the evaluation engine is that it needs to be able to call out to external answer providers for certain predicates.

Most constraints are infinite relations. For example, there are infinitely many pairs of numbers that satisfy the relation $\geq$. Therefore, constraint arguments should not be used as outputs. We set the mode of all constraint arguments to IN, in order to guarantee that the constraint is ground at runtime. The external module that deals with the constraint can therefore be very simple: it only needs to be able to check if a ground constraint is true or false. Complex constraint operations that are required in CLP such as unground satisfaction checking and existential quantifier elimination are thus not needed.

For the same reasons, function arguments are set to IN, apart from the extra output arguments, which are set to OUT. For instance, the nullary function curTime has mode (OUT). Functions may have multiple modes, if there are multiple subsets of arguments that fully determine the other arguments; for instance, subtr has the mode (IN, IN, OUT), and possibly also (OUT, IN, IN), and (IN, OUT, IN), depending on the implementation of the external module that deals with subtr.

Many functions, such as subtr or other arithmetic operations, have an infinite range. Since the output of the function can be fed back into its own input via the rules, this can lead to undecidability and non-termination. For example, with a simple successor function '$\_ + 1$' we could test if $\mathsf{q}(x)$ holds for all integers x: $\mathsf{p}(x) :- \mathsf{q}(x), \mathsf{p}(x+1)$.

This problem only occurs if recursion (p calls itself) is combined with an infinite-range function. But this can be checked statically: infinite-range functions must not occur within a recursive rule. (For example, in the policy $\{\mathsf{r.}, \mathsf{p} :- \mathsf{q.}, \mathsf{q} :- \mathsf{p.}\}$, only the first of the three rules is non-recursive.)

We then have the following result.

Proposition 6. Let $\mathcal{P}$ be a policy with externally evaluated constraints and functions, and Q be a query. If no infinite-range function occurs in a recursive rule and $\mathcal{P}$ and Q are I/O-safe, then there are only finitely many answers to Q with respect to $\mathcal{P}$. Furthermore, if functions and ground constraints can be evaluated in finite time, then the tabled left-to-right resolution strategy is also complete and terminating for evaluating Q.

4.3 Hierarchical Policies

Hierarchies are ubiquitous in policies. Here are a few examples:

1. In Role-Based Access Control (RBAC) [16], a role hierarchy is a partial order that defines a seniority relation between roles. Members of a role automatically inherit permissions from lower-ranked roles.
2. In Mandatory Access Control (MAC) [4], access is based on security labels such as top secret, secret, confidential, etc., attached to users and objects. The labels form a lattice, and users with a given security label can only read objects with an equal or lower label. Furthermore, users can only write objects with an equal or higher label.
3. Policies on file permissions often reflect the hierarchical structure of the file system. Having permission to access a folder may imply permission to access all subfolders.

How could hierarchical structures be combined with a Datalog-based policy language? For each predicate symbol p, we associate each of its argument positions $i \in \{1,...,\mathbf{ar}(p)\}$ with a finite binary relation $\lhd_p^i$ on constants. Intuitively, $\lhd_p^i$ is the hierarchy relation that is applied to the ith argument of p.

Definition 7 (Hierarchical semantics). A ground atom $p(c_1,...,c_n)$ is *hierarchically derivable* from a policy $\mathcal{P}$ (we write $\mathcal{P} \vdash^* p(c_1,...,c_n)$) iff $\mathcal{P} \vdash p(c_1,...,c_n)$, or for all $i \in \{1,...,n\}$, there exists a constant c_i' such that $c_i' = c_i$ or $c_i' \lhd_p^i c_i$, and $\mathcal{P} \vdash^* p(c_1',...,c_n')$.

Since the rule can be applied transitively, we get the property that if $p(c')$ holds, then p also holds for *all* c further down the hierarchy. Every argument position of a predicate is associated with a hierarchy. This also covers the (usual) case where the argument position is non-hierarchical: in this case, we set $\lhd_p^i$ to be the empty relation.

To illustrate the method, we show how the examples above can be expressed in a Datalog-based policy language under the hierarchical semantics.

1. We express the role-permission relation using the predicate hasPerm. For example, hasPerm(`Engineer`,`Read`) states that users in the engineer role have read permission. The first argument position of hasPerm has a non-empty hierarchy relation: let $r_1 \lhd_{\mathsf{hasPerm}}^1 r_2$ whenever role r_2 is strictly more senior than role r_1 (and there exists no role r_3 in between). If we have

   $\texttt{Engineer} \lhd_{\mathsf{hasPerm}}^1 \texttt{SeniorEngineer} \lhd_{\mathsf{hasPerm}}^1 \texttt{PrincipalEngineer}$, and
   $\texttt{SeniorEngineer} \lhd_{\mathsf{hasPerm}}^1 \texttt{DistinguishedEngineer}$,

   then hasPerm(`Engineer`,`Read`) implies hasPerm(`PrincipalEngineer`,`Read`) and hasPerm(`DistinguishedEngineer`,`Read`).

   The derivations require two applications of the second rule in Def. 7.
2. We define the hierarchies $\texttt{TopSecret} \lhd_{\mathsf{readClearance}}^2 \texttt{Secret} \lhd_{\mathsf{readClearance}}^2 \texttt{Confidential}$, and $\texttt{Confidential} \lhd_{\mathsf{writeClearance}}^2 \texttt{Secret} \lhd_{\mathsf{writeClearance}}^2 \texttt{TopSecret}$ (i.e., $\lhd_{\mathsf{writeClearance}}^2 = (\lhd_{\mathsf{readClearance}}^2)^{-1}$). Then the following rules implement MAC:

$$\mathsf{canRead}(x,f) :- \mathsf{label}(f,l), \mathsf{readClearance}(x,l).$$
$$\mathsf{canWrite}(x,f) :- \mathsf{label}(f,l), \mathsf{writeClearance}(x,l).$$
$$\mathsf{readClearance}(x,l) :- \mathsf{label}(x,l).$$
$$\mathsf{writeClearance}(x,l) :- \mathsf{label}(x,l).$$

If Alice has the security label `Secret`, she is able to read files labelled `Secret` and `Confidential`, and write files labelled `Secret` and `TopSecret`.
3. Let $f_1 \lhd^2_{\mathsf{read}} f_2$ whenever f_1 is the immediate parent path of the path f_2. Then the fact read(`A`, `/foo/`) implies read(`A`, `/foo/bar/baz/test.txt`).

How can we evaluate queries under this modified hierarchical semantics, without having to change the existing Datalog evaluation engine? It turns out that we can encode the hierarchical semantics directly in Datalog, while preserving the correctness and termination guarantees, provided that I/O-safeness is enforced.

We do this by treating $\lhd^i_p$ as a binary predicate symbol, with an associated mode set $\mathbf{mode}(\lhd^i_p)$. As in the case of constraints and functions, this requires that the evaluation engine is able to call an external module at runtime that provides answers to $\lhd^i_p$-queries. For example, if $(\text{OUT}, \text{IN}) \in \mathbf{mode}(\lhd^i_p)$, the module implementing $\lhd^i_p$ must be able to enumerate all instantiations of x that satisfy $x \lhd^i_p c$, given any constant c.

In the following, for all normal predicate symbols p occurring in the policy $\mathcal{P}$, let $n = \mathbf{ar}(p)$, and let $x_1, ..., x_n$ and $x'_1, ..., x'_n$ be distinct variables. For $i \in \{1, ..., n\}$, let σ_i be the substitution $[x_i \mapsto x'_i]$, and let $M_i = \{\pi^n_i(\mu) \mid \mu \in \mathbf{mode}(p)\}$ (where π^n_i is the ith projection function on n-tuples).

The algorithm below constructs a policy $\mathcal{P}^*$ that encapsulates the hierarchical semantics from Def. 7. First initialize $\mathcal{P}^* := \mathcal{P}$. Then for each $i \in \{1, ..., n\}$ such that $\lhd^i_p$ is non-empty:

1. If $\text{OUT} \notin M_i$ and $(\text{OUT}, \_) \in \mathbf{mode}(\lhd^i_p)$, add the following rule to $\mathcal{P}^*$:

$$p(x_1, ..., x_n) :- x'_i \lhd^i_p x_i,\ p(x_1\sigma_i, ..., x_n\sigma_i).$$

2. Otherwise, if $\text{OUT} \in M_i$ and $(\_, \text{OUT}) \in \mathbf{mode}(\lhd^i_p)$, add the following rule to $\mathcal{P}^*$:

$$p(x_1, ..., x_n) :- p(x_1\sigma_i, ..., x_n\sigma_i), x'_i \lhd^i_p x_i.$$

3. Otherwise, the algorithm fails.

The following proposition states that $\mathcal{P}^*$ can be used to evaluate queries against $\mathcal{P}$ according to the hierarchical semantics, provided that the original policy is I/O-safe.

Proposition 8. If $\mathcal{P}$ is I/O-safe and $\mathcal{P}^*$ exists, then $\mathcal{P}^*$ is I/O-safe. Furthermore, for all I/O-safe queries Q,

$$\mathcal{P}^* \vdash Q \Longleftrightarrow \mathcal{P} \vdash^* Q.$$

Let us now consider the "natural" modes of the hierarchies from the four examples above:

1. We would set $\mathbf{mode}(\lhd^1_{\mathsf{hasPerm}}) = \{(\text{OUT}, \text{OUT})\}$ if the number of roles is very small. Otherwise, we set it to $\{(\text{IN}, \text{OUT}), (\text{OUT}, \text{IN})\}$, i.e., given a role, we should be able to efficiently enumerate both the more senior and the more junior roles. Neither case imposes a restriction on the mode of the first argument of hasPerm.
2. The hierarchy $\lhd^2_{\mathsf{readClearance}}$ is small, so its only mode is (OUT, OUT). This imposes no restriction on the mode of the second argument of readClearance.

3. Assuming that the file system is large, the mode of $\lhd^2_{\mathsf{read}}$ should be restricted to (OUT, IN), i.e., computing the parent path of a given path. (IN, OUT) is probably not advisable as a directory may contain a large number of files, and (OUT, OUT) is clearly not feasible. If $\mathbf{mode}(\lhd^2_{\mathsf{read}}) = \{(\text{OUT}, \text{IN})\}$, then all modes of read must be of the form $(\_, \text{IN})$. This is a natural choice for read, because there may be a huge number of files that a single user can read.

5 Conclusion

We have shown that replacing Datalog's standard safeness condition by our more liberal I/O-safeness condition facilitates powerful language extensions that retain Datalog's nice complexity and termination properties. The increased expressiveness comes at the price of a slightly more complicated syntactic restriction (which can be automatically checked), and the requirement to specify the input/output mode for each predicate. But since the features discussed in this paper are extremely useful in practice, we believe that this is a good tradeoff. Moreover, in our experience, it is intuitive and natural to write I/O-safe policies: the largest example of a trust management policy to date [1], a hand-written electronic health record policy consisting of 375 constrained Datalog rules, passes the I/O-safeness check — even though it was originally developed for the Cassandra system, which runs under the even more liberal, but generally undecidable, Constraint Logic Programming paradigm, and therefore actually would not require I/O-safeness. Conversely, failure of I/O-safeness is usually an indication of a bug.

References

1. Becker, M.: Information governance in nhs's npfit: A case for policy specification. International Journal of Medical Informatics 76(5-6), 432–437 (2007)
2. Becker, M.Y., Fournet, C., Gordon, A.D.: SecPAL: Design and semantics of a decentralized authorization language. Journal of Computer Security 18(4), 619–665 (2010)
3. Becker, M.Y., Sewell, P.: Cassandra: Flexible trust management, applied to electronic health records. In: IEEE Computer Security Foundations, pp. 139–154 (2004)
4. Bell, D.E., Lapadula, L.J.: Secure computer systems: Unified exposition and Multics interpretation. Technical report, The MITRE Corporation (July 1975)
5. Boley, H., Tabet, S., Wagner, G.: Design rationale of RuleML: A markup language for semantic web rules. In: International Semantic Web Working Symposium (SWWS), pp. 381–402 (2001)
6. Ceri, S., Gottlob, G., Tanca, L.: What you always wanted to know about Datalog (and never dared to ask). IEEE Transactions on Knowledge and Data Engineering 1(1), 146–166 (1989)
7. Dantsin, E., Eiter, T., Gottlob, G., Voronkov, A.: Complexity and expressive power of logic programming. In: CCC 1997: Proceedings of the 12th Annual IEEE Conference on Computational Complexity, p. 82. IEEE Computer Society, Washington, DC (1997)
8. De Bruijn, J., Lausen, H., Polleres, A., Fensel, D.: The web service modeling language WSML: An overview. In: Sure, Y., Domingue, J. (eds.) ESWC 2006. LNCS, vol. 4011, pp. 590–604. Springer, Heidelberg (2006)
9. Debray, S.K., Warren, D.S.: Automatic mode inference for logic programs. Journal of Logic Programming 5(3), 207–229 (1988)

10. Detreville, J.: Binder, a logic-based security language. In: IEEE Symposium on Security and Privacy, pp. 105–113 (2002)
11. Horrocks, I., Patel-Schneider, P., Boley, H., Tabet, S., Grosof, B., Dean, M.: SWRL: A semantic web rule language combining OWL and RuleML. W3C Member Submission (2010)
12. Jaffar, J., Maher, M.J.: Constraint logic programming: a survey. Journal of Logic Programming 19/20, 503–581 (1994)
13. Jim, T.: SD3: A trust management system with certified evaluation. In: Proceedings of the 2001 IEEE Symposium on Security and Privacy, pp. 106–115 (2001)
14. Li, N., Grosof, B., Feigenbaum, J.: A practically implementable and tractable delegation logic. In: IEEE Symposium on Security and Privacy, pp. 27–42 (2000)
15. Li, N., Mitchell, J.C.: Datalog with constraints: A foundation for trust management languages. In: Dahl, V. (ed.) PADL 2003. LNCS, vol. 2562, pp. 58–73. Springer, Heidelberg (2002)
16. Sandhu, R.: Rationale for the RBAC96 family of access control models. In: Proceedings of the 1st ACM Workshop on Role-Based Access Control (1997)
17. Sintek, M., Decker, S.: TRIPLE – a query, inference, and transformation language for the semantic web. In: Horrocks, I., Hendler, J. (eds.) ISWC 2002. LNCS, vol. 2342, pp. 364–378. Springer, Heidelberg (2002)
18. Smolka, G.: Making control and data flow in logic programs explicit. In: ACM Symposium on LISP and Functional Programming, pp. 311–322 (1984)
19. Stärk, R.F.: Input/output dependencies of normal logic programs. Journal of Logic and Computation 4(3), 249 (1994)

Knowledgebase Representation Language Interoperation Tool

Taylor Osmun, Patrick Thébeau, and Yevgen Biletskiy

University of New Brunswick,
Fredericton, New Brunswick, Canada
{w91pq,i202q,biletski}@unb.ca

Abstract. This paper describes the software solution to the Semantic Web's interoperation issue: the Knowledge Representation Language Interoperation Tool. Its fully implemented parsing and engine execution frameworks are presented, touching on how they can be easily used by developers for future expansion. The interoperation method (with the use of the Java Interoperation Object) is explained generally, as well as in the context of Positional-Slotted Knowledge (POSL) and Notation 3 (N3) representations. Additionally, details on the connections found between the relational and graph-oriented paradigms are shown via interoperation of POSL and N3. Finally, an example usage of the system is provided in order to convey the usefulness of the software in the Semantic Web.

Keywords: Euler, Interoperation, Knowledge Representation, Notation 3, OOjDREW, Positional-Slotted Knowledge, Query, Rule Markup Language, Semantic Web.

1 Introduction

The concept of the Semantic Web [1] has been around for the greater part of ten years and during that time, countless projects around the globe have been seeking to be at the forefront of this movement, with some knowledge representations already having industry recognition (e.g. Drools). Despite this, there are little to no implemented products which offer a full suite of interoperability between vast numbers of knowledge representation paradigms, and so a software tool supporting this interoperation would prove to be an innovative addition to this field of computer science. The goal of the present software project is the creation of a software application that both efficiently and easily acts as a general interoperation portal between Semantic Web knowledge representation (KR) languages. Our Knowledgebase Representation Interoperation Tool (KRLIT) succeeds in realizing this goal through the creation of both a knowledge representation interoperation and reasoning engine framework. Both of these frameworks are designed with flexibility in mind, and so have the ability to be extended with any number of knowledge representation languages and reasoning engines, as defined by the developer. Each

F. Olken et al. (Eds.): RuleML 2011 - America, LNCS 7018, pp. 58–65, 2011.

KR is connected to others in the framework via the implementation of a translator to go to and from the central interoperation tool, the Java Interoperation Object (JIO). Currently, KRLIT has implemented support for two different KR viewpoints, each with an individual language: relational knowledge through *Positional-Slotted Knowledge* (POSL) [2], and low-level triple representation through *Notation 3* (N3) [3]. In addition to strict translation of knowledge representations, we also support the querying of supported knowledge bases through a single execution engine for every supported knowledgebase representation language (*OOjDREW* [4] for POSL, and *Euler* [5] for N3).

2 System Architecture

As previously stated, the goal of KRLIT is to create an easy to use and efficient framework for knowledge representation language interoperation. It succeeds in this by using a lightweight model-view-controller architecture that makes packages easy to plug into the system via both strictly defined interface requirements for both parsers and execution engines, and useful library utilities. The use of these interfaces ensures that all additionally developed add-ons will conform to the original specifications and can thus be utilized interchangeably with all other packages.

The parsing and reverse parsing framework (Fig. 1) gives developers the ability to translate their language to the Java Interoperation Object (section 3) as an AtomCollection, as well as transform existing AtomCollection's to their destination representation. It supports the former (translation to JIO) via the use of the *Parser* interface located in the *interfacing* package. This interface (which all Parser's must implement) requires that there be at least one method which allows the user to parse a given *InputObjectCollection* to a single *AtomCollection*. It should now be mentioned that the InputObjectCollection is one of the utilities offered by the KRLIT system. This *InputObjectCollection* contains a list of *InputObject*s; each InputObject's origin can be a String[1], File[2], or URL[3]; consequently, the output of the InputObject can be a String. In addition to the Parsing interface, translation of an AtomCollection to a String is also supported via the use of the *ReverseParser* interface. This interface (which all ReverseParser's must implement) requires that there be at least one method which allows the user to reverse parse a given *AtomCollection* to a single *String*. It should also be noted that there is an additional argument required, *asQuery*. This argument will inform the *ReverseParser* as to whether or not the user wishes the output to be a query (which can look different from a standard request in some knowledge representation languages). Finally, the *Builtins* class of the JIO package is also extended in order to provide the user with a list of the required built-ins which need to be extended in order to provide complete interoperation.

---

1 http://download.oracle.com/javase/1.5.0/docs/api/java/lang/String.html

2 http://download.oracle.com/javase/1.4.2/docs/api/java/io/File.html

3 http://download.oracle.com/javase/1.4.2/docs/api/java/net/URL.html

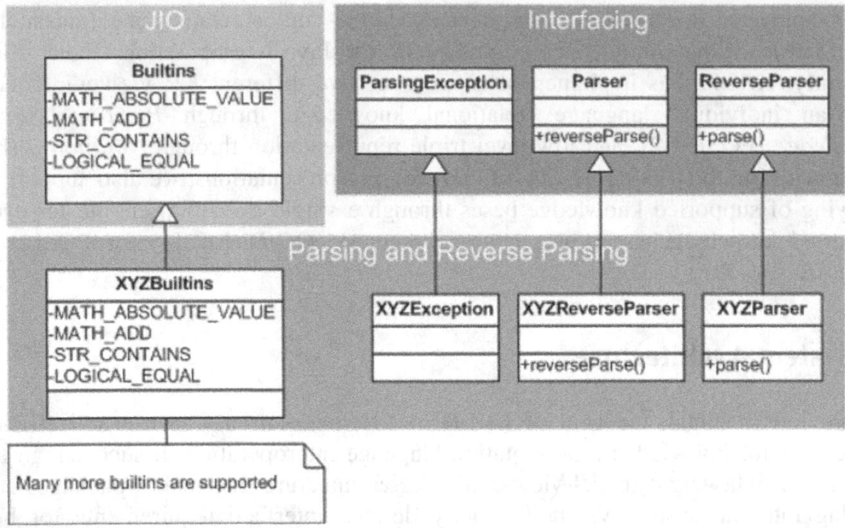

Fig. 1. Parsing and Reverse Parsing Framework Class Diagram. This is the framework which all translation packages use.

The engine execution framework (Fig. 2) gives developers the ability to utilize reasoning engines which support their knowledge representation language. It supports this via the use of the *EngineExecutor* interface located in the *interfacing* package. This interface (which all *EngineExecutor's* must implement) requires that there be at least one method which allows the user to reason a given list of knowledgebases, taxonomies, and queries (all represented via individual *InputObjectCollection*'s) resulting in a single String answer.

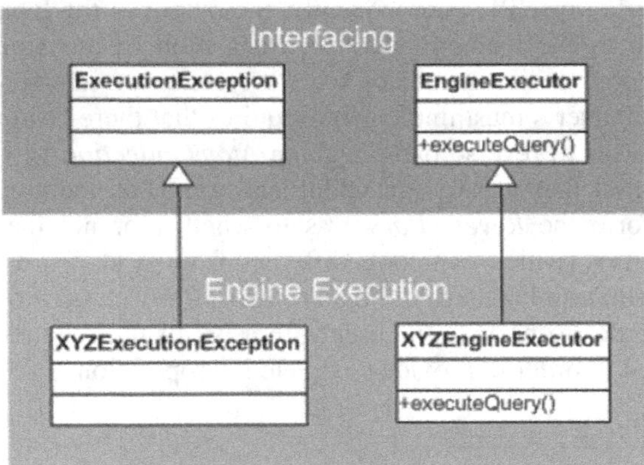

Fig. 2. Engine Execution Framework Class Diagram. This is the framework which all reasoning engine packages use.

3 Java Interoperation Object (JIO)

The Java Interoperation Object is the basis of all interoperation methods found within the framework of KRLIT. The objective of this package is to capture as many aspects of the various knowledge representation paradigms available today (e.g. relational, graph-oriented, etc.) through a universal Java architecture which can support all of them in some fashion. Using RuleML [6] as a building block, KRLIT has successfully created and implemented such a concept, and is now used to translate supported POSL and N3 knowledge bases (sections 4 and 5). It does so by providing developers with a variety of element types which their knowledge base concepts may be stored in.

Typically, atoms are used to represent the smallest element in a knowledgebase, and so this idea was also used in the implementation of the JIO. KRLIT uses Atoms in the JIO to represent the smallest "thing" in a knowledge base (e.g. for POSL this is a relation, for N3 this is a subject). Atoms can be further decomposed into subparts, but those parts can never be referenced without being encapsulated within the atom itself. Fig. 3 depicts how the JIO atom can represent the various data types in a typical knowledge representation language.

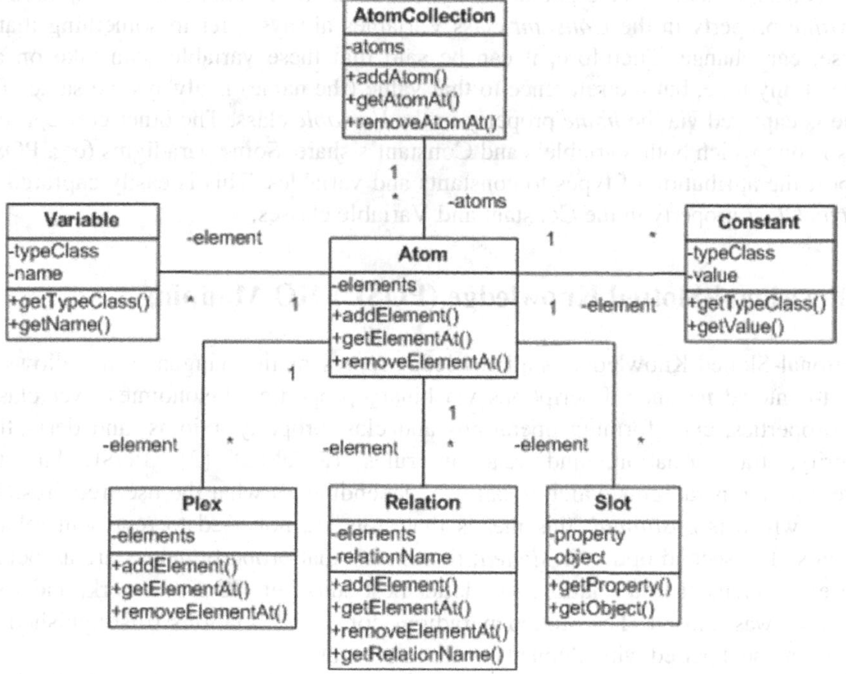

Fig. 3. Atom and Atom Collection Class Diagram. This displays the range of possible Atom contents in the JIO.

As mentioned previously, knowledge representations come in many "shapes and sizes", and so to capture the majority of them, clever use of RuleML's Relation (Rel) and Complex Term (Plex) had to be introduced. A relation in terms of common sense is an abstraction which characterizes two objects together; however, KR paradigms implement this many in different ways. The end result of a translation stores the Relation with a Vector[4] of *elements* and a relation name as *relationName*. This way, the Relation object can be easily associated with its bindings. Complex Terms however, are slightly different than that of a relation. Typically, a complex term is found when you nest a blank node Atom within an existing Atom. This can be captured by a similar structure to that of a Relation object by using a Vector of *elements*, but instead excludes the relation name.

3.1 Slots

A slot is a fairly simple concept to encode. Like an object-oriented programming language, a slot ties a property element (either Variable or Constant) to its value (any element). This is implemented via the use of the *property* and *value* pairs. Like the majority of knowledge representations, variables and constants are the building blocks of reasoning, and are easily implemented with our JIO. Constants always refer to something that is static and true in a knowledge base. Therefore, it can be said that these constants always have one and only one final *value*. This value is captured via the *value* property in the *Constant* class.Variables always refer to something that of course, can change. Therefore, it can be said that these variables can take on any value at any time, but the reference to that value (the name) is always the same. This name is captured via the *name* property in the *Variable* class. The other concept, type class is one which both Variable's and Constant's share. Some paradigms (e.g. POSL) support the attribution of types to constants and variables. This is easily captured via the *typeClass* property in the Constant and Variable classes.

4 Positional-Slotted Knowledge (POSL) JIO Mapping

Positional-Slotted Knowledge is a knowledge representation language that allows for object-centered instance descriptions via binary properties, taxonomies over classes and properties, class-forming operations and class/property axioms, and derivation, integrity, transformation, and reaction rules (RuleML) [2]. POSL has two representation paradigms which it can use, depending on what the user requires. The first of which is *positional*; this means that slots are not used to represent relation contents. The second option is *slotted*; this means that property names are associated with every element in a relation. The latter best suits our JIO framework, and so its paradigm was chosen. The slotted paradigm consist of relations (distinguished via relation names) paired with elements of those relations.

The single existing parser for POSL is also written in Java for OOjDREW [4], and so many concepts were taken from this implementation. The architecture of this

[4] `http://download.oracle.com/javase/1.4.2/docs/api/java/util/Vector.html`

parser is simple; there is a general *parseElement* method, which given a String, will determine its type (e.g. Atom, Constant, etc) and then invoke the appropriate method (e.g. *parseAtom).* The main approach to providing the parseElement method its input was clever usage of Java's built-in StringTokenizer library to cut the knowledge bases into manageable bits. For example, the '.' character was used to grab single Atoms, and the '(' character was used to isolate a single relation within the Atom. Using the methods described, we cut the knowledgebase into manageable pieces. However, these pieces need to be given to the JIO in a standard manner, which is briefly described in the list below:

- **Atom:** Each Atom is delimitated by '.'
- **Relation:** Each Atom has only one relation, which has a single relation name and list of elements
- **Plex:** A complex term can only exist as an element within a relation (which could also be the value of the slot). Like a relation it has a relation name and a list of elements. It is deliminated by '['
- **Slot:** Each slot is deliminated by '->' which has its property on the left, and value on the right
- **Variable:** Each variable is an element deliminated by '?'. Its type class is deliminated by ':'
- **Constant:** Each constant is any element within a relation or Plex which is not a Plex, slot, or variable. Its type class is deliminated by ':'

5 Notation 3 (N3)

Notation 3 is a compact, rule-extended version of RDF's XML syntax [3]; in this way, RDF's complex machine understandable language becomes much more readable to humans. RDF facts and rules are still written with triples (subject, property, and object) and so this language is very expressive in nature, but also great for human comprehension. The N3 parser design is the same to that of the POSL parser (section 4). There is a general *parseElement* method, which given a String, will determine its type (e.g. Atom, Constant, etc) and then invoke the appropriate method (e.g. *parseAtom).* However, what makes the N3 parser vastly different to that of the POSL parser, is in the implementation method behind providing the *parseElement* method with its input. The Prolog interpreter, SWI-Prolog[5], contains a library of RDF utilities. Amongst these utilities is an N3 parser created by Yves Raimond[6] which converts an N3 knowledge base into a Prolog knowledge base. With this tool at hand, an interface to Prolog from Java, JPL[7], is used to allow Prolog to create Java objects corresponding to N3 triples. Upon finishing the Prolog parsing, the N3 parser class now has a list of all triples in the knowledge base. These String representations of these triples are then passed to the *parseElements* method.

---

[5] `http://www.swi-prolog.org/`

[6] `http://moustaki.org/`

[7] `http://www.swi-prolog.org/packages/jpl/java_api/index.html`

Like in its POSL counterpart, we cut the knowledgebase into manageable pieces. However, there are a significant number of constraints used when creating AtomCollections based on these pieces:

- **Atom:** Each Atom is a single triple subject
- **Relation:** Each Atom has only one relation, which has a single relation name (defined by the property *:type*'s object), and list of elements
- **Plex:** A Plex is a BNode (subject without a defined name) is also an object of a current subject are defined to be Plex terms
- **Slot:** Each slot is a property object pair where the property is the triple's property, and value is the triple's object
- **Variable:** A variable can only be a triple's object, and starts with '?'
- **Constant:** Each constant is any triple's object which which is not a Plex, slot, or variable.

6 Example Usage and Conclusion

KRLIT is capable of supporting any kind of knowledge base which is using its supported representation under the individual representation constraints. However, it is useful to see an example usage of the system under a specific context. In this case, we assess two different automobile insurance companies (Mainland Insurance, and Healthy Life) who while using different knowledge representation languages, use the same schema for their facts and rules.Let us assume that *Mainland Insurance* focuses primarily on *Economic* classed customers using an N3 knowledge base. *Healthy Life* on the other hand, caters to *Gold* and *Platinum* classed customers using a POSL knowledge base. Suppose we wish to find the discount policies of both companies, but we are only familiar with the POSL knowledge representation language. Normally, this would prevent the use of Mainland Insurance's knowledgebase, but with KRLIT we are able to query it, and have answers returned in POSL. For example, our POSL query is for finding all discounts. During query processing time, KRLIT's POSLParser class is used to transform this query into a JIO based AtomCollection, which the N3ReverseParser class accepts as input. This provides us with the N3 representation of this POSL query. This is easily fed to OOjDREW, whose answers are returned in POSL. Now that we have an equivalent N3 query, it can be given to Euler as input, whose answers are used by N3Parser to create the JIO based AtomCollection. It is then fed to the POSLReverseParser to provide us with the POSL representation of the N3 answers; these are combined with the OOjDREW results (Fig. 4).

Although the initial work in interoperation among the Semantic Web based rule languages had been previously done [7], there was a gap in a more general technical solution. The present paper has described the Knowledge Representation Language Interoperation Tool as a solution to the Semantic Web's interoperation gap issue. Its framework has been analyzed in detail, providing the reader with an understanding of how developers may expand upon it by programming support for their preferred knowledge base representation language and/or reasoning engine using the parsing and engine execution frameworks in conjunction with the Java Interoperation Object.

```
Discount(company->MainlandInsurance;
        clientID->1:Real;age->19:Real;class->Economic;discount->0.0:Real).
Discount(company->MainlandInsurance;
        clientID->6:Real;age->17:Real;class->Economic;discount->0.0:Real).
Discount(company->MainlandInsurance;
        clientID->2:Real;age->22:Real;class->Economic;discount->0.1:Real).
Discount(company->HealthyLife;
        clientID->3:Real;age->19:Real;class->Gold;discount->0.2:Real).
Discount(company->HealthyLife;
        clientID->5:Real;age->30:Real;class->Gold;discount->0.4:Real).
Discount(company->HealthyLife;
        clientID->4:Real;age->29:Real;class->Platinum;discount->0.7:Real).
```

Fig. 4. POSL representation of OOjDREW and Euler answers (the final result of querying KRLIT with the POSL query)

References

1. Berners-Lee, T., Hendler, J., Lassila, O.: The Semantic Web. Scientific American 284(5), 34–43 (2001)
2. Boley, H.: POSL: An Integrated Positional-Slotted Language for Semantic Web Knowledge (2004), `http://www.ruleml.org/submission/rulemlshortation.html`
3. Berners-Lee, T., et al.: Notation (N3), A readable RDF Syntax, `http://www.w3.org/TeamSubmission/n3/`
4. Ball, M., Boley, H., Hirtle, D., Mei, J., Spencer, B.: The OO jDREW Reference Implementation of RuleML. In: Adi, A., Stoutenburg, S., Tabet, S. (eds.) RuleML 2005. LNCS, vol. 3791, pp. 218–223. Springer, Heidelberg (2005)
5. Euler, `http://eulersharp.sourceforge.net/`
6. Boley, H.: The RuleML Family of Web Rule Languages. In: Alferes, J.J., Bailey, J., May, W., Schwertel, U. (eds.) PPSWR 2006. LNCS, vol. 4187, pp. 1–17. Springer, Heidelberg (2006)
7. Boley, H., Osmun, T.M., Craig, B.L.: WellnessRules: A Web 3.0 Case Study in RuleML-Based Prolog-N3 Profile Interoperation. In: Governatori, G., Hall, J., Paschke, A. (eds.) RuleML 2009. LNCS, vol. 5858, pp. 43–52. Springer, Heidelberg (2009)

Consistency and Provenance in Rule Processing

Eric Jui-Yi Kao

Computer Science Department,
Stanford University,
Stanford, CA 94305,
United States of America
erickao@cs.stanford.edu

Abstract. Open collections of data and rules on the web are typically characterized by heterogeneous quality and imperfect consistency. In reasoning with data and rules on the web, it is important to know where an answer comes from (provenance) and whether the it is reasonable considering the inconsistencies (inconsistency-tolerance). In this paper, I draw attention to the idea that provenance and inconsistency-tolerance play mutually supporting roles under the theme of reasoning with imperfect information on the web. As a specific example, I make use of basic provenance information to avoid unreasonable answers in reasoning with rules and inconsistent data.

1 Introduction

Data and rules on the web are typically characterized by imperfect data, heterogeneity in quality, distributed authorship, semantic misalignments, and inconsistencies. Furthermore, the highly distributed nature of web data storage calls for the replication of data and the caching of computed (or intermediate) results. In reasoning in such a setting, two important requirements emerge:

1. Computed answers must be associated with information on the sources they rely on.
2. Inconsistencies must be tolerated: logical explosion and unreasonable answers must be avoided.

The first requirement calls for the computation and maintenance of provenance information on computed answers. The second requirement can be fulfilled by following an inconsistency-tolerant semantics in reasoning.

Much work has been done on provenance information in web data (for example [26,16,10,11,25]). The processing of inconsistent knowledge on the web has also gained attention [18,23,28,29,3]. In this paper, I draw attention to the idea that provenance and inconsistency-tolerance play mutually supporting roles in the overarching theme of reasoning with imperfect information on the web. As a specific example, I make use of basic provenance information to avoid unreasonable answers in reasoning with rules and inconsistent data.

F. Olken et al. (Eds.): RuleML 2011 - America, LNCS 7018, pp. 66–80, 2011.

In section 2, I give a motivating example. In section 3, I formally develop the *existential answers* semantics. In section 4, I show that the problem of computing existential answers is $\mathcal{NP}$-Complete, ruling out a popular rewriting technique which does not rely on provenance computation. Then, in sections 5 and 6, I give a provenance-based method for computing existential answers. In section 7, I give another characterization of existential answers via answer set programming. Finally, I conclude by discussing related work and future directions.

2 Motivating Example

The data in table 1 will serve as example data. The BirthYear table associates each person with a birth year. Each person has at most one birth year, but in the example data two conflicting birth years are specified for Cody (and David) because they come from two sources, at least one of which is incorrect. The RecessionYear table gives the recessionary years in the United States.

Table 1. Example data

BirthYear

Person	Year
Adam	1980
Brian	1991
Cody	1984
Cody	1991
David	1980
David	1984

RecessionYear

Year
1980
1981
1982
1990
1991

Table 2. Cached/Materialized Results

RecessionBorn

Person
Adam
Brian
Cody
David

Rule:

```
RecessionBorn(X)  :-  BirthYear(X,Y), RecessionYear (Y)
```

OfAge

Person
Adam
Cody
David

Rule:

```
OfAge(X) :- BirthYear(X,Z),Z<1989
```

Consider the following scenario:
For a study, a researcher would like to send out surveys to those who were born during a recessionary year in the United States and are also legally of age. So adding to the rules in table 2, the researcher writes the rule:

```
candidate(X)  :-  RecessionBorn (X) ∧ OfAge(X)
```

Standard datalog semantics, which do not consider the constraints, would produce the answers {`Adam`, `Cody`, `David`}, the natural join between the two intensional relations. By digging down, we see that `RecessionBorn(Cody)` is derived from `BirthYear(Cody, 1991)` and `OfAge(Cody)` is derived from `BirthYear(Cody, 1984)`. But at least one of these two pieces of data is incorrect. We see that `Cody` is not a reasonable answer because whether we choose `BirthYear(Cody, 1984)` or `BirthYear(Cody, 1991)`, `Cody` does not satisfy the criteria intended by the query.

Consider the two conflicting tuples `BirthYear(David, 1980)` and `BirthYear(David, 1984)`. If we chose to believe `BirthYear(David, 1980)`, then `David` is an answer. But if we chose to believe `BirthYear(David, 1984)`, then `David` is not an answer. Since we have no information that leads us to believe one of the two conflicting tuples over the other, `David` is not an unreasonable answer.

The notion of *existential answers* (definition 4 in the next section) formalizes this intuition, admitting answers which are reasonable and rejecting answers which are unreasonable. The idea is to reason from consistent subsets of data so that conflicting pieces of information cannot be combined to give an unreasonable answer.

3 Formal Development

In this section, I develop the formal definitions necessary to define *existential answers*. The development follows the definition of datalog in [1].

Let **dom** be a fixed, countably infinite set which serves as the *underlying domain*. For example, **dom** may be the universe of all possible URI's. A *constant* is an element of **dom**. A schema S is a nonempty, finite set of relation names, each with a fixed arity. An instance of a schema S is a finite set of facts (ground atoms) over S and **dom**.

Let **var** be a fixed, countably infinite set of variables that is disjoint from **dom**. A *tuple* is a vector of elements from **dom**. A *free tuple* is a vector of elements from $\mathbf{dom} \cup \mathbf{var}$. I use $X, Y, Z, U, V, x, y, z, u, v$ and all their subscripted variants to denote variables. All other symbols appearing in a tuple are constants.

Definition 1 (Datalog syntax). *A rule is an expression of the form* $R_1(u_1)\ :-\ R_2(u_2), \ldots, R_n(u_n), \phi(u_\phi)$, *where* $n \geq 1, R_1, \ldots, R_n$ *are relation names,* $u_1, \ldots, u_n, u_\phi$ *are free tuples of appropriate arities, and* ϕ *is a boolean combination of built-in predicates* $(=, \neq, >, \text{etc.})$. *Each variable occurring in* u_1 *or* u_ϕ *must also occur in at least one of* $u_2, \ldots, u_n$. *A datalog program is a finite set of datalog rules.*

To give semantics to datalog programs, one interprets the rules as first-order sentences. Each rule $R_1(u_1) :- R_2(u_2), \ldots, R_n(u_n), \phi(u_\phi)$, is associated with the sentence $\forall x_1 \cdots x_q(\exists x_{q+1} \cdots x_m(R_2(u_2) \wedge \cdots \wedge R_n(u_n) \wedge \phi(u_\phi) \rightarrow R_1(u_1)))$, where $x_1, \ldots, x_q$ are the variables occurring in the head ($R_1(u_1)$) and $x_{q+1}, \ldots, x_m$ are the remaining variables occurring in the rule. For a datalog program P, the set of first-order sentences associated with P is denoted as Σ_P.

Definition 2 (Datalog Semantics). *Let P be a datalog program and D finite set of facts. A model of P in a finite set of facts satisfying Σ_P. The semantics of P on input D, denoted $P(D)$ is the minimum model of P containing D.*[1] *For a fact d, We write $\langle P, D\rangle \vdash_{\mathrm{dl}} d$ to denote that $d \in P(D)$.*

Definition 3 (Denial Constraints). *A denial constraint is a sentence of the form $\forall x_1 \cdots x_m(\neg R_1(u_1) \vee \cdots \neg R_n(u_n) \vee \phi(u_\phi))$, where $n \geq 1, R_1, \ldots, R_n$ are relation names, $u_1, \ldots, u_n, u_\phi$ are free tuples of appropriate arities, ϕ is a boolean combination of built-in predicates ($=, \neq, >$,etc.), and $x_1 \cdots x_m$ are the variables occurring in $u_1, \ldots, u_n, u_\phi$. Each variable occurring in u_ϕ must also occur in at least one of $u_1, \ldots, u_n$. A denial constraint can also be considered a "rule" with an empty head, i.e., $:- R_1(u_1), \ldots, R_n(u_n), \neg\phi(u_\phi))$.*

Definition 4 (Existential Answers). *Given a set of facts D, a set of rules P, and a set of constraints C, a fact d is an existential answers with respect to (D, P, C) if and only if there exists $D' \subseteq D$ such that $P(D')$ is a model of C and $\langle P, D'\rangle \vdash_{\mathrm{dl}} d$. We denote this fact as $\langle P, C, D\rangle \vdash_{\exists\mathrm{dl}} d$.*

Example 1. Here I apply the definition of existential answers to the example in section 2. For brevity, I use the following short-from relation names: `by` for `BirthYear`, `ry` for `RecessionYear`, `oa` for `OfAge`, `rb` for `RecessionBorn`, and `ca` for `candidate`. Let D be the base data (from table 1).

$D = \{$
  by(Adam, 1980), by(Brian, 1991), by(Cody, 1984), by(Cody, 1991),
  by(David, 1980), by(David, 1984), ry(1980), ry(1981), ry(1982),
  ry(1990), ry(1991)
$\}$

Let P be the datalog program.

$P = \{$
  oa(X) :- by(X, Z), Z < 1989,
  rb(X) :- by(X, Y), ry(Y),
  ca(X) :- rb(X), oa(X)
$\}$

Let C be the set of constraints.

$C = \{\forall XY(\neg by(X, Y) \vee \neg by(X, Z) \vee Y = Z)\}$

The collection of subsets D' of D such that $P(D')$ is a models of C are the following: (letting F = {by(Adam, 1980), by(Brian, 1991), ry(1980), ry(1981), ry(1982), ry(1990), ry(1991)})

[1] The minimum model always exists [1, pp 281, Theorem 12.2.3].

1. {by(Cody, 1984), by(David, 1980)} $\cup F$ and all its subsets
2. {by(Cody, 1984), by(David, 1984)} $\cup F$ and all its subsets
3. {by(Cody, 1991), by(David, 1980)} $\cup F$ and all its subsets
4. {by(Cody, 1991), by(David, 1984)} $\cup F$ and all its subsets

The corresponding sets of datalog answers (in the ca relation) are :

1. {ca(Adam), ca(David)} and all its subsets
2. {ca(Adam)} and all its subsets
3. {ca(Adam), ca(David)} and all its subsets
4. {ca(Adam)} and all its subsets

Hence, $\langle P, C, D\rangle \vdash_{\exists \text{dl}}$ ca(Adam) and $\langle P, C, D\rangle \vdash_{\exists \text{dl}}$ ca(David), but $\langle P, C, D\rangle \not\vdash_{\exists \text{dl}}$ ca(Brian) and $\langle P, C, D\rangle \not\vdash_{\exists \text{dl}}$ ca(Cody). The results agree with the intuition in section 2.

I present another example. This example contains recursive rules.

Example 2. A fact link(i, j, t) represents that there is a direct link of type t from i to j. Let the base facts $D = \{$
link(a, b, 1), link(a, c, 2), link(b, d, 2), link(c, d, 3), link(d, e, 1), link(d, f, 2)}

Let the program $P = \{$
aReaches(Y) : − link(a, Y, U),
aReaches(Y) : − aReaches(a, Z, U), link(Z, Y, V)
}.

It defines which nodes are reachable from a.

Furthermore, assume it is known that no two links of the same type can coexist. It can be formalized as the following constraint set $C = \{$
$\forall X_1 Y_1 X_2 Y_2 U(\neg link(X_1, Y_1, U) \vee \neg link(X_2, Y_2, U) \vee X_1 = X_2)$,
$\forall X_1 Y_1 X_2 Y_2 U(\neg link(X_1, Y_1, U) \vee \neg link(X_2, Y_2, U) \vee Y_1 = Y_2)$
}

The collection of subsets D' of D that are models of $C \cup \Sigma_P$ are the following:

1. {link(a, b, 1), link(a, c, 2), link(c, d, 3)} and all its subsets.
2. {link(a, b, 1), link(b, d, 2), link(c, d, 3)} and all its subsets.
3. {link(a, b, 1), link(d, f, 2), link(c, d, 3)} and all its subsets.
4. {link(d, e, 1), link(a, c, 2), link(c, d, 3)} and all its subsets.
5. {link(d, e, 1), link(b, d, 2), link(c, d, 3)} and all its subsets.
6. {link(d, e, 1), link(d, f, 2), link(c, d, 3)} and all its subsets.

The corresponding sets of datalog answers (in the aReaches relation) are :

1. {aReaches(n) : $n \in \{b, c, d\}$} and all its subsets
2. {aReaches(n) : $n \in \{b, d\}$} and all its subsets
3. {aReaches(n) : $n \in \{b\}$} and all its subsets
4. {aReaches(n) : $n \in \{c, d, e\}$} and all its subsets
5. {}
6. {}

Hence, $\langle P, C, D\rangle \vdash_{\exists \text{dl}}$ aReaches(b), aReaches(c), aReaches(d), aReaches(e), but $\langle P, C, D\rangle \not\vdash_{\exists \text{dl}}$ aReaches(f), aReaches(a). Notice that even though $\langle P, D\rangle \vdash_{\text{dl}}$ aReaches(f), it is rejected as an existential answer because it is unreasonable given the constraints.

Based on the definition, a brute-force method for computing existential answers consists of enumerating each set $D' \subseteq D$, checking whether D' is admissible, and finally checking whether $D' \vdash_{\text{dl}} d$. Because the number of subsets of D is $2^{|D|}$, this brute-force method is completely impractical. In section 6, I present a provenance-based method that constructs several special subsets of D and ignore all the other subsets.

4 Complexity and Rewriting

In typical data-oriented applications the set of facts is much larger than the set of rules. It is natural to consider the *data complexity* of rule evaluation. That is, we first fix the program P then consider the complexity of computing the answers given a set of facts as input.

For example, in datalog evaluation, the data complexity for a fixed program P is the complexity of the problem $\Delta_P = \{(D, d) : \langle P, D\rangle \vdash_{\text{dl}} d\}$, where D ranges over the sets of facts and d ranges over the facts.

For a finite set of denial constraints C and a nonrecursive datalog program P, the existential answers problem is $\Xi_{P,C} = \{(D, d) : \langle P, C, D\rangle \vdash_{\exists \text{dl}} d\}$.

If P is restricted to nonrecursive datalog programs, then, given the set of constraints C, it is possible to transform P into another program P' in the same language such that for all finite sets of facts D and all facts d, $\langle P, C, D\rangle \vdash_{\exists \text{dl}} d$ if and only if $\langle P', D\rangle \vdash_{\text{dl}} d$ [17,19][2]. Because datalog evaluation is polynomial time in data complexity, the rewriting result shows that the existential answers problem is also polynomial time in data complexity. That is, given a finite set of denial constraints C and a nonrecursive datalog program P, $\Xi_{P,C}$ is in $\mathcal{P}$.

One may want to apply a similar rewriting approach in the recursive case, rewriting a recursive datalog program P into another datalog program P' such that the standard answers to P' are precisely the existential answers to P. However, we show here that unless $\mathcal{P}$=$\mathcal{NP}$, such a rewriting scheme does not exist for all datalog programs. First, I show that for some datalog program P and finite set of constraints C, $\Xi_{P,C}$ is $\mathcal{NP}$-Hard. If we could rewrite P into a datalog program P' such that for all finite sets of facts D and all facts d, $\langle P, C, D\rangle \vdash_{\exists \text{dl}} d$ if and only if $\langle P', D\rangle \vdash_{\text{dl}} d$, we have reduced the problem $\Xi_{P,C}$ to the problem $\Delta_{P'}$, which is in $\mathcal{P}$. So unless $\mathcal{P}$=$\mathcal{NP}$, such a rewriting does not exist.

[2] The termination of the rewriting algorithm in [17] depends on the finiteness of the resolution closure of $P \cup C$. In the case of nonrecursive datalog P and denial constraints C, the union is essentially a finite set of nonrecursive Horn clauses, which has finite closure under resolution.

4.1 $\mathcal{NP}$-Completeness

First, I show that the existential answer problem is $\mathcal{NP}$-Hard by reduction from MONOTONE-3SAT, a well-known $\mathcal{NP}$-complete problem. I first outline the approach:

1. Fix a datalog program P and a finite constraint set C.
2. Define a polynomial-time transformation from any monotone 3CNF formula Φ to a finite set of facts D_Φ and a query fact d_Φ.
3. Show that for any monotone 3CNF formula Φ, Φ is satisfiable if and only if $\langle P, C, D_\Phi \rangle \vdash_{\exists \mathrm{dl}} d_\Phi$.

MONOTONE-3SAT is like 3SAT except that the input 3CNF formula is further restricted to be monotone, that is, each clause consists of either all positive literals or all negative literals, but never a mix of positive and negative literals. More precisely, a monotone 3CNF formula is a formula $(p_{1,1} \vee p_{1,2} \vee p_{1,3}) \wedge (p_{2,1} \vee p_{2,2} \vee p_{2,3}) \wedge \cdots \wedge (p_{n,1} \vee p_{n,2} \vee p_{n,3}) \wedge (q_{1,1} \vee q_{1,2} \vee q_{1,3}) \wedge (q_{2,1} \vee q_{2,2} \vee q_{2,3}) \wedge \cdots \wedge (q_{m,1} \vee q_{m,2} \vee q_{m,3})$, where each $p_{i,j}$ is a propositional variable and each $q_{i,j}$ is the negation of a propositional variable. Without loss of generality, we can assume $m \geq 1$ and $n \geq 1$.

Consider the datalog program $P = \{$

```
qp(x, y) : − ep(x, y, u, v),
qp(x, y) : − qp(x, z), ep(z, y, u, v),
qn(x, y) : − en(x, y, u, v),
qn(x, y) : − qn(x, z), en(z, y, u, v),
Q(x, y, z) : − qp(x, y), qn(x, z)
```

$\}$

Each $ep(x, y, u, v)$ or $en(x, y, u, v)$ is thought of as an edge from x to y, annotated with u and v. $Q(x, y, z)$ means there is an ep-path from x to y and also an en-path from x to z.

Now consider the constraint $c = \forall x_1 y_1 u_1 v x_2 y_2 u_2 (\neg ep(x_1, y_1, u_1, v) \vee \neg en(x_2, y_2, u_2, v))$. The constraint says that no pair of ep-edge and en-edge can coexist with the same v value.

For each monotone 3CNF formula $\Phi = (p_{1,1} \vee p_{1,2} \vee p_{1,3}) \wedge (p_{2,1} \vee p_{2,2} \vee p_{2,3}) \wedge \cdots \wedge (p_{n,1} \vee p_{n,2} \vee p_{n,3}) \wedge (q_{1,1} \vee q_{1,2} \vee q_{1,3}) \wedge (q_{2,1} \vee q_{2,2} \vee q_{2,3}) \wedge \cdots \wedge (q_{m,1} \vee q_{m,2} \vee q_{m,3})$, we do the following transformation:

Let $a_1, \ldots, a_p$ be the propositional variables. Define $D_\Phi = \{ep(i, i+1, j, k) : i = 1, \ldots, n; j = 1, 2, 3; a_k = p_{i,j}\} \cup \{en(i, i+1, j, k) : i = 1, \ldots, m; j = 1, 2, 3; \neg(a_k) = p_{i,j}\}$

The transformation is clearly polynomial.

Now $\langle P, \{c\}, D \rangle \vdash_{\exists \mathrm{dl}} Q(1, n+1, m+1)$, if and only if there is an ep-path from 1 to $n+1$ and an en-path from 1 to $m+1$ such that no pair of ep-edge and en-edge conflict by sharing the same v-value. Consider choosing each $ep(x, y, u, v)$-edge to be choosing to make $p_{x,u}$ true in the corresponding SAT instance. Also consider choosing each $en(x, y, u, v)$-edge to be choosing to make $q_{x,u}$ true in the corresponding SAT instance. Having an ep-path from 1 to $n+1$ and an en-path from 1 to $m+1$ is equivalent to picking one of $p_{i,1}, p_{i,2}, p_{i,3}$ to be true for all i from 1 to n and one of $q_{i,1}, q_{i,2}, q_{i,3}$ to be true for all i from 1 to m. Furthermore, the fact that the two paths do not conflict by sharing the same v-value is equivalent to that the set of literals picked to be true to not contain a complementary pair. This is exactly the condition required to choose an assignment of truth values that satisfy the formula Φ. We have a polynomial reduction from MONOTONE-3SAT to existential answers.

Hence, the existential answers problem with this fixed query and constraint is $\mathcal{NP}$-Hard.

It is easy to see that $\Xi_{P,C}$ is in $\mathcal{NP}$. For a finite set of facts D and a fact d, $\langle P, C, D\rangle \vdash_{\exists\mathrm{dl}} d$ if and only if there exists an admissible set $D' \subseteq D$ such that $d \in P(D')$. One can nondeterministically guess the appropriate D' and then verify in polynomial time that $d \in P(D')$ and $P(D')$ is a model of C.

Theorem 1 ($\mathcal{NP}$-Completeness). *The existential answer problem $\Xi_{P,C}$ is $\mathcal{NP}$-Complete for some datalog program P and finite set of denial constraints C.*

We conclude that unless $\mathcal{P}$=$\mathcal{NP}$, some existential answer problems over datalog programs and denial constraint cannot be solved by rewriting into datalog (or any other language with polynomial data-complexity, for example, stratified datalog$^\neg$).

Theorem 2 (Non-rewritability into dalalog). *Assuming $\mathcal{P}\neq\mathcal{NP}$, for some datalog program P and finite set of denial constraints C, there does not exist a datalog program P' such that for all finite sets of facts D and all facts d, $\langle P, C, D\rangle \vdash_{\exists\mathrm{dl}} d$ if and only if $\langle P', D\rangle \vdash_{\mathrm{dl}} d$.*

5 Provenance

Provenance of data has received considerable attention. Here, we use the method of Agrawal, Benjelloun, Das Sarma, Halevy, Theobald, and Widom [8,2] to compute and represent data provenance. We briefly review their method here.

Each tuple is associated with a tuple ID. Each computed tuple is associated with a provenance set that gives the set of tuple IDs from which this tuple is derived.

Consider the following example.

Example 3. The base facts D is given by the following table. A fact `link(i,j,t)` represents that there is a direct link from `i` to `j` of type `t`.

link

ID	origin	destination	type	
21	a	b	1	$\lambda(21) = \{\}$
22	a	c	2	$\lambda(22) = \{\}$
23	b	d	2	$\lambda(23) = \{\}$
24	c	d	3	$\lambda(24) = \{\}$
25	d	e	1	$\lambda(25) = \{\}$
26	d	f	2	$\lambda(26) = \{\}$

$P =$
$\{\texttt{aReaches(Y)} : - \texttt{link(a, Y, U)},$
$\texttt{aReaches(Y)} : - \texttt{aReaches(a, Z, U)}, \texttt{link(Z, Y, V)}\}$

The following are the computed facts and their associated provenance information.

aReaches

ID	destination	
31	b	$\lambda(31) = \{21\}$
32	c	$\lambda(32) = \{22\}$
33	d	$\lambda(33) = \{31, 23\}$
34	d	$\lambda(34) = \{32, 24\}$
35	e	$\lambda(35) = \{33, 25\}$
36	e	$\lambda(36) = \{34, 25\}$
37	f	$\lambda(37) = \{33, 26\}$
38	f	$\lambda(38) = \{34, 26\}$

If a fact is produced multiple times from different sets of tuples, the fact is presented as multiple tuples, each with its own tuple ID and associated provenance. The computation of provenance can be embedded in a standard bottom-up datalog evaluation procedure. It is important to note that where regular datalog evaluation (set semantics, no duplicate tuples) has polynomial data complexity, datalog evaluation with provenance computation as shown above can be exponential in the number of facts in the input fact set. The increased complexity is due to the fact that even though the number of unique facts that can be generated is polynomially bounded, the number of unique (fact, provenance) pairs is not.

6 Computing Existential Answers via Provenance

The brute-force method of enumerating each set $D' \subseteq D$ is impractical. In this section, I present a method that uses provenance information to construct several special subsets of D called support sets and then consider only those sets. The IsExistentialAnswer procedure calls on the SupportSet procedure defined immediately after.

IsExistentialAnswer(P, C, D, id, λ)
  $D' :=$ SupportSet(D, id, λ)
  $C^* := \{nogood : - R_1(u_1), \ldots, R_n(u_n), \phi(u_\phi) :$
      $(\forall x_1 \cdots x_m(\neg R_1(u_1) \vee \cdots \neg R_n(u_n) \vee \phi(u_\phi))) \in C\}$
  (Where *nogood* is a new relation name that is not in the current schema)
  if $nogood \in C^*(P(D'))$ **then**
    return FALSE
  else
    return TRUE
  end if

```
SupportSet(D, id, λ)
  Queue Q := empty queue
  D' := {}
  Q.enqueue(id)
  while Q is not empty do
    id' := Q.dequeue()
    if λ(id') == ∅ then
      D' := D' ∪ {fact(id')} (fact(id') gives the fact associated with the ID id')
    else
      for l ∈ λ(id') do
        Q.enqueue(l)
      end for
    end if
  end while
  return D'
```

Theorem 3 (Correctness). *For a datalog program P, a set of facts D, a set of denial constraints C, a fact $d \in P(D)$, and a provenance function λ obtained in evaluating P(D),* $\langle P, C, D\rangle \vdash_{\exists\mathrm{dl}} d$ *if and only if* IsExistentialAnswer (P, C, D, id, λ) *returns TRUE for a tuple ID id of d.*

Example 4. Using the provenance information in example 3 and the datalog program P and constraints C from example 2, I demonstrate the IsExistentialAnswer algorithm.

The tuple ID's associated with the fact `aReaches(f)` $\in P(D)$ are 37 and 38. Running IsExistentialAnswer$(P, D, C, 37, \lambda)$ constructs the set $D' =$ {`link(d, f, 2)`, `link(b, d, 2)`, `link(a, b, 1)`} from the set of base tuple ID's {26, 23, 21}. It also constructs $C^* := \{$
  `nogood : − link'(X1, Y1, U), link'(X2, Y2, U), X1 ≠ X2,`
  `nogood : − link'(X1, Y1, U), link'(X2, Y2, U), Y1 ≠ Y2`
}. Finally, *nogood* $\in C^*(P(D'))$, so the algorithm rejects the tuple of ID 37 as an existential answer tuple.

Running IsExistentialAnswer$(P, D, C, 38, \lambda)$ constructs the set $D' =$ {`link(d, f, 2)`, `link(c, d, 3)`, `link(a, c, 2)`} from the set of base tuple ID's {26, 24, 22}. It also constructs the same C^* as above.
Finally, *nogood* $\in C^*(P(D'))$, so the algorithm also rejects the tuple of ID 38 as an existential answer tuple.

One can conclude that $\langle P, C, D\rangle \not\vdash_{\exists\mathrm{dl}}$ `aReaches(f)`, in agreement with example 2.

Now I examine whether $\langle P, C, D\rangle \vdash_{\exists\mathrm{dl}}$ `aReaches(e)`.The tuple ID's associated with the fact `aReaches(e)` $\in P(D)$ are 35 and 36.

Running IsExistentialAnswer$(P, D, C, 35, \lambda)$ constructs the set $D' =$ {`link(d, e, 1)`, `link(b, d, 2)`, `link(a, b, 1)`} from the set of base tuple ID's {25, 23, 21}. *nogood* $\in C^*(P(D'))$, so the algorithm rejects the tuple of ID 35 as an existential answer tuple.

Running IsExistentialAnswer$(P, D, C, 36, \lambda)$ constructs the set $D' = \{\texttt{link(d,e,1)}, \texttt{link(c,d,3)}, \texttt{link(a,c,2)}\}$ from the set of base tuple ID's $\{25, 24, 22\}$. *nogood* $\notin C^*(P(D'))$, so the algorithm accepts the tuple of ID 36 as an existential answer tuple.

One can conclude that $\langle P, C, D\rangle \vdash_{\exists \mathrm{dl}}$ `aReaches(e)`, in agreement with example 2.

7 Answer Set Programming

Answer set programming (ASP) has received much attention in the logic programming community, the database community, and the rules and ontology community because of its ability to declaratively and succinctly express interesting problems from a wide-range of domains. ASP also offers another way to characterize the existential answers. In this section, I characterize existential answers as the solutions to some answer set programs. The use of disjunctive logic programs to specify changes to data was introduced by Arenas and Bertossi and Chomicki [4]. I assume that the reader is familiar with the basics of answer set programming. For an introduction to answer set programming, I recommend Lifschitz's overview [24].

Let the transformation *primed*(ϕ) take a formula (or rule) ϕ and replace within ϕ each relation name R by R'. For a datalog program P, and a finite set of denial constraints C, we define the transformation into an ASP
`ExistentialASP`$(P) := \{(R'(x) \ :-\ R(x), \mathit{not}\ R'(x)) : R$ a relation name$\}$
$\cup \{\mathit{primed}(r) : r \in C \cup P\}$

Example 5.
Let $P = \{$

```
aReaches(Y) : - link(a, Y, U),
aReaches(Y) : - aReaches(a, Z, U), link(Z, Y, V)}
```

Let $C = \{$

```
  (false) : - link(X1, Y1, U), link(X2, Y2, U), X1 ≠ X2,
  (false) : - link(X1, Y1, U), link(X2, Y2, U), Y1 ≠ Y2
}
```

```
ExistentialASP(P, C) = {
  link'(X, Y, U) : - link(X, Y, U), not link'(X, Y, U),
  aReaches'(X, Y, U) : - aReaches(X, Y, U), not aReaches'(X, Y, U),
  aReaches'(Y) : - link'(a, Y, U),
  aReaches'(Y) : - aReaches'(a, Z, U), link'(Z, Y, V),
  (false) : - link'(X1, Y1, U), link'(X2, Y2, U), X1 ≠ X2,
  (false) : - link'(X1, Y1, U), link'(X2, Y2, U), Y1 ≠ Y2
}
```

Theorem 4. *Given a datalog program P, a finite set of constraints C (written as headless rules), then for any a finite set of facts D and any fact d,*

$\langle P, C, D\rangle \vdash_{\exists dl} d$ if and only if primed(d) is in an answer set to the answer set program `ExistentialASP`(P, C).

The characterization of existential answers as credulous answers to an answer set program gives another method to compute existential answers – reformulate an existential answer problem as an ASP problem, then use an ASP solver to find the credulous answers. However, the cost of this method may be prohibitively high because most general-purpose ASP solvers work by first grounding out the input program[3].

8 Related Work

The importance of adequately processing inconsistencies in reasoning on the web has received wide recognition, but there have been relatively few pieces of work that develop techniques for reasoning with inconsistent knowledge on the web. Notable works in this area include the following [18,23,28,29,3]. None of them take a provenance-based approach to reason in the presence of inconsistencies.

The idea of finding answers from consistent subsets of a theory is due to Elvang-Gøransson and Hunter[14]. The idea is later refined by Kassoff, Zen, Garg, and Genesereth for application to logical spreadsheets [22,20].

Kassoff and Genesereth [21] also proposed a method for computing existential answers based on provenance. However, their method is intended for reasoning with first-order theories and use a general resolution-refutation method rather than one based on standard datalog evaluation. As a result, the method is not guaranteed to terminate (even if restricted to horn clauses, which correspond to datalog).

ULDB [8,2] uses provenance information to compute answers from uncertain databases. The approach is similar to the method presented in this paper. However, the setting they consider is one where all constraints are ground.

As mentioned in section 7, the specification of database repairs using disjunctive logic programs with exceptions first appeared in [4]. Many other works have followed that are based on the same basic idea (some examples include [9,7,5,6,12,13,15]).

9 Future Work

The connection between provenance and trust creates a fertile ground for future work in reasoning on the web in the presence of inconsistencies and uncertainties.

As an example, I define the *prioritized existential answers* to account for the fact that some sources are more trusted than others. Existential answers, as defined in section 3, give all facts equal priority. However, in real applications, some sources are known to be much more reliable than others. In the birth year example in section 2, the tuple `BirthYear(David, 1984)` may be more trusted

[3] [27] is a notable exception.

and hence prioritized over the conflicting tuple BirthYear(David, 1980). Then one would reject David as a candidate.

With this intuition in mind, I define the *prioritized existential answers.*

Definition 5 (Prioritized Existential Answers). *Assume a (possibly empty) partial order $\succ$ on the set of all facts over the schema. (Intuitively, $d \succ d'$ means that d is prioritized over d'.) Given a set of facts D, a set of rules P, and a set of constraints C a fact d is a prioritized existential answers with respect to $(D, P, C, \succ)$ if and only if there exists $D' \subseteq D$ such that*

1. *$P(D')$ is a model of C,*
2. *$(\forall g \in (D - D'))(\forall g' \in D')(g \not\succ g')$,*
3. *and $\langle D', P \rangle \vdash_{\text{dl}} d$.*

We denote this fact as $\langle P, C, D \succ \rangle \vdash_{\exists\text{dl}} d$.

One can check in example 1 that if
BirthYear(David, 1984) $\succ$ BirthYear(David, 1980), then candidate(David) is not a prioritized existential answer.

A direction for future work is to design a provenance-based method to compute prioritized existential answer.

Acknowledgments. I would like to thank Monica Palmirani, Davide Sottara, Frank Olken and the rest of the RuleML 2011 (America) Program Committee for the invitation to submit this paper. I am grateful to Michael Genesereth, Jeff Ullman, Jennifer Widom, Michael Kassoff, Rada Chirkova, Mary-Anne Williams, Carl Hewitt, Lukasz Golab, and attendees of Stanford Logic Group and Stanford Infolab seminars, for their valuable feedback. I would also like to acknowledge the NSERC[4] and Konica-Minolta (via the MediaX project) for their financial support.

References

1. Abiteboul, S., Hull, R., Vianu, V.: Foundations of databases (1995)
2. Agrawal, P., Benjelloun, O., Sarma, A.D., Hayworth, C., Nabar, S., Sugihara, T., Widom, J.: Trio: A system for data, uncertainty, and lineage. In: 32nd International Conference on Very Large Data Bases, VLDB 2006 (demonstration description) (September 2006), http://ilpubs.stanford.edu:8090/776/
3. Alejandro Gmez, S., Ivn Chesevar, C., Simari, G.R.: Reasoning with inconsistent ontologies through argumentation. Applied Artificial Intelligence 24(1-2), 102–148 (2010), http://www.tandfonline.com/doi/abs/10.1080/08839510903448692
4. Arenas, M., Bertossi, L., Chomicki, J.: Specifying and querying database repairs using logic programs with exceptions. In: Flexible Query Answering Systems. Recent Developments, pp. 27–41. Springer, Heidelberg (2000)

[4] Natural Sciences and Engineering Research Council of Canada.

5. Arenas, M., Bertossi, L., Chomicki, J.: Answer sets for consistent query answering in inconsistent databases. Theory and Practice of Logic Programming 3(4), 393–424 (2003)
6. Barcel, P., Bertossi, L.: Repairing databases with annotated predicate logic. In: Ninth International Workshop on Non-Monotonic Reasoning (NMR 2002), Special Session: Changing and Integrating Information: From Theory to Practice, pp. 160–170. Morgan Kaufmann Publishers (2002)
7. Barcel, P., Bertossi, L.: Logic Programs for Querying Inconsistent Databases. In: Dahl, V. (ed.) PADL 2003. LNCS, vol. 2562, pp. 208–222. Springer, Heidelberg (2002)
8. Benjelloun, O., Das Sarma, A., Halevy, A., Theobald, M., Widom, J.: Databases with uncertainty and lineage. The VLDB Journal 17, 243–264 (2008), `http://dx.doi.org/10.1007/s00778-007-0080-z`
9. Bravo, L., Bertossi, L.: Logic programs for consistently querying data integration systems. In: International Joint Conference on Artificial Intelligence (IJCAI), pp. 10–15 (2003)
10. Chebotko, A., Lu, S., Fei, X., Fotouhi, F.: Rdfprov: A relational rdf store for querying and managing scientific workflow provenance. Data Knowl. Eng. 69, 836–865 (2010), `http://dx.doi.org/10.1016/j.datak.2010.03.005`
11. Ding, L., Michaelis, J., McCusker, J., McGuinness, D.L.: Linked provenance data: A semantic web-based approach to interoperable workflow traces. Future Gener. Comput. Syst. 27, 797–805 (2011), `http://dx.doi.org/10.1016/j.future.2010.10.011`
12. Eiter, T.: Data Integration and Answer Set Programming. In: Baral, C., Greco, G., Leone, N., Terracina, G. (eds.) LPNMR 2005. LNCS (LNAI), vol. 3662, pp. 13–25. Springer, Heidelberg (2005)
13. Eiter, T., Fink, M., Greco, G., Lembo, D.: Optimization methods for logic-based query answering from inconsistent data integration systems (2005)
14. Elvang-Gøransson, M., Hunter, A.: Argumentative logics: Reasoning with classically inconsistent information. Data Knowl. Eng. 16(2), 125–145 (1995)
15. Espil, M.M., Vaisman, A.A., Terribile, L.: Revising data cubes with exceptions: A rule-based perspective (2002)
16. Fan, H., Poulovassilis, A.: Tracing data lineage using schema transformation pathways. In: Knowledge Transformation For The Semantic Web, pp. 64–79. IOS Press (2002)
17. Hinrichs, T.L., Kao, J.Y., Genesereth, M.: Inconsistency-tolerant reasoning with classical logic and large databases. In: Proc. of the Eighth Symposium on Abstraction, Reformulation, and Approximation (2009)
18. Huang, Z., van Harmelen, F., ten Teije, A.: Reasoning with inconsistent ontologies. In: Proceedings of the Nineteenth International Joint Conference on Artificial Intelligence (IJCAI 2005), Edinburgh, Scotland, pp. 454–459 (August 2005)
19. Kao, E.J.Y., Genesereth, M.: Query rewriting with filtering constraints. Tech. Rep. LG-2009-02, Stanford University, Stanford, CA (2009), `http://logic.stanford.edu/reports/LG-2009-02.pdf` (updated July 2011)
20. Kassoff, M., Genesereth, M.: Predicalc: A logical spreadsheet management system. Knowl. Eng. Rev. 22(3), 281–295 (2007)
21. Kassoff, M., Genesereth, M.R.: Paraconsistent inference from data using ω-existential entailment. DALI: Workshop on Data, Logic and Inconsistency (2011)
22. Kassoff, M., Zen, L.M., Garg, A., Genesereth, M.: Predicalc: a logical spreadsheet management system. In: VLDB 2005: Proceedings of the 31st International Conference on Very Large Data Bases, pp. 1247–1250. VLDB Endowment (2005)

23. Li, D., Lin, Y., Huang, H., Tian, X.: Linear reduction reasoning with inconsistent ontology. In: 2011 Fourth International Joint Conference on Computational Sciences and Optimization (CSO), pp. 795–798 (April 2011)
24. Lifschitz, V.: What is answer set programming? In: Proceedings of the 23rd National Conference on Artificial Intelligence, vol. 3, pp. 1594–1597. AAAI Press (2008), http://portal.acm.org/citation.cfm?id=1620270.1620340
25. Moreau, L.: Provenance-based reproducibility in the semantic web. Journal of Web Semantics (February 2011), http://eprints.ecs.soton.ac.uk/21992/
26. Moreau, L., Clifford, B., Freire, J., Futrelle, J., Gil, Y., Groth, P., Kwasnikowska, N., Miles, S., Missier, P., Myers, J., Plale, B., Simmhan, Y., Stephan, E., den Bussche, J.V.: The open provenance model core specification (v1.1). Future Generation Computer Systems 27(6), 743–756 (2011), http://www.sciencedirect.com/science/article/pii/S0167739X10001275
27. Dal Palù, A., Dovier, A., Pontelli, E., Rossi, G.: Answer Set Programming with Constraints Using Lazy Grounding. In: Hill, P.M., Warren, D.S. (eds.) ICLP 2009. LNCS, vol. 5649, pp. 115–129. Springer, Heidelberg (2009), http://dx.doi.org/10.1007/978-3-642-02846-5_14
28. Schobach, S., Corner, R.: Non-standard reasoning services for the debugging of description logic terminology. In: IJCAI (2003)
29. Zlatareva, N.P.: Supporting uncertainty and inconsistency in semantic web applications. In: FLAIRS Conference (2009)

D2R2: Disk-Oriented Deductive Reasoning in a RISC-Style RDF Engine

Mohamed Yahya and Martin Theobald

Max-Planck Institute for Informatics,
Saarbrücken, Germany
{myahya,mtb}@mpi-inf.mpg.de

Abstract. Deductive reasoning lies in the expressive intersection of Datalog and Description Logics. In this paper, we present the D2R2 engine, which implements deductive reasoning capabilities based on the Query-Sub-Query (QSQR) algorithm on top of the disk-oriented RDF-3X engine. D2R2 aims to bridge the gap between *rule-oriented* (intensional) reasoning with deduction rules and *data-oriented* (extensional) processing of large joins, over a set of highly tuned, disk-based index structures for large RDF collections. We present a generalization of QSQR, which allows for *dynamic sub-query scheduling* and *chaining of extensional predicates* into atomic join patterns—two key extensions for coupling QSQR with a disk-oriented storage backend. Experiments over a set of recursive queries and a very large knowledge base, consisting of 20 million RDF facts, as well as comparisons to disk-oriented reasoning engines, confirm the practical viability and significant runtime improvements of D2R2 compared to these engines.

Keywords: Deductive reasoning, QSQR, disk-oriented RDF processing.

1 Introduction

A deductive database is a database, in which new facts can be derived from facts explicitly stated in the database using rules [20]. Datalog is the language traditionally used for expressing facts, rules and queries in a deductive database. Datalog has its roots in logic programming, aiming at a balance between expressiveness and efficiency by using rules that are restricted to definite Horn clauses, which each consist of exactly one positive head literal and a set of negated body literals.

Datalog queries can be evaluated in two ways: bottom-up or top-down. Answering a query in a bottom-up fashion involves (i) starting from extensional facts and using the rules to generate all facts that can be inferred by a Datalog program; and (ii) performing a selection on the facts to return answers to the query. In top-down query evaluation, on the other hand, the starting point is a query, and (ideally) only facts relevant to answering the query are generated. Selective-Linear-Definite (SLD) clause resolution [21] is the default method for top-down grounding of recursive queries in Datalog and Prolog. SLD resolution

F. Olken et al. (Eds.): RuleML 2011 - America, LNCS 7018, pp. 81–96, 2011.

processes queries in a manner similar to how a human thinks about answering queries. However, it suffers from one major issue: it is not guaranteed to terminate on an arbitrary Datalog program because it may run into cycles. This issue is solved by approaches based on various forms of tabling (or memoization) in order to both avoid cycles and to cache redundant subgoals. The most prominent example of the use of tabling is the SLG algorithm used in XSB [22]. In our work, we focus on the Query-Sub-Query Recursive (QSQR) algorithm for Datalog query evaluation. QSQR is part of the Query-Sub-Query (QSQ) family of top-down Datalog query evaluation techniques. This family includes both iterative and recursive algorithms, each of which can be applied in a tuple-at-a-time or a set-at-a-time fashion. QSQ is based on SLD resolution, making it relatively intuitive.

An important consideration when evaluating a conjunctive query is the order in which the components of the query are evaluated. In a traditional database setting, this issue is known as *join ordering*, which aims to compile a query pattern into an efficiently evaluable query plan. For our Datalog setting, there is no such notion of a static query plan. Rather, join ordering is done by a dynamic selection function, which, when given a conjunctive query and (partial) binding pattern for the query variables, decides which part of the query (i.e., an individual literal or an entire group of literals) to evaluate next. Having an engine that allows for specifying selection functions, the choice of an appropriate selection function is fundamental for efficient query processing, and can make orders of magnitude difference in reasoning performance.

Current state-of-the art reasoners for the Semantic Web can be roughly divided into two categories: main-memory-based and disk-based approaches. While the top-performing engines in the rule-oriented benchmark tasks of LUBM [7] and OpenRuleBench [23] are main-memory based, these engines usually lack a persistent storage layer and—more importantly—database-style index structures for scalable join processing over large relational input data. In D2R2 (Disk-based Deductive Reasoner for RDF), we aim to bride the gap between rule-oriented and data-oriented reasoning tasks by coupling the disk-oriented RDF-3X engine with deductive reasoning capabilities based on QSQR.

RDF-3X relies on exhaustive indexing and detailed statistics for optimizing queries over billions of RDF triples. RDF-3X follows a RISC-style architecture (in analogy to the "reduced instruction set computer" principle coined in hardware design) by providing only the most principal query operators—based on either merging or hashing index lists—in a highly efficient manner. This architecture allows RDF-3X to remain workload-independent without the need for manual tuning [12], thus focusing on join ordering for query optimization, and processing queries using generic join operators that operate entirely on integer id's.

1.1 Contributions

In this paper, we make the following contributions:

- We extend QSQR, a state-of-the art algorithm for top-down grounding of Datalog-style recursive queries, to handle a *dynamic selection function* and the *chaining of extensional predicates* into efficiently evaluable extensional join patterns, which are two key issues for integrating QSQR with a disk-oriented storage backend for large RDF collections.

– We integrate the extended QSQR framework with RDF-3X, one of the fastest, currently available, open-source query engines for RDF data and non-recursive SPARQL queries. We extend RDF-3X by various *query-time optimizations*, including a *caching* layer which drastically helps to spare redundant page accesses.
– We present an extensive experimental evaluation of D2R2, using a set of handcrafted, recursive queries over the YAGO [15] knowledge base, consisting of 20 million RDF facts, as well as comparative runs with disk-oriented reasoning engines over the LUBM benchmark setting.

2 Related Work

With the increasing demand for scalable reasoning techniques in the context of the Semantic Web, also Datalog-style (deductive) query evaluation strategies have been undergoing a renaissance recently. Specifically, the RuleML [13] standard, which allows for the expression of rules in XML, is the Semantic Web standard for representing rules. It is based on Datalog programs that are restricted to unary and binary predicates.

In [6], the authors introduce Description Logic Programs (DLP), which are contained in the expressive intersection of Datalog and Description Logics. On the other hand, the proposed Semantic Web Rule Language (SWRL) is an effort to create a language combining both OWL-DL and RuleML [8]. DLP is interesting as it shows that Datalog can also be exploited to represent and query ontologies, albeit in a more restricted manner compared to OWL.

In our work, we focus on top-down grounding strategies of Datalog queries. In a large deductive database with millions of facts, we would expect that most of the extensional facts are irrelevant to answering a specific query, and we aim to avoid materializing all deducible facts in an eager bottom-up fashion. Magic Sets [2] is a well-known rule-rewriting technique to optimize top-down query evaluations. Magic Sets performs a rewriting of the rules based on the query, called Magic Sets rewriting. Then, a bottom-up query evaluation strategy, usually semi-naive, is applied to answer the query using the rewritten rules. Moreover, in order to avoid cycles in top-down SLD resolution, various forms of tabling have been introduced [19]. OLDT is the first such algorithm based on SLD resolution [24].

QSQ [17,18,11] was developed shortly thereafter and added set-at-a-time query evaluation. Although QSQ is also based on SLD resolution, it is database-complete, which it achieves through tabling. In general, we call a procedure for answering a query *database-complete* (DB-complete) if, whenever there are finitely many answers to a query, it terminates after returning all the answers [18]. We present a generalized version of QSQR in detail in Section 3.1.

The Semantic Web has led to the development of several reasoning engines which support either classical Datalog-style (rule-based) reasoning, or

RDF/S- and OWL-based reasoning capabilities. These include OntoBroker[1], Jena[2] and IRIS[3], among others. This is in addition to classical logic programming and deductive database implementations such as XSB[4], Yap[5] and DLV[6]. OntoBroker, XSB, Yap and DLV are considered among the top-performing engines in the rule-oriented benchmark tasks of LUBM [7] and OpenRuleBench [23]. They were designed mainly as main-memory based reasoning engines. Tools such as Jena and IRIS were designed with more flexible storage backends, allowing them to work on data that is both main-memory and disk resident. XSB and Yap use top-down processing techniques with tabling, while OntoBroker and DLV are use optimized bottom-up techniques. Jena and IRIS both allow a user to select from a host of evaluation strategies and optimizations to use.

Datalog has recently seen applications outside its immediate domain, such as program analysis and parallel programming. bddbddb [28] is a tool for program analysis, in which all program information are stored as relations, and uses Datalog to analyze the programs. Datalog-inspired languages, such as Overlog and Bloom [27], are being used to simplify parallel programming by making it a data-centric task. Moreover, LogicBlox[7] is a recent implementation of Datalog that is geared towards decision support.

3 Datalog Query Evaluation

D2R2 uses the QSQR algorithm to evaluate Datalog queries. In this section we discuss our generalized QSQR algorithm, which incorporates (i) a selection function for dynamic join ordering and (ii) the chaining of extensional predicates into atomic join patterns.

One of the most cited sources of the QSQR algorithm is [1], which presents the algorithm using the same setting as the one used to present Magic Sets in [2], including adornments and sideways information passing, which are helpful in both understanding and implementing the algorithm. In the context of our work on extending QSQR, we claim that this description of QSQR is incomplete and propose a fix to this problem. To the best of our knowledge, we are the first to detect this incompleteness, which we communicated to the authors of [10], resulting in a modification of their work[8].

In the following, we first introduce basic concepts needed for presenting QSQR [1,5] and then present a generalized, DB-complete version of the algorithm.

[1] http://www.ontoprise.de/en/products/ontobroker/

[2] http://jena.sourceforge.net/

[3] http://www.iris-reasoner.org/

[4] http://xsb.sourceforge.net/

[5] http://www.dcc.fc.up.pt/~vsc/Yap/

[6] http://www.dlvsystem.com/dlvsystem/index.php/Home

[7] http://www.logicblox.com/

[8] See http://www.mimuw.edu.pl/~nguyen/GQSQR-revised-long.pdf, which is a revised and extended version of [10] with proofs for completeness.

3.1 QSQR with Dynamic Join Ordering and Chaining

If we have the sub-query atom $R_0(a, ?y)$, where a is a constant and $?y$ is a variable, we say that the first argument of R_0 in the query is *bound* (^{b}) and the second argument is *free* (^{f}), denoted as R_0^{bf}. The superscript is called an adornment. Generally, if R is an n-ary predicate then an *adornment* γ is an n-tuple of b's and f's, denoted as R^γ, where a b (or f, respectively) indicates that the corresponding argument of the predicate is bound to a constant (or free, respectively) [5].

Given a rule and an adornment for the atom forming the rule's head, an adorned rule is formed by adding adornments to the rule body as follows:

1. All occurrences of each bound variable in the rule head are bound.
2. All occurrences of constants are bound.
3. If a variable $?x$ occurs in the rule body, then all subsequent occurrences of $?x$ in subsequent literals are bound[9].

For example, consider the rule $R_0(?x, ?y) \leftarrow R_1(?x, ?z), R_2(?z, ?w), R_3(?w, ?y)$ and the query $R_0(a, ?y)$. If the rule's head has the adornment R_0^{bf}, then the corresponding adorned rule is $R_0^{bf}(?x, ?y) \leftarrow R_1^{bf}(?x, ?z), R_2^{fb}(?z, ?w), R_3^{bf}(?w, ?y)$.

Two important observations can be made here. First, item 3 in the definition of adorned rules implies that different orderings of the atoms in the rule body imply different adornments. A second observation, also regarding item 3, is that of the idea of *sideways information passing* (SIP). Once a variable has a binding from an atom, it becomes an input (bound) to subsequent atoms, in which it occurs rather than an output (free). A SIP strategy is simply a decision on the order in which atoms in a query will be evaluated [4].

A set of single-atom sub-queries with the same adornment can be denoted as (R^γ, J), where γ is an adornment of the query predicate R, and J is a set of tuples with the values of the entries bound by γ. (R^γ, J) is called a *generalized sub-query.* If R is a predicate and γ is an adornment for R, then *bound*(R, γ) denotes the coordinates of R bound in γ.

Supplementary relations keep track of variable bindings during left-to-right rule evaluation. An adorned rule with n atoms in its body has $n+1$ supplementary relations: sup_0 through sup_n as shown below:

$$\begin{array}{lllll} R_0^{bf}(?x, ?y) \leftarrow & R_1^{bf}(?x, ?z), & R_2^{fb}(?z, ?w), & R_3^{bf}(?w, ?y) & \\ & \uparrow & \uparrow & \uparrow & \uparrow \\ & sup_0[?x] & sup_1[?x, ?z] & sup_2[?x, ?w] & sup_3[?x, ?y] \end{array}$$

The attributes of the 0th supplementary relation, sup_0, are those variables bound in the head of the adorned rule. The attributes of the nth supplementary relation, sup_n, are all the variables in the head of the adorned rule. For $i \in [1, n-1]$, the attribute set of the ith supplementary relation, sup_i, is the set of variables which occur in both (i) sup_0 or one of $B_1, ...B_i$, and (ii) $B_{i+1}, ...B_n$ or sup_n. The role of supplementary relations is to pass variable bindings for bound arguments from

[9] Whether the first occurrence is bound or free depends on item 1.

one atom to the next. sup_i contains only variables whose bindings are needed for evaluating atom j, for $j > i$, or for the final result.

We are now ready to present our generalized QSQR in Algorithm 1, which takes as input a Datalog program and a query over an intensional predicate. This algorithm uses the *global* variables ans_p^δ and $input\_p^\delta$ for each adorned predicate p^δ. Algorithm 1 calls Algorithm 2, which processes a generalized sub-query in a set-at-a-time fashion by calling Algorithm 3 on all rules. *ans_* relations keep track of answers found for an adorned predicate, while *input_* relations keep track of sub-queries that have already been evaluated to avoid running into cycles, as SLD does. Contrary to *ans_* and *input_* relations, the supplementary relation is used as a *local* variable in Algorithm 3.

Algorithm 1. QSQR(D, q)

Input: A Datalog program D and an intensional query q
Input: The global *ans_* and *input_* relations
Output: All answers for q

begin
  Set all *ans_* relations to be empty
  Set (R^γ, J) to be the generalized query corresponding to q
  repeat
    Set all *input_* relations to be empty
    Call QSQR_EVAL_GENERALIZED(D, (R^γ, J))
  until *Until no ans_ relation has changed in the last iteration* ;
  return *All answers for q by performing a selection on ans_R^γ using J*
end

Algorithm 2. QSQR_EVAL_GENERALIZED(D, gq)

Input: A Datalog program D and a generalized query $gq = (R^\gamma, J)$
Input: The global *ans_* and *input_* relations

begin
  Remove from J all tuples in $input\_R^\gamma$
  if *J is empty* **then**
    exit
  $input\_R^\gamma := input\_R^\gamma \cup J$
  foreach *rule φ defining R* **do**
    Call QSQR_EVAL_RULE(D, φ, (R^γ, J))
end

3.2 Join Ordering

The version of QSQR presented in [1,10] assumes a specific selection function, namely, the *left-to-right* selection function, which always selects the atoms based on the order in which they appear in the body of a rule. As we discuss later in Section 3.3, this is not desirable in a declarative language such as Datalog, where the manner in which the rules are written should not dictate how they are

Algorithm 3. QSQR_EVAL_RULE(D, φ, gq)

Input: A Datalog program D, a rule φ and a generalized query $gq = (R^\gamma, T)$
Input: The global *ans_* and *input_* relations

1 **begin**
2 Remove from T all tuples that do not unify with the head of the rule
3 Initialize *sup* from T
4 $SQ_{remaining} = \varphi.body$
5 $SQ_{current} = \phi$
6 **while** $SQ_{remaining} \neq \phi$ **do**
7 $(SQ_{current}, SQ_{remaining})$ = SELECTION_FUNCTION($SQ_{remaining}, \ldots$)
8 $sup = sup \bowtie$ EVALUATE($SQ_{current}$, sup)
9 PROJECT(sup)
10 Add tuples produced for *sup* into the global variable ans_R^γ
11 **end**

Algorithm 4. EVALUATE(C, rel)

Input: A clause C for a sub-query to be evaluated, and relation *rel*
Output: A relation

begin
if *C is extensional* **then**
return *Result of evaluating C against the extensional database with (partial) bindings from rel*
else if *C is intensional composed of a single atom with predicate p* **then**
$gq = (p^\gamma, T)$, where T is initialized from bindings in *rel*
QSQR_EVAL_GENERALIZED(D, gq)
return *ans_p with selection using gq*
end

evaluated. It is not difficult to perform *static reordering* of atoms in the body of the rule using the same algorithms in [1,10]. In this case, the decision on the ordering of the body atoms is made before starting to evaluate the body of the rule. However, we aim to make the algorithm as general as possible by adding two features:

1. *Dynamic join ordering:* The decision about which atom(s) to evaluate next is made only *after* the current atom(s) is evaluated, and not at the start of the evaluation of a rule.
2. *Chaining:* Atoms with extensional predicates can be grouped together for efficient utilization of the underlying storage engine's ability to optimize joins (of extensional predicates).

In Algorithm 3, the (single) supplementary relation is initialized from T after removing from it all tuples that do not unify with the head of the rule φ (lines 2, 3). The remaining query is set to be the entire body of the rule φ (line 4). Next, we iterate until no atoms are left to evaluate (line 6). In every iteration, the selection function returns a clause composed of one or more atoms for evaluation (line 7). This clause is evaluated, with bindings coming from *sup*, and the result is a relation whose schema contains all variables in $SQ_{current}$ (along with other possible variables already in *sup*). The result is then joined with the current value of *sup* to get the new value for *sup*. In line 9, the optional call to PROJECT projects out from *sup* all columns that correspond to variables which will not be needed to evaluate $SQ_{remaining}$. Arguments passed to the selection function depend on the information needed for the function to make its decision on ordering. They can include the supplementary relation, statistics about it, or permissible binding patterns for predicates that require them. Algorithm 3 calls Algorithm 4, which evaluates the clause passed to clause C with bindings in *rel*. EVALUATE returns a relation that contains complete variable bindings for the variables occurring in the clause.

We remark that Algorithms 1–4 are a generalized version of the one presented in [10] (including changes made in the online revision). We claim that our generalized version yields the same results as the original algorithm, as it reconstructs exactly the same intermediate supplementary relations sup_0–sup_m in the original algorithm [1]. That is, for any possible ordering (and chaining) of atoms, Algorithm 3 will change the schema and bindings of *sup* to correspond to sup_0–sup_m, where $m \leq n$, and n is the number of atoms in the body of φ. In the case of chaining, $m < n$, otherwise $m = n$.

3.3 Sub-query Scheduling

The sub-query scheduler is responsible for selecting a sub-query from the current query for evaluation. Our approach to sub-query scheduling is a *dynamic* one: decisions are made iteratively at each recursion step, i.e., whenever a rule is processed for the next grounding step. This allows for the consideration of the query's current bindings, which changes as more sub-queries of the query are evaluated.

The sub-query scheduler calls a selection function on a conjunctive query. The selection function called on a sub-query SQ returns a pair of sets of atoms $\langle SQ_{current}, SQ_{remaining} \rangle$ such that $SQ_{current} \cup SQ_{remaining} = SQ$:

- $SQ_{current}$ is the *chosen sub-query*, which is a conjunctive sub-query that will be evaluated next.
- $SQ_{remaining}$ is the *remaining sub-query*, which is a conjunctive sub-query and which will be evaluated after the chosen sub-query is evaluated successfully.

The chosen sub-query can be composed of a single intensional or of one or more extensional atoms. If the evaluation of the chosen sub-query succeeds, it will result in bindings for variables in the chosen sub-query. These variables will usually occur in the remaining sub-query, which means that the binding pattern of the remaining sub-query changes. Because of this, once the remaining sub-query has to be evaluated, it is sent to the sub-query scheduler with the latest bindings, and a sub-query thereof is chosen.

The *bound-is-easier* selection function is commonly used in recursive query evaluation, where the atom with the largest number of constants is evaluated first, in the hope of returning the smallest intermediate relation [14,16]. One can find extensions of this selection function in the literature, such as in [9] for a Semantic Web setting with binary predicates. There, the position of the bound argument is considered, where atoms with a bound first argument (subject) are preferred over those with a bound second argument (object) for two arguments with the same number of bindings.

4 D2R2 System Architecture

Figure 1 shows a high-level view of the architecture of D2R2. It is composed of the following components:

1. A *rule store*, where rules are kept.
2. A *fact store*, which stores extensionally defined facts. We use RDF-3X [12] as our storage backend for facts.
3. The *sub-query scheduler*, which is responsible for determining the order of evaluation of atoms in a conjunctive query.
4. The *recursive query processor*, which is composed of implementations of two top-down recursive query processing algorithms: SLD resolution and QSQR.

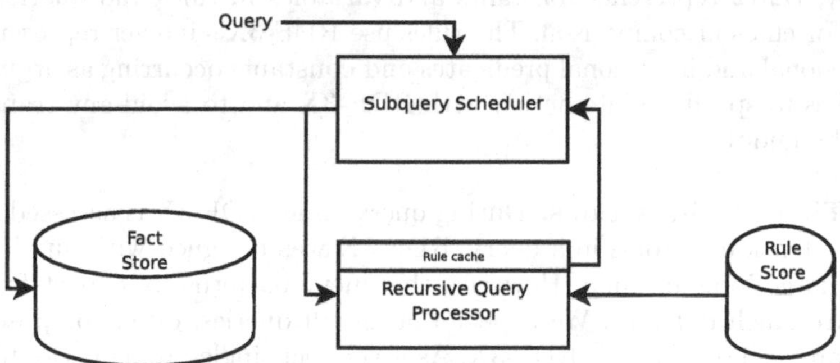

Fig. 1. D2R2 architecture

We assume that the number of rules in our system is much smaller than that of the number of base facts. Based on this, our rules are assumed to be memory resident during query processing.

4.1 RDF-3X

RDF-3X is one of the currently best-performing RDF engines on managing large-scale RDF data with a RISC-style architecture [12,25]. We use RDF-3X as the storage backend for D2R2. Conceptually, RDF-3X uses a single large triplet table composed of the attributes: subject (S), predicate (P) and object (O).

RDF-3X uses index-only relations by maintaining six B^+-trees corresponding to all possible permutations of S, P and O, allowing it to answer any triplet pattern using an index scan, where the constants in the triplet pattern form the prefix of the index. Moreover, RDF-3X maintains partially aggregated and fully aggregated indexes over partial triplet patterns: pairs and single SPO fields to efficiently answer queries, where parts of the full triple are irrelevant to answering the query, and to capture fine-grained statistics to optimize join ordering.

For efficiency, RDF-3X does not index strings directly. Instead, strings are mapped to integer id's and a mapping dictionary is maintained to convert strings to id's, and vice versa. Query plans are generated by RDF-3X using bottom-up dynamic programming, which generates plans for every index that can answer a triplet pattern and later keeps those that are appropriate for subsequent merge-joins between triplet patterns. In order to scale RDF-3X to work with billions of triples, it uses an approach called "ubiquitous sideways information passing" (U-SIP) to allow physical index scan operators to skip reading pages from disk, if they will not contribute to the final query result.

4.2 RDF-3X Integration

A user is assumed to have an RDF-3X database file, which can be compiled from a plain text RDF file in Turtle syntax. The user starts D2R2 by submitting the location of this file along with the rules that will be used for reasoning. Internally, D2R2 represents constants and variables in rules and queries using integers for efficient comparison. The rules use RDF-3X's integer representation for extensional and intensional predicates and constants occurring as arguments. This serves to speed up interaction with RDF-3X and to avoid any translation step in the middle.

Query-Time Optimizations. During query time, RDF-3X is accessed for answering extensional atoms in a query. RDF-3X was designed with queries composed of large joins in mind. However, the query patterns we expect from our setting are much different. We expect that small queries, often composed of a single atom, will be issued to RDF-3X. As we expect single-atom queries to occur frequently, we made sure that they can be performed as fast as possible. When a single-atom query is issued to RDF-3X during recursive query processing, it is handled by a special method, which directly issues an index scan on the appropriate full-triples index. The choice of index is based on the binding pattern of the atom: bound entries of the atom should form a prefix of the chosen index. Issuing an index scan directly avoids logical query plan generation and query optimization in RDF-3X, which are pure overhead for a single-atom query, but are needed for the general case.

For chained queries containing more than a single atom, it is required that RDF-3X's query processing infrastructure is exploited to produce both a good join ordering and a good choice of physical join operators. RDF-3X's query optimizer generates query plans in a bottom-up manner considering every index that can answer a triplet pattern. For us, this means that six indexes have to be considered for all permutations of SPO patterns. The plan generator has to compute the cost of each index scan that can answer such a triplet pattern, which requires disc access because of the manner in which RDF-3X maintains its statistics. Observing that the predicate is always given in our context, we reduced the number of indexes considered from six to two, namely: the PSO and POS indexes. While this can result in some interesting orders not being considered, we have observed that for small join patterns, this restriction helped in reducing the time required for query optimization, as can be seen in Section 5.

Page Caching. In processing SPARQL queries, RDF-3X is unlikely to access the same disk page multiple times. This is very different for recursive queries, where a same disk page can be accessed multiple times. This is due to the manner in which variable bindings propagate and new sub-queries are generated, often sharing the same constants with previous queries. RDF-3X does not maintain any internal caches. It operates on top of a memory-mapped file, which means that the operating system can perform some caching. Index pages are kept compressed on disk and are uncompressed when read into memory. We added caching to RDF-3X's indexes. When caching is enabled, a hash table of cached pages is maintained. The key into this hash table is a page number, and the values are uncompressed pages. Caching can be configured on a per-index basis. If caching is enabled for an index, then, when the page is requested, the hash table is queried for that page. If it exists, then the page is served from cache, otherwise, the page is read into memory, decompressed and then added to the cache.

Moreover, we added caching to RDF-3X's full triples, aggregated, fully aggregated, and statistics indexes. Although the latter three index types are not accessed for answering queries in our setting, they are accessed for statistics when performing join ordering.

4.3 Recursive Query Evaluation

The recursive query processor uses two top-down algorithms: SLD resolution and QSQR. The choice between the two is done by the user, as there is no syntactic characterization of queries that result in cycles to automate this selection [3]. We opted to implement QSQR in a tuple-at-a-time manner mainly because RDF-3X does not support set-at-a-time querying, and we wanted to keep the changes to RDF-3X to a minimum. In choosing a DB-complete strategy to implement, the choice was between QSQR and Magic Sets. We chose to implement QSQR because the of the lack of need for an explicit rule rewriting step. The *ans_* and *input_* relations needed for tabling in QSQR are created during runtime, when they are needed. Hash indexes are kept on each relation's attributes to speed up point queries, which are issued frequently on those relations.

5 Experimental Evaluation

To evaluate our system, we performed experiments over two datasets. The first one is based on the YAGO knowledge base, which knows 20 million facts about 2 million distinct entities and 100 relations [15]. The size of the RDF-3X database for this dataset is 2.0 GB, including indexes and the string dictionary. The second one is based on the LUBM benchmark for evaluating OWL knowledge base systems [7].

D2R2 is implemented entirely in C++ and compiled using GNU GCC version 4.3.2. All experiments were conducted on a Dell Optiplex 760 PC with an Intel Pentium Processor E5200 and 3.2GB main memory, running a 64-bit Linux 2.6.30 kernel. For cold-cache experiments, we used the `/proc/sys/vm/drop_caches` kernel interface before starting each run of an experiment to clear the operating system's buffer cache.

5.1 Handling of Extensional Queries

Figure 2(a) shows the result of issuing eight extensional queries using both RDF-3X's query infrastructure and that of D2R2 with cold cache. Above, we describe how we handle single-atom extensional queries (such as QE1-2), where we skip the query optimizer completely. For queries with multiple atoms (such as QE3-8), we consider only two possible indexes rather than the six which RDF-3X considers, thus reducing the overhead of selectivity estimation, which is performed through disk. This data shows the high cost of query optimization which RDF-3X performs for our setting. We expect join queries issued through D2R2 to be small. For this class of join queries, the data shows that we benefit from considering less index scans and, therefore, less query plans. The eight queries used in this experiment are over the YAGO dataset. They were chosen to be similar to what we expect the storage backend needs to handle.

5.2 Effect of Chaining

To look at the effect of chaining, we measure the *Number of Intermediate Subqueries (NIS)* issued during query processing, which is equivalent to the number of times sub-query scheduling is performed. As expected, NIS falls when chaining is enabled, as can be seen in Figure 2(b). Queries Q1–Q11 are based on YAGO predicates with highly recursive rules.

5.3 YAGO Comparative Runs

We compared D2R2 to two other recursive query processors: Jena using SLG resolution and IRIS using Magic Sets. We used both the queries for YAGO, which were used in the experiments above, and a new set of queries based on the LUBM benchmark.

Figure 2(c) shows the results for four queries based on YAGO using cold (C) and warm (W) cache. Note that we added Q12 and Q13 especially for this test. These two queries are over the well-known ancestor relation. Both systems, Jena and IRIS, could not handle most of our YAGO queries (Q1, Q3–Q9, and Q11) which are highly recursive and are unmanageable without join ordering. For the

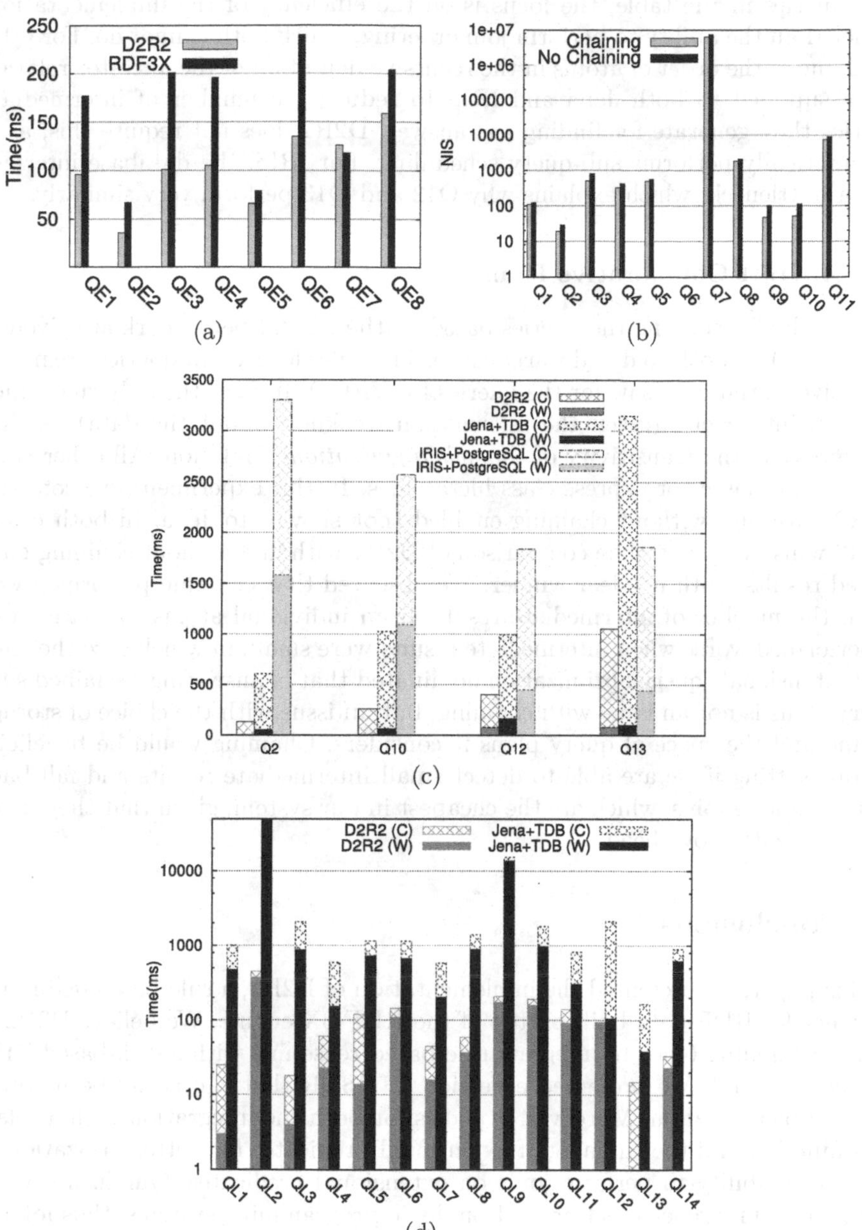

Fig. 2. Experimental results. (a) Results for eight extensional queries over YAGO to show the effects of the changes in dealing with RDF-3X. (b) Effect of chaining for recursive queries based on YAGO. (c) Comparison of D2R2, Jena and IRIS using recurive queries based on YAGO. (d) Comparison of D2R2 and Jena using recurive queries based on LUBM.

four queries in the table, the focus is on the efficiency of the implementation, rather than the ability to perform join ordering, which both cannot do. For Q12, we changed the order of atoms in the recursive definition of the ancestor relation when supplied to both Jena and IRIS to reduce the number of intermediate queries they generate for finding the answer. D2R2 does not require this, as it automatically performs sub-query scheduling. For IRIS, the database interface was a bottleneck, which explains why Q12 and Q13 perform very similarly.

5.4 LUBM Comparative Runs

The results for running the queries based on the LUBM benchmark are given in Figure 2(d) on both cold and warm cache. The rules for LUBM queries are not as recursive as those we saw for the queries for YAGO. In fact, the only rule which can run into cycles (given the information we know about the data), is that of expressing the transitivity of the *subOrganizationOf* relation. All other rules derive new classes or express class hierarchies. In this experiment, we compare D2R2 with and without chaining enabled (not shown) to Jena. In both cases, D2R2 wins over Jena. The comparison of D2R2 with and without chaining gave mixed results, with no clear winner. We observed that chaining performed well when the number of intermediate results from individual atoms was large, but it performed worse when intermediate results were small, in which case the time for (extensional) query optimization dominated that of answering a chained sub-query. This is not an issue with chaining, but an issue with the choice of storage engine and the space of query plans it considers. Chaining would be beneficial for our setting if we are able to detect small intermediate results and fall back on nested loop joins, which are the cheapest in our system, given that they incur no optimization overhead.

6 Conclusions

In this paper, we presented the implementation of D2R2, a rule-based deductive reasoner for RDF data built on top of the RDF-3X engine. We believe D2R2 is a major building block to integrate rule-based reasoning with a disk-based RDF storage backend. We presented a version of QSQR that can easily be mapped to an implementation. Moreover, it allows for both the integration with a selection function and the chaining of extensional predicates for better utilization of RDF-3X's ability to perform joins on extensional predicates. Our future work will focus on more lessons learned from logic programming systems, thus following a WAM-based [26] architecture that also allows for set-at-a-time processing and better integration with the pipeline of RDF-3X. Further topics in our interest include the investigation of distributed deductive reasoning techniques, as well as looking into probabilistic methods to handle uncertain input data and rules.

References

1. Abiteboul, S., Hull, R., Vianu, V.: Foundations of Databases. Addison-Wesley, Reading (1995)
2. Bancilhon, F., Maier, D., Sagiv, Y., Ullman, J.D.: Magic Sets and Other Strange Ways to Implement Logic Programs. In: PODS (1986)
3. Bancilhon, F., Ramakrishnan, R.: An Amateur's Introduction to Recursive Query Processing Strategies. In: SIGMOD (1986)
4. Beeri, C., Ramakrishnan, R.: On the Power of Magic. In: PODS (1987)
5. Ceri, S., Gottlob, G., Tanca, L.: Logic Programming and Databases. Springer, Heidelberg (1990)
6. Grosof, B.N., Horrocks, I., Volz, R., Decker, S.: Description logic programs: combining logic programs with description logic. In: WWW (2003)
7. Guo, Y., Pan, Z., Heflin, J.: LUBM: A benchmark for OWL knowledge base systems. J. Web Sem. 3(2-3) (2005)
8. Horrocks, I., Patel-Schneider, P.F., Boley, H., Tabet, S., Grosof, B., Dean, M.: SWRL: A Semantic Web rule language combining OWL and RuleML. Technical report, World Wide Web Consortium (May 2004)
9. Kaoudi, Z., Kyzirakos, K., Koubarakis, M.: SPARQL Query Optimization on Top of DHTs. In: Patel-Schneider, P.F., Pan, Y., Hitzler, P., Mika, P., Zhang, L., Pan, J.Z., Horrocks, I., Glimm, B. (eds.) ISWC 2010, Part I. LNCS, vol. 6496, pp. 418–435. Springer, Heidelberg (2010)
10. Madalinska-Bugaj, E., Nguyen, L.A.: Generalizing the QSQR Evaluation Method for Horn Knowledge Bases. In: New Challenges in Applied Intelligence Technologies (2008)
11. Nejdl, W.: Recursive strategies for answering recursive queries - the RQA/FQI strategy. In: VLDB (1987)
12. Neumann, T., Weikum, G.: RDF-3X: a RISC-style engine for RDF. In: PVLDB (2008)
13. RuleML. The rule markup initiative (July 2010), `http://ruleml.org/`
14. Stocker, M., Seaborne, A., Bernstein, A., Kiefer, C., Reynolds, D.: SPARQL basic graph pattern optimization using selectivity estimation. In: WWW (2008)
15. Suchanek, F.M., Kasneci, G., Weikum, G.: Yago: a Core of Semantic Knowledge. In: WWW (2007)
16. Ullman, J.D.: Principles of Database and Knowledge-Base Systems. The New Technologies, vol. II. W. H. Freeman & Co., New York (1990)
17. Vieille, L.: Recursive Axioms in Deductive Databases: The Query/Sub-Query Approach. In: Expert Database Conf. (1986)
18. Vieille, L.: A Database-Complete Proof Procedure Based on SLD Resolution. In: ICLP (1987)
19. Warren, D.S.: Memoing for Logic Programs. Commun. ACM 35(3) (1992)
20. Gallaire, H., Minker, J., Nicolas, J.-M.: Logic and Databases: A deductive approach. ACM Comput. Surv. 16(2) (1984)
21. Kowalski, R.A., Kuehner, D.: Linear Resolution with Selection Function. Artif. Intell. 2(3/4) (1971)
22. Sagonas, K.F., Swift, T., Warren, D.S.: XSB as an Efficient Deductive Database Engine. In: SIGMOD (1994)

23. Liang, S., Fodor, P., Wan, H., Kifer, M.: OpenRuleBench: an analysis of the performance of rule engines. In: WWW (2009)
24. Tamaki, H., Sato, T.: Old Resolution with Tabulation. In: Shapiro, E. (ed.) ICLP 1986. LNCS, vol. 225, pp. 84–98. Springer, Heidelberg (1986)
25. Neumann, T., Weikum, G.: Scalable Join Processing on Very Large RDF Graphs. In: SIGMOD (2009)
26. Warren, D.H.D.: An Abstract Prolog Instruction Set. Technical Report 309, AI Center, SRI International (1983)
27. Hellerstein, J.M.: Datalog redux: experience and conjecture. In: PODS (2010)
28. Lam, M.S., Whaley, J., Livshits, V.B., Martin, M.C., Avots, D., Carbin, M., Unkel, C.: Context-sensitive program analysis as database queries. In: PODS (2005)

Principles of the SymposiumPlanner Instantiations of Rule Responder

Zhili Zhao[1], Adrian Paschke[1], Chaudhry Usman Ali[2], and Harold Boley[2,3]

[1] Computer Science Department, Freie Universität Berlin, Germany
{zhili.zhao,paschke}@inf.fu-berlin.de
[2] Faculty of Computer Science, University of New Brunswick, Canada
maniali@gmail.com
[3] Institute for Information Technology, National Research Council of Canada
harold.boley@nrc-cnrc.gc.ca

Abstract. The Rule Responder SymposiumPlanner system supports topic-oriented collaboration between the distributed members of a virtual organization. Each member (or small team of members) is assisted by a semi-autonomous rule-based personal agent, which uses Semantic Web rules to capture aspects of the member's (or team's) derivation and reaction logic. SymposiumPlanner is a series of Rule Responder use cases for supporting the RuleML Symposia (2007-2011) by coordinating personal agents that assist the symposium chairs, intelligently answering questions from people interested in the symposium. In this paper, we introduce principles of SymposiumPlanner and make suggestions about its future development, mainly for RuleML-2012, and about further Rule Responder use cases.

1 Introduction

Rule Responder[1] is a tool for creating virtual organizations as multi-agent systems that support collaborative teams on the Semantic Web. It thus extends the Semantic Web towards a Pragmatic Web infrastructure with collaborative rule-based agent networks realizing distributed inference services, where independent agents engage in conversations by exchanging messages and cooperate to achieve shared goals [3]. Rule Responder's architecture realizes a system of personal agents (PAs), computational agents (CAs), and organizational agents (OAs), accessed via external agents (EAs), on top of an Enterprise Service Bus (ESB) communication middleware. These agents together process events, queries, and requests according to their rule-based decision and behavioral reaction logic. An agent can also delegate subtasks to other agents, collect partial answers, and send the completed answer(s) back to the requester. Since the Rule Responder framework has been conceived, many instantiations of it have been developed

[1] http://responder.ruleml.org

F. Olken et al. (Eds.): RuleML 2011 - America, LNCS 7018, pp. 97–111, 2011.

such as the Health Care and Life Sciences eScience infrastructure [13], Rule-based IT Service Level Management, Semantic Business Process Management (BPM) [14,15], WellnessRules(2) [2], PatientSupporter, and SymposiumPlanner systems.

SymposiumPlanner is a series of Rule Responder instantiations for the Questions&Answers (Q&A) sections of the official websites of the RuleML Symposia. Since 2007 [5], SymposiumPlanner has continued to support the organizing committee of the RuleML Symposium and was continuously developed to support this annual meeting (in 2011, it supports two RuleML Symposia). Symposium organization typically involves organization partner coordination, sponsoring correspondence, panel participants management, etc. Through a collaboration between the organizational agent, personal agents, and the external agent, SymposiumPlanner has assisted the symposium committee with structuring the meeting, and answered various kinds of questions by people interested in the symposium.

In this paper, we introduce the general architecture of the SymposiumPlanner system and present how it is used for symposium organization. In our latest version of SymposiumPlanner-2011, we introduce a user friendlier Rule Responder interface and information integration from external Web data repositories. The new Rule Responder web interface allows users to issue formal queries via web forms and in controlled natural language. Meanwhile, there are large semantic knowledge repositories on the Internet, such as: DBpedia (Deutschland)[2], Freebase[3], YAGO[4], Semantic Web Dog Food[5]. By reusing and integrating existing fact information on the Internet, we avoid redundancy in the knowledge bases of the SymposiumPlanner's agents.

The paper is organized as follows. Section 2 discusses related work. Section 3 describes issues in symposium organization where Rule Responder can help the chairs, and considers what needs to be taken into account when using Rule Responder in symposium organization. Section 4 introduces the conceptual architecture to address these issues. Section 5 presents the Rule Responder implementation architecture. Section 6 concludes the work on Rule Responder SymposiumPlanner and discusses the proof-of concept instantiations.

2 Related Work

To the best of our knowledge, there are no rule-based agent systems focusing on supporting conference planning, but there are a lot of other applications for rule-based multi agent systems. Rule-based agent systems make intelligent decisions quickly and in repeatable form based on their rule based and ontology based knowledge bases. They run specialized rule engines for executing the agent logic. The agent behaviour specification is mainly represented by programming

[2] `http://de.dbpedia.org/`

[3] `http://www.freebase.com/`

[4] `http://www.mpi-inf.mpg.de/yago-naga/yago/`

[5] `http://data.semanticweb.org/`

it in logical rules. Two typical representatives for this category are RC++ [19] and SOAR [11]. Another kind of rule-based agent architectures encompasses approaches that aim at introducing abstract mentalistic notions as agent programming language constructs. These approaches propose specific concerted sets of mental state components and introduce agent programming languages with specific types of rules to operate on the agents components. Prominent representatives of this category are the agent-oriented programming (AOP) [17] and the 3APL/2APL language families. 3APL ("An Abstract Agent Programming Language") and its successor 2APL ("A Practical Agent Programming Language") are developed at the University of Utrecht [9]. Closely related to Rule Responder are agent architectures which directly use expressive rule languages and rule engines as basis for the agent behavior control. Using this kind of architecture basically requires that the rule base is properly connected with the agent's sensors and effectors in order to allow an agent to receive percepts and execute actions. Examples of this domain are e.g. JADE/Jess agent [4], Vivid Agents [16], OPAL Agents [18] and Emerald [10]. While these approaches use their own proprietary agent runtime environments and rule engines, Rule Responder aims at a more general approach using established and highly efficient enterprise service and messaging technologies based on standard Internet transport technologies. For representing the agents knowledge and behaviour it applies standards such as RuleML rules and W3C RDF/OWL ontologies so that the agents logic is declaratively described in a platform-independent manner and can be translated and executed in different platform-specific rule engines deployed as distributed (Web) inference services.

3 Rule Responder for Symposium Organization

Rule Responder has been successfully employed as a distributed query answering framework instantiated for many areas. Two main benefits are gained by alleviating the burden of repetitive tasks and by enabling the automation of rule based organizational processes. SymposiumPlanner assists organizers in managing the meeting and answering queries about it. As Rule Responder uses Semantic Web rules to describe aspects of their owners derivation and reaction logic, it is necessary to extend the SymposiumPlanner system for users who may not have deep knowledge about semantic technologies.

3.1 Issues in Symposium Organization

We are not concerned here with paper submission and reviewing, which are well supported by existing conference management systems such as EasyChair[6] and WitanWeb[7]. Even without those processes, symposium organization involves lots of procedures, and it consumes much energy and time of organizers. Although none of these procedures seems inherently complex, taken together they are non-trivial to manage for meeting chairs. These procedures include:

[6] `http://www.easychair.org/`

[7] `http://witanweb.ca/cascon2010/WitanWebFAQ.jsp`

- coordinating chair responsibilities (responsibility assignment),
- finding contact information about selected chairs of the symposium,
- helping the program and track chairs with mapping planned paper topics to program and track themes,
- helping the program chair to monitor and possibly move important dates,
- helping the liaison chair with special events by symposium partners,
- helping the panel chair with managing panel participants,
- helping the publicity chair with sponsoring correspondence,
- and answering questions of participants about the conference such as important dates, topics addresses, program schedule etc.

3.2 Interaction with Users

For deploying agents on the Web and enabling communication in agent networks, Rule Responder uses an ESB middleware, and utilizes messaging from Reaction RuleML[8] for communication between the distributed agent inference services. While Reaction RuleML/XML has adequate expressiveness for the communication between heterogeneous rule agents in the virtual organization, there are two human-oriented methods to support the interaction between users and Rule Responder.

One method is creating dynamic HTML forms as Web user interface of an organizational agent. A Rule Responder interface description file – itself specified in XML – contains information about the interface name, parameters, and types, which is used to describe the interfaces of the organizational agent. Users are guided to select the appropriate interface and fill in the query parameters. Queries are translated based on the Rule Responder interface description file and the values that users give in the HTML form, as shown in Figure 1. However, it may be difficult for users to identify the desired interface when there are a plenty of interfaces available.

The other method is based on controlled natural language, which allows users to describe queries in controlled English, where a translator maps the controlled English to Reaction RuleML. The benefit is that users do not need to know the available interfaces for various queries. However, the controlled English (e.g. Attempto Controlled English) usually has more types of declarative sentences and some of which are difficult to translate into Reaction RuleML, such as: commands and sentence subordination. In the SymposiumPlanner-2011 system, we thus use both solutions to improve user experience.

3.3 Communication between Distributed Agents

Both centralized rule system and distributed rule system can be used to support the collaboration of distributed members of an organization. A centralized

[8] `http://reaction.ruleml.org`

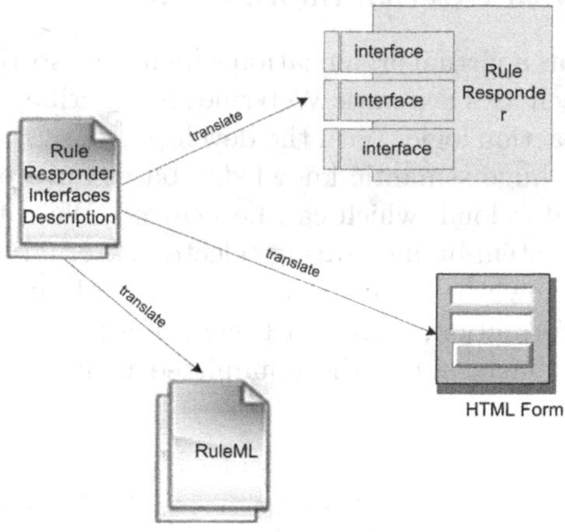

Fig. 1. Rule Responder Interface Description

rule system would contain all of the facts and rules in one knowledge base or in one centralized location. In contrast, the advantages of a distributed rule system over a centralized system include e.g., achieving a fault-tolerant system by using distribution for redundancy, and improved efficiency through distributed processing.

Distributed maintenance allows agents to update their rules and facts without affecting the rule bases of other agents (their consistency, completeness, etc.). If all of the knowledge was stored in one central rule base, problems introduced by one agent would affect the entire system.

Also, if an agent is offline, i.e. a PA is not responding when an OA delegates a query to it, a timeout would be received and either the OA would try another PA that may be able to answer the query or would respond back that the PA is currently offline.

Rule Responder and SymposiumPlanner are implemented as a distributed rule system. It connects OAs and PAs so that they can share knowledge and external agents can query this knowledge. Each PA and OA has its own set of rules and facts. The rules of the PAs correspond to their expert owners while the OA's knowledge describes the virtual organization as a whole. All of the PAs with their rule bases are stored at distributed locations.

In a distributed rule system the knowledge is spread over many different physical locations and communication overhead can become a problem, but the overhead may not be noticeable to external agents. Rules execute faster when there are less clauses for the engine to process, so our distributed approach improves efficiency because we have multiple rule engines working on smaller knowledge modules instead of one rule engine working on a large knowledge base as in a centralized approach.

3.4 Integration with External Information

Rule Responder acts as a virtual organization which consists of many autonomous rule-based agents. Each uses Semantic Web rules to describe aspects of their owners' derivation and reaction logic. With the development of semantic technologies in last decade, many huge semantic knowledge bases have been published, e.g. in the linked open data cloud, which can be utilized. We reduce redundancy of SymposiumPlanner system by integrating selected external semantic knowledge on the Internet, as shown in Figure 2. In SymposiumPlanner 2011 each agent manages personal information, such as a Friend of a Friend (FOAF)-like profile containing a layer of facts about the committee members as well as FOAF-extending rules.

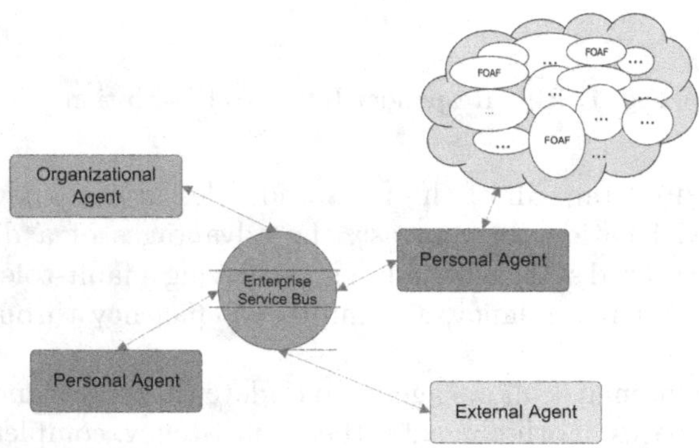

Fig. 2. Integration with External Information

3.5 Role Assignment

Personal agents in Rule Responder are usually loosely coupled and implemented based on their different functionalities. As one possible way for coordination in a virtual organization the Rule Responder framework uses a 'pluggable' Responsibility Assignment Matrix (RAM) to support the OA in its selection of a PA and its optional participating profiles underneath. A RAM describes the responsibility of agent roles in completing certain tasks or deliverables in a virtual organization. A standard RAM is a matrix which describes four key responsibilities most typically used: Responsible, Accountable, Consulted, and Informed.

In the Rule Responder agent topology, a single RAM matrix can be used in the OA to map an incoming query to the PA whose local knowledge base is deemed to be best suited for answering it. The RAM matrix is represented as an OWL ontology (OWL Lite) and can be used by a Rule Responder agent via querying it with the Semantic Web built-ins of Prova, binding the respective roles and their responsibilities to typed variables in the agent's rule logic. Many variants of the RAM with different role distinctions are possible such as RACI (with Consulted agents), RASCI (with Supporting agents) etc. - see, e.g., Table 1.

Table 1. Responsibility Assignment Matrix

	General Chair	Program Chair	Publicity Chair
Symposium	responsible	consulted	supportive
Website	accountable	responsible	
Sponsoring	informed, signs	verifies	responsible
Submission	informed	responsible	

4 Conceptual Architecture

So far, we have presented the major issues addressed in Symposium organization and several critical theoretical considerations in our SymposiumPlanner system. This section introduces the conceptual architecture as a novel design artefact (following the design science research methodology) (see Figure 3). Each committee chair acts as a personal agent. As users usually initialize the queries via a web browser and the SymposiumPlanner client assists users to construct queries and get the answers with web pages. OAs, CAs, PAs and EAs are composed of distributed agent topologies and coordinate with each other to complete users' objectives.

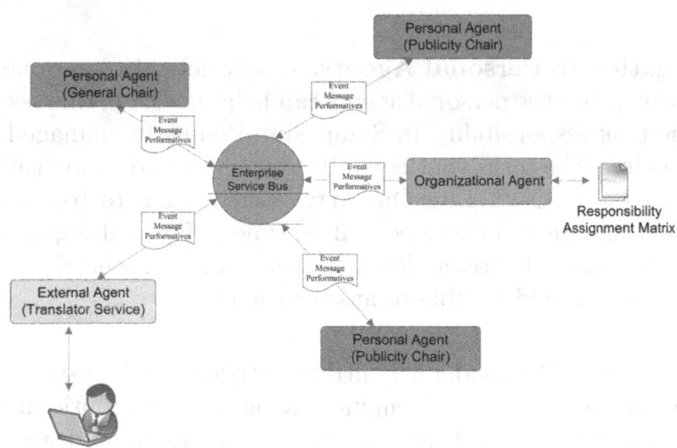

Fig. 3. Conceptual Architecture of SymposiumPlanner

4.1 Organizational Agent

An organizational agent is used to describe the goals shared by its symposium as a whole and contains a knowledge base that describes the symposium's policies, regulations, and opportunities. This knowledge base contains condition/action/event rules as well as derivation rules. An OA manages its local Personal Agents (PAs), providing control of their life cycles and ensuring overall goals and policies of the organization and its semiotic structures. OAs can act as a single point of entry to the managed sets of local PAs to which requests by EAs are disseminated. This allows for efficient implementation of various mechanisms of making sure the PAs functionalities are not abused (security mechanisms) and making sure privacy of entities, personal data, and computation resources are respected (privacy & information hiding mechanisms) [3]. The selection logic for the dissemination of queries to PAs is described by RAM and OA selects responsible agents with a SPARQL query.

4.2 Personal Agents

In the SymposiumPlanner system, each organization committee chair is designed as a personal agent, which contains a knowledge base that represents its chair's responsibilities to answer corresponding queries. Personal agents are chairs' roles in the symposium organization. But, they might also be services or applications in, e.g. a service oriented architecture. A PA runs a rule engine which accesses different sources of local data and computes answers according to the local rule-based decision logic of the PA. Depending on the required expressiveness to represent the personal agents rule logic, arbitrary rule engines can be used as long as they provide an interface to ask queries and receive answers which are translated into the common interchange format in order to communicate with other agents.

Query Delegation to Personal Agents. Query delegation is done by the organizational agent, but the personal agents can help the OA in this responsibility. Currently, the task responsibility in SymposiumPlanner is managed through a RAM, which defines the tasks that committee members are responsible for. The matrix, defined by an OWL Lite Ontology, assigns roles to topics within the virtual organization. Should there be still no unique PA to delegate a query to, the OA needs to make a heuristic delegation decision and send the query to the PA that most likely would be able to answer the query.

Performatives. Rule Responder is multiple distributed rule system, where each rule agent can run a different rule engine having its own proprietary syntax to access different sources of local data. Usually these distributed agents connect and communicate with each other based on a common rule interchange language, which carries pragmatic performatives. These performatives can be used by the receiver agents to understand the pragmatic context of the message.

Query Answering for Personal Agents. In some cases, the OA can try to solve a query from an external agent by itself, but in the following we consider only cases where it delegates queries to PAs. When a PA receives a query, it is responsible for its answering. If there are multiple solutions to a query, the PA attempts to send an enumeration of as many of the solutions to the OA as possible (it is of course impossible when there are infinitely many solutions).

There are different methods for processing multiple solutions to a query. A naive method of the PAs would be to first compute all of the solutions and then send all of the answers back to the OA, one at a time. After the last answer message is sent, an `end-of-transmission` message is sent to let the OA know that there will be no more messages. The main problem with computing all of the answers before sending any of them is obvious: in case of an infinite enumeration of solutions the OA will not receive any answer. The way our implementation addresses the infinite solutions problem is to interleave backtracking with transmission. When a solution is found, the PA immediately sends the answer, and then begins to compute the next solution while the earlier answer is being transferred. When the OA has received enough answers from such a (possibly infinite) enumeration, it can send a `no-more` message to the PA, stopping its computation of further solutions. Once all solutions have been found in a *finite* interleaved enumeration, the PA can send an `end-of-transmission` message.

If a PA receives a query and the agent does not have any solutions for it, a `failure` message is sent right away back to the OA. If this situation or a timeout occurs (i.e., the PA is offline and did not respond back to the OA within the preset time period), then the OA can try to delegate the query to another PA to see if *it* is able to solve the query. If no solution can be found in any of these ways, a `failure` message is sent back to the external agent that states that the OA (representing the entire organization) cannot solve the query.

Communication between Personal Agent and Expert Owner. One problem that can arise when a personal agent works on a query is that the PA may require help or confirmation from its human 'owner'. The PA may not be able to (fully) answer the query until it has communicated with its human owner. The way we approach this problem is to allow PAs to send messages to their owners and vice versa, e.g. in the form of emails. When the owner receives a PA email, he or she can respond to help finding the answer to the external agent. When the personal agent has received the answer from its owner, the PA can use it to complete the answer to the original query.

Agent Communication Protocols. Rule Responder implements different communication protocols which our agents can utilize. The protocols vary by the number of steps involved in the communication. We try to follow message patterns similar to Web Service communication [8]. For example, there can be **in-only**, **request-response**, and **request-response-acknowledge** protocols, as well as entire **workflow** protocols [6]. Most of the instantiations of SymposiumPlanner primarily focus on the request-response protocol.

Translation between the Interchange Language and Proprietary Languages. Having an interchange language is a key aspect in a distributed rule system. Each agent must be able to understand one common language that every other agent can interpret. The interchange language carries performatives that each agent is able to understand and react to. Agents can understand the content of the interchange language by interpreting its semantics and pragmatic performative. Each rule engine can have its own platform specific syntax and, in order to run different rule engines in the Rule Responder agents, there must exist a translator between the platform-independent interchange language and the execution syntax of that rule engine.

5 SymposiumPlanner System

Since 2007, we have implemented five instantiations which support the organizing committee of the RuleML Symposium. We implemented the presented Rule Responder agent architecture using the ESB Mule[9]. We mainly use two representative rule engines, namely Prova[10] and OOjDrew [1] (but furhter extended SymposiumPlanner in 2010 to other engine such as Emerald). The developed prototype proves the applicability of the concept in practice. Figure 4 illustrates the general architecture of SymposiumPlanner instantiations that coordinate symposium chairs and the people who are interested in the meeting.

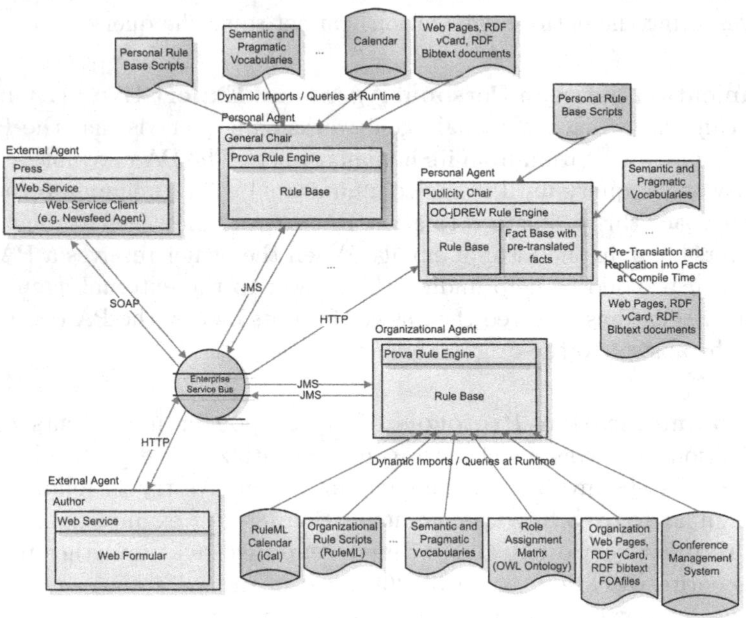

Fig. 4. Main Components of SymposiumPlanner System

9 http://www.mulesoft.org
10 http://prova.ws

5.1 Mule Enterprise Service Bus

To seamlessly handle message-based interactions between the Rule Responder agents/services and other agents/services using disparate complex event processing (CEP) technologies, transports, and protocols, the Mule open-source ESB is used in Rule Responder as the communication middleware. This ESB allows deploying the rule-based agents as highly distributed rule inference services installed as Web-based endpoints on the Mule object broker and supports the communication in this rule-based agent processing network via a multitude of transport protocols. That is, the ESB provides a highly scalable and flexible application messaging framework to communicate synchronously or asynchronously amongst the ESB-local agents and with agents/services on the Web.

Distributed agent services, which at their core run a rule engine, are deployed as Mule components which listen at configured endpoints, e.g., JMS message endpoints, HTTP ports, SOAP server/client addresses or JDBC database interfaces, etc. Reaction RuleML is used as a common platform-independent rule interchange format between the agents (and possible other rule execution/inference services). Translator services are used to translate inbound and outbound messages from platform-independent Reaction RuleML into the platform-specific execution syntaxes of rule engines, and vice versa. Extensible Stylesheet Transformations(XSLT) and ANTLR based translator services are provided as Web forms, HTTP services and SOAP Web services on the Reaction RuleML Web page.

The large variety of transport protocols provided by Mule can be used to transport the messages to the registered endpoints or external applications/tools. Usually, JMS is used for the internal communication between distributed agent instances, while HTTP and SOAP are used to access external Web services. The usual processing style is asynchronous using Staged Event Driven Architecture (SEDA) event queues. However, sometimes synchronous communication is needed. For instance, to handle the communication with external synchronous HTTP clients such as Web browsers where requests, e.g. by a Web from, are sent through a synchronous channel. In this case, a synchronous bridge component dispatches the requests into the asynchronous messaging framework and collects all answers from the internal service nodes, while keeping the synchronous channel with the external service open. After all asynchronous answers have been collected, they are sent back to the still connected external service via the HTTP-synchronous channel.

5.2 Platform-Specific Rule Responder Agents

Each agent service might run one or more arbitrary rule engines to execute the interchanged queries, rules and events and derive answers on requests. Prova is a highly expressive Semantic Web rule engine which we used in our reference implementation for agents with complex reaction workflows, decision logic and dynamic access to external Semantic Web data sources. Another rule engine which we applied was the OOjDrew rule engine [1] in order to demonstrate rule interchange between various rule engines. Further rule engines and event correlation engines (CEP engines) are used in the Rule Responder project in other applications.

Prova follows the spirit and design of the recent W3C Semantic Web initiative and combines declarative rules, ontologies and inference with dynamic object-oriented Java API calls and access to external data sources via query languages such as SQL, SPARQL and XQuery.

One of the key advantages of Prova is its separation of logic, data access, and computation and its tight integration of Java and Semantic Web technologies. Due to the natural integration of Prova with Java, it offers a syntactically economic and compact way of specifying agents' behaviour while allowing for efficient Java-based extensions to improve performance of critical operations.

The main language constructs of messaging reaction rules in Prova are: sendMsg predicates to send messages, reaction rcvMsg rules which react to inbound messages, and rcvMsg or rcvMult inline reactions in the body of messaging reaction rules to receive one or more context-dependent multiple inbound event messages.

5.3 Reaction RuleML

For SymposiumPlanner System we use Reaction RuleML as our interchange language between agents. Reaction RuleML [12] is a general, practical, compact and user-friendly XML-serialized sublanguage of RuleML for the family of reaction rules. It incorporates various kinds of production, action, reaction, and KR temporal/event/action logic rules as well as (complex) event/action messages into the native RuleML syntax using a system of step-wise extensions.

Rule Responder permits agents to use local languages and engines, only requiring that all rule bases, queries, and answers be translated to RuleML for transmitting them to other agents over the Mule ESB. The RuleML Interface Description Language (RuleML IDL) as sublanguage of Reaction RuleML describes the signatures of public rule functions together with their mode and type declarations and narrative human-oriented meta descriptions.

Reaction RuleML provides a translator service framework with Web form interfaces accepting controlled natural language input or predefined selection-based rule templates for the communication with external (human) agents on the computational independent level, as well as Servlet HTTP interfaces, and Web service SOAP interfaces, which can be used for translation into and from platform-specific rule languages such as Prova. On the platform-independent and platform-specific level, the translator services are using different translation technologies such as XSLT stylesheet, Java Architecture for XML Binding (JAXB), etc. to translate from and to Reaction RuleML as a general rule interchange format.

5.4 SymposiumPlanner User Client

One of the main advantages of SymposiumPalnner is that it answers users queries promptly and reduces users' burden of finding the interested information by themselves. The queries include the information about the symposia and the procures mentioned in section 3.1. For its usability, the SymposiumPlanner user client provides an interface to distributed personal agents, allowing users to query the available interfaces, describe and submit the queries, and retrieve the answers from a standard web browser.

SymposiumPlanner user client allows users to query the SymposiumPlanner agents via the SymposiumPlanner interface either by HTML forms or by a controlled natural language.

The first solution uses the XML based Rule Responder interfaces description file to create HTML forms which present users with the information of interface in detail, such as interface name, parameter and its descriptions, and etc. The translator service will combine the structure of Reaction RuleML message from the Rule Responder interfaces description file with values which users initialize to construct the Reaction RuleML message.

The translation between the used controlled English language and Reaction RuleML is based on domain-specific language translation rules in combination with a controlled English translator service. In SymposiumPlanner, we use Attempto Controlled English [7] which is a rich subset of standard English designed to serve as knowledge representation language. Queries to Rule Responder are formulated in Attempto Controlled English and the ACE2RML translator forwards the text to the Attempto Parsing Engine (APE), which translates the text into a discourse representation structure (DRS) and/or advices to correct malformed input. The DRS gives a logical/structural representation of the text. It is fed into an XML parser which translates it into a domain-specific Reaction RuleML representation of the query. Besides parsing and processing the elements of the DRS, the parser additionally employs domain-specific transformation rules to correctly translate the query into a public interface call of a Rule Responder OA.

6 Conclusion

Following a design science research methodology, we introduced the design principles, conceptual model and component architecture of the Rule Responder SymposiumPlanner agent system. SymposiumPlanner allows users to issue queries to the RuleML conference organisation committee members which are represented by their SymposiumPlanner agents.

SymposiumPlanner is a Semantic Web infrastructure for distributed rule-based event processing multi-agent eco-systems. Based on modern enterprise service technologies and Semantic Web technologies for implementing intelligent rule-based agent services that access data and ontologies, receive and detect events (e.g., for complex event processing in event processing agent networks), and make rule-based inferences and (semi-) autonomous pro-active decisions for reactions based on these representations. The core rule agents of Symposium-Planner implement the decision and behavioural reaction logic of the agents roles and manage the symposium organization effectively.

SymposiumPlanner instantiations span various implementations from initial state in 07,08,09 to Emerald based instantiation in 2010 to the 2011 double-instantiation using the latest Mule and Prova with a more user friendly interface involving 3 OA's instead of just one for the sake of clarity (although future implementation could see reunification of business logics into one OA as in the initial instantiations).

In SymposiumPlanner, distributed agent instances follow SEDA style, which decomposes a complex, event-driven application into a set of stages connected by event queues. This design decouples event and thread scheduling from application logic and avoids the high overhead associated with thread-based concurrency models. However, although event queues decouples the execution of distributed components, it increases response time correspondingly.

Future implementation will focus on increased automation of processes as well as better support from human operators to add flexibility (e.g. the system already contacts human operator in case the query is not solvable by the agent itself). Further improvements will be also in the form of better support through systems in order to achieve automation in terms of responses from agents as they replace actual human users and try to respond to increasingly complex queries. This might also lead to the need of communication between personal agents in order to help each other in answering queries posed by external agents. However, a single PA might not be able to answer a query as a whole. Another extension to query delegation would thus be query decomposition, followed by delegation of its decomposed parts to multiple PAs, and finally re-integration of the PAs' answers before being sent back to the OA.

References

1. Ball, M., Craig, B.: Object Oriented java Deductive Reasoning Engine for the Web, `http://www.jdrew.org/oojdrew/`
2. Boley, H., Osmun, T., Craig, B.: Social semantic rule sharing and querying in wellness communities. In: Gómez-Pérez, A., Yu, Y., Ding, Y. (eds.) ASWC 2009. LNCS, vol. 5926, pp. 347–361. Springer, Heidelberg (2009), `http://dx.doi.org/10.1007/978-3-642-10871-6_24`
3. Boley, H., Paschke, A.: Rule responder agents framework and instantiations. In: Eli, A., Kon, M., Orgun, M. (eds.) Semantic Agent Systems. SCI, vol. 344, pp. 3–23. Springer, Heidelberg (2011), `http://dx.doi.org/10.1007/978-3-642-18308-9_1`
4. Cardoso, H.L.: Integrating jade and jess (2007), `http://jade.tilab.com/doc/tutorials/jade-jess/jade_jess.html`
5. Craig, B.L.: The OO jDREW Engine of Rule Responder: Naf Hornlog RuleML Query Answering. In: Paschke, A., Biletskiy, Y. (eds.) RuleML 2007. LNCS, vol. 4824, pp. 149–154. Springer, Heidelberg (2007)
6. Craig, B.L., Boley, H.: Personal agents in the rule responder architecture. In: Bassiliades, N., Governatori, G., Paschke, A. (eds.) RuleML 2008. LNCS, vol. 5321, pp. 150–165. Springer, Heidelberg (2008), `http://dx.doi.org/10.1007/978-3-540-88808-6_17`

7. Fuchs, N.E., Kaljurand, K., Schneider, G.: Attempto controlled english meets the challenges of knowledge representation, reasoning, interoperability and user interfaces. In: Sutcliffe, G., Goebel, R. (eds.) FLAIRS Conference, pp. 664–669. AAAI Press (2006), `http://dblp.uni-trier.de/db/conf/flairs/flairs2006.html#FuchsKS06`
8. Gudgin, M., Lewis, A., Schlimmer, J.: Web Services Description Language (WSDL) Version 1.2 Part 2: Message Patterns, `http://www.w3.org/TR/2003/WD-wsdl12-patterns-20030611/`
9. Hindriks, K.V., De Boer, F.S., Van Der Hoek, W., Meyer, J.-J.C.: Agent programming in 3apl. Autonomous Agents and Multi-Agent Systems 2, 357–401 (1999)
10. Kravari, K., Kontopoulos, E., Bassiliades, N.: Emerald: A multi-agent system for knowledge-based reasoning interoperability in the semantic web. In: Konstantopoulos, S., Perantonis, S., Karkaletsis, V., Spyropoulos, C.D., Vouros, G. (eds.) SETN 2010. LNCS, vol. 6040, pp. 173–182. Springer, Heidelberg (2010)
11. Lehman, J.F., Laird, J., Rosenbloom, P.: A gentle introduction to soar, an architecture for human cognition. In: Sternberg, S., Scarborough, D. (eds.) Invitation to Cognitive Science. MIT Press (1996)
12. Paschke, A., Kozlenkov, A., Boley, H.: A homogenous reaction rules language for complex event processing. In: International Workshop on Event Drive Architecture for Complex Event Process (2007), `http://ibis.in.tum.de/staff/paschke/`
13. Paschke, A.: Rule responder hcls escience infrastructure. In: Proceedings of the 3rd International Conference on the Pragmatic Web: Innovating the Interactive Society, ICPW 2008, pp. 59–67. ACM, New York (2008), `http://doi.acm.org/10.1145/1479190.1479199`
14. Paschke, A., Bichler, M.: Knowledge representation concepts for automated sla management. CoRR abs/cs/0611122 (2006)
15. Paschke, A., Kozlenkov, A.: A rule-based middleware for business process execution. In: Multikonferenz Wirtschaftsinformatik (2008)
16. Schroeder, M., Wagner, G.: Vivid agents: Theory, architecture, and applications. Applied Artificial Intelligence 14(7), 645–675 (2000)
17. Shoham, Y.: Agent-oriented programming. Artif. Intell. 60(1), 51–92 (1993)
18. Wang, M., Purvis, M., Nowostawski, M.: An internal agent architecture incorporating standard reasoning components and standards-based agent communication. In: Proceedings of the IEEE/WIC/ACM International Conference on Intelligent Agent Technology, IAT 2005, pp. 58–64. IEEE Computer Society, Washington, DC (2005), `http://dx.doi.org/10.1109/IAT.2005.43`
19. Wright, I., Marshall, J.: The execution kernel of rc++: Rete*, a faster rete with treat as a special case. International Journal of Intelligent Games and Simulation 2 (2003)

Extended Rules in Knowledge-Based Data Access

Jaroslaw Bak, Grażyna Brzykcy, and Czeslaw Jedrzejek

Institute of Control and Information Engineering,
Poznan University of Technology,
M. Sklodowskiej-Curie Sqr. 5, 60-965 Poznan, Poland
firstname.lastname@put.poznan.pl

Abstract. We present a method for an efficient knowledge-based access to relational data. Knowledge is represented as a set of rules (basic rules) and describes a source data at concept (ontological) level. Forward chaining in the integrated system is performed with extended rules, which are obtained by a goal- and dependency-directed transformation of the basic rules. The novel feature of our method is generality - every rule is generated so that includes all possible binding of the head predicates, and variable dependencies, while in many implementations of the magic method the succession of bindings depends on a query. We demonstrate a query answering algorithm and our prototypical implementation of the system coupled with the Jess engine. The results of performance evaluation are presented and compared to the results described in our previous works.

Keywords: Rule-based system, magic transformation, Rete algorithm, ontology, relational database access.

1 Introduction

Nowadays, the most of data processed in modern applications come from relational databases. Data stored in such sources are described only by their schema (a structure of data). Without strictly defined semantics there is often a mismatching problem with table and column names in databases. Moreover, it is rather difficult to query data at a more abstract level than only in a language of database relations and attributes. A lack of conceptual knowledge can be overcome by introducing ontologies. For the evaluation purposes, an ontology (and other knowledge) can be transformed into a set of rules. The additional rule-based knowledge allows reasoning and query answering at an appropriate abstract layer. Moreover, it simplifies to pose a question than using structural constructions from SQL. In our approach a knowledge base is derived from the Horn-SHIQ ontology [1] transformed into a set of rules.

In rule-based systems a query answering process, based on the forward chaining, is generally inefficient. The report of OpenRuleBench initiative [2] shows that the performance results of pure rule-based engines are surpassed by tabling Prolog and deductive database technologies. Therefore, we propose a modified magic transformation algorithm which together with the Rete Pattern Matching algorithm increases speed and scalability of rule-based systems with the forward chaining. Our

F. Olken et al. (Eds.): RuleML 2011 - America, LNCS 7018, pp. 112–127, 2011.

method is based on dependencies between variables appearing in predicates inside each rule. Our approach generates rules to be processed by the Rete-based engine.

An important step in our procedure consists of linking data stored in a relational database to the knowledge base. We accomplish this by creating a special rules which contain simple SQL queries in their bodies. We also propose a grouping algorithm to improve the database query answering process. This paper makes the following contributions:

- We define an algorithm for semantically equivalent rules transformation where rules from a knowledge base are transformed into goal- and dependency-oriented rules,
- We propose a mapping construction method that is used to relate knowledge predicates and the corresponding database,
- We evaluate our approach with the prototypical implementation performed on the model presented in [3] with the comparison to the results achieved in the RuleML-2010 Challenge [4].

Section 2 presents overview of our rule-based system and reasoning schemes. Our query answering process with a rule-based system and relational database is presented in Section 3. The next part contains a performance evaluation and comparison to the results achieved in the RuleML-2010 Challenge. Related work is presented in the Section 5 before concluding remarks and future work.

2 Rule-Based System and Reasoning Scheme

2.1 Rules and Facts

We apply the following form of a rule:

$$p_1(\bar{X}_1), p_2(\bar{X}_2), \ldots, p_n(\bar{X}_n), AP => h(\bar{X}_h) \quad (1)$$

where each p_i (and h) is a predicate symbol, and $\bar{X}_i$ represents a vector of variables and constants, which appear in the atom $p_i(\bar{X}_i)$ as arguments. We assume that only unary or binary predicates are used in our system. For example, in atom *p(x, ?y)* there appears a constant *x* and a variable *?y*. *AP* denotes a set of additional predicates, which are used for comparisons and tests, for example: $x < 2$, $y \geq x$, etc.

Every rule consists of the two parts: the left-hand-side, which is called the body, and the right-hand-side, which is called the head. In general, both parts are represented by sets of atoms interpreted conjunctively. In the body of the rule we use premises (patterns, conditions), which have to be satisfied by appropriate atoms (facts) to allow a rule to be fired and to produce conclusions from the rule's head. We assume that the body of a rule may be empty. In this case, the rule is called a fact.

Rules of the form (1) belong to the class of Horn clauses [5] (if there are several predicates in the head, a rule can be easily transformed into Horn clauses with the Lloyd-Topor transformation [5]). Moreover, we assume that only DL-safe rules are taken into account.

Arguments in atoms, particularly pertaining to the same variables, play a significant role, as they form information channels between atoms. In order to efficiently verify satisfaction of conditions from the rule body and infer a conclusion specified in the head, we are interested in finding dependencies between the atoms (predicates). Let us define a subset *Dep(B,P)* of atoms from a set B which share a variable or a constant with some atom in the set of atoms *P*, e.g.,

$$Dep(\{p(x, y), q(z)\}, \{r(y), s(w)\}) = \{p(x, y)\}.$$

2.2 Rule-Based System

A rule-based system is used as a way to derive new facts from the given ones according to the defined set of rules. Such a system consists of few elements:

- A list of rules (rule base), which forms a kind of a knowledge base.
- A working memory, which contains facts. The working memory changes during the reasoning process.
- An inference engine, which generates a new fact (or takes an action) based on an interaction between facts and the rule base.
- A user's interface (e. g., a console).

Usually, a rule-based system processes data only in its working memory. According to a forward chaining mechanism, commonly used in reasoning tasks, a user gets information as a set of inferred facts. In this set it is hard to find a fact or facts which the user is interested in. Thus, the user has to pose a query to the rule-based system to obtain the necessary facts. This is a better way than looking through the working memory manually.

The forward chaining approach needs reasoning about all facts in the working memory. Therefore, some of the inferred facts are useless and many rules are fired unnecessarily. It has a negative impact on efficiency of the answering process. Moreover, as all facts should exist in the working memory, the scalability of reasoning tasks is poor due to the limited RAM memory.

The Rete algorithm, used to match atoms (facts) and rules (patterns) in the rule-based systems, is fast and efficient. The algorithm was invented by Dr Charles Forgy [6]. The performance of the Rete algorithm is weakly dependent of the number of rules in the system. In the Jess engine [7, 8], which is a Rete-based system, the computational complexity is between $O(RF^P)$ and $O(RFP)$ [7], where R is the number of rules, F is the number of facts in the working memory, and P is the average number of patterns per rule body. Therefore, it is better to create more rules but with smaller number of patterns per rule.

One way of increasing efficiency and scalability of a deduction process is to use a backward chaining method. This scheme of reasoning is implemented, for instance, in the Prolog engine, as the Selective Linear Definite clause resolution (SLD). By the backward reasoning technique facts are obtained only when they are needed in derivations.

2.3 Magic Transformation

In systems with facts and rules deduction processes are often performed with the bottom-up scheme of evaluation. But effective query answering process should be combined with a goal-directedness (top-down reasoning). To fulfill the requirement a transformation of a program *P* and a query *Q* into a new program, *magic(P* $\cup$ *Q)*, is defined (as is presented in [9]).

Bottom-up evaluated magic program avoids a blind generation of conclusions by inserting special conditions into each rule of the program *P*. The new predicates – *call_p* for each original predicate *p* – are used in [9] to define the conditions. In magic transformation for each rule:

$$p_1(\bar{X}_1), p_2(\bar{X}_2), \ldots, p_n(\bar{X}_n) => h(\bar{X}_h)$$

a set of new rules is defined in the following way:

$$call\_h(\bar{X}_h), p_1(\bar{X}_1), p_2(\bar{X}_2), \ldots, p_n(\bar{X}_n) => h(\bar{X}_h)$$
$$call\_h(\bar{X}_h), p_1(\bar{X}_1), p_2(\bar{X}_2), \ldots, p_{i-1}(\bar{X}_{i-1}) => call\_p_i(\bar{X}_i)$$

where $i \epsilon \{1, n\}$.

Definition 1. *Atoms call_p are called magic templates and can be interpreted as needed or called atoms. In our approach magic templates (or called atoms) are differentiated from proper ones by annotation with C symbol.*

One can see the new rules as plans for the rule's head evaluation, but plans augmented with goal of the evaluation.

The magic transformation of slightly modified rule (1) (the *AP* atoms are refused) yields the following set of rules:

$$h_1(?x, ?w)^C, p_1(?x, ?y),\ p_2(?y, ?z),\ p_3(?z, ?w)\ => h_1(?x, ?w)$$
$$h_1(?x, ?w)^C\ => p_1(?x, ?y)^C$$
$$h_1(?x, ?w)^C, p_1(?x, ?y)\ => p_2(?y, ?z)^C$$
$$h_1(?x, ?w)^C, p_1(?x, ?y), p_2(?y, ?z)\ => p_3(?z, ?w)^C$$

The magic approach has been shown to be sound and complete [9, 10].

The original magic transformation is strongly connected with order of premises in the body of the rule. It is worth to notice, that any permutation of atoms in the body gives a semantically equivalent rule. Therefore, we can built different sets of magic rules for diverse sequences of the atoms. This flexibility may be very important in building efficient plans of a goal evaluation. Properly chosen subsets of magic rules form the basis of the extended rules in our system.

2.4 Sideways Information Passing and Adorned Rules

A magic transformation is done with respect to the particular sideways information passing strategy (sip strategy) which indicates how bindings in the head of a rule should be passed to the body of that rule, and in which order body atoms should be evaluated [10]. For a set of rules *P* and a query *Q*, there usually exist many different sip strategies. Without evaluating all of them, it is not easy do decide whether a chosen sip strategy is better or worse than another one [11].

Definition 2. *An adornment of a predicate is a sequence of b's (bound) and f s (free) indicating the status of the arguments of the predicate. The adorned rule is obtained by replacing each atom in the rule by its adorned version.*

For example, to indicate that in predicate *p(?x, ?y)* only the variable ?x is bound, we write $p^{bf}(?x, ?y)$. In the magic transformation, for each adorned predicate p^a and for each rule, where *p* occurs in the head, we should choose the sip and use it to generate an adorned version of the rule. Since predicates may appear with several adornments, we may attach several distinct sips to several versions of the same rule, one to each version. Such process of creating adorned rules starts from the given query. For the query predicate *q* we replace it by the adorned version of *q* where adornment is determined by bindings of variables in the query. Next, the adorned rules are generated according to the chosen sip and adornment of *q*. For example, for the following rule:

$$p(?x,?y) => q(?x,?y) \text{ and the query: } q(10,?y)$$

the following adorned rule is generated (magic predicates are omitted):

$$p^{bf}(?x,?y) => q^{bf}(?x,?y) \quad (2)$$

Definition 3. *In our approach an adornment of a rule is expressed by the use of* ***nil*** *value which represents free variable. A variable that is bound is represented only by its name and a condition that checks if the variable's value is different from* ***nil****. Variables that are indicated only by ? can be bound or free.*

For example, rule (2) is transformed into the following rule:

$$p(?x,nil), ?x \neq nil => q(?x,nil)$$

We use *?* sign when there is no matter if a value is bound or not. The following rule: $p(?x,?y) => q(?x)$ can be replaced by another one: $p(?x,?) => q(?x)$. In this case, these two rules are equal.

3 Query Answering with a Rule-Based System

3.1 Overview of the Method

In this Section we present the overview of our approach for a database query answering with a rule-based system, which is built over the forward chaining and enhanced magic transformation.

In our approach we apply rules that are obtained from a given Horn-SHIQ ontology. The TBox reasoning is performed by the Pellet engine [12]. Next, a classified form of the ontology (inferred class/property hierarchy, domain/range restrictions) is transformed into rule definitions in the Jess language. SWRL [13] DL-safe [14] rules are also transformed to the Jess language with SWRL Built-ins [15] used as comparison predicates.

From now on, we do not differentiate which rules were created based on a given ontology and which were not.

In the current state of our work we use only unary and binary predicates. Nevertheless, our approach can be extended for predicates with an arbitrary number of arguments.

The presented method consists of the following elements:

- Two sets of facts: one including *called* facts (goals in a goal-directed reasoning, annotated with *C*) and the *proper* ones.
- Set of the basic rules.
- Set of the extended rules.
- Set of the mapping rules.
- Query algorithm.

The division of the facts is very important in our approach. *Proper facts* are directly derived from a relational database, or are inferred by rules from other proper facts. *Called facts* reflect *goals*. They are used to prevent firing more rules than is required in the query evaluation process.

With the usage of the combination of proper and called facts, we can infer with the forward chaining scheme like with the backward one, where the reasoning is a goal-driven process.

The set of basic rules consists of rules which constitute the knowledge base. The set forms input data in our algorithm for the automatic generation of the extended rules. The set of extended rules is semantically equivalent to the set of basic rules. Together with the mapping rules, the extended ones are used in the query answering algorithm.

3.2 Generation of the Extended Rules

The extended rules are generated on the basis of the basic rules. In principle, we transform rules according to the magic transformation, the enhancement is proposed by the use of the dependent predicates (see Section 2.1).

During the generation process the special symbol *C* (for *called* atoms) can be added to predicates in rules. If a predicate does not contain any symbol it means that it matches only proper facts. If a predicate is annotated with *C* symbol, it matches only called facts. For example, the annotated predicate $p_1(?x, ?y)^C$ with variables *?x* and *?y*, can match the following called facts: $p_1(x, y)^C$, $p_1(x, nil)^C$, $p_1(nil, y)^C$ or $p_1(nil, nil)^C$ where x and y are constants, and nil is a special value denoting an unbound variable.

Now we describe the generation process (an Algorithm 1) of the extended rules. It is worth noticing, that each variable from the rule head should occur in the rule's body (the Datalog [16] safety restriction is used to guarantee algorithm decidability).

Every basic rule consists of the body *B*, additional predicates *AP* and the head predicate *H*. In order to denote that *B* matches only proper or called facts, we mark it as *B* and B^C respectively. In the same way we indicate the head of the rule: *H* (adds proper facts) or H^C (adds called facts). Therefore, each basic rule is represented as follows:

$$B, AP \Rightarrow H \tag{3}$$

In accordance with magic transformation, the body of the rule (3) is first augmented with the called predicate H^C to indicate an expected goal of the rule. To describe the needed (called) fact, one has to identify its arguments. Moreover, to define other extended rules for the basic rule (3) (due to magic transformation), one can compose the appropriate subsets of different proper, called and dependent facts.

The algorithm defining a specialized magic transformation is based on the sip goal- and dependency-directed strategy. As our strategy is query-independent (the extended rules are generated only once), we call it the general sip (gsip) strategy. This algorithm is the main result of the work.

Algorithm 1. The gsip strategy for the generation of the extended rules.

Step 1. For each basic rule (3) a rule of the following form is created:

$$B, AP, H^C => H$$

where H^C contains patterns of attributes (the attributes may be bound or stay unbound).

Step 2. For each basic rule (3) a new set of rules is generated, where none of the variables in the head predicate annotated with C symbol is bound. In this case, all variables are replaced by the *nil* value and rules are generated of the following form:

$$H^C => P_i^C$$

where P_i is a predicate from the body of a basic rule.

Step 3. For each basic rule (3) a new set of rules is generated according to the bindings of variables in the head. Get a set $D = Dep(B,H)$ of predicates from the set B, which depend on the bound variables in the head H, and create one rule for each dependent predicate D_i from the set D:

$$H^C => D_i^C$$

Step 4. For each basic rule (3) a new set of rules is generated according to the bindings of variables in the head and dependent predicates that are connected to the head by a chain of variables. This set contains rules in which called predicates are mixed with the proper ones with respect to the dependencies between variables.

We stress out that all *AP* predicates are added to the body of each created rule if all variables appearing in predicates from *AP* also appear in the body.

Example 1. Applying Algorithm 1 to the following rule:

$$p_1(?x, ?y),\ p_2(?y, ?w),\ p_3(?w), ?w \neq ?x => h_1(?x, ?w)$$

we obtain the following sets of rules which correspond to the steps of the algorithm:

1. One rule which is generated by adding the goal connected with the head predicate:

   $$p_1(?x, ?y), p_2(?y, ?w), p_3(?w), ?w \neq ?x,\ h_1(?x, ?w)^C => h_1(?x, ?w) \quad (4)$$

2. The set of rules with dependent predicates from the set $Dep(\{p_1(?x, ?y), p_2(?y, ?w), p_3(?w)\}, \{h_1(?x, ?w)\}) = \{p_1(?x, ?y), p_2(?y, ?w), p_3(?w)\}$, where all the variables from the head are unbound. In such case, the variables are replaced by the *nil* value:

   $$h_1(nil, nil)^C => p_1(nil, nil)^C$$
   $$h_1(nil, nil)^C => p_2(nil, nil)^C$$
   $$h_1(nil, nil)^C => p_3(nil)^C$$

3. The set of rules with dependent predicates and different binding patterns of the head predicate:

   $$h_1(?x, ?w)^C, ?x \neq nil => p_1(?x, nil)^C$$

$h_1(?x,?w)^C, ?w \neq nil => p_2(nil,?w)^C$
$h_1(?x,?w)^C, ?w \neq nil => p_3(?w)^C$

4. The set of rules with dependencies between proper and called predicates:

$h_1(?x,?)^C,\ p_1(?x,?y) => p_2(?y,nil)^C$ (5)
$h_1(?,?w)^C,\ p_2(?y,?w) => p_1(nil,?y)^C$
$h_1(?,?w)^C,\ p_2(?y,?w) => p_3(?w)^C$
$h_1(?,?w)^C,\ p_3(?w) => p_2(nil,?w)^C$
$h_1(?x,?)^C,\ p_1(?x,?y), p_2(?y,?w) => p_3(?w)^C$
$h_1(?,?w)^C,\ p_1(?x,?y), p_2(?y,?w) => p_3(?w)^C$

Each extended rule is generated to pass only one binding of a variable from a proper fact to a called one. In such case, called predicates are mixed with the proper ones with bindings that are passed through a chain of variables from the head and dependent predicates. In result we will obtain all possible bindings of variables that are strictly connected with a goal (in this case $h_1(...)$). For example, in the rule (5) we pass the variable *?x* through the predicate p_1 (which reflects a proper fact) to obtain a binding of the variable *?y* in the predicate p_2 (such fact is asserted to the engine's working memory as a called fact).

3.3 Mapping between Predicates and Relational Data

This section presents a method for mapping creation between terms of rule-based system and relational data. The terms come from the "essential" predicates with the *C* symbol which express that appropriate facts are needed in the reasoning process. We assume that every "essential" predicate has a corresponding SQL query. "Essential" means that the instance of the predicate cannot be derived from the rules. Instead, it can be obtained only in the direct way as a result of the SQL query evaluation in the database. For example, in the OWL [17] hierarchy of classes *ChairmanOfTheBoard is-a CompanysPrincipal is-a PersonConectedToCompany is-a Person*, where the class *ChairmanOfTheBoard* is a subclass of the class *CompanysPrincipal* etc. The class *ChairmanOfTheBoard* is represented as an "essential" predicate.

A predicate-database mapping is defined as a set of rules, where each rule is of the following form:

SQL query => essential predicate

A body of each mapping rule contains SQL query which is defined manually by a user. The body contains also other parameters that are used in our algorithm of grouping SQL queries, but details are omitted here.

We assume that every SQL query has the following form:

SELECT [R] FROM [T] <WHERE> <C, AND, OR>

where:

- *R* are the attributes (columns) – one or two according to the unary or binary terms (OWL Class, OWL DataProperty or OWL ObjectProperty),
- *T* are the tables which are queried,
- *WHERE* is an optional clause to specify the constraints,

- *C* are the constraints in the following form: <attribute, comparator, value>, for example: *Age > 21*,
- *AND, OR* – are the optional SQL commands.

Only such queries are currently available in our system. As an example, assume that we have a table *Employee* with the following attributes: *ID, Name, CompanyID* and *Position*. The example of SQL query for the concept *ChairmanOfTheBoard* can be defined as follows: *SELECT ID FROM Employee WHERE Position=' Chairman'*. When we want to apply more constraints, we may use *OR* / *AND* clauses.

The mapping process requires defining SQL queries for all "essential" classes and properties. Take the example of the mapping of the property *isSignedBy*:

SELECT IDDoc, IDEmp FROM Signature. (6)

The execution of the query (6) results in obtaining all instances of the relation between *IDDoc* of the document and *IDEmps* of the employees that signed this document. If the query is executed, the results are added to the working memory as proper facts.

In the reasoning process many SQL queries are generated. We developed an algorithm which groups queries that correspond to the same essential predicate. These queries are aggregated and only one SQL query is executed. For example, if we have the following called facts: *isSignedBy (5, nil)*^{c} and *isSignedBy (10, nil)*^{c} , and the mapping query (6), our grouping algorithm will create a query:

SELECT IDDoc IDEmp FROM Signature AND (IDDoc='5' Or IDDoc='10').

We assume also that the ontology, which is used, is properly constructed and defined (the taxonomy is computed and classified; without inconsistencies). Next, a user defines SQL queries for essential predicates and then the mapping rules are automatically generated and saved as a Jess script file.

3.4 Reasoning and the Query Algorithm

In our query answering method a user poses a query to a rule-based system. The query is constructed from the predicates available in the knowledge base and from the additional predicates used for comparisons (<, ≠, etc.). An answer is obtained as a result of the reasoning process using the forward chaining method.

We assume that the engine contains a knowledge base constructed from extended and mapping rules. Facts are stored in a relational database.

Algorithm 2. The reasoning and query algorithm is performed in the following way:

1. Create a special (technical) rule from a given query and name it *QUERYRULE*. The query constitutes the body of the rule. The head contains invocation of the Java method, which remembers bindings of the variables in the query when the rule is fired. The number of firings of the rule is the number of different results. Add *QUERYRULE* to the Jess engine.
2. For every predicate p_i appearing in the query do the following:

a) Add predicate p_i with the C symbol and bound variables (if exist) to the engine's working memory. Replace all variables that are not bound with the *nil* value.
b) Run the engine – it reasons about facts in the working memory and generates partial SQL queries, which are grouped by the defined mapping.
c) When reasoning stops, for every group of SQL queries, one aggregated SQL query is created and executed. The results are added as the instances of the according predicates (facts) to the working memory.
d) If there are activations of the rules in the engine, go to the point b), or else go to the point e).
e) Remember the bindings of the variables appearing in the predicate p_i.

3. Return the results and remove *QUERYRULE* from the engine.

4 Query Implementation and Performance Evaluation

4.1 Implementation

We implemented presented approach in the SDL (Semantic Data Library) tool [18]. Previously implemented method was based on the hybrid reasoning algorithm (using both forward and backward chaining) [18]. In this section we introduce the implementation details of the current approach and present a brief overview of our tool. The implementation language is Java.

Our SDL tool is split into two modules:

- SDL-API (Application Programming Interface), which provides all functions,
- SDL-GUI (Graphical User Interface), which exploits SDL-API functions for defining the mapping between ontology terms and relational data; and provides automatic transformation of ontology into rules and the generation of Jess scripts (with basic, extended and mapping rules).

SDL supports interaction with the Pellet engine (for TBox reasoning with ontology), exploits OWL API [19] (for handling OWL files) and uses JDBC library for MS SQL 2008 Server access. SDL contains also many functions for the Jess management and scripts generation in the Jess language. The taxonomies of ontology classes and properties are classified by SDL-GUI with Pellet 2.2.1 and prepared for a user, who can define SQL mapping queries on these calculated taxonomies.

We implemented our approach according to the described algorithms. All sets of rules are generated automatically. Basic set of rules is generated from a given ontology. Extended set of rules is generated from the basic one. Mapping rules are generated from the defined mappings. In Jess scripts we use a *triple* template to represent facts. The triple consists of tree slots: *subject*, *predicate*, *object*. This template is augmented with a slot called *kind* used to represent proper or called facts in the extended set of rules. For better understanding of the representation we show an example of one of the generated rules for obtaining instances of the class *ContractDocument* (we omit URIs in the example):

```
(defrule MAIN::Rule14
 (triple (kind P) (predicate "rdf:type") (subject ?d) (object "Document"))
 (triple (kind P) (predicate " isSignedBy") (subject ?d) (object ?p1))
 (triple (kind P) (predicate "rdf:type") (subject ?p1) (object "CompanysPrincipal"))
 (triple (kind P) (predicate " isSignedBy") (subject ?d) (object ?p2))
 (test (neq ?p1 ?p2))
 (triple (kind P) (predicate "rdf:type") (subject ?p2) (object "CompanysPrincipal"))
 (triple (predicate "rdf:type") (subject ?d) (object "ContractDocument") (kind C))
 =>
 (assert (triple (predicate "rdf:type")(subject ?d)(object "ContractDocument")(kind P))))
```

We implemented our approach in the Jess engine, but it is directly applicable (not counting an interface modifications) to every engine, which exploits the Rete algorithm.

4.2 Performance Evaluation

This section presents the example use of the SDL library. We compared our current approach with the results presented in [4] where we used hybrid reasoning method [18]. The description of the knowledge base and relational data can be found in [4]. Figure 1 depicts five test queries.

These queries test different aspects of the query answering mechanism. The first query contains only variables (without any values) and exploits hierarchy rules. The second query contains variables and values; it exploits ontological rules (for inComplicityWith symmetric property). The third query contains only variables and

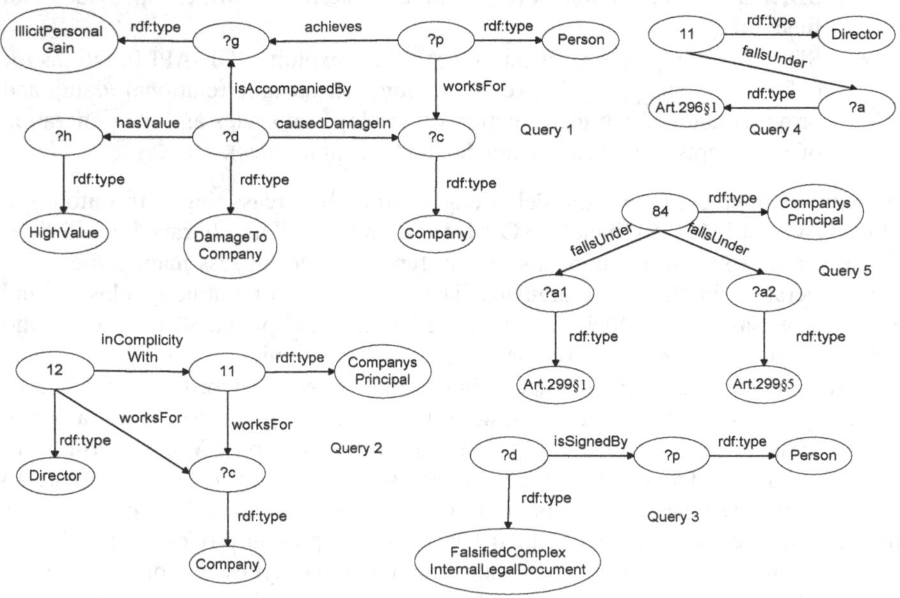

Fig. 1. The test queries

exploits hierarchy rules. The fourth and fifth queries contain variables and values, and exploit various characteristics of the knowledge base as coded by rules. The last two queries are computationally demanding - the property *fallsUnder* needs almost all rules to be fired, because it requires evidence why a person falls under a given article. It is obvious that a rule can be fired more than once (if appropriate facts exist in the Jess working memory).

Results are presented in Table 1., where number 2010 means that results come from our RuleML-2010 Challenge Demo [4], whereas number 2011 indicates our current approach.

All tests were executed on PC machine with the following configuration:

- Intel Core2 Duo 2,0 GHz processor, 4MB cache memory,
- 2 GB of RAM memory, 667MHz,
- Microsoft SQL Server 2008,
- Java Heap Space was set at 1024 MB.

Results presented in the Table 1 show that our current approach beats the hybrid one. Since we did not apply all possible optimizations (including suplementary magic sets, more efficient implementation, counting, rule-dependent sips), we are convinced that the efficiency of our method can be improved. Moreover, we notice that the Algorithm 1 generates a number of excess rules. If we are able to remove such rules we will increase the performance of Algorithm 2.

Table 1. Results of queries execution and comparison to the RuleML Challenge 2010 results

Query and info		Database 20		Database 100		Database 200	
		2010	**2011**	**2010**	**2011**	**2010**	**2011**
Query 1	[ms]	781	219	1 328	891	1 922	969
Results	[number]	54	54	474	474	1036	1036
Rules Fired	[number]	74	251	441	1 630	796	3 001
Query 2	[ms]	2 734	437	37 141	4 125	163 968	19 391
Results	[number]	1	1	1	1	1	1
Rules Fired	[number]	1076	1 506	36 260	13 179	225 381	29 593
Query 3	[ms]	2 875	359	36 344	14 938	183 047	116 593
Results	[number]	18	18	322	322	1004	1004
Rules Fired	[number]	1 367	2 005	38 457	41 755	232 583	359 681
Query 4	[ms]	5 437	1 859	128 719	35 656	Time	347 110
Results	[number]	1	1	1	1	exceeded	1
Rules Fired	[number]	2 040	5 467	57 091	58 520	10 minutes	597 711
Query 5	[ms]	9 312	1 234	Time	34 500	Time	343 469
Results	[number]	1	1	exceeded	1	exceeded	1
Rules Fired	[number]	2 540	5 828	10 minutes	61 199	10 minutes	608 925

A comparison of our results with pure forward and backward reasoning in Jess system is presented in the Table 2. The times of executing queries are measured for the same database (loaded from the files) and juxtaposed in the table under, respectively, **F** letter (for forward) and **B** letter (for backward). Numbers below *F* and *B* indicate times of data loading into working memory in miliseconds. While loading data from the third database, the size of the Java heap space was reached (in both engines), so the queries could not be executed. It seems obvious that for small databases, it is better to store data (facts) in the engines' working memory. But for the bigger databases, the problem with scalability occurs. In such cases our approach seems promising.

Table 2. Results of queries execution and comparison to the pure forward and backward Jess engines

Query and info		Database 20			Database 100			Database 200		
		F 375	B 534	2011	F 14 665	B 183 704	2011	F –	B –	2011
Query 1	[ms]	281	328	219	15938	19906	891	–	–	969
Results	[number]	54	54	54	474	474	474	–	–	1036
Rules Fired	[number]	1873	1873	251	15567	15567	1 630	–	–	3 001
Query 2	[ms]	234	266	437	14875	19344	4 125	–	–	19 391
Results	[number]	1	1	1	1	1	1	–	–	1
Rules Fired	[number]	1820	1820	1 506	15094	15094	13 179	–	–	29 593
Query 3	[ms]	250	281	359	14516	19688	14 938	–	–	116 593
Results	[number]	18	18	18	322	322	322	–	–	1004
Rules Fired	[number]	1837	1837	2 005	15415	15415	41 755	–	–	359 681
Query 4	[ms]	250	250	1 859	14319	19718	35 656	–	–	347 110
Results	[number]	1	1	1	1	1	1	–	–	1
Rules Fired	[number]	1820	1820	5 467	15094	15094	58 520	–	–	597 711
Query 5	[ms]	250	266	1 234	14559	20065	34 500	–	–	343 469
Results	[number]	1	1	1	1	1	1	–	–	1
Rules Fired	[number]	1820	1820	5 828	15094	15094	61 199	–	–	608 925

Presented results confirm that our approach significantly improves a scalability of a rule-based system. It is a very important issue, because in the forward chaining rule-based systems, facts have to be stored in the working memory which is, in general, limited by the RAM memory (we call it the traditional approach). If we store facts outside of the memory and load them only when they are needed, we achieve better scalability. Unfortunately, in a case when we pose a query without any bound variable, we have to load all data from a database. In such a case our method will achieve worse results than the traditional one, because we lose some time for data loading.

5 Related Work

In this paper attention is focused on efficient integration of systems built of a rule-based component and a relational database. Particularly, we confront a problem how to improve knowledge-based access in the rule-based Jess system. Our first solution was presented in [18], where the hybrid system is described which consists of two reasoning engines, and relatively complex and costly data flow.

More generally, we can find different strategies for processing logic queries in relational databases. Most of the work, including that of Bancilhon, Ramakrishnan [20] and others [21, 10] was done in eighties, when knowledge based systems were created for the first time. Various strategies of bottom-up, top-down and combined evaluation of queries are analysed by the authors together with different optimization techniques, such as magic set transformation of rules, or efficient counting and filtering.

A very close work is presented in [22] where data-driven backward chaining is described. With automatically generated goals, a capability to represent unbound variables in goals and support for unification a system presented in the paper satisfies a lot of requirements of rule-based query answering systems. The main difference of our approach is that we modify a set of rules, whereas in [22] they modified also a reasoning engine (architecture of a rule system).

Along the same lines contemporary efforts are also undertaken in view of the important task of data and systems integration. Two computation paradigms, namely relational databases and rule systems, need to be tightly and smoothly linked to better satisfy requirements of database and web programmers. This amounts for deriving queries from ontologies and thus deal with the semantic aspects of data. With standard languages of description logics the semantic web initiative contributes to a grow up of various rule systems. A thorough analysis of different technologies, performance and scalability results of the systems can be found in OpenRuleBench report [23].

Rule systems and reasoning engines form an interesting multiparadigm research area, where different methods and ideas are successfully applicable. Such significant examples are, for instance, ontology-based data access system, QuOnto [24] and Dlog [21] systems, specialized for Prolog.

6 Conclusions and Future Work

In this work the practical method of building a query answering system with the rule-based ontological knowledge is presented. This technique is defined over source data from a relational database, and with the Rete-based forward chaining reasoning over extended, goal- and dependency-directed rules. Our approach is more efficient than a query answering with standard forward or backward evaluation, outperforming the state of the art hybrid approach that was presented in [18]. Finally our approach is more flexible and more scalable.

The novel approach is its generality. Extended rules of the system are constructed independently of a query, for all the binding patterns. Rule generation is performed only once, but with possibility to define diverse, specialised strategies. Such approach increases also a scalability of a pure reasoning engine.

The user of our system gets an easier way to pose queries (due to ontology origin of rules) than using structural constructions from SQL. The creation of queries, presented in the performance evaluation, is extremely difficult when we want to use pure SQL constructions.

Our method largely removes a deficiency of the pure Jess engine mentioned on page 11 of [23]. We aim at making detailed comparisons with systems using variants of magic transformation [25]. Ultimately we would like also to apply the system to the OpenRuleBench [23] suite of benchmarks. It is worth noticing that engines are tested with all data in RAM memory, whereas our system is a complete platform that fetches only needed data to the working memory. This fact would be advantageous if combined rules execution and loading times were tested.

In future, we plan to improve execution of the aggregated SQL queries and to implement the explanation service, which can present individual reasoning steps to a user and can explain the results of the given query. We will extend our approach to handle predicates with an arbitrary number of arguments. We will also develop algorithms that would be rule-dependent in the generation of the extended rules (rule-dependent sip strategy).

Acknowledgements. This work was supported by PUT DS 45-083/11 grant.

References

1. Hustadt, U., Motik, B., Sattler, U.: Data Complexity of Reasoning in Very Expressive Description Logics. In: Proceedings of the 19th International Joint Conference on Artificial Intelligence, pp. 471–477. Morgan Kaufmann Publishers (2005)
2. Liang, S., Fodor, P., Wan, H., Kifer, M.: OpenRuleBench: An Analysis of the Performance of Rule Engines. In: Proceedings of the 18th International Conference on World Wide Web, pp. 601–610. ACM (2009)
3. Bak, J., Jedrzejek, C.: Application of an Ontology-based Model to a Selected Fraudulent Disbursement Economic Crime. In: Casanovas, P., Pagallo, U., Sartor, G., Ajani, G. (eds.) AICOL-II/JURIX 2009. LNCS (LNAI), vol. 6237, pp. 113–132. Springer, Heidelberg (2010)
4. Bak, J., Jedrzejek, C., Falkowski, M.: Application of the SDL Library to Reveal Legal Sanctions for Crime Perpetrators in Selected Economic Crimes: Fraudulent Disbursement and Money Laundering. In: Palmirani, M., Omair Shafiq, M., Francesconi, E., Vitali, F. (eds.) Proceedings of the 4th International RuleML 2010 Challenge, Washington, DC, USA, October 21-23, vol. 649 (2010)
5. Lloyd, J.W.: Foundations of logic programming, 2nd extended edn. Springer series in symbolic computation. Springer, New York (1987)
6. Forgy, C.: Rete: A Fast Algorithm for the Many Pattern/Many Object Pattern Match Problem. Artificial Intelligence 19, 17–37 (1982)
7. Jess (Java Expert System Shell), `http://jessrules.com/`
8. Friedman-Hill, E.: Jess in Action. Manning Publications Co. (2003)
9. Nilsson, U., Maluszynski, J.: Logic, programming and Prolog, 2nd edn. John Wiley & Sons Ltd., Chichester (1995)
10. Beeri, C., Ramakrishnan, R.: On the Power of Magic. J. Log. Program., 255–299 (1991)
11. Sippu, S., Soisalon-Soininen, E.: Multiple SIP strategies and bottom-up adorning in logic query optimization. In: Abiteboul, S., Kanellakis, P.C. (eds.) ICDT 1990. LNCS, vol. 470, pp. 485–498. Springer, Heidelberg (1990)
12. Pellet Reasoner, `http://clarkparsia.com/pellet/`
13. Horrocks, I., Patel-Schneider, P.F., Boley, H., Tabet, S., Grosof, B., Dean, M.: Swrl: A semanticweb rule language combining owl and ruleml. W3C Member Submission (May 21, 2004), `http://www.w3.org/Submission/SWRL/`
14. Eiter, T., Ianni, G., Polleres, A., Schindlauer, R., Tompits, H.: Reasoning with Rules and Ontologies. In: Barahona, P., Bry, F., Franconi, E., Henze, N., Sattler, U. (eds.) Reasoning Web 2006. LNCS, vol. 4126, pp. 93–127. Springer, Heidelberg (2006)
15. SWRL Built-ins,
`http://www.w3.org/Submission/2004/SUBM-SWRL-20040521/`

16. Gallaire, H., Minker, J. (eds.): Logic and Data Bases, Symposium on Logic and Data Bases, Centre d'études et de recherches de Toulouse, 1977. Advances in Data Base Theory. Plenum Press, New York (1978)
17. McGuinness, D., van Harmelen, F.: Owl web ontology language overview. W3C Recommendation (February 10, 2004), `http://www.w3.org/TR/owl-features/`
18. Bak, J., Jedrzejek, C., Falkowski, M.: Usage of the Jess engine, rules and ontology to query a relational database. In: Governatori, G., Hall, J., Paschke, A. (eds.) RuleML 2009. LNCS, vol. 5858, pp. 216–230. Springer, Heidelberg (2009)
19. Horridge, M., Bechhofer, S.: The OWL API: A Java API for Working with OWL 2 Ontologies. In: 6th OWL Experienced and Directions Workshop, OWLED 2009, Chantilly, Virginia (2009)
20. Bancilhon, F., Ramakrishnan, R.: An Amateur's Introduction to Recursive Query Processing Strategies. In: Proceedings of ACJW SIGMOD Conference, pp. 16–52 (1986)
21. Lukacsy, G., Szeredi, P.: Efficient Description Logic Reasoning in Prolog: The DLog system. Theory and Practice of Logic Programming 09(03), 343–414 (2009)
22. Haley, P.: Data-driven backward chaining. In: International Joint Conferences on Artificial Intelligence, Milan, Italy (1987)
23. Liang, S., Fodor, P., Wan, H., Kifer, M.: OpenRuleBench: Detailed Report (May 29, 2009), `http://projects.semwebcentral.org/docman/view.php/158/69/report.pdf`
24. Poggi, A., Lembo, D., Calvanese, D., De Giacomo, G., Lenzerini, M., Rosati, R.: Linking Data to Ontologies. Journal on Data Semantics 10, 133–173 (2008)
25. Brass, S.: Implementation Alternatives for Bottom-Up Evaluation. In: 26th International Conference on Logic Programming, ICLP (Technical Communications), Edinburgh, pp. 44–53 (2010)

Standards for Complex Event Processing and Reaction Rules

Adrian Paschke[1], Paul Vincent[2], and Florian Springer[3]

[1] Computer Science Department,
Freie Universitaet Berlin,
Germany
paschke@inf.fu-berlin.de
[2] Tibco, London, UK
pvincent@tibco.com
[3] Senacor Technologies,
Germany
Florian.Springer@senacor.com

Abstract. In Rule-based Event Processing and Complex Event Processing (CEP), many areas of software development re-use existing technologies and methodologies, allowing their related standards to be re-used. Other standards may be required to be developed to replace or augment existing standards. This paper introduces a general reference model for CEP standards with which existing and required standards will be discussed.

1 Introduction

Standards are used throughout business and IT for many reasons, including achieving a common understanding, enabling good communication, and promoting an easier interchange across organizations and tools.

Such achievements in turn lead to reduced training, a higher-quality and safer productivity, reduced costs, and increased customer confidence.

In Rule-based Event Processing and Complex Event Processing (CEP), many areas of software development re-use existing technologies and methodologies, allowing their related standards to be re-used. Other standards may be required to be developed to replace or augment existing standards. This paper introduces a general reference model for CEP standards with which existing and required standards from the business as well as the technical perspective will be discussed.

The paper is organized as follows. Section 2 introduces our CEP Standards Reference Model which we use for discussion of the event processing and reaction rule standards. Section 3 gives an overview on the existing standards and identifies benefits, standardization gaps and required actions in standardization research. Section 4 gives a summary and concludes with an outlook on the future of CEP standards.

F. Olken et al. (Eds.): RuleML 2011 - America, LNCS 7018, pp. 128–139, 2011.

2 The CEP Standards Reference Model

To understand the positioning of existing and required standards in Event Processing and Complex Event Processing it is necessary to understand the multiple viewpoints and business and technology areas to which standards may be applied. A CEP Standards Reference Model (abbreviated forthwith to CSRM) can be used to assist with this understanding. The CSRM model in Figure 1 uses the OMG Model Driven Architecture viewpoint to describe standardisation areas.

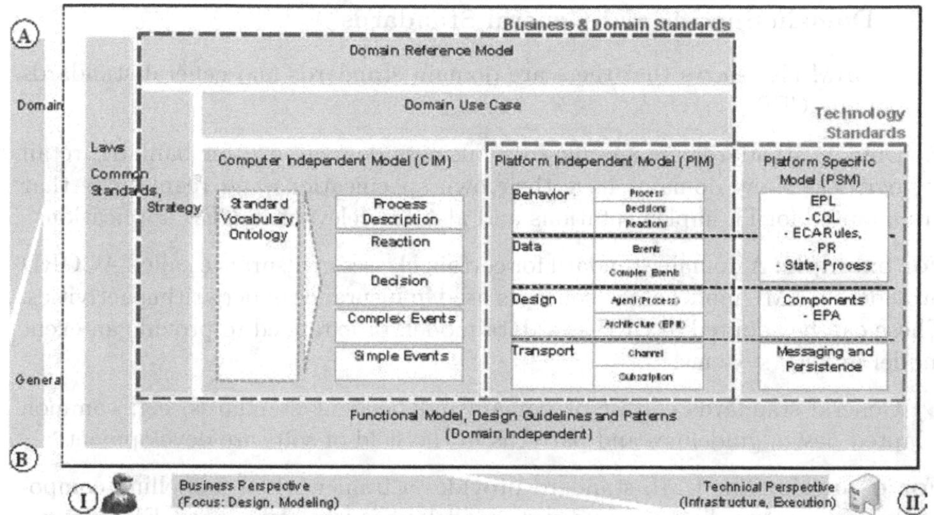

Fig. 1. a CEP Standards Reference Model version 1 - CSRMv1

2.1 Business and Technical Perspective

The CSRM describes a set of components influencing the development, implementation and deployment of CEP applications, where CEP is considered as a superset of general event processing. The model extends the Model Driven Architecture (MDA) where a sequence of models are defined from a Business or Computer Independent Model (CIM) and then progressively detailed / transformed with IT perspectives to the Platform Independent (PIM) and then to the Platform Specific Model (PSM). These models explicitly distinguish between the business and the technical perspectives.

I) On the one hand, in the business perspective, the aim is to define the domain terminology independent of any specific technology in a specification sheet. This provides business users and managers / decision makers, and for IT systems the developers, with a common understanding about the general definitions of a system from which requirements can be abstracted. These models are often augmented by business use cases. The abstraction from business model to IT system requires answers to questions such as: What functionality has to be realized? What limitations have to be considered? What best practices should be considered?

II) On the other hand, in the technical perspective, the aim is to describe in increasing detail the implementation techniques and technologies for developing some automated aspect of the business perspective. The target groups here are the software architects, designers and developers. The main questions here are: What technologies have to be used? What technical guidelines and patterns should be considered? What technical conditions have to be considered?

2.2 Domain Specific and General Standards

The CSRM also shows that there are domain standards and general standards supporting CEP.

A) Domain standards are specific to a business domain, e.g. for banking, retail or logistics. Many domains have their own specifications and regulations that are adopted for IT implementations and also are relevant in CEP applications.

For example: A domain standard for certain classes of insurance called ACORD provides an XML model of the concepts used in insurance underwriting activities. These can be adopted in CEP as a data model, or extended to provide an event model in CEP systems.

B) General standards consist of domain independent standards, e.g. common adapted design guidelines and patterns in the field of software development.

For example: The UML standard provides a framework of modelling components such as class diagrams and state models that are relevant to CEP systems.

2.3 Standards per the CSRM Classification

This subsection provides a short introduction of all CSRM component standards that influence CEP applications.

Common Standards, Laws. Common standards and laws provide conditions and regulations which have to be considered in the business, e.g. laws for stock trading. Development of a software application has to follow these laws.

Domain Reference Model. Domain Reference Models provide a subset of best practices, reference business processes, etc. for a specific business domain. These models help adaptors in defining a proper application based on well proven best practices, e.g. a well proven reference business process for the manufacturing domain.

Domain Use Case. The use case describes how a problem can be solved, e.g. how to detect fraud in stock trading. It is often derived out of the business strategy and the reference model.

Strategy. The strategy defines the individual business strategy of a company which has to be considered in developing new applications. The strategy consists of business (business motivations, goals, policies, rules) as well of technical (applications infrastructure, allowed frameworks) conditions.

Functional Model. The functional model provides domain independent best practices and guidelines helping to design and develop a proper application, e.g. "Design Patterns - Elements of Reusable Object-Oriented Software"

Computer Independent Model. The Computer Independent Model (CIM) describes the business functionality or system without reference to IT specifics. CIM should provide a common understanding between business users and software developers. In the CEP model it consists of following components:

Standard Vocabulary, Ontology. The ontology provides a set of definitions and terms enabling a common understanding for all stakeholders. The concept is like a glossary. The aim is, that every participant has to use the same word for a defined term.

Process description. Description of activities and its flow to produce a specific product or service enhanced with events occurring in it or influencing it.

Reaction. Definition of the activities which have to be initiated based on the previous taken decision.

Decision. Definition of rules, what has to be done if a relevant situation was detected by a pattern matching.

Complex Events. Definition of event correlations for detection of relevant situations defined by patterns representing knowledge from source events, e.g. for detection of fraud.

Simple Events. Definition of attributes and types consisting of a simple event, e.g. the event "Stock Price" consists of the fields WKN, amount, etc.

Platform Independent Model Standards (PIM). The Platform Independent Model layer represents behaviour, data, design, and messaging, independent from a particular EP platform. This PIM abstractions supports

- increased portability and platform independence
- cross-platform interoperability and interchange between domain boundaries.

Event-Driven Behaviour. Effects of events lead to some (state) changes in the properties of the world which can be abstracted into situations. Decisions represent the choices a system can take in certain situations. Actions might be triggered / performed as reactions based on the decisions and changes in states / situations as an effect of events.

Event Data. Platform-independent representation of events and their data is crucial for the interoperation between EP tools and between domain boundaries.

- Interoperation between different EP products to exploit benefits, e.g. stream + rule processing component
- Interchange of events in a distributed heterogeneous EPN
- Interchange of events over domain boundaries, e.g. cross-organizational processes.

Event Processing Design. Platform-independent (reference) architecture and design models addressing different views for different stakeholders are means for, e.g.

- furnishing abstractions and reference generalizations to manage technical complexity
- providing structure for solving design problems
- experimenting to explore multiple solutions, including best practice solutions such as design patterns, reference architecture descriptions that model the abstract architectural design elements, and architectural reference models which describes the important concepts and relationships in the design space.

Messaging. PIM Messaging is addressing transport protocols and routing, coordination / negotiation mechanisms.

3 Standards in CSRM Areas

Tables 1, 2, 3 provide an overview about the main standards existing for the components described in the CSRM standards model. They describe the benefits of the available standards, identify gaps which need to be closed by new standards or by extensions of existing ones, and propose actions to be taken in CEP standardization research.

Table 1. Overview Common and Domain Independent Standards

Area	Available Standards	Benefits	Gap	Research Action
Common Standards	Several laws (often country specific), e.g. BrsG for stock trading in Germany	No direkt benefit for CEP	None	None, because not CEP specific
Domain Reference Model	Various per domain for data.	Efficient design and development of CEP applications for specific domains	Rarely handles events, just data.	Extend to common events as required.
Domain Use Case	Covered by UML Use Case [18], EPTS Use-Case Template [3]	Create common understanding between business user and software developer	Misses event aspect.	Improve Use Case templates.
Strategy	Usually a textual description. Partial coverage in OMG BMM [11]	Clarify business strategy	May need more emphasis on events	None, because CEP unspecific
Functional Model	- EPTS Fn Ref Architecture [23,24,28] - lot of different ones in the field of software development	Helps implementing a proper application	Specific functional patterns for CEP not available	Create and improve functional models for CEP

Table 2. Overview Business and Domain Standards

Standard Vocabulary	- text based glossary - KR Ontologies (e.g. in OWL) [27] - OMG SBVR [16]	Common understanding for all stakeholders involved	ontologies for events, time, situations etc.	Integrated top level ontologies for general CEP concepts
Process Description	- BPMN [12] - EPC [6]	Create a common understanding between business user and software developer on a "big picture"	Insufficient detail on events for CEP applications	Extend BPMN with sufficient support for modelling simple and complex events
Reaction	Can be an event update through to a service definition	Common understanding for all stakeholders involved	None	None, text based description is sufficient
Decision	None but - Decision Table, Tree etc (OMG DMN [13] proposed)	Common understanding for all stakeholders involved	None	None, because CEP unspecific

Table 3. Overview CEP Models and Technology Standards

Complex Events	None but - OMG EMP [14] proposed	Better understanding of relation between involved events and roles	No structured way to describe complex events	New standard required
Simple Events	- UML - Design language used in NEAR [FS1]	Create a common understanding across business users / event sources, and developers	Not sufficient for needs of event processing	Improve modelling languages eg NEAR [29]
Event-Driven Behaviour	- Reaction RuleML [25] and W3C RIF [32] - OMG PRR [15] - OMG UML Behavioural View Diagrams [18] - OMG BPEL [8], W3C WS Choreography [31], and further EDA standards [9]	Declarative, explicit representation of behavioural/reactive logic Publication and interchange of decisions and reactive behaviour	Standards for specific domains: rule-based event processing languages (RuleML) [25], Web Service Execution (BPEL, WS-C,) [9]	- Rules: further standardization in RuleML / W3C RIF [25,30] - Standards for other domains needed, e.g. stream processing - Interoperation, e.g. rule standards with BPEL
Event Data	- Software Engineering: UML Structural View diagrams - Knowledge Representation: many event ontologies exist (e.g. in OWL) - Rules: W3C RIF/RRuleML [25,30] - OASIS WS Notification, W3C WS Eventing, OASIS WS Topics [9] - OMG Event Meta Model [14] - OASIS Common Base Event	- Declarative representation, translation and interchange of events - Interoperation between different platform specific tools and domain boundaries (requires semantics)	Standards for specific domains: rule-based event processing languages (RuleML), Web Service Events (WS X), Enterprise applications (OASIS CBE)	- Rules: further standardization in W3CRIF/RuleML - Standards for other domains needed, e.g. stream processing - Interoperation, e.g. rule standards with other event standards/ontologies
Event Processing Design	- UML 2 Implementation View Diagrams - ISO/IEC 42010:2007 Recommended Practice for Architectural Description of Software-intensive Systems [7] - Agents: OMG Agent Metamodel [10]; [5]; ... - Workflow Management Coalition Reference Model [33]	- Abstraction from the PSM design increases understandability and reusability - Agent model is an abstraction from technical IT components to role-based agents on a more abstract level	Current standards are not specialized for event processing design	Reuse and extend existing standards for event processing design descriptions
Messaging	- Many transport protocols: JMS, JDBC, TCP, UDP, multicast, http, servlet, SMTP, POP3, file, XMPP - Message Routing Patterns	Platform-independent messaging	None - existing standards can be reused for transporting and messaging events	None

Gaps and research actions arise in particular in the direct standardization of CEP-related models and technologies. In the following we will drill down into them.

3.1 CEP Reference Architecture and CEP Design Patterns

The Event Processing Technical Society (EPTS) Reference Architecture Working Group has developed a functional reference architecture that describes the functions of typical event processing (EP) / complex event processing (CEP) operations. [23,24,28] This includes design and administration as well as runtime considerations - see Figure 2. The EPTS Reference Architectures predefines a common frame of standard reference with a set of architectural best practices, which can be customized to obtain architectures for specific applications in a domain. Future research might describe best practice solutions as standard functional models and design patterns for recurring functions in EP/CEP. [28]

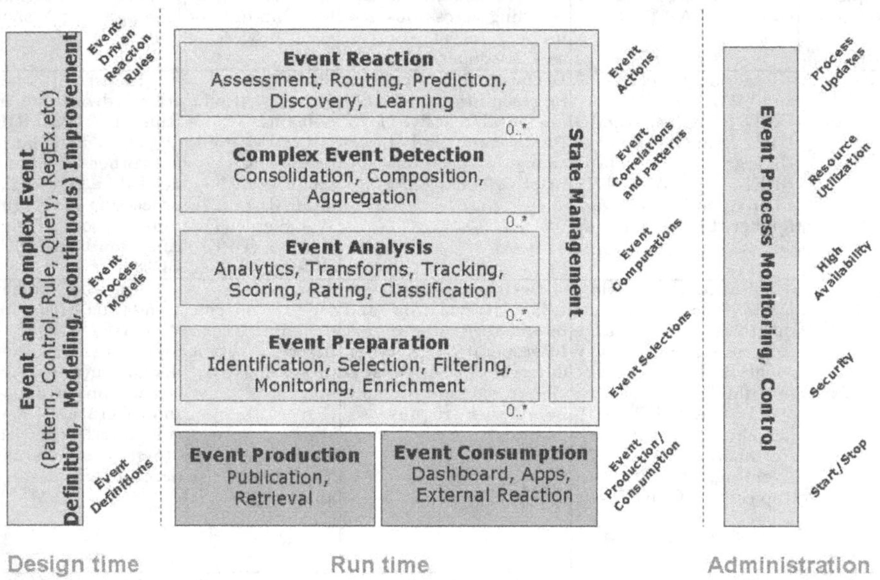

Fig. 2. The Event Processing Technical Society Reference Architecture

3.2 Standard CEP Vocabularies and Semantic Ontologies

Standard vocabularies for typical concepts in event processing such as events, time, space, situations, etc. help to establish a common understanding for all stakeholders involved. This standardization among many others facilitates integration and interchange. Moreover, the formalization in terms of machine-readable knowledge representations (KR) such as ontologies, gives a formal semantics to concepts relevant in event processing, e.g. tense, spatio, state, etc.

This allows semantic complex event processing (SCEP) engines to semantically understand what is happening in terms of events and rule-based reactions. The event engine can know what reactions and processes it can invoke and what events it can signal.

For representation of events and their relationships several Semantic Web event ontologies have been proposed. Shaw R. et al. provide in [26] a comparison of existing event ontologies like CIDOC CRM[1], ABC Ontology[2], Event Ontology[3],EventsML-G[4], DOLCE + DnS Ultralite[5], and OpenCYC Ontology[6], based on their main constituent properties like, type, time, space, participation, causality and composition. Other ontologies have been specifically developed for representing time [7] or spatio-temporal relations [2].

On the computational independent level with the OMG Semantics and Business Vocabulary Representation (SBVR) [16] there exists a standard to define domain-specific business vocabularies for business rules. Current extension of SBVR address a Standard Business Vocabulary for Date and Time Concepts, [17].

However, none of these ontologies are developed specially for complex event processing or are used in combination with CEP technologies. An general modular ontology model for semantic CEP (see Figure 3 is proposed in [27].

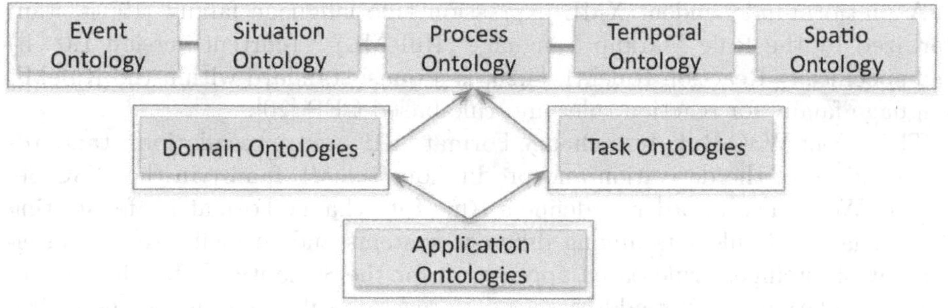

Fig. 3. Top Ontologies for Complex Event Processing

Future work in standardization of vocabularies and ontologies for (Semantic) CEP needs to address the transformation from one format into another, e.g. SBVR ontologies into OWL ontologies (and vice versa) and the integration of separated domain, task, and application ontologies into a general semantic model of CEP.

---

1 `http://cidoc.ics.forth.gr/OWL/cidoc_v4.2.owl`
2 `http://metadata.net/harmony/ABC/ABC.owl`
3 `http://motools.sourceforge.net/event/event.html`
4 `http://www.iptc.org/EventsML`
5 `http://www.loa-cnr.it/ontologies/DUL.owl`
6 `http://www.opencyc.org/`
7 e.g. `http://www.w3.org/TR/owl-time/`

3.3 Computational Independent Standard for Simple and Complex Event Modeling

Although there exist general standards for computational independent modeling (CIM) such as the Unified Modeling Language (UML) and the Business Process Modeling Notation (BPMN), there exist no specialized standard for modeling simple and complex events. The request for proposal (RFP) for an Event Metamodel and Profile (OMG EMP) [14] is a first activity into this direction. Additionally, with OMG SBVR [16] there exists an established standard for business rules which can be extend with business event descriptions (based on a business event vocabulary) on the CIM level.

3.4 CEP Technology Standards

Event Processing technologies have many different roots and standards for distributed event based systems (DEBS), reaction rule systems (see [21,19,20] for an overview) and event driven architectures (EDA) (see [9] for an overview on EDA/CEP related standards).

With OMG Production Rules Representation (PRR) there exists a general standard for modeling production rules. However, PRR currently does not address extensions of productions rules for complex event processing.

A platform-independent XML expression rule language family [19] is standardized by the Rule Markup Language (RuleML) [8] (current version 1.0 [4]) and specifically Reaction RuleML [4,25] is a quasi-standard within the RuleML language family for reaction rules and rule-based CEP [20].

The recent W3C Rule Interchange Format (RIF) recommendation, standardizes a subset of the derivation and production RuleML family in the W3C Semantic Web stack, in order to define a Rule Interchange Format for facilitating the exchange of rule sets among different systems and to facilitate the development of intelligent rule-based application for the Semantic Web. The current recommendation does not address events in reaction rules, but later standardization of a Reaction Rules Dialect [30], following the proposal of Reaction RuleML, might further extend the W3C RIF standard.

Besides CEP reactions rule standardization further standards for other domains are needed, e.g. for stream processing. Research is also need on the interaction of these standards with existing standards for event-driven / event-based systems and applications, e.g. for event-driven BPM (edBPM) extending, e.g. the OASIS Business Process Execution Language (BPEL) and BPMN with events and CEP / rule semantics (see e.g. [22,1]).

4 Conclusion

The CEP Standards Reference Model shows much overlap with existing standards for business and software at multiple levels. It is likely that as event based

[8] http://ruleml.org/

(/real-time) considerations become more important in information technology, the existing models will be adapted and extended to better accommodate event processing principles.

As examples of the latter, we could expect to see domain-specific models start to develop "event information"; this is already apparent in new standards proposals such as for Dobb-Frank Wall Street Reform and Consumer Protection Act compliance monitoring that involves trade-manipulation events inside banks. Such Domain Information Models could well be extended to include useful complex events that are understood and common at the business level.

Standards specific for event processing constructs particularly at the computation-independent level - are likely to be developed as appropriate ontologies, as ontological research expands to cover basic modelling needs. Platform specific constructs for specifics such as continuous queries are certainly needed, but there are signs of "standards fatigue" from the major vendors that is delaying the onset of such work. It is expected that the Event Processing Technical Society as a user, vendor and researcher collaboration organisation , as well as RuleML - as vendor-neutral body for (Web) rule standardization research - may help instigate developments here.

References

1. Barnickel, N., Böttcher, J., Paschke, A.: Incorporating semantic bridges into information flow of cross-organizational business process models. In: I-SEMANTICS (2010)
2. Batsakis, S., Petrakis, E.: Sowl: A framework for handling spatio-temporal information in owl 2.0. In: Bassiliades, N., Governatori, G., Paschke, A. (eds.) RuleML 2011 - Europe. LNCS, vol. 6826, pp. 242–249. Springer, Heidelberg (2011)
3. Bizarro, P.: Epts use case wg report, at epts virtual symposium, arlington, va usa (March 24, 2011)
4. Boley, H., Paschke, A., Shafiq, O.: Ruleml 1.0: The overarching specification of web rules. In: Dean, M., Hall, J., Rotolo, A., Tabet, S. (eds.) RuleML 2010. LNCS, vol. 6403, pp. 162–178. Springer, Heidelberg (2010)
5. FIPA. Foundation for intelligent physical agents (fipa) specifications (2005), `http://www.fipa.org/specifications/` (accessed April 2011)
6. Scheer, A.W., Keller, G., Nttgens, M.: Semantische processmodellierung auf der grundlage ereignisgesteuerter processketten (epk). Verffentlichungen des instituts fur wirtschaftsinformatik, heft 89, University of Saarland (1992) (in german)
7. ISO. Recommended practice for architectural description of software-intensive systems, iso/iec 42010: Ieee std 1471 (2007), `http://www.iso-architecture.org/ieee-1471/` (accessed April 2009)
8. OASIS. Oasis web services business process execution language, wsbpel (2011), `http://www.oasis-open.org/committees/wsbpel/` (accessed March 2011)
9. OMG. Existing eda/cep standards v2.1 (March 1, 2007), `http://soa.omg.org/soa-docs/eda-standards.htm` (accessed April 2007)
10. OMG. Agent metamodel and profile (amp) rfp (2011), `http://www.omgwiki.org/amp-team/` (accessed April 2011)

11. OMG. Business motivation model (bmm) version 1.1 (2011), http://www.omg.org/spec/bmm/1.1/ (accessed March 2011)
12. OMG. Business process model and notation (bpmn) version 2.0 (2011), http://www.omg.org/spec/bpmn/ (accessed March 2011)
13. OMG. Decision model and notation rfp (2011), http://www.omgwiki.org/dmn-rfp/ (accessed April 2011)
14. OMG. Event metamodel and profile (emp) rfp (2011), http://www.omgwiki.org/soaeda/ (accessed April 2011)
15. OMG. Production rule representation (prr), version 1.0 (2011), http://www.omg.org/spec/prr/ (accessed March 2011)
16. OMG. Semantics of business vocabulary and rules (sbvr), version 1.0 (2011), http://www.omg.org/spec/sbvr/ (accessed March 2011)
17. OMG. Standard business vocabulary for date and time concept, rfp (2011), http://www.omg.org/techprocess/meetings/schedule/date-time_foundation_vocabulary_rfp.html (accessed March 2011)
18. OMG. Uml 2 use cases (2011), http://www.omg.org/spec/uml/2.4/ (accessed March 2011)
19. Paschke, A., Boley, H.: Rule Markup Languages and Semantic Web Rule Languages. In: Giurca, A., Gasevic, D., Taveter, K. (eds.) Handbook of Research on Emerging Rule-Based Languages and Technologies: Open Solutions and Approaches, pp. 1–24. IGI Publishing (May 2009)
20. Paschke, A., Boley, H.: Rules Capturing Events and Reactivity. In: Giurca, A., Gasevic, D., Taveter, K. (eds.) Handbook of Research on Emerging Rule-Based Languages and Technologies: Open Solutions and Approaches, pp. 215–252. IGI Publishing (May 2009)
21. Paschke, A., Kozlenkov, A.: Rule-based event processing and reaction rules. In: Governatori, G., Hall, J., Paschke, A. (eds.) RuleML 2009. LNCS, vol. 5858, pp. 53–66. Springer, Heidelberg (2009)
22. Paschke, A., Teymourian, K.: Rule based business process execution with bpel+. In: I-SEMANTICS (2009)
23. Paschke, A., Vincent, P.: A reference architecture for event processing. In: DEBS (2009)
24. Paschke, A., Vincent, P., Moxey, C., Alves, A., Palpanas, T.: The epts event processing architecture, debs 2011 tutorial (2010), http://www.slideshare.net/isvana/debs2010-tutorial-on-epts-reference-architecture-v11c (accessed December 2011)
25. RuleML. Reaction ruleml (2009), http://reaction.ruleml.org/ (accessed October 2009)
26. Shaw, R., Troncy, R., Hardman, L.: Lode: Linking open descriptions of events. In: Gómez-Pérez, A., Yu, Y., Ding, Y. (eds.) ASWC 2009. LNCS, vol. 5926, pp. 153–167. Springer, Heidelberg (2009)
27. Teymourian, K., Streibel, O., Paschke, A., Alnemr, R., Meinel, C.: Towards semantic event-driven systems. In: NTMS, pp. 1–6 (2009)
28. Vincent, P., Alves, A., Moxey, C., Paschke, A.: Architectural and functional design patterns for event processing. In: DEBS, pp. 363–364 (2011)
29. von Ammon, R., Emmersberger, C., Ertlmaier, T., Etzion, O., Paulus, T., Springer, F.: Existing and future standards for event-driven business process management. In: Proceedings of the Third ACM International Conference on Distributed Event-Based Systems, DEBS 2009, pp. 24:1–24:5. ACM, New York (2009)

30. W3C. W3c reaction rules dialect, proposal (2009), http://www.w3.org/2005/rules/wiki/rrd (accessed July 2009)
31. W3C. W3c web services choreography, working draft (2009), http://www.w3.org/2002/ws/chor/ (accessed October 2009)
32. W3C. W3c rule interchange format, recommendation (2010), http://www.w3.org/2005/rules/wiki/rif_working_group (accessed October 2010)
33. WfMC. Workflow management coalition reference model (1999), http://www.wfmc.org/reference-model.html (accessed April 2011)

Supporting Data Consistency in Concurrent Process Execution with Assurance Points and Invariants

Susan D. Urban[1], Andrew Courter[2], Le Gao[2], and Mary Shuman[3]

[1] Department of Industrial Engineering
[2] Department of Computer Science,
Texas Tech University, Lubbock, TX
{susan.urban,s.courter,le.gao}@ttu.edu
[3] Department of Computer Science,
University of North Carolina, Charlotte, Charlotte, NC
mary.shuman@gmail.com

Abstract. This research has developed the concept of invariant rules for monitoring data in a service-oriented environment that allows concurrent data accessibility with relaxed isolation. The invariant rule approach is an extension of the assurance point concept, where an assurance point is a logical and physical checkpoint that is used to store critical data values and to check pre and post conditions related to service execution. Invariant rules provide a stronger way of monitoring constraints and guaranteeing that a condition holds for a specific duration of execution as defined by starting and ending assurance points, using the change notification capabilities of Delta-Enabled Grid Services. This paper outlines the specification of invariant rules as well as the invariant monitoring system for activating invariants, evaluating invariant rule conditions, and deactivating invariants. The system is supported by an invariant evaluation web service that uses materialized views for more efficient re-evaluation of invariant rule conditions. The research includes a performance analysis of the invariant evaluation Web Service. The strength of the invariant rule technique is that it provides a way to monitor data consistency in an environment where the coordinated locking of data items across multiple service executions is not possible.

Keywords: web services, invariants, data consistency, data monitoring, concurrent data access.

1 Introduction

In service-oriented computing, business processes are composed by executing Web Services [12]. Although each Web Service is autonomous and self-contained, composing business processes and achieving a correct global solution is a difficult and sometimes error-prone task, especially in the context of concurrently executing processes that access shared data.

In traditional distributed transaction systems, the two-phase commit (2PC) protocol [5] has been used to support the properties of atomicity, consistency, isolation, and

F. Olken et al. (Eds.): RuleML 2011 - America, LNCS 7018, pp. 140–154, 2011.

durability. Moreover, the concept of serializability is supported by using the two-phase locking protocol [5]. In service-oriented computing, however, it is generally not feasible to support ACID properties and serializability at the process level. An individual service invoked by a process can lock data for the duration of the service execution. But due to the autonomy of each service, the commit of the service and thus release of the locks on relevant data accessed by the service cannot be coordinated with the globally executing process through a procedure such as 2PC. This is especially true for long-running processes, causing processes to execute using a relaxed form of isolation *in between* service executions. As a result, the correctness of one process might be affected by the recovery of another concurrently running process if both processes are invoking services that access shared data. Insuring data consistency at the process level in a service-oriented environment with relaxed isolation is a challenging task.

This paper presents the concept of *invariants* for monitoring data in a service-oriented environment that allows concurrent data accessibility with relaxed isolation. The invariant technique is an extension to the concept of an *assurance point* (AP) as defined in [14, 19]. An AP is a logical checkpoint created in between the service calls of a process, defining a named point that can be used to store critical data values, to express a post-condition for completed services, and to express a precondition for the next service to execute. APs are also used as intermediate rollback points to assist with backward and forward recovery actions when process failure occurs.

An invariant is expressed as a rule that must remain true during process execution in between two different APs. An invariant rule is specifically designed for use in processes where 1) critical data items cannot be locked across multiple service executions, and 2) it is critical to monitor constraints for the data items that cannot be locked. The data monitoring functionality provided by the work with Delta-Enabled Grid Services (DEGS) [2, 18] makes it possible to declare and monitor invariant conditions. As described in [2], a DEGS is a Grid Service that has been enhanced with an interface that stores the incremental data changes, or deltas, that are associated with service execution in the context of globally executing processes. Using the DEGS approach, when a change to the source database is made by a Grid service, the delta is captured and inserted into a delta repository.

This research has defined the specification of invariant rules as well as the design and development of a prototype invariant monitoring system. After a process declares an invariant rule, if a concurrent process modifies a data item of interest in an invariant rule condition, the process that activated the invariant is notified by the monitoring system built on top of Delta-Enabled Grid Services. If the invariant condition is violated during the specified execution period, the process can invoke recovery procedures as defined in [19]. The monitoring system includes the design of a Web Service for evaluating invariants. Since an invariant may need to be evaluated several times between the starting and ending APs of an invariant, the invariant evaluation Web Service was designed to make use of materialized views for more efficient re-evaluation of invariant conditions [15]. The research includes a performance analysis of the invariant evaluation Web Service, illustrating the benefits of using materialized views. Whereas the original work with APs allows data consistency conditions to be checked at specific points in the execution, invariant rules provide a stronger way of monitoring constraints to determine if a condition holds for a specific duration of execution. This is especially useful for long-running processes with consistency constraints involving data that cannot be locked across multiple service invocations.

The remainder of this paper is organized as follow. After outlining related work in Section 2, Section 3 provides an overview of the Delta-Enabled Grid Services and Assurance Point concepts that provide the basis for supporting the invariant rule. Section 4 presents an overview of the design and functionality of the Invariant Monitoring System. A prototype of the Invariant Monitoring System is described in Section 5, followed by a discussion of the testing and evaluation results in Section 6. The paper concludes in Section 7 with a summary and discussion of future research.

2 Related Work

Past research with transactional workflows has investigated the need to relax ACID properties for long running workflow activities [21]. The Saga transaction model was proposed as a base model for long-running activities and defines a chain of transactions as a unit of control [6]. The Saga model relaxes the requirement of the entire transaction as an atomic action by releasing a resource before it completes without sacrificing the consistency of the database. Models similar to the Saga model are called Advanced Transaction Models (ATMs). A model that has been used to define and study transactional workflow is the ConTracts model [20].

Several new approaches for addressing transactional issues have been defined in the context of web services. A goal of the Promises project [7] is to make sure that certain values are not overwritten or changed by concurrently executing Web Services. A promise is an agreement between a client application and a service or promise maker. The promise maker guarantees that some set of conditions will be maintained over a set of resources for a specified period of time. Another similar method is the reservation-based approach [22]. The reservation-based approach reserves resources that meet the criteria of what the Web Service has requested. Only the required amount of a resource is reserved, rather than locking the database record or the entire resource for an extended period of time.

Transactional Attitudes are used as a framework to handle the transactional reliability issue in Web Services. Transactional Attitudes establish a separation of transactional properties from other aspects of a service description. In [13], the WSTx framework uses transactional attitudes that make Web Service providers declare their individual transactional capabilities and semantics, and Web Service clients declare their transactional requirements.

The work in [1] uses monitoring rules woven inside of a WS-BPEL process to dynamically control the execution during runtime. The monitoring rules are annotated in the source code using assertion languages, such as Anna (Annotated Ada) [11] and

JML (Java Modeling Language) [10] . User-defined constraints are blended with the WS-BPEL process at deployment time and are defined externally to allow separation of the different functionalities.

The work presented in [3] uses aspect-oriented concepts to address the modularity issues in workflow languages. A prototype extension to BPEL using aspect-oriented workflow concepts (AO4BPEL) [4] was developed to validate their work. A well known aspect-oriented programming language, AspectJ [9], uses three key concepts: join points, pointcuts, and advice, to support the aspect portion of the aspect-oriented workflows and AO4BPEL described in [3].

Using the techniques describes in this section, constraint conditions cannot be monitored during a specific execution duration. The focus of the research presented in this paper is to present a system to extend the Assurance Point architecture to allow monitoring of critical data conditions during specific execution periods in a process. Providing this capability allows a more optimistic approach to concurrent process execution but also allows data inconsistencies to be more quickly recognized.

3 Background for the Use of Invariants

Before presenting the Invariant Monitoring System, it is first necessary to provide background on the supporting framework provided by Delta-Enabled Grid Services (DEGS) and Assurance Points.

3.1 Delta-Enabled Grid Services

A DEGS is a Grid Service that has been enhanced with an interface that stores the incremental data changes, or *deltas*, that are associated with service execution in the context of globally executing processes. A DEGS uses the OGSA-DAI Grid Data Service for database interaction. The DEGS functionality was originally defined in [2] and has been used to determine data dependencies among concurrently executing processes to support process recovery actions [18].

Using the DEGS approach, a database captures deltas using capabilities provided by most commercial database systems. The work in [2, 18] experimented with triggers and with the use of Oracle Streams as a way to capture data changes. Oracle Streams is a feature that monitors database redo logs for changes and publishes these changes to a queue to be used for data sharing [16].

Using the DEGS approach, when a change to the source database is made by a Grid service, the delta is captured and inserted into a delta repository. The delta repository has a separate table for inserts, deletes, and updates to each source database table, allowing information about each type of change to be kept separate. Additionally, a table mapping each delta to information about the Grid service that made the change is kept.

A Java stored procedure deployed in the source database is automatically called to notify a listening Grid service that there are new deltas in the table that was just modified. The listening Grid service then looks for new deltas in delta repository tables. These deltas are compiled into an XML format and then relayed to any other system that has registered to receive the delta information, such as the Invariant Monitoring System described in this paper.

3.2 Service Composition and Recovery with APs

As described in [19], an Assurance Point (AP) is a logical and physical checkpoint for storing data and using rules, known as *integration rules* (IRs), to check pre and post conditions at critical points in the execution of a process. Inserting APs at critical points in a process is important for checking consistency constraints and potentially reducing the risk of failure or inconsistent data.

An AP can also be used as a rollback point for backward recovery. Three different forms of backward recovery are described in [19], with the different forms supporting either full backward recovery or a combination of backward and forward recovery. APRetry is a recovery action that is used when a running process needs to be backward recovered to a previously-executed AP. APRollback is a recovery action that is used when the overall process has more severe errors and must be recovered back to the beginning of the process. APCascadedContingency is a hierarchical backward recovery technique that continues to compensate nested processes, checking each AP that is encountered for a possible contingent procedure that can be used to correct an execution error.

The most basic use of an AP together with integration rules is shown in Figure 1, which illustrates three composite groups (i.e., code segments that invoke services) and an AP between each composite group. The shaded box on the right shows the functionality of an AP using AP2 as an example. When AP2 is reached, the post-condition rule, the pre-condition rule, and any conditional rules are checked sequentially. If the post-condition or the pre-condition is violated, then a recovery action is invoked. If the pre and post conditions are not violated, then the AP will invoke any conditional rules to check additional, application-oriented conditions.

One of the limitations of the original AP functionality is that constraints are checked at a single point in the execution of a process. When the execution continues, data accessed by the constraint checking procedure can be modified to no longer satisfy the constraint. As a result, the checking of pre and post-conditions is insufficient in situations where the constraint must hold but data cannot be locked over the invocation of several services. The Invariant Monitoring System extends the functionality of Assurance Points by adding an additional invariant rule type, where an invariant rule allows the specification of a critical data condition that can be monitored in between two AP occurrences. The Invariant Monitoring System therefore supports concurrent activity but allows a process to be notified if a critical data condition is violated.

4 Invariant Monitoring System

This section presents an overview of the functionality of the Invariant Monitoring System. The format for invariant rule specification is then presented using two examples that will be used throughout the remainder of the paper.

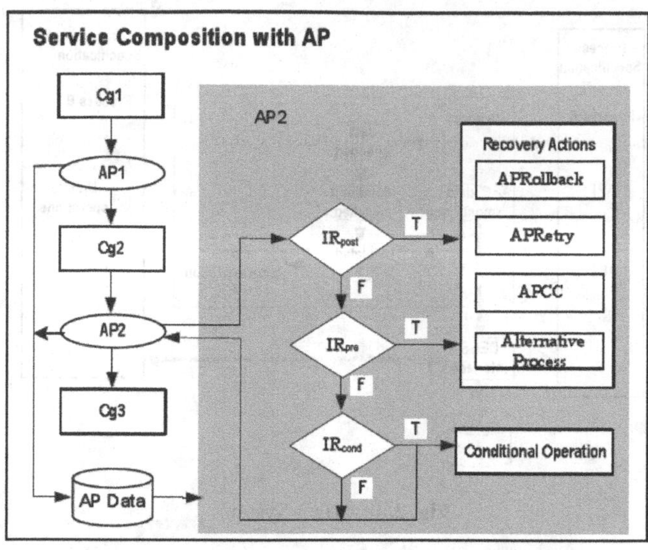

Fig. 1. Assurance Points and Integration Rules [14]

4.1 Overview

Using the invariant technique, a process declares an invariant condition when it reaches a specific AP in the process execution, also declaring an ending AP for monitoring of the invariant condition. When a concurrent process modifies a data item of interest in an invariant condition, the process that activated the invariant is notified by a monitoring system built on top of Delta-Enabled Grid Services. If the invariant condition is violated during the specified execution period, the process can invoke the recovery procedures of Rollback, Retry, and APCascadedContingency as defined in the previous section.

An invariant definition has an identifier, two AP specifications (AP_s as a starting AP and AP_e as an ending AP), and optional parameters that are necessary in the condition specification. Once AP_s is reached, the invariant rule condition becomes active. The condition is specified as an SQL query. The condition is initially checked and the action is executed if the invariant condition is violated. If the invariant condition holds, the rule condition goes into monitoring mode using the DEGS capability. The condition monitoring continues until AP_e is reached or until the invariant condition is violated.

As shown in Figure 2, when an invariant condition goes into monitoring mode, the data items of interest in the invariant condition are registered with a monitoring service. The monitoring service subscribes to the DEGSs that contain the relevant data items referenced in an invariant. For example, if the condition to be monitored in process A at AP1 is a + b > 10, then process A registers the condition when it reaches AP1 and the relevant DEGS that provide interfaces for access to a and b will notify process A of any changes to a or to b by a concurrent process, such as process B. Any deltas that are forwarded to the monitoring service will cause the invariant condition (a + b > 10) to be rechecked. As long as the condition still holds, then there is no interference among the concurrent process executions. If the condition is violated, then the recovery action of the invariant rule for process A will be executed.

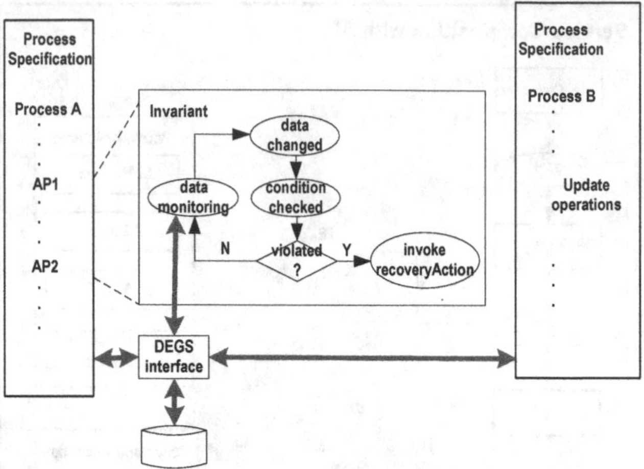

Fig. 2. Invariant System

4.2 Invariant Specification

Assurance Points use the Event-Condition-Action (ECA) format to define different types of integration rules. These ECA rules are based on previous work with using integration rules to interconnect software components [8, 17].

Each invariant begins with a create rule statement that defines an invariant identifier. The event component of the rule identifies the starting AP as well as the ending AP and any parameters needed for the rule condition specification. When a process reaches an AP in the execution process, it generates an event indicating the AP that has been reached. This status event is used to trigger invariant rules that specify the AP as a starting AP. In the condition section of the invariant rule structure, the condition is expressed as not exists (select * from ...), where the select statement returns the tuples that satisfy the invariant condition. If the select statement returns tuples that satisfy the condition, then not exists evaluates to false and no recovery action is triggered. However, if the SQL condition returns no tuples, then not exists will return true, indicating that the invariant condition is not satisfied. In this case, the process is notified and the recovery procedure in the action is invoked.

Hotel Room Reservation Monitoring Example

Figure 3 provides an example of an invariant for a travel planning process, where the process is scoping out available hotel and airline options before finalizing the plans. The full details of the process are not presented here, but the invariant is triggered when the process reaches the BeginTravelPlanning AP as specified in the EVENT component of the invariant rule. The first parameter of the event specifies that the invariant is deactivated when the process reaches the ReadyToBook AP. The invariant condition checks a specific hotel for the availability of a seaside room that is less than a specified price, where the hotelID and price are passed as additional parameters from the BeginTravelPlanning AP. Expression of the invariant allows the process to continue checking the availability of other travel options, such as airline reservations, but to be notified if the room availability changes. If the process reaches the ReadyToBook AP and the desired room type and price are still available, then the process continues past the ReadyToBook AP, making the appropriate reservations after deactivating the HotelRoomMonitoring invariant. If at anytime between the BeginTravelPlanning AP and the ReadyToBook AP the room is no longer available, the invariant monitoring system will notify the process instance that owns the invariant condition. If the condition is violated for the first time, the first action APRetry will be invoked. Otherwise, if the violation happens again, the second action APRollback takes place.

```
create rule        HotelRoom Monitoring :: inv
event              BeginTravelPlanning (ReadyToBook,
                   hotelID, price)
condition          (Not exists (select * from Rooms R
                   where R.roomPrice < '"+ price +"'and
                   R.roomType = 'seaview' and
                   R.hid = '"+hotelID+"'))
recoveryAction1    APRetry
recoveryAction2    APRollback
```

Fig. 3. Invariant for a Hotel Room Reservation Request

Bank Loan Application Monitoring Example

As another example, consider the invariant in Figure 4, where the LoanAmountMonitoring invariant is to be monitored between the LoanAppCreation AP (i.e., the starting AP for the monitoring process) and the LoanCompletion AP (i.e., the ending AP for the monitoring process). The process represents a loan approval process, where the process is creating a loan application for a customer at a bank that already has an account at that bank. Figure 4 shows an invariant that is activated when the LoanAppCreation AP is reached and checks to make sure the loan applicant has a tenth of the requested loan amount in the account, where the customerId is passed as a parameter from the LoanAppCreation AP. The monitoring process is started if the condition is satisfied. If the process reaches the LoanCompletion AP and the applicant's account balance still meets the necessary criteria, then the process continues past the LoanCompletion AP, completing the loan application after deactivating the LoanAmountMonitoring invariant. If at anytime between the LoanAppCreation AP and the LoanCompletion AP, the applicant's account balance falls below the necessary criteria, the invariant monitoring system will notify the process, which will execute the recovery action.

5 Prototype of the Invariant Monitoring System

This section outlines the relevant components of the invariant monitoring system that we have prototyped as part of this research.

```
create rule        LoanAmountMonitoring::inv
event              LoanAppCreation(LoanCompletion, customId)
condition          (Not exists (select * from loan where loan.applicantID =
                     '"+customId+"' and loan.status='pre-qualified' and
                     loan.amount < (select 10*balance from account where
                     account.customId = '"+customId+"'))
recoveryAction1    APRetry
recoveryAction2    APRollback
```

Fig. 4. Invariant for a Bank Loan Approval Process

5.1 Registration of Invariants and Monitored Objects

Invariant rules are parsed and processed to extract the SQL condition and the monitored objects from the invariant rule definition. Monitored objects are acquired from the SQL condition of an invariant by extracting the table names together with the attributes and relevant conditions. Changes to these extracted objects can affect the result of the query. The Invariant Monitoring System may need to re-evaluate the SQL condition when it detects a change in monitored objects.

As an example, consider the SQL query from Figure 4. The two tables in this query are the Loan table and the Account table. There are three conditions in the where clause of the outer SQL query associated with the Loan table. As a result, there are three monitored objects from this table: "applicantId = +customerId+", "status = 'pre-qualified'", and "amount < (select ...)". To simplify the monitored object related to the amount attribute, the object is converted into "amount < calc" since multiple tables cannot be analyzed during the delta filtering. The calc keyword is used to signify that this is a calculated value that must be re-evaluated. In the first condition, customerId is a parameterized value that is acquired from the parameters of the AP.

The Account table of the inner query has one condition in the where clause, "customerId = +customerId+", where customerId is a parameterized value. This query also illustrates a relevant monitored object in the select clause for the balance attribute of the Account table. Balance is identified as a calculated value since, if this attribute changes, it will change the output of the inner query and could potentially violate the invariant condition.

After parsing an invariant rule, an object structure is used to forward information about the invariant to an Invariant Agent, which validates the condition and registers the invariant and its list of monitored objects with the system if the condition is satisfied. There is a many-to-many relationship between monitored objects and invariants. If an invariant no longer needs to be monitored, then it is deactivated and deleted. If the objects related to that invariant are not related to another invariant, they will also be removed.

5.2 The Invariant Evaluation Web Service

An important component of the Invariant Monitoring System is the Invariant Evaluation Web Service [15]. The Web Service is used to initially evaluate the SQL query of an invariant to determine if the condition is satisfied. Since the invariant may need to be re-evaluated several times between the starting and ending APs, the Web Service was designed to make use of materialized views to provide an efficient way of checking the invariant.

A materialized view is a database object that contains the results of a query. After populating a materialized view when an invariant is initially evaluated, the view is automatically updated after any table that is associated with the query is changed. In Oracle, this is referred to as the FAST refresh option. As a result, simply counting the number of tuples from the materialized view is faster and more efficient than re-executing the SQL query when an invariant must be re-evaluated. As long as the count is greater than zero, the constraint is still satisfied. An empty view indicates that the constraint is not satisfied.

Figure 5 illustrates the functionality of the Invariant Evaluation Web Service. After creating any necessary log files needed for the FAST refresh option, the Invariant Evaluation Web Service determines if the materialized view exists. If the view does not exist, the materialized view is populated by executing the query of the invariant for the first time. If the materialized view already exists, then the number of tuples is queried from the view instead of re-executing the query.

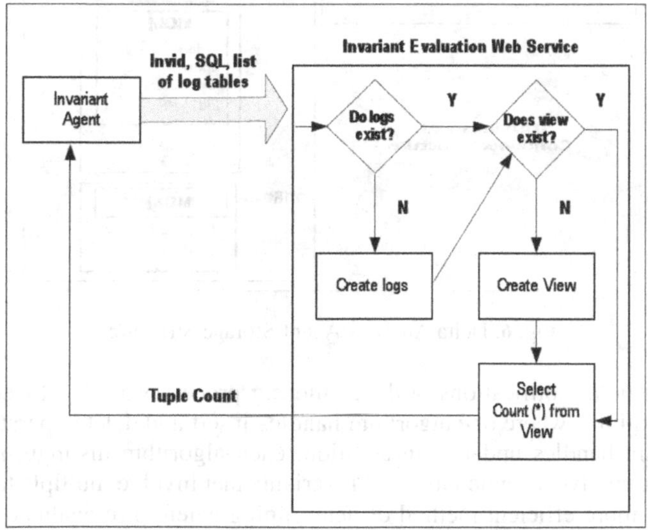

Fig. 5. Evaluation Web Service Functionality

5.3 The Delta Analysis and Filtering Process

The Delta Analysis Agent of the Invariant Monitoring System invokes the filtering of delta information received from DEGS against the monitored objects. To support the delta filtering process, a storage container for the monitored objects is required. Figure 6 shows the Delta Analysis Agent (DAA) Invariant Storage Container, which consists of two hashtables. The first hash table is the table/attribute hashtable containing a vector of invariant identifiers that have monitored objects containing the same table/attribute combination as the key. For example, if an invariant is monitoring the price attribute in the orders table, then the key would be orders/price and the invariant identifier of that invariant would be inserted into the container of that key in the table/attribute hashtable. The second hashtable, or invariant hashtable, uses the invariant identifier as the key and relates that key to a container of monitored objects of that invariant. The first entry in the container contains information about the number of tuples that the last evaluation of the invariant found, the current number of violations found against that invariant identifier, and the invariant identifier. The rest of the container holds the monitored objects that are related to that invariant so that all conditions related to that invariant can be checked at the same time.

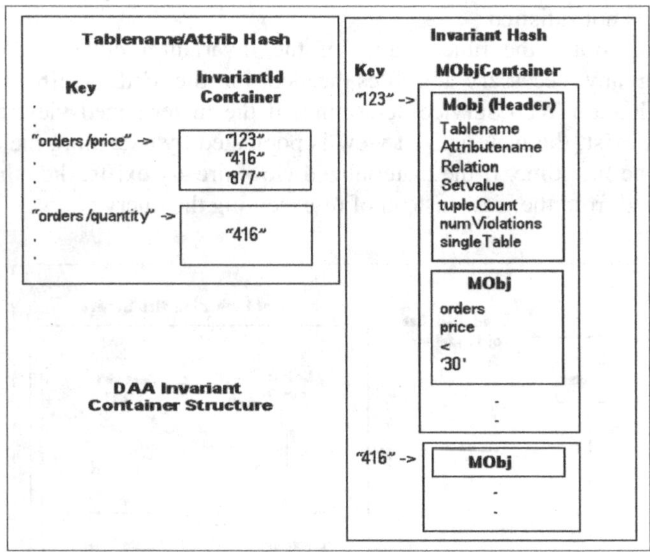

Fig. 6. Delta Analysis Agent Storage Structure

To process delta notifications, a delta filtering process was developed using two different algorithms, where one algorithm handles insert and delete operations and the other algorithm handles updates. In addition, each algorithm distinguishes between invariants that involve a single table and invariants that involve multiple tables.

To allow a more efficient method of determining when to re-evaluate an invariant that applies to a single table, a variable containing the number of tuples returned from the SQL query was introduced. Since all of the monitored objects are evaluated over a single table, the filtering process can use tuple counts to determine when an invariant is violated. Tuple counts are initialized with the first execution of the query. In the case of an invariant condition associated with a single table, a violation of the condition occurs when a tuple that previously satisfied the invariant condition is deleted. The delta information for the deleted tuple is sent to the delta filtering agent, where the conditions of the invariant are applied. As a result, a deleted tuple that previously satisfied the invariant condition can be discovered in the delta filtering process. Similar violations can be discovered when a tuple is updated. If the number of tuples equals the number of violations found, then the Delta Analysis Agent can deduce that there are no more tuples that satisfy the invariant.

Example 1: Single table insert and delete

Invariant: "select r.price from room r where r.price < '30' and r.roomType = 'seaview' and r.hotelid = '234'"

Monitored Objects: [(room, price, <, '30'), (room, roomType, =, 'seaview'), (room, hotelid, =, '234')]

Number of Satisfying Tuples: 1

Discussion: If a tuple satisfying all of the monitored object conditions is inserted into the room table, then the number of tuples is incremented by one. If one of the monitored object conditions is not satisfied by the inserted tuple, then the number of tuples is not incremented (i.e., the inserted data has not affected the contents of the view). If a tuple that satisfies the invariant is deleted by an external process, then the number of violations will be incremented. Since the number of tuples will equal the number of violations, notification will be sent to the process monitoring the invariant condition. The invariant will be removed from the monitoring process, and the process will be informed of the violation.

When monitoring multiple tables, a threshold value is used instead of comparing the number of tuples and the number of violations found. Invariants that involve join conditions and, therefore multiple tables, require rechecking the invariant condition. A tuple from one table can join with multiple tuples from another table. As a result, an insert, delete, or update can cause multiple tuples to enter or leave the result of the invariant. Furthermore, depending on the number of tuples in the invariant result, these changes do not necessarily violate the invariant condition. It is not desirable to check the invariant after each change to a relevant table. A threshold value is used as a way to periodically initiate a re-evaluation, where the value is a percentage of the number of tuples that determines when to re-evaluate the invariant condition. This research has initially used a threshold value of 25% of the invariant tuples. Further research is needed to dynamically discover a relevant threshold value.

Example 2: Multiple table insert and delete

Invariant: "select r.price from room r, hotel h where r.price < '30' and r.roomType = 'seaview' and r.hotelid = h.hotelid and h.state = 'Texas'"

Monitored Objects: [(room, price, <, '30'), (room, roomType, =, 'seaview'), (hotel, state, =, 'Texas')]

Number of Satisfying Tuples: 25

Threshold: 25%

Discussion: All inserts into multiple table invariants are ignored. Inserting tuples can potentially increase the size of the number of tuples that satisfy the invariant condition, but will not cause a violation. If seven tuples from the room table satisfying the invariant condition are deleted, then the number of violations will be incremented after each deletion. After the seventh deletion, the number of violations will be greater than the threshold (7 > .25*25). The invariant condition will then be re-evaluated. If tuples are found that satisfy the invariant condition, the invariant will update the number of tuples found in the view, reset the number of violations to zero, and continue monitoring. If the process continues and after another re-evaluation no more tuples are found, a notification will be sent to the process monitoring the invariant condition and the invariant will be removed.

6 Testing and Evaluation

The focus of the evaluation was on the performance of the Invariant Evaluation Web Service to determine if the use of materialized views improves the performance of the re-evaluation process. The testing example used was the Hotel monitoring example, which involves the Hotel and Room tables, with DEGS created to monitor changes to all columns of each table. A process with Assurance Points was created for activating and deactivating different test invariants. Another concurrent process was also created to modify the monitored data in the source database.

Since re-evaluation occurs primarily in the context of multiple table invariants, the focus of the evaluation was on invariants that involve join conditions. The first test case updated 25 tuples, with changes ranging from satisfying the invariant condition to not satisfying the invariant condition. These updates triggered the invariant condition to be re-evaluated, but the test was designed so that the invariant condition was still satisfied and, as a result, the invariant was not removed. The second test case updated all of the tuples with the changes ranging from satisfying the invariant condition to not satisfying the invariant condition. This test group was designed so that the invariant was violated and, as a result, monitoring of the invariant was removed to evaluate the time associated with removal of the monitored invariant.

Table 1 describes different measurements that were taken and the times associated with each measurement. The measurements taken include:

- The time for creating the materialized view, where the time includes creating the view and extracting the number of tuples from the newly created view.
- The total time of the Invariant Evaluation Web Service, which includes checking and creating any logs, and either creating and querying from the materialized view or just querying tuple counts from the materialized view if it already exists.
- The time to evaluate the invariant from the Invariant Agent, which includes the time to call and receive feedback from the re-evaluation function in the Invariant Agent for evaluating the invariant condition the first time,
- The time to evaluate the invariant from the Delta Analysis Agent, which is the time is takes to call and receive feedback from the re-evaluation function in the Invariant Agent. The time taken can also include the time it takes to remove the invariant condition if there are no more tuples in the view.
- The time to select tuple counts from the materialized view.
- The time to execute an invariant query of instead of materializing a view.

Both multiple table test cases were executed 25 times and an average time in microseconds was recorded for all measurements. During testing, the Oracle database used had at least 100 tuples that satisfied the invariant condition on the initial evaluation. The machine used for testing was a Dell Precision T3400 with 2.99GHz Intel Core 2 Extreme processor and 4GB of RAM, running Microsoft Windows XP Professional x64 Edition.

Materialized view creation and total evaluation time was about the same in both multiple table test cases. The values that are significantly different are the times for evaluating from the Delta Analysis Agent. The invariant condition is removed in the case with invariant removal before returning back from the Delta Analysis Agent evaluation, indicating the time required for deactivation of the invariant.

An observation from Table 1 is that the time difference between creating the materialized view and selecting tuple counts from an existing materialized view is significantly different. The time it takes to query tuple counts from a materialized view is also much less than the time required to repeatedly re-execute the invariant query. If a process is long running between the starting and ending APs of an invariant and might potentially re-execute the invariant query often, then creating the materialized view is beneficial. Otherwise, directly re-evaluating the query is a better choice for a shorter process to avoid the overhead of establishing the materialized view.

Table 1. Performance of Multiple Test Cases

Measurement Description	Avg Time (Microsec) with Invariant Removal	Avg Time (Microsec) without Invariant Removal
Creating Materialized View	**249492**	**269974**
EvalWS Total Time	**371234**	**371025**
Evaluating from Invariant Agent	**575150**	**603457**
Select from Existing Materialized View	**452**	**443**
EvalWS Total Time (without creating materialized view)	**107844**	**117455**
Evaluating from Delta Analysis Agent	**618913**	**292364**
Executing Select Query	**2143**	**2079**

7 Summary and Future Work

This paper has introduced invariant rules that are capable of monitoring data constraint conditions in a process, using the AP concept from [19] as a way to define the monitoring period. A web service was developed that makes use of materialized views and is invoked by delta filtering algorithms to improve the efficiency of the invariant re-evaluation process. Invariant rules provide a way to monitor data consistency in an environment where the coordinated locking of data items across multiple service executions is not possible, thus providing support for user-defined correctness conditions among concurrent processes. Future research is needed to more accurately define the threshold that is used to determine when to invoke the invariant evaluation web service. The web service could also be enhanced to make dynamic decisions regarding the use of materialized views vs. direct re-execution of the invariant query. Using DEGS to directly monitor the materialized views instead of the delta repository tables could provide a more efficient solution to monitoring multiple tables.

Acknowledgments. This research has been supported by NSF Grants CCF-0820152 and CNS-1005212. Opinions, findings, conclusions or recommendations expressed in this paper are those of the author(s) and do not necessarily reflect the views of NSF.

References

1. Baresi, L., Guinea, S.: Towards Dynamic Monitoring of WS-BPEL Processes. In: Benatallah, B., Casati, F., Traverso, P. (eds.) ICSOC 2005. LNCS, vol. 3826, pp. 269–282. Springer, Heidelberg (2005)
2. Blake, L.: The Design and Implementation of Delta-enabled Grid Services. Arizona State University (2006)
3. Charfi, A., Mezini, M.: Aspect-Oriented Workflow Languages. In: Meersman, R., Tari, Z. (eds.) OTM 2006. LNCS, vol. 4275, pp. 183–200. Springer, Heidelberg (2006)
4. Charfi, A., Mezini, M.: Ao4bpel: An Aspect-Oriented Extension to BPEL. World Wide Web 10(3), 309–344 (2007)
5. Elmasri, R., Navathe, S.B.: Fundamentals of Database Systems, 6th edn. Addison-Wesley Longman Publishing Co., Inc., Amsterdam (2010)
6. Garcia-Molina, H., Salem, K.: Sagas. ACM SIGMOD Record 16, 249–259 (1987)
7. Jang, J., Fekete, A., Greenfield, P.: Delivering Promises for Web Services Applications. In: IEEE International Conference on Web Services, Salt Lake City, Utah, USA (2007)
8. Jin, Y.: An Architecture and Execution Environment for Component Integration Rules. PhD Dissertation, Arizona State University (2004)
9. Kiczales, G., Hilsdale, E., Hugunin, J., Kersten, M., Palm, J., Griswold, W.: An Overview of AspectJ. In: Lee, S.H. (ed.) ECOOP 2001. LNCS, vol. 2072, pp. 327–354. Springer, Heidelberg (2001)
10. Leavens, G.T., Baker, A.L., Ruby, C.: Preliminary Design of JML: A Behavioral Interface Specification Language for Java. ACM SIGSOFT Software Engineering Notes 31, 1–38 (2006)
11. Luckham, D.: Programming with Specifications: An Introduction to ANNA. In: A Language for Specifying Ada Programs. Springer, New York (1990)
12. Martens, A.: Analyzing Web Service Based Business Processes. In: Cerioli, M. (ed.) FASE 2005. LNCS, vol. 3442, pp. 19–33. Springer, Heidelberg (2005)
13. Mikalsen, T., Tai, S., Rouvellou, I.: Transactional Attitudes: Reliable Composition of Autonomous Web Services. In: Conference Transactional Attitudes: Reliable Composition of Autonomous Web Services (2002)
14. Shrestha, R.: Using Assurance Points and Integration Rules for Recovery in Service Composition. MS Thesis, Texas Tech University (2010)
15. Shuman, M.: A Database Service for Checking Invariants. Technical Report, Department of Computer Science, Texas Tech University (2010)
16. Tumma, M.: Oracle Streams: High Speed Replication and Data Sharing. Rampant TechPress (2004)
17. Urban, S.D., Dietrich, S.W., Na, Y., Jin, Y., Sundermier, A., Saxena, A.: The IRules Project: Using Active Rules for the Integration of Distributed Software Components. In: Proceedings of the 9th IFIP Working Conference on Database Semantics: Semantic Issues in E-Commerce Systems, Hong Kong, pp. 265–286 (April 2001)
18. Urban, S.D., Xiao, Y., Blake, L., Dietrich, S.W.: Monitoring Data Dependencies in Concurrent Process Execution through Delta-Enabled Grid Services. International Journal of Web and Grid Services 5, 85–106 (2009)
19. Urban, S., Gao, L., Shrestha, R., Courter, A.: Achieving Recovery in Service Composition with Assurance Points and Integration Rules. In: Meersman, R., Dillon, T.S., Herrero, P. (eds.) OTM 2010. LNCS, vol. 6426, pp. 428–437. Springer, Heidelberg (2010)
20. Wächter, H., Reuter, A.: The Contract Model. Universität, Fakultät Informatik (1991)
21. Worah, D., Sheth, A.: Transactions in Transactional Workflows. In: Kershberg, S.J.a.L. (ed.) Advanced Transaction Models and Architectures, pp. 3–34 (1997)
22. Zhao, W., Moser, L.E., Melliar-Smith, P.M.: A Reservation-Based Coordination Protocol for Web Services. In: IEEE International Conference on Web Services. IEEE Computer Society, Orlando (2005)

Probabilistic Event Calculus Based on Markov Logic Networks

Anastasios Skarlatidis[1,2], Georgios Paliouras[1],
George A. Vouros[2], and Alexander Artikis[1]

[1] Institute of Informatics and Telecommunications
NCSR "Demokritos", Athens 15310, Greece
{anskarl,paliourg,a.artikis}@iit.demokritos.gr

[2] Department of Information and Communication Systems Engineering,
University of the Aegean, Samos, Greece
georgev@aegean.gr

Abstract. In this paper, we address the issue of uncertainty in event recognition by extending the Event Calculus with probabilistic reasoning. Markov Logic Networks are a natural candidate for our logic-based formalism. However, the temporal semantics of Event Calculus introduce a number of challenges for the proposed model. We show how and under what assumptions we can overcome these problems. Additionally, we demonstrate the advantages of the probabilistic Event Calculus through examples and experiments in the domain of activity recognition, using a publicly available dataset of video surveillance.

1 Introduction

Symbolic event recognition has received attention in a variety of application domains, such as health care monitoring, public transport management, activity recognition etc [2]. The aim of a symbolic event recognition system is to recognise high-level events (HLE) of interest, based on an input stream of time-stamped symbols, that is low-level events (LLE).

HLE are defined as relational structures over other subevents, either HLE or LLE. Logic-based methods, such as the Event Calculus [12], can naturally and compactly represent relational HLE definitions [4]. These methods, however, cannot handle uncertainty, which naturally exists in real-world applications.

In this paper, we present a probabilistic extension to Event Calculus [12], using Markov Logic Networks [8]. Event Calculus (EC) is a formalism for representing events and their effects, with formal and declarative semantics. Markov Logic Networks (MLN) is a statistical relational framework, which combines the expressivity of first-order logic with the formal probabilistic semantics of graphical models. Thus, MLN are a natural candidate for a probabilistic EC – see [18] for a survey on first-order logic probabilistic models. However, the temporal semantics of EC introduce a number of challenges. We show how and under what assumptions, the Event Calculus axioms can be efficiently represented in MLN. Moreover, we show the effect of probabilistic modelling on some of the most interesting properties of EC, such as the persistence of HLE.

F. Olken et al. (Eds.): RuleML 2011 - America, LNCS 7018, pp. 155–170, 2011.

To demonstrate the proposed approach, we apply it to activity recognition, a subfield of event recognition. The definitions of HLE are domain-dependent rules that are naturally defined by humans. Each rule is expressed in first-order logic using the EC language and is associated with a degree of confidence. The knowledge base of the activity recognition system, consists of these domain-dependent rules, as well as the domain-independent axioms of the EC. The input of the system is a sequence of LLE. Probabilistic inference is performed, to recognise HLE.

The remainder of the paper is organised as follows. First, we present a succinct description of the EC in first-order logic. Then in section 3, we show how we can efficiently represent the EC axioms in MLN. In section 4, we explain how the probabilistic nature of MLN affects the EC semantics. In section 5, we demonstrate the benefits of probabilistic modelling, through examples and experiments in the domain of activity recognition. In section 6, we present related work. Finally, we outline directions for further research.

2 Event Calculus: A Succinct Presentation

The Event Calculus (EC), originally introduced by Kowalski and Sergot [12], is a many-sorted first-order predicate calculus for reasoning about events and their effects. A number of different dialects have been proposed and implemented using either logic programming or classical logic — see [20,14] for a survey. Most EC dialects, however, share the same ontology and core domain-independent axioms. The ontology consists of timepoints, events and fluents. A timepoint represents an instant of time. The underlying time model is often linear and it may represent timepoints as real or integer numbers. A fluent is a property, whose value may change over time. When an event occurs, it may change the value of a fluent. The core domain-independent axioms define whether a fluent holds or not at a specific timepoint. Moreover, the axioms incorporate the common sense *law of inertia*, according to which fluents persist over time, unless they are affected by the occurrence of some event.

In this work we model uncertainty in EC with the use of Markov Logic Networks (MLN), which employ first-order logic as a representation language. As a result, we base our model on an axiomisation of EC in classical first-order logic. As a starting point, we use a subset of the Full Event Calculus, proposed by Shanahan [20]. For simplicity and without loss of generality the predicate *releases* is excluded. This predicate, is domain-dependent and defines under which conditions the *law of inertia* for a fluent is disabled. All fluents, therefore, are subject to inertia at all times. Table 1 summarizes the elements of the EC that we use. Variables (starting with an upper-case letter) are assumed to be universally quantified unless otherwise indicated. Predicates, function symbols and constants start with a lower-case letter. Fluents and events are represented by functions and involve domain objects as variables. In the context of activity recognition, for instance, the event that a person id_1 is walking, is represented by the function $walking(id_1)$. The domain of all variables and functions, that is the domain of fluents $\mathcal{F}$, events $\mathcal{E}$ and timepoints $\mathcal{T}$, is finite.

Table 1. Event Calculus predicates in classical logic

Predicate	Meaning
$happens(E, T)$	Event E occurs at time T
$initially_P(F)$	Fluent F holds from time 0
$initially_N(F)$	Fluent F does not hold from time 0
$holdsAt(F, T)$	Fluent F holds at time T
$initiates(E, F, T)$	Event E initiates fluent F at time T
$terminates(E, F, T)$	Event E terminates fluent F at time T
$clipped(F, T_0, T_1)$	Fluent F is terminated some time in the interval $[T_0, T_1]$
$declipped(F, T_0, T_1)$	Fluent F is initiated some time in the interval $[T_0, T_1]$

The axioms that determine when a fluent holds, are defined below:

$$\begin{aligned} holdsAt(F, T) \leftarrow & \\ & initially_P(F) \wedge \\ & \neg clipped(F, 0, T) \end{aligned} \tag{1}$$

$$\begin{aligned} holdsAt(F, T) \leftarrow & \\ & happens(E, T_0) \wedge \\ & initiates(E, F, T_0) \wedge \\ & T_0 < T \wedge \\ & \neg clipped(F, T_0, T) \end{aligned} \tag{2}$$

According to axiom (1), a fluent holds at time T if it held initially and has not been terminated in the interval 0 to T. Alternatively, in axiom (2), a fluent holds at time T if it was initiated at some earlier time T_0 and has not been terminated between T_0 and T.

The axioms that determine when a fluent does not hold, are defined below:

$$\begin{aligned} \neg holdsAt(F, T) \leftarrow & \\ & initially_N(F) \wedge \\ & \neg declipped(F, 0, T) \end{aligned} \tag{3}$$

$$\begin{aligned} \neg holdsAt(F, T) \leftarrow & \\ & happens(E, T_0) \wedge \\ & terminates(E, F, T_0) \wedge \\ & T_0 < T \wedge \\ & \neg declipped(F, T_0, T) \end{aligned} \tag{4}$$

Axiom (3) defines that a fluent does not hold at time T if it did not held initially and has not been initiated in the interval 0 to T. Axiom (4) defines that a fluent does not hold at time T if it was terminated earlier at T_0 and has not been initiated between T_0 and T.

The auxiliary domain-independent predicates *clipped* and *declipped*, are defined as follows:

$$\begin{aligned} clipped(F, T_0, T_1) \leftrightarrow & \\ \exists\, E, T \;\; & happens(E, T) \wedge \\ & T_0 \leq T \wedge T < T_1 \wedge \\ & terminates(E, F, T) \end{aligned} \tag{5}$$

$$
\begin{aligned}
\mathit{declipped}(F, T_0, T_1) \leftrightarrow & \\
\exists\, E,\, T\ \mathit{happens}(E, T) \wedge & \\
T_0 \leq T \wedge T < T_1 \wedge & \\
\mathit{initiates}(E, F, T) &
\end{aligned}
\tag{6}
$$

According to axiom (5), a fluent is clipped when the occurrence of an event terminates the fluent in the interval T_0 to T_1. In the same manner, axiom (6) defines that a fluent is declipped when the occurrence of an event initiates the fluent in the interval T_0 to T_1.

3 Event Calculus in Markov Logic Networks

Event Calculus (EC) can compactly represent complex event relations, but as a logic-based formalism cannot handle uncertainty. A knowledge base of EC axioms and high-level event (HLE) definitions is defined by a set of first-order logic formulas. Each formula imposes a (hard) constraint over the set of possible worlds, that is, Herbrand interpretations. A missed or an erroneous low-level event (LLE) detection can have a significant effect on the event recognition results.

Markov Logic Networks (MLN) [8] soften these constraints by associating a weight value w_i to each formula F_i in the knowledge base. The higher the value of w_i, the stronger the constraint represented by F_i. In contrast to classical logic, all worlds in MLN are possible with a certain probability. The main concept behind MLN, is that the probability of a world increases as the number of formulas it violates decreases. A knowledge base in MLN, however, may contain both hard and soft-constrained formulas. Hard-constrained formulas are associated with an infinite weight value and capture the knowledge which is assumed to be certain. Therefore, an acceptable world must at least satisfy these hard constraints. Soft constraints capture imperfect knowledge in the domain, allowing for the existence of worlds where this knowledge is violated. The domain-independent axioms of EC need to be specified as hard constraints, in order to ensure that all acceptable worlds in the set of possible worlds satisfy them.

A knowledge base L of weighted formulas together with a finite domain of constants C can be transformed into a ground Markov network $M_{L,C}$, which defines a probability distribution over possible worlds. All formulas are converted into *clausal form* and each clause is grounded according to the domain of its distinct variables. The nodes in $M_{L,C}$ are Boolean random variables, each one corresponding to a possible grounding of a predicate that appears in L. The predicates of a ground clause, form a clique in the $M_{L,C}$. Each clique is associated with the corresponding weight w_i and a Boolean *feature*, taking the value 1 when the ground clause is true and 0 otherwise. More formally, the probability distribution over possible worlds is represented as follows:

$$
P(X = x) = \tfrac{1}{Z} exp\left(\sum_i^{|F_c|} w_i n_i(x)\right) \tag{7}
$$

where $x \in \mathcal{X}$ represents a possible world, F_c is the set of clauses, w_i is the weight of the i-th clause and $n_i(x)$ is the number of true groundings of the

i-th clause in x. Z is the partition function used for normalisation, that is, $Z = \sum_{x \in \mathcal{X}} exp(\sum_i^{|F_c|} w_i n_i(x))$, where $\mathcal{X}$ is the set of all possible worlds.

For example, the EC axiom (1) produces one clause and has two distinct variables F and T. Therefore, the number of its groundings is defined by the Cartesian product of the corresponding variable-binding constants, that is $\mathcal{F} \times \mathcal{T}$. Assuming that the domain of variable F is relatively small compared to the domain of T, the number of groundings of axiom (1) grows linearly to the number of timepoints. Axioms (5) and (6), however, are triply quantified over timepoint variables (T_0, T_1 and T) and therefore, the number of their groundings has a cubic relation to the number of timepoints. In addition, the variables E and T are existentially quantified. During MLN grounding, existentially quantified formulas are replaced by the disjunction of their groundings [8]. This leads to clauses with a large number of disjunctions and a combinatorial explosion of the number of clauses that are generated from axioms (5) and (6). Therefore, representing the presented EC directly in MLN is not practical for real-world event recognition, as its axioms lead to an unmanageably large Markov network.

To eliminate the triply quantified axioms that lead to an explosion of the number of groundings, a discrete version of EC [16] can be used instead. The Discrete Event Calculus (DEC) has been proven to be logically equivalent with EC, when the domain of timepoints is limited to integers [16]. In a similar manner to the EC presented in section 2, we focus on the corresponding domain-independent axioms of DEC. The axioms of DEC utilize a subset of the EC elements (Table 1), that is *happens*, *holdsAt*, *initiates* and *terminates*.

The axioms that determine when a fluent holds, are defined as follows:

$$\begin{aligned} holdsAt(F, T+1) \leftarrow \\ & happens(E, T) \wedge \\ & initiates(E, F, T) \end{aligned} \tag{8}$$

$$\begin{aligned} holdsAt(F, T+1) \leftarrow \\ & holdsAt(F, T) \wedge \\ & \neg\exists\ E\ happens(E, T) \wedge \\ & teminates(E, F, T) \end{aligned} \tag{9}$$

According to axiom (8), when an event E that initiates a fluent F occurs at time T, the fluent holds at the next timepoint. Axiom (9) implements the inertia of fluents, dictating that a fluent continues to hold unless an event terminates it.

The axioms that determine when a fluent does not hold, are defined similarly:

$$\begin{aligned} \neg holdsAt(F, T+1) \leftarrow \\ & happens(E, T) \wedge \\ & terminates(E, F, T) \end{aligned} \tag{10}$$

$$\begin{aligned} \neg holdsAt(F, T+1) \leftarrow \\ & \neg holdsAt(F, T) \wedge \\ & \neg\exists\ E\ happens(E, T) \wedge \\ & initiates(E, F, T) \end{aligned} \tag{11}$$

Axiom (10) defines that when an event E that terminates a fluent F occurs at time T, then the fluent does not hold at the next timepoint. Axiom (11) specifies that a fluent continues not to hold unless an event initiates it.

Compared to EC, DEC axioms are defined over successive timepoints. Additionally, the DEC axioms are quantified over a single timepoint variable. Therefore the number of ground clauses is substantially smaller than EC. Axioms (9) and (11), however, contain the existentially quantified variable E. Each of these axioms will be transformed into $2^{|\mathcal{E}|}$ clauses, each producing $\mathcal{F} \times \mathcal{T}$ groundings. Moreover, each ground clause will contain a large number of disjunctions, causing large cliques in the ground Markov network. To overcome the creation of $2^{|\mathcal{E}|}$ clauses, we can employ the technique of subformula renaming [17], as it is used in [16]. According to this technique, the subformula $happens(E,T) \wedge initiates(E,F,T)$ in (11), is replaced by a utility predicate that applies over the same variables, e.g. $startAt(E,F,T)$. A corresponding utility formula, i.e $startAt(E,F,T) \leftrightarrow happens(E,T) \wedge initiates(E,F,T)$, is then added to the knowledge base. With this replacement, the axiom produces a single clause and the utility formula produces three clauses. However, the existential quantification remains in the axiom, causing large cliques in the ground network.

In order to eliminate the existential quantification and reduce further the number of variables, we adopt a similar representation as in [3], where the arguments of initiation and termination predicates are only defined in terms of fluents and timepoints — represented by the predicates *initiatedAt* and *terminatedAt* respectively. As a result, the domain-independent axioms of DEC presented above are universally quantified over fluents and timepoints.

The axioms that determine when a fluent holds are thus defined as follows:

$$\begin{aligned} holdsAt(F,T+1) \leftarrow& \\ &initiatedAt(F,T) \end{aligned} \tag{12}$$

$$\begin{aligned} holdsAt(F,T+1) \leftarrow& \\ &holdsAt(F,T) \wedge \\ &\neg teminatedAt(F,T) \end{aligned} \tag{13}$$

Axiom (12) defines that when a fluent F is initiated at time T, then it holds at the next timepoint. Axiom (13) specifies that a fluent continues to hold unless it is terminated.

The axioms that determine when a fluent does not hold, are defined similarly:

$$\begin{aligned} \neg holdsAt(F,T+1) \leftarrow& \\ &terminatedAt(F,T) \end{aligned} \tag{14}$$

$$\begin{aligned} \neg holdsAt(F,T+1) \leftarrow& \\ &\neg holdsAt(F,T) \wedge \\ &\neg initiatedAt(F,T) \end{aligned} \tag{15}$$

Axiom (14) defines that when a fluent F is terminated at time T then it does not hold at the next timepoint. According to axiom (15), a fluent continues not to hold unless it is initiated.

The predicates *happens*, *initiatedAt* and *terminatedAt* are defined only in a domain-dependent manner. Specifically, the predicate *happens* provides the input evidence, determining the occurrence of an event at a specific timepoint. The predicates *initiatedAt* and *terminatedAt*, specify under which circumstances a fluent is to be initiated or terminated at a specific timepoint. According to the representation proposed by [3], a domain-dependent rule, e.g. the initiation of a fluent $fluent_1$ over objects X and Y, has the following general form:

$$\begin{aligned} & initiatedAt(fluent_1(X,Y),T) \leftarrow \\ & \qquad happens(event_1(X),T) \wedge \ldots \wedge \\ & \qquad Conditions[X,Y,T] \end{aligned} \tag{16}$$

where $Conditions[X,Y,T]$ is a set of predicates that introduce further constraints in the definition, referring to time T and the domain-dependent objects X and Y. The initiation and termination of a fluent can be defined by more than one rule, each capturing a different initiation and termination case.

As an example, consider the following definition of the meeting activity between two persons. The rules represent the conditions under which the HLE *meet* is initiated or terminated.

$$\begin{aligned} & initiatedAt(meet(ID_1,ID_2),T) \leftarrow \\ & \qquad happens(active(ID_1),T) \wedge \\ & \qquad \neg happens(running(ID_2),T) \wedge \\ & \qquad close(ID_1,ID_2,25,T) \end{aligned} \tag{17}$$

$$\begin{aligned} & initiatedAt(meet(ID_1,ID_2),T) \leftarrow \\ & \qquad happens(inactive(ID_1),T) \wedge \\ & \qquad \neg happens(running(ID_2),T) \wedge \\ & \qquad \neg happens(active(ID_2),T) \wedge \\ & \qquad close(ID_1,ID_2,25,T) \end{aligned} \tag{18}$$

$$\begin{aligned} & terminatedAt(meet(ID_1,ID_2),T) \leftarrow \\ & \qquad happens(walking(ID_1),T) \wedge \\ & \qquad \neg close(ID_1,ID_2,34,T) \end{aligned} \tag{19}$$

$$\begin{aligned} & terminatedAt(meet(ID_1,ID_2),T) \leftarrow \\ & \qquad happens(running(ID_1),T) \end{aligned} \tag{20}$$

$$\begin{aligned} & terminatedAt(meet(ID_1,ID_2),T) \leftarrow \\ & \qquad happens(exit(ID_1),T) \end{aligned} \tag{21}$$

Predicate *close* is a preprocessed spatial constraint, stating that the distance between the persons ID_1 and ID_2 at time T must be below a specified threshold in pixels, e.g. in (17) the threshold is 25 pixels.

4 The Law of Inertia in Probabilistic Event Calculus

A knowledge base with domain-dependent rules in the form of (16), describes explicitly the conditions under which fluents are initiated or terminated. It is usually impractical to define also when a fluent is *not* initiated and *not* terminated.

However, the open-world semantics of first-order logic result to an inherent uncertainty about the value of the fluent for many timepoints. In other words, if at a specific timepoint no event that terminates or initiates a fluent happens, we cannot rule out the possibility that the fluent has been initiated or terminated. As a result, it cannot be determined whether a fluent holds or not, causing the loss of the inertia.

This is also known as the frame problem and one solution for EC and DEC in classical logic is the use of circumscription [13,19,7]. The aim of circumscription, is to automatically rule out all those conditions which are not explicitly entailed by the given formulas. Hence, circumscription introduces a closed world assumption to first-order logic. We perform circumscription by predicate completion, as in [19,16]. Technically, predicate completion is a syntactic transformation, in which formulas are translated into logically stronger ones.

As an example, consider a knowledge base of domain-dependent rules in the form of (16), containing, among others, the definition of HLE *meet* (17) - (21). The application of circumscription over the predicates *initiatedAt* and *terminatedAt* will transform all domain-dependent rules into the following form:

$$
\begin{aligned}
& initiatedAt(F,T) \leftrightarrow \\
& \qquad \exists\, ID_1,\ ID_2\ (F = meet(ID_1, ID_2) \land \\
& \qquad happens(active(ID_1), T) \land \\
& \qquad \neg happens(running(ID_2), T) \land \\
& \qquad close(ID_1, ID_2, 25, T)\ ) \lor \\
& \qquad \exists\, ID_1,\ ID_2\ (F = meet(ID_1, ID_2) \land \\
& \qquad happens(inactive(ID_1), T) \land \\
& \qquad \neg happens(running(ID_2), T) \land \\
& \qquad \neg happens(active(ID_2), T) \land \\
& \qquad close(ID_1, ID_2, 25, T)\ ) \lor \\
& \qquad \ldots \\
& terminatedAt(F,T) \leftrightarrow \\
& \qquad \exists\, ID_1,\ ID_2\ (F = meet(ID_1, ID_2) \land \\
& \qquad happens(walking(ID_1), T) \land \\
& \qquad \neg close(ID_1, ID_2, 25, T)\ ) \lor \\
& \qquad \exists\, ID_1,\ ID_2\ (F = meet(ID_1, ID_2) \land \\
& \qquad happens(running(ID_1), T)\ ) \lor \\
& \qquad \exists\, ID_1,\ ID_2\ (F = meet(ID_1, ID_2) \land \\
& \qquad happens(exit(ID_1), T)\ ) \lor \\
& \qquad \ldots
\end{aligned}
\tag{22}
$$

The resulting rules (22), define explicitly the unique condition, under which each fluent is initiated or terminated. Any other event occurrence cannot affect any fluent, as it is impossible to cause any initiation or termination. However, the presence of existentially quantified variables causes combinatorial explosion to the number of grounded clauses, as explained above.

To address this problem we make the assumption that every fluent of interest is defined in terms of at least one initiation and one termination rule. Additionally, we assume that the variables that appear in the head of the *initiatedAt* and *terminatedAt* rules are the only variables in these rules. Therefore, each domain-dependent rule is implicitly universally quantified over these variables. These assumptions are reasonable in event recognition applications. The assumptions allow to compute the circumscription for each fluent separately, rather than computing the circumscription of the entire knowledge base over the predicates *initiatedAt* and *terminatedAt*. Furthermore, the knowledge base is enriched with additional formulas.

For example, the domain-dependent rules about the initiation of *meet* (rules (17) and (18)) are translated into the following form:

$$
\begin{aligned}
\Sigma &= \left\{
\begin{array}{l}
\mathit{initiatedAt}(\mathit{meet}(ID_1, ID_2), T) \leftarrow \\
\qquad\qquad \mathit{happens}(\mathit{active}(ID_1), T)\ \wedge \\
\qquad\qquad \neg\mathit{happens}(\mathit{running}(ID_2), T)\ \wedge \\
\qquad\qquad \mathit{close}(ID_1, ID_2, 25, T) \\
\mathit{initiatedAt}(\mathit{meet}(ID_1, ID_2), T) \leftarrow \\
\qquad\qquad \mathit{happens}(\mathit{inactive}(ID_1), T)\ \wedge \\
\qquad\qquad \neg\mathit{happens}(\mathit{running}(ID_2), T)\ \wedge \\
\qquad\qquad \neg\mathit{happens}(\mathit{active}(ID_2), T)\ \wedge \\
\qquad\qquad \mathit{close}(ID_1, ID_2, 25, T)
\end{array}
\right. \\
\Sigma' &= \left\{
\begin{array}{l}
\mathit{initiatedAt}(\mathit{meet}(ID_1, ID_2), T) \rightarrow \\
\qquad\qquad (\mathit{happens}(\mathit{active}(ID_1), T)\ \wedge \\
\qquad\qquad \neg\mathit{happens}(\mathit{running}(ID_2), T)\ \wedge \\
\qquad\qquad \mathit{close}(ID_1, ID_2, 25, T)\ )\ \vee \\
\qquad\qquad (\mathit{happens}(\mathit{inactive}(ID_1), T)\ \wedge \\
\qquad\qquad \neg\mathit{happens}(\mathit{running}(ID_2), T)\ \wedge \\
\qquad\qquad \neg\mathit{happens}(\mathit{active}(ID_2), T)\ \wedge \\
\qquad\qquad \mathit{close}(ID_1, ID_2, 25, T)\ )
\end{array}
\right.
\end{aligned}
\tag{23}
$$

Compared to the rules in (22), the rules in (23) are simpler, as they do not involve any existentially quantified variable. Compared to (17) - (21), the axioms in (23) introduce additional formulas, indicated by Σ', which eliminate the possibility that worlds not described by the original knowledge base can satisfy the theory.

By assigning a weight to a formula in MLN it automatically becomes a soft constraint, allowing some worlds that do not satisfy this formula to become likely. This is desirable in event recognition, in order to allow for imperfect HLE definitions. In the presence of soft constraints, however, the behaviour of circumscribed formulas changes. To illustrate this, consider that a knowledge base of domain-dependent rules, in the form of (23), is separated into a set Σ of the original rules and a set of additional formulas Σ' that result from circumscription. By treating the formulas in these sets as either hard or soft constraints, we may distinguish the following four general cases:

1. The formulas in both sets are hard-constrained. This will produce the same results as crisp logic and there are no differences or benefits to be gained.

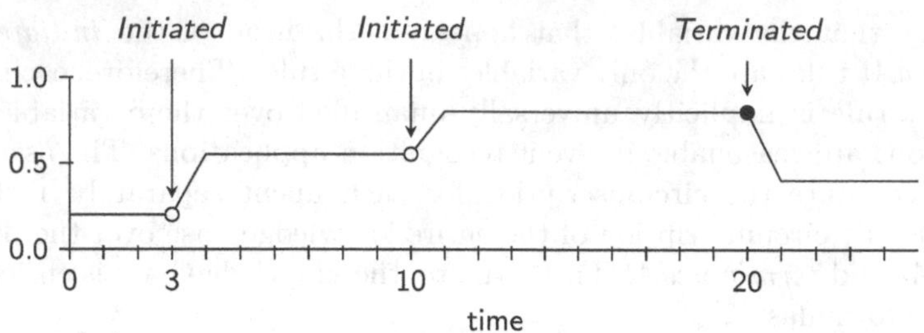

Fig. 1. The probability of *meet*

2. Only the formulas in Σ are soft-constrained and thus worlds that violate these constraints become probable. This situation reduces the certainty of a fluent being initiated or terminated, when all the required conditions are met. As a result, fluents hold with some probability, instead of absolute certainty. Moreover, given a fluent that holds with some probability, when the initiating conditions are met the probability increases. Similarly, when the terminating conditions are satisfied, the probability that a fluent holds decreases. At the same time, the worlds that violate the formulas in Σ' are rejected and therefore the inertia is retained. Consider, for example, that the fluent *meet* holds at time 0 with some probability. At time 3, the fluent is initiated by (18). Thereafter at time 10 it is initiated again by (17) and finally at time 20 it is terminated by (19). The probability of *meet* will increase at time 4. Since the inertia is retained, the probability of *meet* will persist in the interval 4 to 10. Similarly, at time 11, the probability of *meet* will increase again and persist until time 20. Thereafter, the probability that *meet* holds will decrease (see figure 1).
3. Only formulas in Σ' are soft-constrained. A fluent is initiated or terminated with certainty when the corresponding conditions of the rules in Σ are satisfied by the evidence. The formulas imposed by circumscription, however, can be violated. Therefore, the closed-world assumption is softened and the initiation or the termination of a fluent when irrelevant events happen becomes likely. The lower the value of the weight on the constraint, the more probable worlds that violate the constraint become. As a result, the value of the weight affects the persistence of inertia. In other words, strong weight values in Σ' cause the inertia to persist for longer time periods than weak ones. Despite that the fluent in this case is initiated or terminated with certainty, the softened formulas in Σ' causes the fluent to hold with some probability.
4. All formulas are soft-constrained in both Σ and Σ' sets. Fluents will be initiated or terminated with some probability, as in the second case. Also the persistence of inertia is controlled by the weight of the formulas in Σ', as in the third case.

In (23) we could have chosen a more compact representation, using equivalence, as commonly done in circumscription. However, the expanded form of the rules allows us to control separately our confidence level for each domain-dependent rule and the inertia of each fluent.

5 Application to Activity Recognition

To demonstrate our method (DEC-MLN)[1], we present examples and experiments[2] from the domain of video activity recognition, using the publicly available dataset of the CAVIAR project[3]. The dataset comprises 28 surveillance videos, where each frame is annotated by human experts, providing two levels of activity information. The first level contains the low-level event (LLE) annotation for individual objects or persons, using the tags *active, inactive, walking* and *running*. The second level contains the high-level events (HLE) between people and objects, using the tags *meeting, moving, fighting* and *leaving an object*. The former level provides the input LLE for our approach, while the latter the ground truth HLE. The aim of the experiments is to recognise HLE that occur among people and objects, by providing a sequence of LLE as evidence. In EC terminology, events and fluents correspond to LLE and HLE, respectively.

For comparison purposes, we use as a baseline method the activity recognition method proposed in [4] (EC-LP). EC-LP implements EC using logic programming and contains a knowledge base of HLE definitions for the CAVIAR dataset. The experiments are performed using the same HLE definitions as EC-LP, translated into first-order logic syntax using the formulation proposed in section 3 (e.g. formulas (17) - (21)) and computing the circumscription as presented in section 4. Details about the activity recognition application and a description of the HLE definitions, can be found in [4].

The input to both DEC-MLN and EC-LP consists of a sequence of LLE, along with their timestamps. Additionally, the first and the last time that a person or an object is tracked is provided as the LLE *enter* and *exit*. The input to EC-LP contains also the coordinates of the people tracked at each time-point. In DEC-MLN, the value of the *close* predicates is precomputed.

The output of both methods consists of a sequence of ground *holdsAt* predicates, indicating which HLE are recognised. EC-LP performs crisp reasoning, and thus all HLE are recognised with absolute certainty. On the other hand, DEC-MLN performs conditional probabilistic inference. Consequently, all recognised HLE are associated with a probability. In the following experiments, we consider any result with probability above 0.5 as a recognised HLE.

In the first experiment, we wanted to confirm that our method behaves like a crisp EC method, if required. For this purpose, we assigned the same strong weight value (high confidence) to each HLE definition in Σ and hard-constrained the resulting formulas of circumscription in Σ'. As expected, DEC-MLN produced exactly the same results as EC-LP in this experiment.

---

[1] The HLE definitions of the method can be found in: `http://www.iit.demokritos.gr/~anskarl`

[2] For our experiments we used the open-source MLN framework Alchemy, which can be found in: `http://alchemy.cs.washington.edu`

[3] The CAVIAR dataset can be found in: `http://homepages.inf.ed.ac.uk/rbf/CAVIARDATA1`

Table 2. Results for HLE "*meet*" using soft constraints. Number of True Positives (TP), False Positives (FP), False Negatives (FN), Precision and Recall rates are measured per frame.

Method	TP	FP	FN	Precision	Recall
EC-LP	3099	2258	525	0.578	0.855
DEC-MLN$_a$	3048	1762	576	0.633	0.841
DEC-MLN$_b$	3048	1154	576	0.725	0.841

In the second experiment, we demonstrate the effect of soft constraints on event recognition. For this purpose, we adjusted the weight values for the HLE *meet* and studied two cases. The first case (DEC-MLN$_a$) demonstrates the benefits of having soft-constrained domain-dependent definitions only in Σ. The second case (DEC-MLN$_b$) demonstrates a potential use of soft-constrained circumscription rules in Σ', in addition to the soft-constrained rules of DEC-MLN$_a$. The evaluation results are presented in Table 2.

In the DEC-MLN$_a$ case, each initiation and termination rule in (17) - (21) is associated with a weight value that indicates its confidence. More specifically, the HLE *meet* is rarely initiated rule (18) and therefore this rule is assigned a weak weight value, indicating low confidence. On the other hand, the initiation rule (17), as well as the termination rules (19) - (21), are assigned weight values that indicate high confidence, as they are tightly associated with the HLE. The additional formulas that result from circumscription are hard-constrained, in order to fully retain the inertia. Compared to EC-LP, the low confidence value in rule (18) reduces significantly the number of false positives. The cost is a small loss of true positives, as can be seen in Table 2. As a result, precision is improved by 5.5 percentage points, while recall falls by 1.4 points, without any effect on the recognition of other HLE.

As noted in [4], the definitions of HLE *meet* and *move*, share the same termination constraints in the knowledge base. As a result, the HLE *meet* and *move* that are detected by EC-LP may overlap. According to the HLE annotation, however, *meet* and *move* do not happen concurrently. Consider, for example, a situation where two people meet for a while and thereafter they move together. During the interval where *move* is detected, *meet* will also remain detected, as it is not terminated and the *law of inertia* holds. However, there are no LLE that initiate *meet* in this interval and its probability is not reinforced. By softening the circumscription formulas for terminating *meet* in Σ', worlds not satisfying these rules will become likely. As a result, when there is no further evidence from LLE that initiates *meet*, e.g. when *move* starts in the above example, the detection of *meet* will gradually become less likely as desired. As a side effect, this change reduces the detection probability of *meet* in cases where *meet* is initiated. To overcome this issue, we increased the weight values of the initiation rules in Σ. In summary, in the DEC-MLN$_b$ case the circumscription of termination rules in Σ' for HLE *meet* are soft-constrained, while the circumscription of initiation rules remain hard-constrained and the weights of the initiation rules in Σ are soft-constrained. Compared to EC-LP, the number of false positives is further reduced, increasing the precision rate by 9.2 percentage points, without any loss of recall or any effect on the recognition of other HLE.

The two cases presented here, DEC-MLN$_a$ and DEC-MLN$_b$, illustrate the benefits to be gained by softening the constraints and performing probabilistic logical reasoning in event recognition.

6 Related Work

Symbolic methods can naturally and compactly represent high-level event (HLE) definitions for event recognition and model complex event relations, such as concurrency and persistency — see [2] for a list of applications. The chronicle recognition system [9], for example, is a symbolic event recognition method that can efficiently recognise HLE. Event Calculus (EC) is another logic-based formalism that has been recently applied to event recognition [4,3]. The formal declarative semantics of symbolic methods, allow the compact representation of structured HLE, as well as the integration of background domain knowledge that helps to improve the event recognition performance. However, symbolic methods cannot handle uncertainty, which naturally exists in many real-world applications and may seriously compromise the event recognition results. In our work, we combine EC and Markov Logic Networks (MLN) in a method that supports the definition of HLE in EC and performs probabilistic event recognition with MLN. Unlike crisp-logic EC [4,3], our method allows to control the level of the persistency of fluents. As noted in section 5, we have used the same HLE definitions as in [4], preprocessed appropriately to fit the MLN representation and computation.

Probabilistic graphical models, such as Hidden Markov Models and Dynamic Bayesian Networks have been successfully applied to event recognition in a variety of applications where uncertainty exists (e.g. [6,22]). Compared to symbolic methods, such models can naturally handle uncertainty but their propositional structure provides limited representation capabilities. To model HLE that involve a large number of domain objects (e.g. interactions between multiple persons), the structure of the model may become prohibitively large and complex. The lack of a formal representation language makes the definition of such HLE complicated and the integration of domain background knowledge is very hard.

A logic-based method that handles uncertainty is presented in [21]. The method incorporates rules that express HLE in terms of input low-level events (LLE). Each HLE or LLE is associated with two uncertainty values, indicating a degree of information and confidence respectively. The underlying idea of the method is that the more confident information is provided, the stronger the belief about the corresponding HLE becomes. Accordingly, in our work, the more initiations (or terminations) we have, the higher (or lower) the probability that the corresponding HLE holds. In contrast to that method, our work employs MLN that provide formal probabilistic semantics, as well as EC to represent complex HLE.

Recently, MLN have also been used for event recognition. The method in [5], uses MLN to combine the information from low-level classifiers, in order to recognise HLE. A more expressive method that can represent persistent and concurrent HLE, as well as their starting and ending points, is proposed in [10]. However, that method has a quadratic complexity to the number of timepoints. Also, the methods in [5] and [10] focus on HLE that do not involve relations among multiple domain objects. Additionally, they cannot handle situations where nothing is happening, as their axioms require that at each timepoint at least one HLE must occur. Due to those limitations, these methods are difficult to scale up in real-world event recognition applications.

In [23,11] a knowledge base of common sense rules, expressing HLE, is defined in first-order logic. Each rule is associated with a weight value that indicates its confidence. Additionally, the method takes into account the confidence value of the input LLE, which may be due to noisy sensors. Probabilistic inference is performed by MLN, in order to recognise the HLE. Although, the method represents HLE that involve relations among multiple domain objects, the HLE definitions have a limited temporal representation. A more expressive method that uses interval-based temporal relations, is proposed in [15]. The aim of the method is to determine the most consistent sequence of HLE, based on the observations of low-level classifiers. Similar to [23,11], the method expresses HLE using common sense rules. However, it employs temporal relations that are based on Allen's Interval Algebra (IA) [1]. In order to avoid the combinatorial explosion of possible intervals that IA may produce, as well as to eliminate the existential quantifiers in HLE definitions, a bottom-up process eliminates the unlikely HLE hypotheses. That process can only be applied to domain-dependent axioms, as it is guided from the observations and the IA relations. In our work, we address the combinatorial explosion problem in a more generic manner, by representing the EC domain-independent axioms efficiently.

7 Conclusions

In this work, we address the issue of uncertainty that naturally exists in many levels of event recognition, such as the input LLE and the imprecise HLE definitions. We propose a probabilistic extension of Event Calculus (EC) based on Markov Logic Networks (MLN). The method has formal, declarative semantics and inherits the properties of the EC. The domain-independent axioms of EC are hard-constrained, while the domain-dependent HLE definitions can be associated with a confidence level. Moreover, by exploiting the probabilistic nature of MLN, we show how the persistency of fluents can be controlled. We place emphasis on the efficiency and effectiveness of our approach to meet the requirements of real-world applications, by simplifying the axioms of the EC and therefore reducing the size of the underlying ground network built by MLN.

Due to the use of MLN, our method lends itself naturally to learning the weights of event definitions from data. We believe this is an important next step, as the manual setting of weights is suboptimal and cumbersome. Furthermore, we plan to perform additional experiments with other real-world datasets, in order to demonstrate further the potential of our method.

Acknowledgements. This work has been partially funded by EU, in the context of the PRONTO project (FP7-ICT 231738).

References

1. Allen, J.F.: Maintaining knowledge about temporal intervals. Commun. ACM 26(11), 832–843 (1983)
2. Artikis, A., Paliouras, G., Portet, F., Skarlatidis, A.: Logic-based representation, reasoning and machine learning for event recognition. In: DEBS, pp. 282–293 (2010c)
3. Artikis, A., Sergot, M., Paliouras, G.: A logic programming approach to activity recognition. In: ACM Workshop on Events in Multimedia (2010b)
4. Artikis, A., Skarlatidis, A., Paliouras, G.: Behaviour recognition from video content: a logic programming approach. IJAIT 19(2), 193–209 (2010a)
5. Biswas, R., Thrun, S., Fujimura, K.: Recognizing activities with multiple cues. In: Elgammal, A.M., Rosenhahn, B., Klette, R. (eds.) Human Motion 2007. LNCS, vol. 4814, pp. 255–270. Springer, Heidelberg (2007)
6. Brand, M., Oliver, N., Pentland, A.: Coupled hidden markov models for complex action recognition. In: CVPR, pp. 994–999. IEEE Computer Society (1997)
7. Doherty, P., Lukaszewicz, W., Szalas, A.: Computing circumscription revisited: A reduction algorithm. J. Autom. Reasoning 18(3), 297–336 (1997)
8. Domingos, P., Lowd, D.: Markov Logic: An Interface Layer for Artificial Intelligence. Morgan & Claypool Publishers (2009)
9. Dousson, C., Maigat, P.L.: Chronicle recognition improvement using temporal focusing and hierarchization. In: Veloso, M.M. (ed.) IJCAI, pp. 324–329 (2007)
10. Helaoui, R., Niepert, M., Stuckenschmidt, H.: Recognizing interleaved and concurrent activities: A statistical-relational approach. In: PerCom, pp. 1–9. IEEE (2011)
11. Kembhavi, A., Yeh, T., Davis, L.S.: Why did the person cross the road (there)? scene understanding using probabilistic logic models and common sense reasoning. In: Daniilidis, K., Maragos, P., Paragios, N. (eds.) ECCV 2010. LNCS, vol. 6312, pp. 693–706. Springer, Heidelberg (2010)
12. Kowalski, R., Sergot, M.: A logic-based calculus of events. New Generation Computing 4, 67–95 (1986)
13. McCarthy, J.: Circumscription - a form of non-monotonic reasoning. Artificial Intelligence 13, 27–39 (1980)
14. Miller, R., Shanahan, M.: Some alternative formulations of the event calculus. In: Kakas, A.C., Sadri, F. (eds.) Computational Logic: Logic Programming and Beyond. LNCS (LNAI), vol. 2408, pp. 452–490. Springer, Heidelberg (2002)
15. Morariu, V.I., Davis, L.S.: Multi-agent event recognition in structured scenarios. In: Computer Vision and Pattern Recognition (CVPR)
16. Mueller, E.T.: Event calculus. In: Handbook of Knowledge Representation, FAI, vol. 3, pp. 671–708 (2008)
17. Nonnengart, A., Weidenbach, C.: Computing small clause normal forms. In: Handbook of Automated Reasoning, vol. 1, pp. 335–367 (2001)

18. de Salvo Braz, R., Amir, E., Roth, D.: A survey of first-order probabilistic models. In: Innovations in Bayesian Networks. SCI, pp. 289–317 (2008)
19. Shanahan, M.: Solving the frame problem: a mathematical investigation of the common sense law of inertia. MIT Press, Cambridge (1997)
20. Shanahan, M.: The event calculus explained. In: Artificial Intelligence Today: Recent Trends and Developments, pp. 409–430 (1999)
21. Shet, V.D., Neumann, J., Ramesh, V., Davis, L.S.: Bilattice-based logical reasoning for human detection. In: CVPR (2007)
22. Shi, Y., Bobick, A.F., Essa, I.A.: Learning temporal sequence model from partially labeled data. In: CVPR (2), pp. 1631–1638. IEEE Computer Society (2006)
23. Tran, S.D., Davis, L.S.: Event modeling and recognition using markov logic networks. In: Forsyth, D., Torr, P., Zisserman, A. (eds.) ECCV 2008, Part II. LNCS, vol. 5303, pp. 610–623. Springer, Heidelberg (2008)

On Applying Temporal Database Concepts to Event Queries

Foruhar Ali Shiva[1] and Susan D. Urban[2]

[1] School of Computing, Informatics, and Decision Systems Engineering, Arizona State University,
Foruhar.Shiva@ASU.EDU
[2] Department of Industrial Engineering, Texas Tech University,
Susan.Urban@TTU.EDU

Abstract. Temporal databases and query languages have been a subject of research for more than 30 years and are a natural fit for expressing queries that involve a temporal dimension. This paper makes an argument for an event query language that incorporates temporal relational operators to provide a higher degree of expressivity for event queries. The proposed event query language is based on relational algebra with extensions from the XChange^{EQ} event query language. After an overview of temporal database operators, example use cases are presented to illustrate the benefits of integrating event and temporal query language concepts. Challenges to the approach and potential solutions are also presented.

Keywords: Temporal Queries, Event Processing, Temporal Databases.

1 Introduction

The increasing availability of network infrastructure and bandwidth has increased the prevalence of system designs in which system components share data through the use of events. Application areas include Homeland Security, Supply Chain Management and any other environment where sensor readings are continually forwarded for processing. Subsequently, processing of event streams has garnered considerable attention in the research community.

Originally, events in active databases consisted of simple or primitive events. Later work supported specification of patterns of different events over time, called composite or complex events [1]. Complex events are formed through the use of event composition operators. Most of the recent work in the area of event stream processing also uses composition operators as a basis for their languages [2-4], although exceptions such as [5] exist, with a language that is based on temporal logic.

While the meaning of sequence and other composition operators seems straightforward at first glance, in reality different approaches have been used for defining their semantics. A thorough investigation of issues with the sequence operator and composition operators in general can be found in [6], [7]. These issues

F. Olken et al. (Eds.): RuleML 2011 - America, LNCS 7018, pp. 171–178, 2011.

have led to an increase in adoption of an interval-based model. With the move towards interval semantics in event processing, simple sequence operators are no longer sufficient to capture temporal relationships that are possible between different composite events. Operators based on temporal relationships as defined in Allen [8] have been proposed in some languages [9], [10]. However, direct querying of the temporal aspects of interval-based events has not been supported in previous work.

Temporal databases and, by consequence, temporal query languages have been a subject of research for the last 30 years. The objective of temporal databases is to enable correct modeling and expressive querying of data that changes over time.

This paper proposes adoption of operators developed in the context of temporal databases for querying interval-based event data to enable a new dimension for expressing event queries. We utilize these operators presented in [11] to present example use cases where temporal operators can be used for event processing.

To utilize temporal operators developed in the database context, it is necessary to use a relational framework for event processing. XChange^{EQ} is an event processing language that uses relational algebra as a basis for formalizing its operational semantics [7], [9]. We examine the relational framework introduced in XChange^{EQ} and propose an extension to support the application of temporal operators.

2 Temporal Database Operators

Temporal databases are databases that maintain historical data [11], which is data with an temporal axis. Two operators are used in temporal database queries: PACK and UNPACK [3]. Both operators take a relation that has an interval attribute as input and produce a relation with the same heading and representing the same semantic information. Informally, the UNPACK operator expands each tuple into multiple tuples, such that each of the new tuples has the same value for the non-interval attributes as the original tuple, and the interval attribute for each new tuple reflects one unit from the original tuple's interval value. Figure 1 panels (A) and (B) show an example for a relation called department and the result of applying UNPACK.

(A) Department

id	dept	During
e1	CSE	[1001:1003]
e2	CSE	[1002:1003]
e3	ECE	[1006:1008]

(B) Unpack

id	dept	During
e1	CSE	[1001:1001]
e1	CSE	[1002:1002]
e1	CSE	[1003:1003]
e2	CSE	[1002:1002]
e2	CSE	[1003:1003]
e3	ECE	[1006:1006]
e3	ECE	[1007:1007]
e3	ECE	[1008:1008]

(C) Temporal Project

dept	During
CSE	[1001:1001]
CSE	[1002:1002]
CSE	[1003:1003]
ECE	[1006:1006]
ECE	[1007:1007]
ECE	[1008:1008]

(D) Pack

dept	During
CSE	[1001:1003]
ECE	[1006:1008]

Fig. 1. Demonstration of Temporal Project using PACK and UNPACK

The relation of panel (A) reflects the periods of time during which an employee was present in a department. In Figure 1, id is the employee identifier, dept is the name of the department, and the during attribute displays the validity duration for each tuple.

As can be seen in panel (B), UNPACK expands the interval attribute for each department so that in the resulting relation, each tuple is associated with a "unit interval". The PACK operator takes tuples that are temporally adjacent or overlapping, and have the same values for non-interval attributes, and merges them into a single tuple.

Panels (C) and (D) of Figure 1 illustrate the result of projecting the department name and validity interval on the unpacked relation and the result of applying PACK, respectively. Panel (C) illustrates a projection of the dept and during attributes. In panel (D) the PACK operation has been applied to the result of the projection. The sequence of UNPACK, PROJECT, and PACK together is called a temporal projection which, answers the query: "Return continuous periods of time during which any employee was present in each department". JOIN, SELECT, PROJECT, UNION, INTERSECT, MINUS all have temporal counterparts and are defined in a similar fashion. The following section presents use cases to demonstrate the use of temporal operators for querying event streams.

3 Example Use Cases

The following examples use a simplified version of the linear road example from [12] to demonstrate the use of temporal operators for querying event data. A single input event stream called PosSpeedStr2, exists which contains notifications sent by a vehicle while it is being driven through different highway segments:

PosSpeedStr2(vehicleId,speed,segment,dir,hwy,[b:e])

In PosSpeedStr2, vehicleId is the identifier for the vehicle, speed reflects its speed, dir is the direction of the vehicle's movement, and hwy is the highway number. Each highway is divided into one mile segments. Events are generated when a vehicle enters a segment, and reports the segment number. An interval attribute is used for the timestamp. The attribute named 'During,' of type interval, holds the primary timestamp value for any event. An interval type attribute has two components, 'b' and 'e', which reflect the begin and end time of that interval. Where there is no risk of confusion, the b and e values are accessed directly for the sake of brevity. Because PosSpeedStr2 reflects an instantaneous reading, the length assigned to the interval is zero. i.e. b=e. To focus on concepts rather than syntax, queries are presented in a style inspired by Rel^{EQ}, which is an intuitive syntax used in $XChange^{EQ}$ to formalize its relational semantics.

Interval query: The following event query forms the basis for the temporal queries in the rest of this section and reflects the periods of time that each vehicle spent in each segment. This interval is defined as a vehicle entering a segment followed by the same vehicle entering the next segment.

Query 1: Return interval-based events reflecting the amount of time that a vehicle spent in each segment:

```
segStr (P1.vehicleId,P1.segment,P1.dir,P1.hwy,[P1.b:P2.b]) <-
  P1: PosSpeedStr2(vehicleId,segment,dir,hwy,[b:e]),
  P2: PosSpeedStr2(vehicleId, segment,dir,hwy,[b:e])
  P1 before P2,  P1.vehicleId = P2.vehichleId, P1.segment+1 = P2.segment
```

The above query performs a self-join of PosSpeedStr2 over the vehicleId number, with P1 and P2 serving as the two different aliases of PosSpeedStr2. P1 needs to occur before P2 and P2 needs to belong to the segment immediately after P1. The output interval-based event is called segStr, which retains the values of vehicleId, direction and highway number from P1. The output event stream uses the entry segment number to tag the entire segment. The output timestamp duration takes its begin timestamp from P1 and its end timestamp from P2 to reflect the period during which the vehicle was present in the segment.

Windows and Temporal Projection: Temporal operators need to be specified over a time window, as will be explained in section 4. The window is specified using an operator called WINDOWED_SOURCE. WINDOWED_SOURCE acts as an event source to the rest of the query. It has four operands:

```
WINDOWED_SOURCE((interval_source_alias, [b_offset, o_offset]), {window attributes},
[temporal_ query| [[COLLECT|NOT] event_source]])
```

The first operand is an input event stream, which forms the basis for the window interval. The interval of the window can be modified using the second operand which can be used to specify offsets to the begin and end timestamps of the input event stream. The third operand specifies the attributes that need to be projected from the window statement, and form the attributes for the window output. Besides these attributes each window has a mandatory During attribute which takes its value from the offsets applied to the input event stream. The fourth and final operand is the statement that is temporally bound by the window. This can be a temporal query or a negation or aggregation operation. Now we look at temporal projection:

Query 2: Every 5 minutes, return continuous periods during which any vehicle was present in a segment.

```
seg_Busy(segment, carSegDuring, [W.b:W.e]) <-
  W:windowed_source (5_minute_timer, [0:0], {*}
                    t_project {segment, segStr.During as carSegDuring}
                      segStr(vehicleId, segment,dir,hwy,[b:e]))
```

This example uses two input event streams: the segStr stream which is the output of Query 1, and a timer event called 5_minute_timer. The 5_minute_timer event is a system generated event that occurs every 5 minutes. Every hour, the begin time of the interval is aligned to the first second of the hour and the beginning second of every fifth minute after that. Subsequently, the end time points to the last second of every five minute interval.

To answer the query, we perform a temporal projection of the segment attribute over segStr. The interval attribute is also projected and renamed to avoid naming conflict with the window interval. The temporal projection is then enclosed within a 5 minute window. Finally the segment number and the interval resulting from the temporal projection are included in the output. The window interval is assigned as the output interval of the event.

The behavior of the temporal projection operator is to aggregate overlapping events together when they have the same values for projected attributes. This is useful in situations where we are interested in distinct values of a subset of event attributes. In contrast to a standard projection, we avoid generation of redundant notifications of events corresponding to intervals that overlap or subsume each other.

Temporal Intersect and Difference: Define two sub streams of segStr which correspond to two specific vehicles with identifiers x and y. For the vehicle with vehicleId=x, we define:

```
x_SegStr (P1.segment,P1.dir,P1.hwy,[P1.b:P2.e]) <-
  P1: PosSpeedStr2(vehicleId,segment,dir,hwy,[b:e]),
  P2: PosSpeedStr2(vehicleId, segment,dir,hwy,[b:e])
  P1 before P2,  P1.vehicleId = x, P2.vehichleId=x, P1.segment+1 = P2.segment
```

y_SegStr is defined similarly. Now consider the intersection query below.

Query 3 (intersect): Every 5 minutes, return periods during which car x and y were simultaneously in the same segment.

```
x_intersect_y_segStr (segment, intersectDuring, [W.b:W.e]) <-
  W:windowed_source (5_minute_timer, [0:0], {during as intersectDuring, segment}
                     x_SegStr t_intersect y_SegStr)
```

We again make use of the windowed source and the 5_minute_timer event discussed above. The t_intersect operator returns periods of time during which x_SegStr and y_SegStr share all values and their intervals overlap with each other. The window specification projects the segment number and renames the interval attribute to avoid conflict with the window interval attribute. The query output consists of the segment number and the intersecting durations and has the same output timestamp as the window. Intersection is useful when we want to know when two interval-based event streams were ongoing during the same period of time. Difference works in a similar manner to specify when one event was active but not the other.

Temporal Restrict: Restrict is used for specifying interesting points of time.

Query 4: Every five minutes, return the cars that were in section z at the instant [5:5].

```
z_at_5_segStr (vehichleId, [W.b:W.e]) <-
  W:windowed_source (5_minute_timer, 0, {vehicleId}
                     segStr t_restrict during = Interval_Constructor ([5:5]))
```

Since the restrict operation occurs over the unpacked version of segStr, any event interval that includes the time point [5:5] will be included in the result.

4 A Relational Framework for Temporal Event Queries

XChange^{EQ} is an event processing language that uses a special version of relational algebra called Composite Event Relational Algebra, or CERA [7], to formalize its operational semantics. In CERA, event histories are treated as relations, with timestamps being included in relation headings as attributes. Directly applying the database query model to event processing by continuously re-running the query at every instant is not possible, since results generated at a specific step of a query might be incompatible with previously generated results. This is due to the fact that not all relational operations are monotonic. For example, a difference operation might need to retract previously generated results due to arrival of new data in its second operand.

One approach to address this issue is to restrict the semantics of the query language in such a way that at any given instant of time, results can be calculated using available data only. In other words, events that arrive in the future should not affect query results generated at the current or previous instants of time. In the following subsections, we look at how CERA implements these requirements and note extensions that are required for enabling temporal queries.

4.1 Relational Algebra for Temporal Queries

CERA introduces a number of limitations to relational algebra that together ensure that a) non-monotonic or blocking operators are not allowed in an unrestricted way, b) timestamp values are not modified or omitted, and c) the timestamp of the output of an event query spans the duration of all events participating in that result. Collectively, these properties are called Temporal Preservation in [7].

Temporal preservation ensures that current results can always be calculated using available data. However, disallowing any kind of modification of the output timestamp is too restrictive. To deal with this issue we extend the merge operator of CERA into a *merge function.* The merge function calculates the output interval similar to the merging operator of CERA. Additionally, the user can specify offsets on the values of the output duration, which are applied to the default output of the merge operation: merge(b_offset, e_offset). The b_offset can be any integer value, but to uphold temporal preservation, the e_offset can only take non-negative values. If the end time of an event is allowed to be reduced, that would mean that an event is being generated in the past, which could have an effect on the output of other events that reference this event. As such shifting the occurrence time of an event at the current instant of time to a value less than the current instant of time should not be allowed.

To support temporal operators, it should be noted that PACK is not a monotonic operation. Consider the example in Figure 1, assuming that the table containing the result of the projection is made available to the PACK operator over time, applying the operator would produce a result that is only correct at that instant in time. As more tuples arrive, the previous output of PACK is no longer correct. This makes PACK, and by extension, all temporal relational operators, non-monotonic. As such temporal relational operators need to be defined within a window. Rel^{EQ} includes a number of window operators to support negation and aggregation. We unify the CERA window operators into a single operator and extend it to support temporal operators. The unified window mechanism is the WINDOWED_SOURCE presented in Section 4.

4.2 Incremental Evaluation of Temporal Queries

The relational expressions used to formulate event queries need to be evaluated in a continuous, step-wise manner. To avoid re-computing a query result, XChange^{EQ} uses a technique called finite differencing. In the evaluation step, the underlying data is categorized into two distinct sets: the historical data that existed in the relevant histories prior to the current instant of time, and the delta, or the newly arrived data.

(A) Input stream

id	dept	During
e1	CSE	[1001:1003]
e2	CSE	[1002:1003]
e3	ECE	[1006:1008]

(B) Modified Unpack

id	dept	temp_During	During
e1	CSE	[1001:1001]	[1001:1003]
e1	CSE	[1002:1002]	[1001:1003]
e1	CSE	[1003:1003]	[1001:1003]
e2	CSE	[1002:1002]	[1002:1003]
e2	CSE	[1003:1003]	[1002:1003]
e3	ECE	[1006:1006]	[1006:1008]
e3	ECE	[1007:1007]	[1006:1008]
e3	ECE	[1008:1008]	[1006:1008]

(C) Modified Temporal Project

dept	temp_During	During
CSE	[1001:1001]	[1001:1003]
CSE	[1002:1002]	[1001:1003]
CSE	[1003:1003]	[1001:1003]
ECE	[1006:1006]	[1006:1008]
ECE	[1007:1007]	[1006:1008]
ECE	[1008:1008]	[1006:1008]

(D) Pack

dept	During
CSE	[1001:1003]
ECE	[1006:1008]

Fig. 2. Modified UNPACK and Temporal PROJECT with Temporal Preservation

Using finite differencing, CERA expressions, are rewritten based on the history and delta relations. Any new operators added to CERA need to support temporal preservation so that they can be correctly split into history and delta relations. As seen in panel (B) of Figure 1, UNPACK does not adhere to the temporal preservation since it loses the original timestamp values. At any instant, applying the delta operator, which returns tuples belonging to the current instant of time, would discard other new tuples that should belong in the same delta. Turning to panel (C), since the project is operating on the unpacked version, deltas cannot be correctly applied to it.

Figure 2, panels (A) and (B) show a solution to the above problem by modifying the behavior of the UNPACK and temporal PROJECT. The modified UNPACK tags each tuple it outputs with the original timestamp. The original interval is called During, and the result of unpack is called temp_During. Panels (C) and (D) show the modified temporal projection and subsequent UNPACK. The temporal projection's result is equivalent to the result of Figure 1, including the added interval attribute. The interval attribute for each tuple is a merge of the time intervals that were used to produce that tuple. The added attribute preserves the original timestamp values and, as a result, deltas can be correctly applied.

5 Summary and Future Work

This paper has presented use cases to motivate application of temporal operators in an event query language. Extensions needed to the XChange^{EQ} relational framework to support temporal operators were also presented. Our future work includes developing an SQL-like syntax to express event queries that have been enhanced with the temporal database query language features described in [3]. The complete specification of the language and the development of a prototype of the evaluation engine, with support for incremental evaluation are part of the future research plan.

References

1. Chakravarthy, S., Mishra, D.: Snoop: An expressive event specification language for active databases. Data & Knowledge Engineering 14(1), 1–26 (1994)
2. Wu, E., Diao, Y., Rizvi, S.: High-performance complex event processing over streams. In: Proc. of the 2006 ACM SIGMOD Int. Conf. on Management of Data, Chicago, IL, USA, pp. 407–418 (2006)
3. Mei, Y., Madden, S.: Zstream: a cost-based query processor for adaptively detecting composite events. In: Proc. of the 35th SIGMOD Int. Conf. on Management of Data, pp. 193–206 (2009)
4. Barga, R.S., Caituiro-Monge, H.: Event Correlation and Pattern Detection in CEDR. In: Grust, T., Höpfner, H., Illarramendi, A., Jablonski, S., Fischer, F., Müller, S., Patranjan, P.-L., Sattler, K.-U., Spiliopoulou, M., Wijsen, J. (eds.) EDBT 2006. LNCS, vol. 4254, pp. 919–930. Springer, Heidelberg (2006)
5. Cugola, G., Margara, A.: TESLA: a formally defined event specification language. In: Proc. of the 4th ACM Int. Conf. on Distributed Event-Based Systems, Cambridge, United Kingdom, pp. 50–61 (2010)
6. White, W., Riedewald, M., Gehrke, J., Demers, A.: What is next in event processing? In: Proc. of the 26th ACM SIGMOD-SIGACT-SIGART Symp. on Principles of Database Systems, pp. 263–272 (2007)
7. Eckert, M.: Complex Event Processing with XChangeEQ: Language Design, Formal Semantics, and Incremental Evaluation for Querying Events. PhD Dissertation, Ludwig-Maximilians-Universitat Munchen (2008)
8. Allen, J.F.: Maintaining knowledge about temporal intervals. Communications of the ACM 26(11), 832–843 (1983)
9. Bry, F., Eckert, M.: Rule-based composite event queries: the language XChangeEQ and its semantics. In: Proc. of the 1st Int. Conf. on Web Reasoning and Rule Systems, Innsbruck, Austria, pp. 16–30 (2007)
10. Roncancio, C.L.: Toward Duration-Based, Constrained and Dynamic Event Types. In: Andler, S.F., Hansson, J. (eds.) ARTDB 1997. LNCS, vol. 1553, pp. 176–193. Springer, Heidelberg (1999)
11. Date, C.J., Darwen, H., Lorentzos, N.A.: Temporal Data and the Relational Model. Morgan Kauffman Publishers (2002)
12. Arasu, A., et al.: Linear road: a stream data management benchmark. In: Proc. of the 30th Int. Conf. on Very Large Data Bases, Toronto, Canada, vol. 30, pp. 480–491 (2004)

Lexicalized Ontology for a Business Rules Management Platform: An Automotive Use Case*

Nouha Omrane[1], Adeline Nazarenko[1], Peter Rosina[2], Sylvie Szulman[1], and Christoph Westphal[2]

[1] LIPN, Université Paris 13 & CNRS (UMR 7030), France
[2] AUDI AG, Germany

Abstract. This paper describes a platform that helps industrial domain experts to preserve the connection between textual sources and formalized business rules by using lexicalized ontologies both for links and for storage of the conceptual knowledge.

Business Rules Management Systems (BRMSs) are used to update and query business rules of an automotive use case. They rely strongly on domain ontologies, which model the business knowledge and provide a conceptual vocabulary for the formalization of the rules that are expressed in written policies. We show that lexicalized ontologies are a key component of such BRMSs and how such knowledge can be encoded.

Our proposed solution supports domain experts in the automotive industry in understanding and maintaining their business rules by presenting the relevant source documents that were used to create the ontological concepts. The use case is based on a car development scenario that models the connection between car testing scenarios, e.g., safety tests, and the methods and tools used to analyze and prepare these tests. The intended solution has been developed in the ONTORULE project and is still work in progress.

Keywords: Business rules, domain ontology, semantic annotation.

1 Introduction

Business Rules Management Systems (BRMSs) are software applications that help organizations to separate their application code from their business knowledge. BRMSs help the users to author and maintain business rules and apply decision logic that reflects this business knowledge. The business rules can have different origins, such as regulations, policy documents or business logic directly entered by domain experts. This business logic expresses both development processes and coherence between different events, including conditions and the resulting conclusions.

* This work was realised as part of the FP7 231875 ONTORULE project (`http://ontorule-project.eu`). We thank our partners for the fruitful discussions, especially to Audi for the collaboration on their use case.

F. Olken et al. (Eds.): RuleML 2011 - America, LNCS 7018, pp. 179–192, 2011.

One of the main advantages of expressing the logic in business rules is that the domain knowledge is independent of the application code that uses this logic. In such way, there is no need to alter the application code itself, when business logic evolves, new policies are applied, already introduced policies change or retire. Thus, the use of BRMSs leads to increased flexibility and agility of the organization.

In the ONTORULE project, Audi uses OntoBroker as the execution environment for its business rules which are formalized in Objectlogic[1]. The OWL representation of the domain ontology has been developed in parallel for the research purposes described in this paper.

Domain experts who are not also business rules experts may have difficulties expressing their knowledge in formalized logic languages. Supporting them in their management of the knowledge needed to write these rules is one of the goals of the ONTORULE project.

We propose building an ontology as a formal model for representing conceptual vocabulary that is used to express business rules in written policies. Using a normalized vocabulary helps domain experts in writing rules more efficiently and is less costly than managing controlled vocabulary. Such ontologies are shared conceptual models, so experts can share the same vocabulary. We use the OWL-DL language to represent concepts and properties of the domain ontology. In addition,, the ontology is linked to the lexicon used to express rules in the text, so experts can query source documents. This calls for a formalism to link linguistic elements to conceptual ones. We opt to use the SKOS[2] language which provides basic elements to link domain concepts to terms from the text. The combination of OWL entities, SKOS concepts and their related information form a lexicalized ontology which supports the semantic annotation of documents.

The paper is organized as follows. Section 2 describes the Audi use case and Audi's expectations of using a lexicalized ontology. Section 3 explains the choice of OWL and SKOS as languages to support the lexicalized ontology. Section 4 reports the experimentations. Section 5 describes the related work in linking ontology to lexicon and semantic information retrieval. Section 6 presents the conclusion and future work.

2 The Audi BRMS or Platform

Nowadays, the development of new cars has become very challenging and many different process steps are involved. Computer Aided technologies (CAx), like virtual modeling, simulations or the analysis and planning of physical testing, need to be integrated even tighter to satisfy the higher requirements and reduced time-to-market which also shortens the development cycles.

---

[1] Ontology, rule and query language introduced by ontoprise as successor of F-Logic. Main language supported by the semantic web ontology repository and inference engine OntoBroker.

[2] Simple Knowledge Organization System.

In the ONTORULE project Audi is developing a prototype application that makes use of ontologies and business rules that includes and visualizes the context of the following use case.

The development of a car typically follows a process starting with product planning, runs over concept development to testing (virtual & physical) until a car can be launched for production. This long process is strongly supported by different Computer Aided technologies, e.g., Computer Aided Design (CAD), Computer Aided Engineering (CAE), and Computer Aided Testing (CAT):

- CAD: This branch provides methodologies for the virtual design of the parts of a car - e.g., digital mock-up (DMU) methods, parametric design methods, - and verification of the design concerning the geometry when integrated into a car.
- CAE: The main task of CAE is to provide methodologies for simulating the behaviour of a car and its functions - e.g., finite element analysis (FEA) for crash simulation, computational fluid dynamics for thermal management, and multi body simulation (MBS) for driving dynamics.
- CAT: Methodologies for performing physical tests of cars are provided by CAT - e.g., vehicle management, job control, testing control, and test result analysis.

Ontologies together with business rules help Audi to keep abreast of technology advances and use them in its R&D IT applications. Especially the interweaving of the various CAx technologies will help Audi to reduce development time and cost.

One of the first steps in the development cycle of a new car model is the definition of properties, i.e., features that can be experienced by customers, like driving comfort, safety or sportiness that the desired car has to fulfill. These target properties are listed in catalogs, that describe the car's required and mandatory behavior in various granularities.

At a later stage in the development cycle, engineers begin to design new or modify already existing Computer Aided Design models, that have to comply with Audi's high quality expectations. These models are then used in simulations (Computer Aided Engineering) or serve as a model for the physical parts which are tested in Computer Aided Testing. For example, new electronic components, like an Electronic Stability Control (ESC), are tested in Hardware in the Loop (HiL) simulations that make use of virtual models that behave like the related dynamic systems.

The entirety of all these attempts and approaches, physical and virtual, is called CAx Methods. The different CAx Methods ensure either that the desired properties are achieved, or that legal requirements are fulfilled. Components, such as ESC, are referred to as "Solution Concepts" (cf. Fig. 1). They affect the customer experience or vehicle property directly.

The knowledge about the initial relation between a property that was defined in the beginning of the development cycle and a CAD part with its related

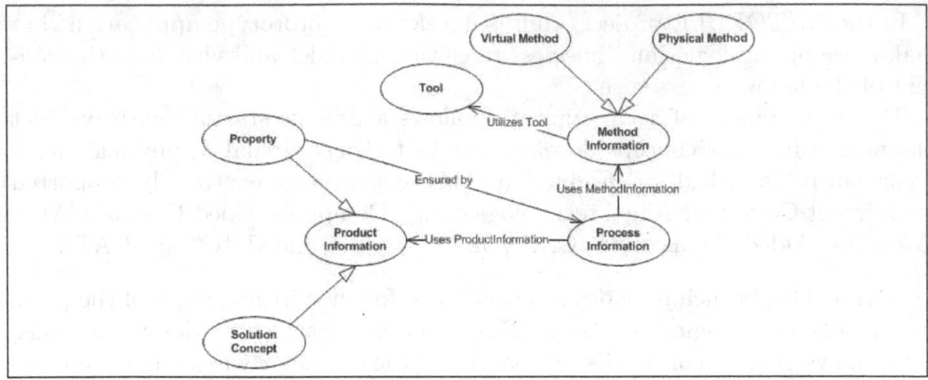

Fig. 1. Simplified extract of the intended Audi R&D ontology

CAx Methods often perishes during the progression of the vehicle's design and construction. In addition, requirements and targeted properties may change over time.

By modeling the described scenario in an ontology, and formulating and processing the relevant rules in a BRMS, Audi expects to reduce the knowledge gap between the various process steps for the involved employees and departments and thus to benefit from a tighter CAx integration. Sharing the knowledge by using a common tool and shared data will reduce time-consuming data acquisition and ensures that the personnel involved will access identical data which will help speed up the development and innovation cycles [7].

For example, with the help of business rules, we are calculating the duration of processes (*processDuration*) that involve different CAx methods (cf. rule example below). Every CAx Method has an assigned attribute for either an estimated or an actual value for its lead time, cost and maturity. Testing if the requirements for one vehicle property are fulfilled normally takes several process steps. As an example, the execution of a CAE simulation may take only minutes - the preparation, the modeling, and so on might take several weeks.

Every process, e.g., an analysis or the validation of such an analysis, makes use of a CAx Method (cf. Fig. 1). The function *processDuration* calculates the whole process duration: the relevant attribute *time* is queried with the function *methodDuration* (which is defined in another rule) from all the methods involved in the relevant subprocesses.

With this rule, the application is able to visualize different durations involving different methods that all test one specific vehicle property. These indications will support managers when planning their projects, so that they can choose whichever process is best suited for their work.

```
processDuration(?X,?Y,?totalTime) :-
    methodDuration(?X,?Y,?totalTime).
processDuration(?X,?Z,?totalTime) :-
    methodDuration(?Y,?Z,?time) AND
```

```
processDuration(?X,?Y,?previousTime) AND
?totalTime = ?time + ?previousTime.
```

(Rule example, that calculates the total process duration.)

One of the difficulties with business knowledge rules is that various departments or roles sometimes use different vocabularies for the same things so they cannot understand each other immediately. Addionally, formalized rules per se are often not easy to understand.

Using an ontology as a unified model for a heterogeneous vocabulary and annotating the rules and the underlying ontology has another advantage: it will reduce misunderstandings and ensure that people are discussing the same thing. Also, the users can easily confirm and verify the appropriateness of the modeled semantic relations. The prototype that is to be developed will handle links between source documents, such as policies and internal documents, i.e. policies or internal documents, and the concepts and instances of the ontology. Also, if a business rule originates directly from a legal document, the relevant passage will be linked to the rule in the same way.

3 The Role of the Lexicalized Ontology in BRMS

A BRMS of the kind described here relies strongly on domain knowledge that is encoded in a lexicalized ontology. This section shows how OWL-DL and SKOS standards support the needs for formalization, document annotation, normalization and documentation that business experts face when designing a business rule application.

3.1 Formalization of Domain Knowledge

The idea of the ontology as a conceptual model was explicitely introduced by [6] affirming that an ontology is: "the specification of a conceptualization". The ontology is a set of concepts that are formally defined. We opted for the for OWL-DL[3] language to express domain concepts or classes and their properties.

Such an ontology not only gives the vocabulary to be used in expressing the rules, it also provides a structured vocabulary that encodes relationships between concepts and supports cheking for inconsistencies. The following example describes the concept *BuckleTest*, its related SKOS concept

```
<rdf:Description rdf:about="http://lipn.univ-paris13.fr/RCLN/
    terminae/Audi#BuckleTest">
```

having as label "buckle test" in the text:

```
<owl:Class rdf:about="&onto;#BuckleTest">
  <rdfs:subClassOf rdf:resource="&onto;#PhysicalMethod"/>
```

[3] http://www.w3.org/TR/owl-guide/

```
</owl:Class>
<rdf:Description rdf:about="http://lipn.univ-paris13.fr/RCLN/
   terminae/Audi#BuckleTest">
  <skos:prefLabel>buckle test</skos:prefLabel>
  <rdf:type rdf:resource="http://www.w3.org/2004/02/skos/
   core#Concept"/>
</rdf:Description>
```

Formalizing the business rule vocabulary in an ontology gives a structure to, and enables querying of, the rule base. For example, we can display all the roles involving physical methods by querying only the parent concept of all physical method concepts.

Experts can also query the ontology itself to search, e.g., for a test that verifies a property and is related to some constraints, as soon as these properties are encoded as concept roles. The following example shows a query written in ObjectLogic to query the ontology. The concept *ProductInformation* is used in the verification process (*ProcessInformation*) and every *ProcessInformation* uses a designated method (i.e., physical or virtual method). The concept *MethodInformation* has as subconcepts all the physical and virtual methods (cf. Fig. 1). The result of this query displays all *ProductInformation* (i.e., car parts, functions, etc) and the tools that use them.

```
@{Systemanalysis_ManagedProductInformation, options[outorder(
  ?Tool,?ProductInformation),fillNull]}
?- ?MethodInformation:MethodInformation[utilizes_Tool->?Tool]
  AND ?ProcessInformation:ProcessInformation[
  uses_ProductInformation->?ProductInformation,uses_Method->
  ?MethodInformation]
  AND ?ProductInformation:ProductInformation.
```

Finally, using the OWL-DL language supports reasoning on the ontology. This is useful for searching for hidden information that is implicit in the rules, for inferring new knowledge, updating the rule base and ultimately improving the business of the organization. For example, experts may recognize that a safety test is less costly with some specific parameters.

For example, the concept *SeatBelt* which describes the seat belt, is related through the role *assuredBy* to the tests *CorrosionTest* and *SeatBeltFlipTest*, which are used to test its safety:

```
<owl:Class rdf:about="&onto;#SeatBelt">
  <assuredBy rdf:resource="&onto;#CorrosionTest"/>
  <assuredBy rdf:resource="&onto;#SeatBeltFlipTest"/>
</owl:Class>
```

3.2 Semantic Annotation of Documents

A key issue for experts in managing a rule base is to recognize that the meaning of formal rules and natural language sources, such as written policies and documentation is a precious source of information. It is also important to update the business rules as organizations often modify their policies according to internal or external constraints.

It is therefore important to be able to mine textual sources to understand how a given concept is used in business documents, what rules are related to it and how those concepts and rules evolve when the policies are updated. This is achieved through the semantic annotation of the documents in which the mentions of the ontological entities (concepts, instances and roles) are highlighted and can be searched for.

Semantic annotation means that ontological entities are related to the terms that can be used to mention them in the texts and calls for designing lexicalized ontologies. When the ontology has been created from textual source, as for the Audi ontology, it is easy to keep track of the terms that denote the various conceptual entities. The resulting lexicalized ontology is used to annotate source documents and to query them.

Our aim is to save the terms related to the conceptual vocabulary that is used to express the business rules. We don't need to encode sophisticated information such as the morphological structure of terms since we do not perform a deep analysis of the documents. We simply need to save the various linguistic units that denote a concept, instance or role. We use SKOS for that.

SKOS supports encoding of *SKOS concepts* that represent the links between the OWL concepts and their related terms, which are encoded as *skos labels*[4]. This relation is described by <`rdf:Description rdf:about`>.

3.3 Normalization of Vocabularies

When designing and updating business rules, experts face the problem of the heterogeneity of information sources and multilingualism. *SKOS* also supports that normalization of vocabularies.

SKOS enables association of a given SKOS concept with the various terms or labels that denote it in the texts or any other information source. For a given concept, *SKOS* supports distinguishing one preferred label and as many alternative labels as necessary, using the <`skos:prefLabel`> and <`skos:altLabel`> properties. In the Audi ontology, for example, the SKOS concept *LowTemperatureChamber* is linked to two terms: *low temperature chamber* is encoded as the preferred label and *refrigerated cabinet* as its alternative form:

```
<rdf:Description rdf:about="http://lipn.univ-paris13.fr/RCLN/
    terminae/Audi#LowTemperatureChamber">
  <skos:prefLabel>low temperature chamber</skos:prefLabel>
  <skos:altLabel>low-temperature chamber</skos:altLabel>
  <skos:altLabel>refrigerated cabinet</skos:altLabel>
  <rdf:type rdf:resource="http://www.w3.org/2004/02/skos/core#
    Concept"/>
</rdf:Description>
```

[4] http://www.w3.org/2004/02/skos/

Alternative labels are used to encode linguistic variants (e.g., seat belt which is a belt) or unify different vocabularies (e.g., low temperature chamber actually has the same meaning as refrigerated cabinet). The following example shows that the SKOS concept *SeatBelt* is related to two terms *seat belt* and *belt* in the text:

```
<rdf:Description rdf:about="http://lipn.univ-paris13.fr/RCLN/
    terminae/Audi#SeatBelt">
  <skos:prefLabel>seat belt</skos:prefLabel>
  <skos:altLabel>belt</skos:altLabel>
  <rdf:type rdf:resource="http://www.w3.org/2004/02/skos/core#
    Concept"/>
</rdf:Description>
```

SKOS also supports the encoding of multilingual information. The information about the language used is described by <`rdf:lang=‘‘en‘‘`>. For example, the SKOS concept *TrolleyTest* has a preferred label ”trolley test“ which is mentioned in English in the text.

```
<rdf:Description rdf:about="http://lipn.univ-paris13.fr/RCLN/
    terminae/Audi#TrolleyTest">
  <skos:prefLabel df:lang="en">trolley test</skos:prefLabel>
  <rdf:type rdf:resource="http://www.w3.org/2004/02/skos/core#
    Concept"/>
</rdf:Description>
```

PR : TrolleyTest means ”‘Schlittentest”’ in German.

Thanks to the alternative labels and language tags, *SKOS* therefore helps experts managing the heterogeneity of the vocabulary of their sources and controlling the vocabulary used for designing rules.

3.4 Documentation of the Shared Knowledge

Since experts often have to manage a large volume of information but do not always formally describe all the concepts, it is important to add informal documentation when it is available. Defining concepts in natural language is very important to understand what concepts mean, especially if they have ambiguous or implicit labels.

Since legal documents such as policies often define their terminology precisiely, we propose to extract those definitions from the source documents when designing the ontology and to associate them with the related SKOS concepts using the label <`skos:definition`>.

Source documents are exploited to find definition for existing concepts in the Audi ontology. For example, the concept *ReferenceZone* is described as follows:

```
<rdf:Description rdf:about="http://lipn.univ-paris13.fr/RCLN/
    terminae/Audi#ReferenceZone">
  <rdf:type rdf:resource="http://www.w3.org/2004/02/skos/core#
```

```
   Concept"/>
  <skos:definition>"Reference zone" means  the space between two
    vertical longitudinal planes , 400 mm apart and symmetrical
    with respect planes , 400 mm apart and symmetrical with
    respect to the H point , and  defined by rotation from
    vertical to horizontal of the head form apparatus.
  </skos:definition>
  <skos:prefLabel>reference zone</skos:prefLabel>
</rdf:Description>
```

3.5 Formalism for the Audi Lexicalized Ontology

The Audi ontology is a formal representation of the conceptual vocabulary used to express business rules in written policies. In the Audi use case, we use OWL-DL to describe concepts and their roles. Structuring the vocabulary and normalizing it supports querying of the ontology in order to manage the knowledge base, infer new knowledge and detect inconsistency. As the Audi ontology is lexicalized, the domain concepts and their occurrences in the text can be matched onto one another thanks to the linkage of OWL entities, SKOS concepts and labels.

This is a simple efficient way to represent lexicalized ontologies and we show in the following section its benefit for the Audi BRMS. Figure 2 describes how the Audi ontology is linked to the lexicon and annotated text.

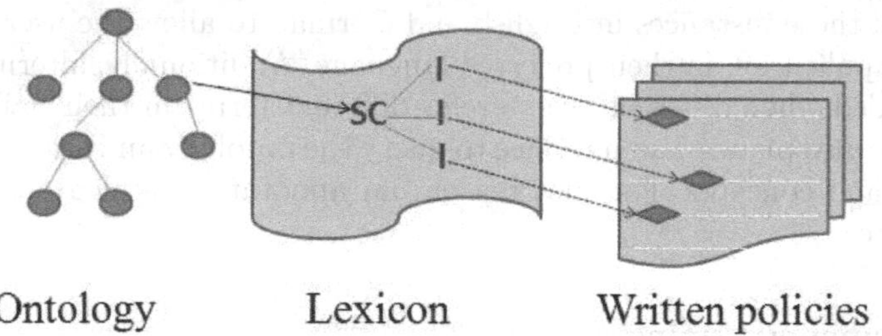

Fig. 2. A lexicalized ontology for annotating source documents. Each concept from the ontology is linked to a SKOS concept *SC* and each SKOS concept is related to its labels *l*. The annotations link some text entities to these labels.

4 Experiments in the Audi Use Case

This section presents the Audi ontology and illustrates the benefit in the Audi use case of having such a lexicalized ontology.

4.1 The Audi BRMS Ontology

The Audi ontology has been built in two steps. At first, the goal was to integrate the various existing knowledge sources in a single one. This resulted into a small conceptual model (around 30 concepts) associated with a large knowledge base (thousands of instances).

In a second step, in order to better fits the experts' needs for semantic querying and document mining, the initial ontology has been restructured and lexicalized. It also appeared useful to increase the granularity of the domain model so as to represent not only the various types of tests but also their actual occurrences in the car manufacturing process (instances that are related to the different tests applied to specific vehicle models).

This led to encoding of various elements as concepts rather than instances (90 concepts were added). Modeling tests as concepts supports, for instance, querying of the Audi ontology in such a way as to detect implicit relationships between tests, tools and parameters, which are important for the safety of vehicles. The conceptual structure has been reorganized (4 subsumption levels instead of 1). A SKOS resource has been associated with this resulting ontology: each concept is related to at least 1 preferred label and up to 5 alternative labels. In addition, using a subset of the initial ontology for the exploration of written policies showed that 10 of the mentioned tests were missing in the initial ontology and led us to enrich it [9].

4.2 Semantic Querying

The knowledge base of our ontology currently consists of several thousands of instances separated into more than 30 concepts. It currently reflects only a small part of the whole use case and will be enhanced over time. We have annotated a subset of these instances in English and German to allow the users to use the aimed-at application in their preferred language. Additionally, alternative labels can be added when different users prefer different terms in their daily work.

We have also planned an interface to query the ontology and search for specific instances and concepts. For that reason, an annotated ontology is much more appropriate.

4.3 Document Mining

We enrich the Audi ontology with new concepts and link conceptual elements to linguistic ones from the Audi documents. We obtain a lexicalized ontology that contains 90 SKOS concept, 90 preferred terms and 16 alternatives labels. For example, we create the SKOS concept *BreakingStrengthOfStrapTest* that describes a specific test of the seat belt and link the preferred and alternative labels which are mentioned in source documents.

```
<rdf:Description rdf:about="http://lipn.univ-paris13.fr/RCLN/
    terminae/Audi#BreakingStrengthOfStrapTest">
  <skos:prefLabel>breaking strength test</skos:prefLabel>
  <skos:altLabel>test of breaking strength</skos:altLabel>
  <skos:altLabel>breaking strength of strap test
  </skos:altLabel>
```

```
  <skos:altLabel>test of breaking strength of strap
  </skos:altLabel>
  <rdf:type rdf:resource="http://www.w3.org/2004/02/skos/core#
    Concept"/>
</rdf:Description>
```

Once the ontology is lexicalized, domain experts can query source documents to search for fragments of texts that describe specific concepts mentioned in rules. For example, they can find all references of the concept *BreakingStrengthOfStrapTest* in the text, wherever it is mentioned in the documents:

```
prefix schema:<http://lipn.univ-paris13.fr/RCLN/terminae/schema#>
prefix onto:<http://lipn.univ-paris13.fr/RCLN/terminae/Audi#>
prefix skos:<http://www.w3.org/2004/02/skos/core#Concept>
select ?sentence
where
{  ?sentence rdf:type schema:sentence
   ?sentence schema:annotatedBy ?concept
   ?concept schema:realized concept <onto:
     BreakingStrengthOfStrapTest>
   ?skos skos:skosConcept ?concept
   ?skos skos:preflabel "test of breaking strength"
}
```

We can also search for all sentences where the physical methods are mentioned in the text. As the concepts expressing tests are sub-concepts of the concept "MethodInformation", we query the text by searching about all subconcepts of "MethodInformation". The following example shows the query:

```
prefix schema:<http://lipn.univ-paris13.fr/RCLN/terminae/schema#>
prefix onto:<http://lipn.univ-paris13.fr/RCLN/terminae/Audi#>
prefix skos:<http://www.w3.org/2004/02/skos/core#Concept>
select ?sentence
where
{  ?sentence rdf:type schema:sentence
   ?sentence schema:annotatedBy ?concept
   ?concept schema:realized concept <onto:MethodInformation>
   ?conceptfils rdfs:subClassOf ?concept
   ?skos skos:skosConcept ?conceptfils

}
```

Thanks to the labels of concepts, the ontology can be used to annotate the documents. Figure 3 shows an example of texts where all the mentions of known concepts are emphasized.

This supports experts in browsing of documents.

```
Two belts or restraint systems are required for the buckle inspection, the
low-temperature buckle test, the low-temperature test described in
paragraph 7.5.4. below where necessary, the buckle durability test, the belt
corrosion test, the retractor operating tests, the dynamic test and the
buckle-opening test after the dynamic test. One of these two samples shall be used
for the inspection of the belt or restraint system.
```

Fig. 3. A fragment of text annotated by the lexicalized ontology

5 Related Work

Many research activities have tackled the problem of linking an ontology to a lexicon. Two major areas are of interest.

The first is the NLP domain which aims at adding some semantic structure to a lexicon by linking its elements to ontology's elements. There are several ways to combine a lexicon with an ontology. We describe the most popular ones.

LMF[5] standard [5] aims at detecting the relation between the words used to express objects and their formalization in the ontology. The mapping is assured by axioms declared in the ontology. *LMF* has the merit of assessing large scale lexical resources. *TMF*[6] is a standard ISO that allows describing the terms of a lexicon within a formal language. The supported language is based on the definition of a meta-model and a set of features used to represent elements of the lexicon (e.g., related class, language, lexical information). *OLIF*[7] is an open standard for exchange format that allows to represent morphological, syntactic and semantic data categories. *LMM*[8] is a formal language described in OWL-DL. It integrates linguistic knowledge resources (e.g., FrameNet) and foundational ontology (e.g., DOLCE). It has the advantage of dealing with multi-lingual resources.

The other family trys to link an ontology to a lexicon by introducing models for representing linguistic information for ontologies. [11] defines a meta model to distinguish terms and concepts. Terms are linked to concepts through a semantic relation "denote". *LexOnto* proposed by [2] supports definition of the lexicon by using all the expresseiveness of OWL. *LexOnto* considers a term as an "OWL: class" and presents a meta model that supports linking of terms to concepts. The relation between the elements can be simple or complex (e.g., sub-category-of).

LingInfo [1] define a meta class to link the linguistic properties to the concept or to its Data/Object properties. The meta class contains the associated term, its language and the morpho-syntactic structure of the term. [8] introduces a set of annotation rules to link an existing ontology to its lexicon that is described in the text. The authors consider a standard OWL-DL ontology that they extend and, for each domain ontology, propose to define a set of annotation rules that link each concept to its linguistic representations in the text.

[5] Lexical Markup Framework.
[6] Terminological Markup Framework.
[7] Open Lexicon Interchange Format.
[8] Linguistic Meta Model.

LIR [10] supports storage of linguistic information in a lexical ontology and linkage to domain concepts via ontology relations.

From a practical point of view, the choice of one model or another depends on the aimed application and the task. Our aim is to build a lexicalized ontology to allow annotating the technical documents and thus to help the expert in exploring documents by querying its set of annotations explained above. We use for that a W3C standard *SKOS* that links linguistic to semantic knowledge. *SKOS* introduces especially the properties: *skos:prefLabel* and *skos:altLabel* to link preferred and alternative terms to each concept in the ontology.

Usually users query documents by entering keywords that occur in the target documents in Information Retrieval (IR). But searching relevant information through a keyword-based approach very often provides limited results. Therefore, IR adopts a conceptual search-approach to capture the user needs on a semantic level [4]. Information retrieval uses ontologies as formal models to query knowledge data base [3]. It takes into account these keywords and tries to match them with their corresponding concepts in the ontology. To do so, ontologies need to be linked to a rich lexicon as in lexicalized formalism described above so that the result obtained matches the query of users.

The ability to link an ontology to a lexicon is very important for annotation of documents. Annotating documents supports linking of textual units to their corresponding concepts in an ontology, and showing the relationship between these concepts and the terms that are related to them. Such a lexicalized ontology helps the exploration of texts through semantic queries once they are annotated with the ontology.

6 Conclusion

The proposed integration of CAx systems will increase the flexibility of the development process, allowing Audi to meet the increasing market demand for product diversification.

This integration relies on the design of an application that is currently under development and is based on a BRMS.

Our approach for the acquisition and management of the knowledge embodied in such BRMS relies on a lexicalized ontology which unifies and normalizes the various vocabularies and links the conceptual knowledge to the source policies and regulation written in natural language.

Using a lexicalized ontology enables experts to determine the most suitable CAx Methods from given functional requirements and to query sources documents.

These new approaches, standards and technologies are already partially integrated in some processes. During the next years Audi will continue to incorporate the ONTORULE platform in their landscape which will lead to even less time-consuming, cheaper and higher quality processes in the innovation and development cycles.

References

1. Buitelaar, P., Sintek, M., Kiesel, M.: A Multilingual/Multimedia Lexicon Model for Ontologies. In: Sure, Y., Domingue, J. (eds.) ESWC 2006. LNCS, vol. 4011, pp. 502–513. Springer, Heidelberg (2006)
2. Cimiano, P., Haase, P., Herold, M., Mantel, M., Buitelaar, P.: LexOnto: A Model for Ontology Lexicons for Ontology-based NLP. In: Proceedings of OntoLex - From Text to Knowledge: The Lexicon/Ontology Interface (Workshop at the International Semantic Web Conference) (2007)
3. Davies, J., Duke, A., Kiryakov, A.: Semantic Search. In: Information Retrieval, Searching in the 21st Century. Wiley
4. Fernández, M., Cantador, I., López, V., Vallet, D., Castells, P., Motta, E.: Semantically enhanced Information Retrieval: An ontology-based approach (2010), http://dx.doi.org/10.1016/j.websem.2010.11.003
5. Francopoulo, G., Be, N., George, M., Calzolari, N., Monachini, M., Pet, M., Soria, C.: Lexical markup framework: ISO standard for semantic information in NLP lexicons. In: Workshop of the GLDV Working Group on Lexicography at the Biennial Spring Conference of the GLDV (2007)
6. Gruber, T.R.: Toward principles for the design of ontologies used for knowledge sharing. In: Formal Ontology in Conceptual Analysis and Knowledge Representation. Available as Stanford Knowledge Systems Laboratory Report. Kluwer Academic (March 1993)
7. Kiss, E., Albert, P., Korf, R., Rosina, P., Hoppenbrouwers, J., Njissen, S.: Market Intelligence Report, D8.4 ONTORULE Project Deliverable. Tech. rep. (2011)
8. Ma, Y., Audibert, L., Nazarenko, A.: Ontologies étendues pour l'annotation sémantique. In: 20mes Journées Francophones d'Ingénierie des Connaissances, IC 2009 (2009)
9. Omrane, N., Nazarenko, A., Szulman, S.: Les entités nommées: éléments pour la conceptualisation. In: 22mes Journées Francophones d'Ingénierie des Connaissances, IC 2011 (2011)
10. Peters, W., Espinoza, M., Montiel-Ponsoda, E., Sini, M.: Multilingual and localization support for ontologies. Technical report, D2.4.3 Neon Project Deliverable. Tech. rep. (2009)
11. Reymonet, A., Thomas, J., Aussenac-Gilles, N.: Modélisation de ressources termino-ontologiques en OWL. In: Trichet, F. (ed.) Journées Francophones d'Ingénierie des Connaissances (IC), Grenoble, pp. 169–180 (July 2007)

Towards Directly Applied Ontological Constraints in a Semantic Decision Table

Yan Tang and Robert Meersman

Semantic Technology and Application Research Laboratory (STARLab),
Department of Computer Science, Vrije Universiteit Brussel,
Building G-10, Pleinlaan 2, 1050 Elsene, Belgium
{yan.tang,robert.meersman}@vub.ac.be

Abstract. Decision tables have been a powerful tool for business people since a long time ago. A semantic decision table (SDT) is a decision table properly annotated with domain ontologies. It contains a set of formal agreements called *commitments*, which is a result from group decision making processes involving a community of business stakeholders. In this paper, we focus on validation and verification issues (V&V) for SDT. In particular, we deal with directly applied ontological constraints that are stored as SDT commitments. With them, we can detect inconsistency in an SDT. We also show how an SDT commitment can be stored in Semantic Decision Rule Markup Language (SDRule-ML). In the meanwhile, we illustrate the mapping between SDRule-ML and RDFs/OWL.

Keywords: semantic decision table, validation and verification, semantic decision rule markup language (SDRule-ML), RDFs, OWL.

1 Introduction

In the business domain, one of the favorite decision tools used by non-technical business people is decision tables. A decision table provides a clear way to visualize conditions and actions and the relations between them.

A semantic decision table (SDT, [12]) is a decision table properly annotated with domain ontologies. Thanks to the modern ontology engineering technology, a semantic decision table allows rule modelers, knowledge engineers or evaluators to analyze a decision table using domain semantics.

An important analysis issue is validation and verification (V&V, [3]), the goal of which is to ensure the quality of the modeled decision rules. *Validation* is a process of checking whether or not the decision rules are correctly modeled according to certain meta-rules (or models). During the process of *verification*, rule auditors need to confirm that the decision rules are correctly built. V&V is a mandatory step towards ensuring the *correctness* of a decision table.

In this paper, we illustrate how we can use ontologies to validate and verify the decision rules in a decision table. We first transform a decision table into an SDT. During this process, the domain experts (e.g., rule editors and business people) specify hidden rules and meta-rules of this decision table into a set of ontological commitments (e.g., axioms and constraints). Those commitments, in this paper, are

F. Olken et al. (Eds.): RuleML 2011 - America, LNCS 7018, pp. 193–207, 2011.

stored in Semantic Decision Rule Markup Language (SDRule-ML, [13]). We will as well show how RDFs/OWL constraints are mapped to SDRule-ML.

This paper is organized as follows. Sec. 2 is the paper background. The main contribution of this paper is illustrated in Sec. 3, which covers six types of directly applied ontological constraints. We illustrate the related work in Sect. 4. In Sec. 5, we present the discussion and our future work and conclude the paper.

2 Background: Semantic Decision Tables

A decision table has three constituents: *conditions*, *actions* and *decision rules* [1]. Each condition has a *condition stub* and a *condition entry*. Each action has an *action stub* and *action entry*. A decision rule, which is represented as a table column, is a combination of a set of conditions and actions.

Table 1. A decision table example used in a ubiquitous system (example taken from [14])

Condition	1	2	3	4
People move Ear	Yes	No	Yes	No
Pressure on Crib	Yes	Yes	No	No
Action				
Screen shows Message	Message1			
iPhone rings			RingTone1	

Table 1 is a decision table example for a smart home. It is to decide which messages a screen will show and which ring tones an iPhone will ring, depending on whether the ear of a smart rabbit is moved or not, and whether there is pressure on a crib or not. "People move Ear" and "Pressure on Crib" are the two condition stubs. "Yes" and "No" are the two condition entries. A condition can be, for instance, $\langle People\ move\ Ear, Yes\rangle$ (see columns 1 and 3). "Screen shows Message" and "iPhone rings" are the two action stubs. "Message1", "RingTone1" and "" are the action entries. An action can be, for instance, $\langle iPhone\ rings,\ RingTone1\rangle$ (see column 3) or $\langle Screen\ shows\ Message,\ \ \rangle$ (see columns 2, 3 and 4). Columns 1~4 are the decision rules. A decision rule (e.g., column 1) can be written as follows.

$$\{\langle People\ move\ Ear, Yes\rangle, \langle Pressure\ on\ Crib, Yes\rangle\} \rightarrow \{\langle Screen\ shows\ Message, Message1\rangle, \langle iPhone\ rings,\ \ \ \rangle\}$$

A semantic decision table (SDT, [12]) contains three parts – a *decision table*, a set of *lexons* and *commitments*. A lexon is a binary fact type, which has the format of $\langle \gamma, t_1, r_1, r_2, t_2\rangle$. t_1 and t_2 are the two terms that represent two concepts in a natural language; r_1 and r_2 are the two roles that the two concepts presented by t_1 and t_2 can possibly play with. γ is the context identifier that points to the document where t_1 and t_2 are originally defined, and where r_1 and r_2 are meaningful. A context identifier can be, e.g. a URI.

We show an example of lexon as follows.

$$\langle \gamma_1, Bunny, has, is\ of, Ear\rangle$$

A commitment specifies how to use a lexon or a set of lexons based on the agreements made by a user community. A commitment can be

1) Instantiation of a concept (e.g., "Bunny" is the Nabaztag Rabbit with tag 123XYZ) or a lexon (e.g., Nabaztag Rabbit with tag 123XYZ has a right ear with tag EAR123);
2) A constraint, e.g., EACH Bunny has EXACTLY TWO Ears;
3) Selecting/grouping lexons from one or several contexts;
4) Instantiation of a value for a concept if its value range is defined in a constraint;
5) Articulation, which is a mapping between $\langle \gamma, t \rangle$ and the glosses defined in a glossary, dictionary and thesaurus in a particular language or languages;
6) Interpretation and implementation of a role pair $\langle r_1, r_2 \rangle$, for instance, the role pairs $\langle is\ a, superType\ of \rangle$ and $\langle isA, subsumes \rangle$ can be both interpreted as a "is-a" taxonomical relationship;
7) Alignment of t and r, e.g., the terms "rabbit" and "cony" are aligned with "Bunny". The roles "subtype of" and "subclass of" are aligned with "is-a".

As an example, the SDT from Table 1 contains the lexons and commitments as shown in Table 2. Note that here we omit the context identifiers in the lexons.

Table 2. The lexons and commitments in the SDT for Table 1 (example taken from [14])

SDT Lexons	
Lexon 1	$\langle Bunny, has, is\ of, Ear \rangle$
Lexon 2	$\langle Bunny, has, is\ of, Name \rangle$
Lexon 3	$\langle Ear, is\ moved\ by, move, People \rangle$
Lexon 4	$\langle Crib, has, is\ of, Name \rangle$
Lexon 5	$\langle Screen, shows, is\ shown\ by, Message \rangle$
Lexon 6	$\langle iPhone, rings\ with, is\ rang\ with\ by, RingTone \rangle$
SDT Commitments	
Commitment 1	EACH Bunny has EXACT ONE name.
Commitment 2	EACH Crib has EXACT ONE name.
Commitment 3	EACH Screen shows AT LEAST ONE Message
Commitment 4	Each iPhone rings with AT LEAST ONE Ring Tone.

The basic characteristics of decision tables are *completeness* and *correctness* [3]. The completeness of a decision table is ensured by exhaustively list all the possible combinations of the conditions. Hence the completeness is a problem that can be easily solved. Yet the issue of correctness has always been the challenge.

Validation and Verification (V&V) is a classical process, with which we can ensure the correctness of a decision table, e.g. as shown in [8], [10] and [15]. We will discuss the related work in detail in Sec. 4. In this paper, we take an approach that is different from the existing ones. We transform a decision table into an SDT. During this transformation process, rule modelers (such as business decision makers) are asked to specify the hidden semantics of this decision table. A knowledge engineer takes these specifications and transforms them into lexons and commitments. Note that our ontologies are also modeled in lexons and commitments. We can check the correctness of this decision table by checking the consistency of the commitments.

In the following section, we will illustrate how different kinds of ontological constraints can be used for SDT V&V.

3 Directly Applied Ontological Constraints

The constraints of *value*, *uniqueness*, *mandatory*, *cardinality and frequency*, *exclusive-or* and *subtyping* are the ones that can be used for SDT V&V.

3.1 Value Constraint

A value constraint, sometimes called *domain constraint*, indicates which values are allowed in a concept (in the case that this concept represents a value type) or role ([2], pp. 216-221).

There are three kinds of value constraints: *enumeration*, *range* and *multiple*. With enumeration, we list all the possible values, e.g. the commitment "VALUE of Gender is {M, F}". If we can list the values in a continuous order, then we can specify it with a range, e.g. commitment 1 in Table 3. The range can as well be unbounded, e.g. "VALUE of Age is [0..)". Multiple value constraint combines enumeration and range, e.g. commitment 2 in Table 3.

Table 3. An SDT on deciding whether to accept to process or not based on the value received from a temperature sensor, the age and the login state of a user

Condition	1	2	3	4	…	n	…
Age	>=18	>=18	>=18	>=18	…	>=100, <=350	
Temperature Sensor	>=0,<30	>=0,<30	>=0,<30	>=-10,<0	…	>=0,<30	
Login State	Yes	No	Maybe	Yes	…	Yes	…
Action							
Accept	*		*	*		*	
SDT Lexons							
Lexon 1	$\langle Person, has, is\ of, Age\rangle$						
Lexon 2	$\langle Temperature\ Sensor, mesure, is\ measured\ by, Temperature\rangle$						
Lexon 3	$\langle Person, has, is\ of, Login\ State\rangle$						
Lexon 4	$\langle Login\ State,\ has\ value\ type, is\ value\ type\ of, Boolean\rangle$						
SDT Commitments							
Commitment 1	VALUE of Age is [0..200]						
Commitment 2	VALUE of Temperature Sensor is {[-100,-20),[0..100]}						

Commitment 1 in Table 3 can be stored in RDFs/OWL and SDRule-ML, which is illustrated in Fig. 1.

Note that we can also specify value constraints indirectly by annotating a condition stub with existing value types, such as Float, Boolean and Integer. The annotation is stored as lexons (e.g. lexon 4 in Table 3). The value ranges of a Float and Integer are $[Float.MIN, Float.MAX]$ and $[Integer.MIN, Integer.MAX]$. We use any of the following value enumerations as the default value constraint for a Boolean: {Yes, No}, {Y, N}, {True, False}, {T, F}, and {1, 0}.

Fig. 2 shows how an annotation like lexon 4 from Table 3 can be stored in SDRule-ML.

RDFs/OWL

```
...
<DataPropertyRange>
<DataProperty URI="has_age"/>
<DatatypeRestriction>
<Datatype URI="&xsd;integer"/>
<DatatypeFacetRestriction facet="&xsd;maxInclusive">
<Constant datatypeURI="&xsd;integer">200</Constant>
</DatatypeFacetRestriction>
<DatatypeFacetRestriction facet="&xsd;minInclusive">
<Constant datatypeURI="&xsd;integer">0</Constant>
</DatatypeFacetRestriction>
</DatatypeRestriction>
</DataPropertyRange>
...
```

SDRule-ML

```
...
<Predicate id="Lexon1">
<Object_Role ID="Lexon1_forward" Object="Person"
Role="has"/>
<Object_Role ID="Lexon1_backward" Object="Age"
Role="is of"/>
</Predicate>
<Constraint Object="Age">
<ValueConstraint ValueConstraintType="Range"
LowerBound="0" UpperBound="200"
lowerBoundOpen="false" upperBoundOpen="false"/>
</Constraint>
...
```

Fig. 1. Commitment 1 from Table 3 stored in RDF/OWL and SDRule-ML

```
...
<annotated corole="is value type of" relation="has value type of">
<DecisionItem xsi:type="xs:string">Login State </DecisionItem>
<Target conceptName="Integer" context="VALUE_TYPE"/>
</annotated>
...
```

Fig. 2. Lexon 4 from Table 3 in SDRule-ML

When we verify Table 3, column 3 is considered invalid because "Login State" has Boolean values (see lexon 4 in Table 3) and "Maybe" is not a default Boolean value. Column 4 is inconsistent with commitment 2 in Table 3 and hence is invalid. Column n does not satisfy commitment 1 in Table 3; therefore, it is also not valid.

3.2 Cardinality and Occurrence Frequency

A cardinality constraint can be either an *object cardinality* or a *role cardinality* ([2], p. 289). Object cardinality is applied to a lexon term when we want to restrict the number of members or instances of the population of the type that this lexon term points to. For example, if we want to allow at most three X-Box humidity sensors, then we design a commitment as "AT MOST 3 X-Box Humidity Sensors ARE ALLOWED IN ANY CASES".

Role cardinality is comparable to a constraint of occurrence frequency, which is applied to a lexon (co-)role when we want to restrict the number of members of the instance of a role. Researchers sometimes distinguish cardinality from frequency when cardinality is only used to specify the number of objects in some type. Frequency is to specify how many times, within the same state, a given object can play some role. To make it clearer (and follow the OWL definition of cardinality), we use cardinality for specifying the numbers of objects. We use frequency instead of role cardinality.

For instance, if we have a lexon$\langle\gamma, Room, has, is\ of, X-Box\ Humidity\ Sensor\rangle$ and we want to allow at most two X-Box humidity sensors in one room, then we design a commitment as "EACH Room has AT MOST 2 X-Box Humidity Sensors", which contains a frequency constraint.

Note that the two commitments "AT MOST 3 X-Box Humidity Sensors ARE ALLOWED IN ANY CASES" (cardinality) and "EACH Room has AT MOST 2 X-Box Humidity Sensors" (frequency) are different. The former emphasizes that in any cases, at most three X-Box humidity sensors are allowed; while the latter specifies that only in the case of in a room, at most two X-Box humidity sensors are allowed.

Note also that if we want to apply cardinality on one object and frequency on a lexon that plays a near role[1] with this object, then the cardinality range of the constraint for the object cardinality must be overlapped with the one for frequency. For example, the commitment "EACH Room has AT LEAST 5 X-Box Humidity Sensor" is invalid because it is inconsistent with the commitment "AT MOST 2 X-Box Humidity Sensors ARE ALLOWED IN ANY CASES".

Table 4. An SDT on deciding whether or not to turn on Actuator x based on the availability of X-Box557, X-Box120 and MS Xbox 360

Condition	1	2	3	4	5	6	7	8
X-Box 557	Yes	Yes	Yes	Yes	No	No	No	No
X-Box 120	Yes	Yes	No	No	Yes	Yes	No	No
MS Xbox 360	Yes	No	Yes	No	Yes	No	Yes	No
Action								
Actuator x	*		*		*	*		*
SDT Lexons								
Lexon 1	$\langle Room, has, is\ of, X-Box\ Humidity\ Sensor\rangle$							
Lexon 2	$\langle X-Box\ Humidity\ Sensor, has\ value\ type, is\ value\ type\ of, Boolean\rangle$							
SDT Commitments								
Commitment 1	VALUE of X-Box Humidity Sensor is {X-Box557, X-Box120, MS Xbox360}.							
Commitment 2	EACH Room has AT MOST 2 X-Box Humidity Sensors							

Given a concept C, a list of condition stub $C_1, C_2, \ldots, C_i$ and the below conditions

- $C_1, C_2, \ldots, C_i$ are the members of C (which we write as $C_1, C_2, \ldots, C_i \in C$)
- $C_1, C_2, \ldots, C_i$ have the value type of Boolean
- C is represented by the lexon term t_x

We say the SDT contains invalid decision rules if the below conditions are met

Situation 1 (≤):

- The near role of t_x is played at most n times and/or at most n instances from C are allowed in any cases.
- There are more than n combinations of $\langle C_j, Yes\rangle$, $C_j \in \{C_1, C_2, \ldots C_i\}$, in one column and this column contains an action.

[1] In a lexon $\langle\gamma, t_1, r_1, r_2, t_2\rangle$, we call r_1 is the near role of t_1 and r_2 is the far role of t_1; $r_2$is the near role of t_2 and $r_1$is the far role of t_1.

Or, situation 2 (≥):

- The near role of t_x is played at least n times and/or at least n instances from C are allowed in any cases.
- There are less than n combinations of $\langle C_j, Yes\rangle$, $C_j \in \{C_1, C_2, \dots C_i\}$, in one column and this column contains an action.

The situations for $<, >, =$ can be designed in a similar way.

Table 4 shows an example for situation 1. According to commitment 2 from Table 4, column 1 in this table does not satisfy the specified constraint of frequency.

Fig. 3 shows how commitment 2 from Table 4 can be stored in RDFs/OWL and SDRule-ML. Note that currently OWL only deals with constraints of frequency, not constraints of object cardinality. SDRule-ML supports both.

RDFs/OWL	SDRule-ML
…<ObjectPropertyDomain> <ObjectProperty URI="has_X-Box_Humidity_Sensors"/> <ObjectAllValuesFrom> <ObjectProperty URI="has_X-Box_Humidity_Sensors"/> <Class URI="Room"/> </ObjectAllValuesFrom> </ObjectPropertyDomain> <ObjectPropertyRange> <ObjectProperty URI="has_X-Box_Humidity_Sensors"/> <ObjectMaxCardinality cardinality="2"> <ObjectProperty URI="has_X-Box_Humidity_Sensors"/> <Class URI="XBox_Humidity_Sensor"/> </ObjectMaxCardinality> </ObjectPropertyRange>…	… <Object Name="Room"/> <Object Name="X-Box Humidity Sensors"/> <Predicate id="lexon1"> <Object_Role ID="lexon1_forward" Object="Room" Role="has"/> <Object_Role ID="lexon1_backward" Object="X-Box Humidity Sensors" Role="is of"/> </Predicate> <Constraint> <CardinalityConstraint cardinalityConstraintType="RoleCardinality" Object_Role="lexon1_forward" cardinalityValue="<=2"></CardinalityConstraint> </Constraint>…

Fig. 3. Commitment 2 from Table 4 in RDFs/OWL and SDRule-ML

```
…
<Object CI="SmartHome" Name="X-Box Humidity Sensors" type="NOLOT"/>
…
<Constraint>
 <CardinalityConstraint cardinalityConstraintType="ObjectCardinality" Object="X-Box Humidity
Sensors" cardinalityValue="&lt;=3"></CardinalityConstraint>
</Constraint>
…
```

Fig. 4. An example of object cardinality constraint in SDRule-ML

We store the commitment "AT MOST 3 X-Box Humidity Sensors ARE ALLOWED IN ANY CASES" in SDRule-ML as illustrated in Fig. 4.

In the following two subsections, we will discuss two specific cases of frequency. They are the constraints of mandatory and uniqueness.

3.3 Mandatory

A lexon role can be *mandatory* or *optional*. A mandatory is mandatory iff it is played by every member of the population of its connected object type, otherwise, it is optional ([2], p. 162). A mandatory constraint is equivalent to an "AT LEAST ONE" frequency constraint.

Suppose we have a commitment that contains a uniqueness constraint, which is "EACH Room has AT MOST ONE X-Box Humidity Sensor". If we apply this commitment to Table 4, then column 8 is invalid.

The discussed example illustrates how a mandatory constraint can be used when the condition stubs represent value members of an object type and their entries are Boolean values.

Table 5 is another SDT example, which uses a mandatory constraint when an object type is a condition stub and its value members are used as its condition entries.

Table 5. An SDT on deciding whether or not to turn on Actuator x based on the availability of X-Box Humidity Sensors (diverted from Table 4)

Condition	1	2	3
X-Box Humidity Sensor	{X-Box557, X-Box120}	{X-Box557, MS Xbox360}	N/A
Action			
Actuator x	*		*
	SDT Lexons		
Lexon 1	$\langle Room, has, is\ of, X - Box\ Humidity\ Sensor\rangle$		
Lexon 2	$\langle X - Box\ Humidity\ Sensor, has\ value\ type, is\ value\ type\ of, Set\rangle$		
Lexon 3	$\langle N/A, is, is, EMPTY\ SET\ \rangle$		
	SDT Commitments		
Commitment 1	VALUE of X-Box Humidity Sensor is {X-Box557, X-Box120, MS Xbox360}.		
Commitment 2	EACH Room has AT LEAST ONE X-Box Humidity Sensor		

Given a concept C, which is a set and is represented by a lexon term t.We say the SDT contains invalid decision rules if the below conditions are met:

- The near role of t is a mandatory role
- t is a condition stub
- A decision column contains a condition $\langle t, \emptyset\rangle$ where $\emptyset$ denotes an empty set, and this column contains an action

In the example illustrated in Table 5, $\emptyset$ is mapped to N/A using lexon 3 (see Table 5). Accordingly, column 3 in Table 5 is invalid.

Note that we can use the following combinations for a mandatory constraint:

- Combination one: condition stubs represent value members of an object type and their entries are Boolean values
- Combination two: an object type is a condition stub and its value members are used as its condition entries

But we should try to avoid combination two (see above) for a normal role cardinality constraint. It is because the members in a set, by default, have a relationship of "or" instead of "and". Let us look at one example, if we want to apply the commitment "EACH Room has AT LEAST 2 X-Box Humidity Sensors" on Table 5, the validity of column 1 can not be checked because this condition implies the following three situations:

- Room has X-Box557 but not X-Box120
- Room has X-Box120 but not X-Box557
- Room has X-Box557 and X-Box120

Among these situations, only the last one is valid.

RDFs/OWL uses cardinality to deal with the mandatory constraint. SDRule-ML provides two possibilities to deal with the mandatory constraint: one way is to use a frequency constraint and the other is to use a mandatory constraint specified in its XML schema. Fig. 5 shows how commitment 2 from Table 5 is stored in RDFs/OWL and SDRule-ML using its specific mandatory constraint specification.

RDFs/OWL	SDRule-ML
...<owl:ObjectProperty rdf:about="#has_X- Box_Humidity_Sensors"> <rdfs:subPropertyOf rdf:resource="#has"/> <rdfs:range> <owl:Restriction> <owl:onProperty rdf:resource="#has_X- Box_Humidity_Sensors"/> <owl:onClass rdf:resource="#XBox_Humidity_Sensor"/> <owl:minQualifiedCardinality rdf:datatype="&xsd;nonNegativeInteger">1 </owl:minQualifiedCardinality> </owl:Restriction> </rdfs:range> <rdfs:domain> <owl:Restriction> <owl:onProperty rdf:resource="#has_X- Box_Humidity_Sensors"/> <owl:allValuesFrom rdf:resource="#Room"/> ...	... <Object>Room</Object> <Object>X-Box Humidity Sensor</Object> <Predicate id="Lexon1"> <Object_Role ID="Lexon1_forward" Object="Room" Role="has"/> <Object_Role ID="Lexon1_backward" Object="X- Box Humidity Sensor" Role="is of"/> </Predicate> <Constraint><MandatoryConstraint Object_Role="Lexon1_forward"></M andatoryConstraint> </Constraint> ...

Fig. 5. Commitment 2 from Table 5 in RDFs/OWL and SDRule-ML

In this subsection, we have discussed the constraint of mandatory, which is a specific case of frequency. In the next subsection, we will illustrate another specific case, which is the constraint of uniqueness.

3.4 Uniqueness

A uniqueness constraint is used when we need to ensure a (co-)role from one lexon or a combination of (co-)roles from several lexons is played at most once.

Situation 1: Given a concept C, a list of condition stub $C_1, C_2, \dots, C_i$ and if the following conditions are met, then we say the table contains invalid columns.

- $C_1, C_2, \dots, C_i$ are the members of C (which we write as $C_1, C_2, \dots, C_i \in C$)
- $C_1, C_2, \dots, C_i$ have the value type of Boolean

- C is represented by the lexon term t_x
- The near role of t_x has a uniqueness constraint
- There are more than one combinations of $\langle C_j, Yes\rangle$, $C_j \in \{C_1, C_2, \dots C_i\}$, in one column and this column contains an action

For example, if we have a uniqueness constraint as "EACH Room has AT MOST ONE X-Box Humidity Sensor" for Table 4. Columns 1, 3 and 5 are then considered invalid.

The above example shows how we can use a uniqueness constraint with Boolean condition entries. In what follows, we will discuss how to verify decision columns when condition entries are sets.

Situation 2: Given two condition stubs S_1 and S_2, which are two sets. A table column is invalid if the following conditions are met.

- $S_1 \cap S_2 \neq \emptyset$ (S_1 is overlapped with S_2)
- S_1 is represented by a lexon term t_1, the near role of which is a unique role
- The condition entry of S_1 is not empty in this column
- The condition entry of S_2 is not empty in this column
- There exists a member s where $s \in S_1$ and s is in the condition entry of S_2 in this column

Table 6. An SDT on deciding whether or not to turn on Actuator x and Actuator y based on the availability of Sensors

Condition	1	2	3	...	n
Humidity Sensor	{X-Box557, X-Box120}	{ MS Xbox360}	{X-Box557, Xbox360}	...	{ MS Xbox360}
Sensor	{EZEYE 1011A}	{EZEYE 1011A}	{X-Box120}	...	{E1, X-Box557}
Action					
Actuator x	*		*		
Actuator y		*	*		*

SDT Lexons	
Lexon 1	$\langle Room, has, is\ of, Humidity\ Sensor\rangle$
Lexon 2	$\langle Humidity\ Sensor, has\ value\ type, is\ value\ type\ of, Set\rangle$
Lexon 3	$\langle Sensor, has\ value\ type, is\ value\ type\ of, Set\rangle$
SDT Commitments	
Commitment 1	VALUE of Humidity Sensor is {X-Box557, X-Box120, MS Xbox360}.
Commitment 2	EACH Room has AT MOST ONE Humidity Sensor
Commitment 3	VALUE of Sensor is { E1, X-Box557, X-Box120, MS Xbox360, EZEYE 1011A}

Table 6 shows an example of situation 2. Columns 3 and n are considered invalid because X-Box120 is a humidity sensor and only one humidity sensor is allowed in one room.

Note that we also need to add exclusiveness for the set members of Humidity Sensor and Sensors in Table 6. Otherwise, column 1 from Table 6 is also invalid because the room can have X-Box557 and X-Box120 (two humidity sensors) at the same time, which is not allowed by commitment 2.

RDFs/OWL	SDRule-ML
…<owl:ObjectProperty rdf:about="#has_Humidity_Sensor"> <rdfs:subPropertyOf rdf:resource="#has"/> <rdfs:range><owl:Restriction> <owl:onProperty rdf:resource="#has_Humidity_Sensor"/> <owl:onClass rdf:resource="#Humidity_Sensor"/> <owl:maxQualifiedCardinality rdf:datatype="&xsd;nonNegativeInteger">1</owl:maxQualifiedC ardinality> </owl:Restriction></rdfs:range><rdfs:domain> <owl:Restriction> <owl:onProperty rdf:resource="#has_Humidity_Sensor"/> <owl:allValuesFrom rdf:resource="#Room"/> </owl:Restriction></rdfs:domain> </owl:ObjectProperty>…	…<Predicate id="Lexon1"> <Object_Role ID="Lexon1_forward" Object="Room" Role="has"/> <Object_Role ID="Lexon1_backward" Object="Humidity Sensor" Role="is of"/> </Predicate> <Constraint><UniquenessConstraint Object_Role="Lexon1_forward"> </Constraint> …

Fig. 6. Commitment 2 from Table 6 in RDFs/OWL and SDRule-ML

Similar to the constraint of mandatory, the uniqueness constraint is stored in RDFs/OWL using the cardinality constraint. In SDRule-ML, it can be stored as a frequency constraint or a uniqueness constraint (see Fig. 6).

3.5 Exclusive-Or

In an information system, an exclusive-or constraint is used to ensure that two sets do not overlap each other. We use it for two situations.

Situation one: we use exclusive-or to check the combination of *conditions.*

Given two concepts C_1 and C_2, which are represented by the lexon terms t_1 and t_2 respectively. Both C_1 and C_2 are condition stubs. If the following conditions are satisfied, then an invalid decision rule will be detected.

- The lexons $\langle \gamma, t_1, r_1, r_1', t_3 \rangle$ and $\langle \gamma, t_2, r_2, r_2', t_3 \rangle$ are in the SDT lexon set
- $r_1' = r_2'$ and the role pair $\langle r_1', r_2' \rangle$ has external exclusive-or relationship
- C_1 and C_2 have the value type of Boolean
- The conditions $\langle C_1, Yes \rangle$ and $\langle C_2, Yes \rangle$ appear in the same column
- There is an activated action in the mentioned column

Situation two: we use exclusive-or to check the combination of *actions.*

Given two concepts C_1 and C_2, which are represented by the lexon terms t_1 and t_2 respectively. C_1 (C_2) is a set that contains one member, which is an action stub. Allow us to indicate these two sets as - $C_1 = \{a_1\}$ and $C_2 = \{a_2\}$ where a_1 and a_2 are two action stubs. If the following conditions are satisfied, then an invalid decision rule will be detected.

- There are two lexons - $\langle \gamma, t_1, is\ a, is, ACTION \rangle$ and $\langle \gamma,\ t_2,\ is\ a,\ is,\ ACTION \rangle$ - in the SDT lexon set
- An action can be either t_1 or t_2, but not both
- The actions $\langle C_1, * \rangle$ and $\langle C_2, * \rangle$ appear in the same column

Table 7 shows an example of the above two situations. Column 1 is invalid because it does not satisfy commitment 1. Column 3 is invalid because it does not satisfy commitment 2.

Fig. 7 shows how to store commitment 1 from Table 7 in RDFs/OWL and SDRule-ML.

Table 7. An SDT on deciding whether or not to turn on Actuator x and Actuator y based on the availability of Humidity Sensor and Light Sensor

Condition	1	2	3	4
Humidity Sensor	Yes	Yes	No	No
Light Sensor	Yes	No	Yes	No
Action				
Actuator x	*		*	
Actuator y			*	
	SDT Lexons			
Lexon 1	$\langle Room, has, is\ of, Humidity\ Sensor\rangle$			
Lexon 2	$\langle Humidity\ Sensor, has\ value\ type, is\ value\ type\ of, Boolean\rangle$			
Lexon 3	$\langle Room, has, is\ of, Light\ Sensor\rangle$			
Lexon 4	$\langle Light\ Sensor, has\ value\ type, is\ value\ type\ of, Boolean\rangle$			
Lexon 5	$\langle X, is\ a, is, ACTION\rangle$			
Lexon 6	$\langle Y, is\ a, is, ACTION\rangle$			
	SDT Commitments			
Commitment 1	EACH Room has EITHER Humidity Sensor OR Light Sensor, BUT NOT BOTH			
Commitment 2	EACH ACTION can EITHER BE X OR Y, BUT NOT BOTH			
Commitment 3	VALUE of X is {Actuator X}			
Commitment4	VALUE of Y is {Actuator Y}			

RDFs/OWL	**SDRule-ML**
… <owl:ObjectProperty rdf:about="#has_Humidity_Sensor"> <rdfs:subPropertyOf rdf:resource="#has"/> <owl:propertyDisjointWith rdf:resource="#has_Light_Sensor"/> … </owl:ObjectProperty> …	…<Predicate id="Lexon1"> <Object_Role ID="Lexon1_forward" Object="Room" Role="has"/> <Object_Role ID="Lexon1_backward" Object="Humidity Sensor" Role="is of"/></Predicate> <Predicate id="Lexon2"><Object_Role ID="Lexon2_forward" Object="Room" Role="has"></Object_Role> <Object_Role ID="Lexon2_backward" Object="Light Sensor" Role="is of"></Object_Role></Predicate> <Constraint><ExclusiveOrConstraint> <Object_Role ID="Lexon1_forward"></Object_Role> <Object_Role ID="Lexon2_forward"></Object_Role> </ExclusiveOrConstraint></Constraint>…

Fig. 7. Commitment 1 from Table 7 in RDFs/OWL and SDRule-ML

3.6 Subtyping

The "is-a" subtype/taxonomical relationship is probably one of the mostly used ontological relations. A subtype is an object type, each of whose instances belong to an encompassing type.

We use subtyping to check the validity of a combination of conditions. Given two concepts C_1 and C_2, which are represented by the lexon terms t_1 and t_2, a decision rule is considered to be invalid when the following conditions are met.

- C_1 and C_2 are two condition stubs
- The condition entries for C_1 and C_2 have the value type of Boolean
- C_1 is a subtype of C_2
- The conditions $\langle C_1, Yes\rangle$ and $\langle C_2, No\rangle$ appear in one column and there is an activated action in this column

Table 8 shows an example of subtyping. As Humidity Sensor is a subtype of Sensor, the condition $\langle Humidity\ Sensor, Yes\rangle$ implies that there is a sensor in the room. Therefore, it is impossible to execute a decision rule, which contains the condition $\langle Sensor, No\rangle$. Accordingly, column 2 is invalid.

Fig. 8 shows how this "is-a" relationship is stored in RDFs/OWL and SDRule-ML.

Table 8. An SDT on deciding whether or not to turn on Actuator x based on the availability of Humidity Sensor and Sensor

Condition	1	2	3	4
Humidity Sensor	Yes	Yes	No	No
Sensor	Yes	No	Yes	No
Action				
Actuator x	*	*	*	
SDT Lexons				
Lexon 1	$\langle Room, has, is\ of, Humidity\ Sensor\rangle$			
Lexon 2	$\langle Room, has, is\ of, Sensor\rangle$			
Lexon 3	$\langle Humidity\ Sensor, has\ value\ type, is\ value\ type\ of, Boolean\rangle$			
Lexon 4	$\langle Sensor, has\ value\ type, is\ value\ type\ of, Boolean\rangle$			
Lexon 5	$\langle Humidity\ Sensor, is\ a, is, Sensor\rangle$			
SDT Commitments				
Commitment 1	Humidity Sensor IS SUBTYPE OF Sensor			

RDFs/OWL	SDRule-ML
<owl:Class rdf:about="#Humidity_Sensor"> <rdfs:subClassOf rdf:resource="#Sensor"/> </owl:Class>	<Object>Sensor</Object> <Object SuperType="Sensor">Humidity Sensor</Object>

Fig. 8. Commitment 1 from Table 8 in RDFs/OWL and SDRule-ML

In this section, we have discussed directly applied ontological constraint for SDT V&V. In the next section, we will illustrate our related work.

4 Related Work

There are a few existing V&V approaches for decision tables. Shwayder [10] proposes to use the Quine-McCluskey method to combine decision columns in a decision table in order to reduce redundancies. Pooch [8] illustrates a survey on decomposition and conversion algorithms of translating decision tables in order to check for redundancy, contradiction and completeness.

Recently, Vanthienen et al. [15] illustrate how to use PROLOGA (a decision table tool) to discover two kinds of tabular anomalies: intra-tabular and inter-tabular anomalies. The intra-tabular anomaly is caused by a cyclic dependence between a condition and an action. The inter-tabular anomaly is caused by redundancy, ambivalence and deficiency. Qian et al. [9] use an approach called approximation reduction to managing incomplete and inconsistent decision tables. Using their approach, incomplete and inconsistent decision tables are reduced into complete and consistent sub tables.

Other related work can be found in [4] [5] [6].

Compared to their work, our approach is focused on using ontological constraints as the meta-rules for V&V. As an ontology is shareable and community-based, the SDT V&V process thus supports group activities in a nature way. Decision modellers and rule auditors share their common view through this process. By doing so, misunderstanding is minimized and the cost of V&V is consequently reduced.

5 Discussion, Conclusion and Future Work

As an extension to decision tables, SDT provide extra advantages while using it for V&V:

- It supports multiple decision modellers (also called "decision group") to create, validate and verify a decision table.
- It contains semantically rich meta-rules for its self-organization.
- Its analysis functions take advantages of modern ontology engineering technologies, such as the formality, shareability, interoperability and community-based.

It is important to ensure the correctness of SDTs; especially a community of decision modellers is involved. This problem belongs to V&V for decision making systems.

In this paper, we have discussed SDT V&V issues concerning ontology-based consistency checking. We identify the constraints of value, uniqueness, mandatory, cardinality and frequency, exclusive-or and subtyping as the ones that can be directly applied. The graphical notations of the discussed constraints for the examples that are illustrated in this paper can be found in [11].

The SDT creation method used in this paper is to create an ontology that stores the meta-rules for V&V. This creation phase can be replaced by importing existing ontologies, which requires an extra effort during the annotation process.

We have designed an SDT rule engine for checking the validity of decision columns in an SDT. We are still working on the implementation. We are currently busy with the implementation of the mapping between SDT commitments, RDFs/OWL and SDRule-ML. In the future, we will study how to use combined ontological constraints for SDT V&V.

Acknowledgments. The work has been supported by the EU ITEA-2 Project 2008005 "Do-it-Yourself Smart Experiences", founded by IWT 459.

References

[1] CSA: Z243.1-1970 for Decision Tables, Canadian Standards Association (1970)

[2] Halpin, T., Morgan, T.: Information Modeling and Relational Databases, 2nd edn. The Morgan Kaufmann Series in Data Management Systems. Morgan Kaufmann (March 17, 2008) ISBN-10: 0123735688, ISBN-13: 978-0123735683

[3] Henry Beitz, E., Buck, N.H., Jorgensen, P.C., Larson, L., Maes, R., Marselos, N.L., Muntz, C., Rabin, J., Reinwald, L.T., Verhelst, M.: A modern appraisal of decision tables, a Codasyl report. ACM, New York (1982)
[4] Hewett, R., Leuchner, J.: Restructuring decision tables for elucidation of knowledge. Data & Knowledge Engineering 46(3), 271–290 (2003)
[5] Ibramsha, M., Rajaraman, V.: Detection of logical errors in decision table programs. Communications of the ACM 21(12) (December 1978)
[6] Lew, A.: Optimal conversion of extended-entry decision tables with general cost criteria. Communications of the ACM 21(4) (April 1978)
[7] Murrell, S.T., Plant, R.: A survey of tools for the validation and verification of knowledge-based systems: 1985-1995. Journal of DS Sys. 21(4), 307–323 (1997)
[8] Pooch, U.W.: Translation of Decision Tables. Journal of ACM Computing Surveys (CSUR) Surveys 6(2) (June 1974)
[9] Qian, Y., Liang, J., Li, D., Wang, F., Ma, N.: Approximation reduction in inconsistent incomplete decision tables. Knowledge-Based Systems 23(5) (2010)
[10] Shwayder, K.: Combining decision rules in a decision table. Communications of the ACM 18(8) (August 1975)
[11] Tang, Y.: Directly Applied ORM Constraints for Validating and Verifying Semantic Decision Tables. In: Proc. of OTM 2011 (upcoming, 2011)
[12] Tang, Y., Meersman, R.: Towards Building Semantic Decision Tables with Domain Ontologies. In: Chan, M.C., et al. (eds.) Challenges in Information Technology Management. World Scientific (2008) ISBN 978-981-281-906-2, 981-281-906-1
[13] Tang, Y., Meersman, R.: SDRule Markup Language: Towards Modeling and Interchanging Ontological Commitments for Semantic Decision Making. In: Handbook of Research on Emerging Rule-Based Languages and Technologies: Open Solutions and Approaches. IGI Publishing, USA (2009) ISBN: 1-60566-402-2
[14] Tang, Y., Debruyne, C., Criel, J.: Onto-DIY: A Flexible and Idea Inspiring Ontology-based Do-It-Yourself Architecture for Managing Data Semantics and Semantic Data. In: Meersman, R., Dillon, T., Herrero, P. (eds.) OTM 2010. LNCS, vol. 6427, pp. 1036–1043. Springer, Heidelberg (2010)
[15] Vanthienen, J., Mues, C., Aerts, A.: An Illustration of Verification and Validation in the Modeling Phase of KBS development. Journal of Data & Knowledge Engineering 27(3), 337–352 (1998)

Representing and Solving Rule-Based Decision Models with Constraint Solvers

Jacob Feldman

OpenRules, Inc., 75 Chatsworth Ct.,
Edison, NJ 08820, USA
jacobfeldman@openrules.com

Abstract. This paper describes how constraint solvers could serve as rule engines in the context of modern business decision management systems. Decision models are based on rule families oriented to business users and frequently represented as Excel decision tables. The proposed approach uses exactly the same representation of decision models as a rule engine. The developed Rule Solver loads a decision model from multiple Excel files, generates a constraint satisfaction problem, and then validates it for consistency, diagnosing possible conflicts. Finally, it solves the problem, delivering results using the same terms as business rules. In fact, a user may switch between a rule engine and a constraint solver without changing the rules themselves. Additionally, Rule Solver can find solutions or find an optimal decision when business rules only partially define a problem. Rule Solver is implemented as an advanced component of the popular open source business decision management system "OpenRules".

Keywords: Decision Model, Rule Family, Constraint Satisfaction, Rule Engine, Constraint Solver.

1 Introduction

In recent years, decision management services have become key components of real-world business applications in banking, insurance, healthcare, telecommunication, advertising, and many other industries. They are frequently based on predictive analytics, business rules management, complex event processing, optimization, and other business intelligence technologies. According to IDC [1] the decision management software market is expected to exceed $10B by 2014 – doubling in the five years from 2009. Business rules management systems (BRMS) and rule engines are already "must-have" components for decision management. At the same time, constraint programming (CP) has been successfully used for years to find optimal solutions for complex industrial problems. However, it is only now CP is starting to penetrate the world of business decision support applications. In this paper, we show how existing CP solvers can be effectively used as an execution mechanism for complex decision models.

F. Olken et al. (Eds.): RuleML 2011 - America, LNCS 7018, pp. 208–221, 2011.

There are two major implementations of rule engines available on the market today:

1) Inferential rule engines that support a pure declarative representation of business rules;
2) Sequential rule engines that rely on user-defined sequencing of rules and rule families.

The famous Rete algorithm was invented by Charles Forgy almost 40 years ago [2] and it still remains the major foundation for most implementations of inferential rule engines [4], [5], [6], [7]. Sequential rule engines are used by many commercial and open source engines ([20], [21], [8], [9]), which recognized that in many practical applications manual rules sequencing is a preferred mode. Even vendors of the major Rete-based rule engines added special sequential modes to more effectively compete with their sequential counter-parts. However, the newest decision management methodologies ([3], [22]) without insisting on any particular rule engine implementation, require that there should be no rules ordering within rule sets, and between rule sets. These declarative principles simply cannot be supported by sequential rule engines which makes Rete again the dominating implementation approach.

Over the years, Rete went through many enhancements, but until now there were no practical alternatives to Rete for implementation of non-sequential rule engines in the business rules world. At the same time, Prolog-based tools and different constraint solvers (see the list of products in [23]) have been successfully used for years to resolve complex optimization problems defined in terms of rules and constraints. However, these tools usually require a deep understanding of the underlying technologies, and are mainly oriented to software developers, not to subject matter experts. This fact limits the real-world acceptance of these technologies. Making these tools available to business users through their favorite interfaces such as Excel-based decision tables and/or different BRMS rule editors, can bring constraint-based technologies to the practical decision management world.

In this paper we propose a new, constraint-based approach to the implementation of inferential rule engines that can execute rule-based decision models [3]. The proposed approach is functionally similar to Rete-based rule engines in its support of declarative principles for business rules organization. On the one hand, it allows a user to execute decision models using exactly the same business rules without any additional coding. On the other hand, it does not require explicit sequencing of rules inside a rule family or a strict execution order of related rules families. For every input dataset, a constraint-based rule engine executes all related business rules and either infers a decision or diagnoses conflicts among rules and input data. Additionally, it can find solutions when business rules only partially define a problem. When an optimization objective is defined by the rules, it also can find an optimal decision instead of forcing a user to specify enormous amount of rules to compare different decisions. The proposed approach is implemented as a component of the open source business decision management system "OpenRules" [8], in which it is called "Rule Solver". We will use this name throughout this paper when referring to the proposed approach and its implementation.

2 The Decision Model

Rule Solver does not deal with any particular rule language, but rather executes rule-based decision models created by business users in accordance with the methodological approach known as "The Decision Model" [3]. The Decision Model was introduced two years ago by Barbara von Halle and Larry Goldberg and quickly gained popularity as a practical methodology for developing Business Decision Management Systems (BDMS) for large financial services, insurance, health care, and other industries. According to the authors, "The decision model is a representation of fact-based business logic within a scope of a single business decision". Examples of such decisions are "Determine Loan Eligibility", "Define Insurance Premium" or "Determine Medical Treatment". The Decision Model is oriented to subject matter experts (business analysts who are not software developers) providing them with a strictly defined notation, as well as concepts and principles that they should follow to build maintainable decision support systems. The Decision Model is defined as technology agnostic, meaning that different BRMS products may provide different implementations of the same decision models.

The Decision Model is defined in [3] as "an intelligent template for perceiving, organizing, and managing business logic behind a business decision (specifically, a representation of business logic statements that together lead to a single business decision, and which complies with the 15 Decision Model principles)". The rigor of the Decision Model is embodied in these 15 principles that are divided into structural, declarative, and integrity principles. In particular, they specify how to organize and to connect Rule Families.

2.1 Rule Families

Rule Families are the heart of the Decision Model and they are defined as traditional decision tables but with certain limitations. A Rule Family is a decision table that consists of 0 or more conditions and only one conclusion. If there is more than one condition, then all of them are connected by the logical operator "AND". Examples of Rule Families are shown in Figures 1 and 2.

RuleFamily PersonLikelihoodOfDefaultingOnLoan									
Condition		Condition		Condition		Condition		Conclusion	
Person Employment History		Person Mortgage Situation		Person Miscellaneous Loans Assessment		Person Outside Credit Score		Person Likelihood of Defaulting on a Loan	
Is	Poor	Is	Poor	Is	Medium			Is	High
Is	Good					>=	650	Is	Low
Is	Poor	Is	Poor	Is	Low	>=	650	Is	Medium
						<	650	Is	High

Fig. 1. Rule Family "PersonLikelihoodOfDefaultingOnLoan"

This Rule Family consists of four AND'ed condition columns and a single conclusion column. Each column is associated with one fact type (e.g. "Person Employment History"). Multiple rows (rules) specify the fact using an operator (e.g."<=" or "Is") and a value (e.g. "Poor").

RuleFamily PersonEmploymentHistory					
Condition		Condition		Conclusion	
Person Years at Current Employer		Person Number of Jobs in Past Five Years		Person Employment History	
<	1	>	5	Is	Poor
<	1	<=	5	Is	Average
Within	[1;2]	>	5	Is	Poor
Within	[1;2]	<=	5	Is	Average
>	2	<=	4	Is	Good
>	2	Within	(4;6]	Is	Average
>	2	>	6	Is	Poor

Fig. 2. Rule Family "PersonEmploymentHistory"

Conditions and conclusions may use different business fact types shared by different Rule Families. The fact types used in conditions of one Rule Family may be defined by conclusions of other Rule Families. For example, Figure 2 shows a Rule Family that specifies the value for the fact "Person Employment History" used by the dependent Rule Family in Figure 1. This is an example of so called "inferential relationships". According to the "Declarative Inferential Relationship" principle [3], there should be no implied sequence in the path among Rule Families related through such inferential relationships.

The Decision Model includes other important principles that support the integrity of Rule Families, among which are some that are especially important for automatic execution of the Decision Model.

The "Declarative Body" principle states that "the entries in the body of a Rule Family are unordered" [3]. In particular, it means that a user may insert new rules into a Rule Family without worrying about any particular order. This principle imposes very strong requirements not only upon the rule engine that will execute the Decision Model, but also on the designer of Rule Families. It excludes the (sometimes very convenient) ability override rules and forces a Rule Family author to consider almost all possible combinations among condition values.

The "Rule Family Consistency" principle states that "a Rule Family should be free of inconsistencies such as overlapping conditions or more than one conclusion" [3]. The conditions need to cover only a subset of the fact type's domains that are within scope of a Rule Family. At the same time, a Rule Family must result in at least one conclusion value for any set of valid input values for condition fact types.

2.2 Business Glossary

Fact types used by all Rule Families are collected in one special table called the "Business Glossary". Usually a glossary defines the following information about fact types:

- Business names of the fact types defined exactly in the same way they are used in Rule Families;
- Business Concepts to which these fact types belong;
- Domains with all possible values of the fact types;
- Technical names of fact types for integration of the Decision Models with actual business object models used by programmers.

Figure 3 shows an example of the business glossary for rule families presented in Figures 1 and 2.

Glossary glossary			
Fact Type	**Business Concept**	**Business Concept Attribute**	**Domain**
Person Employment History	Person	employmentHistory	Good,Average,Poor,Undefined
Person Likelihood of Defaulting on a Loan		likelihoodOfDefaulting	High,Medium,Low,Undefined
Person Mortgage Situation		mortgageSituation	Good,Average,Poor,Undefined
Person Miscellaneous Loans Assessment		miscLoansAssessment	High,Medium,Low,Undefined
Person Outside Credit Score		outsideCreditScore	0-999
Person Years at Current Employer		yearsAtCurrentEmployer	0-50
Person Number of Jobs in Past Five Years		numberOfJobsInPastFiveYears	0-20

Fig. 3. Example of a Business Glossary

2.3 Top-Down Design

The Decision Model promotes a top-down design approach that starts with a top-level decision which can be described through sub-decisions and their associated Rule Families. For the above examples of Rule Families, the proper Decision table is presented in Figure 4.

Decision DetermineLikelihoodOfDefaultingOnLoan	
Decisions	**Execute Rule Families**
Define Person Employment History	:= PersonEmploymentHistory()
Define Person Likelihood Of Defaulting On Loan	:= PersonLikelihoodOfDefaultingOnLoan()

Fig. 4. The Decision Model "DetermineLikelihoodOfDefaultingOnLoan"

The Decision Model can be considered as a hierarchy of decisions presented in a graphical form [3] or a tabular form [8]. For example, using the table of the type "Decision" we may present a top-level decision and its sub-decisions in Excel tables similar to the ones on Figure 5.

Decision DecisionMain	
Decisions	Execute
Define Fact 1	:= RuleFamilyFact1()
Define Fact 2	:= RuleFamilyFact21()
Define Fact 2	:= RuleFamilyFact22()
Define Fact 3	:= DecisionFact3()
Define Fact 4	:= RuleFamilyFact4()

Decision DecisionFact3	
Decisions	Execute
Define Fact 3.1	:= RuleFamilyFact31()
Define Fact 3.2	:= RuleFamilyFact32()
Define Fact 3.3	:= RuleFamilyFact33()

Fig. 5. Decisions and Sub-Decisions

The first table specifies a top-level decision using 5 sub-decisions and Rule Families that implement their business logic. For instance, the decision "Define Fact 2" is defined by two Rule Families "RuleFamilyFact21" and "RuleFamilyFact22". At the same time, the decision "Define Fact 3" is defined using a separate decision table "DecisionFact3".

According to the Decision Model [3], there should be no inferential dependencies among inferentially related Rule Families. Correspondingly, the order of fact definitions inside the above decision tables should not matter during the execution of these models.

The decision can be also defined through other decisions using different conditions. For example, Figure 6 demonstrates a situation when the first sub-decision validates your data and the second sub-decision executes complex calculations but only if the data validation was successful.

Decision Apply1040EZ			
Condition		ActionPrint	ActionExecute
1040EZ Eligible		Decisions	Execute
		Validate	:= ValidateTaxReturn(decision)
Is	TRUE	Calculate	:= DetermineTaxReturn(decision)
Is	FALSE	Do Not Calculate	

Fig. 6. Conditional Sub-Decisions

2.4 Test Cases and Real Data

The test cases like Rule Families and all other components of the Decision Model can be defined by business people directly in Excel. Figure 7 shows an Excel table that defines a data type for the business concept "Person" (defined in the glossary in Figure 3 above.)

Datatype Person	
String	fullName
String	SSN
String	employmentHistory
String	mortgageSituation
String	miscLoansAssessment
boolean	additionalDebtResearchNeeded
String	likelihoodOfDefaulting
int	outsideCreditScore
int	yearsAtCurrentEmployer
int	numberOfJobsInPastFiveYears

Fig. 7. An example of a Datatype table used for Decision Model testing

Instead of an Excel-based data type, we may use a regular Java class Person that is defined as a Java bean by the Java application in which this Decision Model is going to be incorporated. Figure 8 shows an Excel table that contains concrete test instances of type Person called "borrowers".

Data Person borrowers									
Full Name	SSN	Employment History	Mortgage Situation	Misc Loans Assessment	Additional Debt Research Needed	Outside Credit Score	Years At Current Employer	Number Of Jobs In Past Five Years	Likelihood Of Defaulting
Peter N. Johnson	111-22-3333	Poor	Poor	Low	No	640	3	4	Undefined
Mary K. Brown	444-55-6666	Poor	Average	Low	Yes	520	1	5	Undefined

Fig. 8. An example of a Data table with test instances

When the Decision Model is integrated with a Java or .NET application, actual data instances can be used by the same Decision Model without any changes in the business logic.

The described components of the Decision Model "DefinePersonLikelihoodOf DefaultingOnLoan" are sufficient for Rule Solver to either execute this model inferring a correct decision or to inform a user about possible inconsistencies.

3 Constraint-Based Implementation

Formally, the Decision Model can be described as follows:

- There is a set of business objects $X = \{ X_1, \ldots, X_n \}$
- Each business object X_i has fact types $F_i = \{ f_1, \ldots, f_m \}$ with possible values $D_j = \{ v_{j1}, \ldots, v_{jk} \}$ for each property f_j
- There is a set of rules $R = \{ R_1, \ldots, R_r \}$, where a rule R_k defines relationships between different fact types by specifying the allowed combinations for all fact types in that rule.

The rules from set R are grouped into Rule Families that are organized in accordance with the Decision Model principles. Execution of the Decision Model should cause the assignment of values to all fact types that satisfy the rules.

This representation demonstrates that the Decision Model is quite similar to a typical constraint satisfaction problem (CSP) where fact types F_i correspond to constrained variables with known domains D_j and where rules R_k correspond to conditional constraints.

Thus, to use a constraint solver as a rule engine that is capable of executing a decision model compliant with The Decision Model principles, we need a tool that can do the following:

- read the decision model created by business analysts directly from the rule repository (i.e. from a set of Excel files) without requiring the manual transfer of the model into any CP language
- generate a CSP that corresponds to this decision model
- validate the consistency of the model by checking the consistency of the generated CSP and point to possible conflicts using the business terms of the initial decision model
- execute the decision model against concrete data using the following steps:
  - instantiating all constrained variables for which input data is defined
  - posting all constraints that correspond to rules from all Rule Families
  - if constraint propagation by itself does not find single values for all fact types (does not instantiate all constrained variables), then run a constraint solver's search strategy that finds one or more solutions.

OpenRules Rule Solver provides the described functionality by downloading all decision model tables directly from Excel files and then automatically generating and solving a corresponding constraint satisfaction problem. Rule Solver is based on the standard Java Constraint Programming API defined by the Java Specification Request (JSR) 331 [19]. The use of the JSR 331 allows a user to not commit to a particular CP vendor and to try different underlying solvers before choosing the most suitable one based on its technical and business applicability. A user may switch between different underlying CP solvers compliant with the JSR 331 without any changes in the code. Below we will use a simple example to describe how Rule Solver works.

3.1 Fact Types as Constrained Variables

First, Rule Solver creates a CSP instance using the class RuleSolver inherited from the JSR 331 class Problem:

```
RuleSolver rs = new RuleSolver();
```

Then it iterates through the glossary and for each fact type it creates a constrained variable of one of the following types:

- Var for integer constrained variables
- VarBool for Boolean constrained variables
- VarReal for real constrained variables
- VarString for string constrained variables.

Rule Solver automatically converts fact type domains from the glossary, to the domains of the constrained variables as they are specified by JSR 331. While the glossary does not specify a particular type of the fact types, the concrete types of variables are defined based on the provided data instances. For example, a constrained variable that corresponds to the fact type "Person Outside Credit Score" will be created using the following JSR 331 method:

```
rs.variable("Person Outside Credit Score", 0, 999);
```

The Decision Model may use aggregated fact types, for example arrays of strings. Consider the Rule Family in Figure 9 that specifies up-selling rules.

RuleFamily DefineUpSellProducts							
Condition		Condition		Condition		Conclusion	
Customer Profile		Customer Products		Customer Products		Offered Products	
Is One Of	New,Bronze,Silver	Include	Checking Account	Do Not Include	Saving Account	Are	Saving Account, Debit/ATM Card, Web Banking
Is One Of	New,Bronze,Silver	Include	Checking Account, Overdraft Protection	Do Not Include	CD with 25 basis point increase, Money Market Mutual Fund, Credit Card	Are	CD with 25 basis point increase, Money Market Mutual Fund, Credit Card
Is One Of	New,Bronze,Silver	Include	Checking Account, Saving Account	Do Not Include	CD with 25 basis point increase, Money Market Mutual Fund, Credit Card	Are	CD with 50 basis point increase, Money Market Mutual Fund, Credit Card, Debit/ATM Card, Web Banking
Is One Of	Gold	Include	Checking Account	Do Not Include	CD with 25 basis point increase, Money Market Mutual Fund, Web Banking	Are	CD with 50 basis point increase, Money Market Mutual Fund, Credit Card, Debit/ATM Card, Web Banking, Brokerage Account
Is One Of	Platinum	Include	Checking Account, Saving Account	Do Not Include	CD with 25 basis point increase, Money Market Mutual Fund, Web Banking	Are	CD with 50 basis point increase, Money Market Mutual Fund, Credit Card with no annual fee, Debit/ATM Card, Web Banking with no charge, Brokerage Account

Fig. 9. An example of a Rule Family with aggregated fact types

Here the fact type "Customer Products" is an array of strings that represents banking products that a customer already has. The fact type "Offered Products" represents additional products a bank is ready to offer to a customer based on the customer's profile and the set of existing products. Rule Solver represents such fact types using constrained set variables (the JSR 331 standard type VarSet) and posts the proper constraints defined on these set variables.

3.2 Rules as Conditional Constraints

While processing the Decision Model tables and related Rule Families, Rule Solver creates conditional constraints in the form:

```
conditionConstraints.implies(conclusionConstraint)
```

where "conditionConstraints" are accumulated by using the method "and" defined for the JSR-331 class Constraint. For example, the rule

```
IF Person Years at Current Employer < 1
AND Person Number of Jobs in Past Five Years > 5
THEN Person Employment History = Poor
```

may be implemented in Java using the JSR-331 interface:

```
Var var1 = rs.getVar("Person Years at Current Employer");
Constraint c1 = rs.linear(var1, "<", 1);

Var var2 = rs.getVar("Person Number of Jobs in Past Five Years");
Constraint c2 = rs.linear(var2, ">", 5);

Constraint conditionConstraints = c1.and(c2);

VarString var3 = rs.getVarString("Person Employment History");
Constraint conclusionConstraint = rs.linear(var3, "=", "Poor");

rs.add(conditionConstraints.implies(conclusionConstraint));
```

However, Rule Solver never generates Java or any other code. Instead, at run-time, it simply creates an instance of different JSR 331 classes and adds them to the already created constraint satisfaction problem (an instance of the class "RuleSolver"). All instances of constrained variables and constraints are added to the problem "on the fly". How does Rule Solver actually generate this CSP? It does not use any special code parser and/or generator. Instead, it effectively relies on the existing OpenRules's templatization mechanism.

OpenRules uses different rule templates to implement all tables included into the default (not constraint-based) implementation of the Decision Model. Such tables as "Decision", "RuleFamily", and "Glossary" are actually implemented based on rule templates defined in several configuration Excel files. For example, the file "RuleFamilyExecuteTemplates.xls" contains a template with the fixed name "RuleFamilyTemplate" and all Rule Families are created based on it. This template is a regular OpenRules "single-hit" rules table. It means that it is trying to execute rules in top-down order by evaluating their conditions. When all conditions inside a rule are evaluated as TRUE, the rule's conclusion (and possibly other related actions) will be executed and all remaining rules will be ignored.

Rule Solver provides another configuration file “RuleFamilySolveTemplates.xls” that substitutes the template “RuleFamilyTemplate” with a different implementation that is actually a special “multi-hit” rules table. This rule table executes all rules inside every Rule Family. However, instead of evaluating rule conditions it simply creates new constraints similar to `c1` and `c2` above, and then “AND”s all previously defined conditions similarly to `c1.and(c2)`. Thus, all conditions from one rule will form a constraint `conditionConstraints` described in the previous example. Then the conclusion will be converted to the `conclusionConstraint` that is based on the constrained variable associated with the conclusion’s fact type, operator, and value. Finally, Rule Solver creates a new constraint `conditionConstraints.`**`implies`** `(conclusionConstraint)` and adds it to the problem. According to the JSR 331, this constraint states that if the constraint `conditionConstraints` is satisfied then the constraint `conclusionConstraint` also should be satisfied.

While the “RuleFamilyTemplate” may contain more complicated constructions, the very fact that the generated CSP can be reconfigured by simply changing the template directly in Excel, makes this approach extremely flexible, extensible, and customizable for different needs.

3.3 Consistency Validation

Rule Solver provides a user (a business analyst who creates and maintains the rules within the Decision Model) with several consistency validation modes.

Mode 1. Validate rules consistency. In this mode, Rule Solver simply posts all already added constraints one-by-one with constraint propagation turned on. If a constraint fails to be posted, a user will be notified that the associated rule is in conflict with the rules, for which the corresponding constraints were previously posted.

Mode 2. Validate rules consistency using test data. In this mode, before posting any constraints, Rule Solver is trying to instantiate constrained variables, for which the proper test data is defined. If an error occurs, the user will be informed about invalid data. If there are no errors in the data, then Rule Solver will try to post all automatically defined constraints for all involved Rule Families. The constraints again will be posted one-by-one with constraint propagation on. If a constraint fails to be posted, the user will be notified that the associated rule is in conflict with previously posted constraints (rules). To help a user find the reason for the conflict, Rule Solver will display the current state of all instantiated (or only partially instantiated) variables corresponding to the fact types.

Mode 3. Validate rules completeness. If the previous modes do not produce errors, Rule Solver validates whether the Rule Family consistency principle has been satisfied. This principle states that “a Rule Family must result in at least one conclusion value for any set of valid input values.” So, Rule Solver determines whether all constrained variables have been instantiated for all conclusion fact types. If all Rule Families have been fully defined in accordance with the Decision Model principles, constraint propagation will be sufficient to determine a decision.

In real-world decision management environments, not all Rule Families are created at the same time, and as a result, the Decision Models frequently can be found to be incomplete, but still producing satisfactory results on the data that have been used. However, a user may not even know about potential problems with such decision models. In this case Rule Solver provides a user with a list of fact types that remain undefined. These fact types are displayed with all remaining possible values from their domains that may have been reduced. This information prompts a user to identify which rules should be extended to cover the remaining situations.

It is important to emphasize that Rule Solver validates consistency of not only one Rule Family but of all Rule Families included in the Decision Model and related through inferential relationships! Otherwise, it may be extremely difficult for the author of the rules to predict how adding or modifying a single rule in one Rule Family may affect the execution logic of dependent Rule Families. There could be hundreds and even thousands of Rule Families in real-world decision support applications, and it would be humanly impossible to maintain their consistency relying only on test cases. Rule Solver helps business users to keep their entire Decision Models in a consistent state.

3.4 Finding Solutions for Partially Defined Decision Models

In some practical situations a creator of a decision model cannot strictly specify all possible combinations of values for all conditions. Instead, users frequently cover only a subset that according to the Decision Model is "within scope" [3]. Unfortunately, this means that such incomplete Decision Models will not produce any decision for certain data sets. Rule Solver helps a user to deal with this problem by simply executing the default search strategy after all data and rule constraints have been posted. Rule Solver offers a user the following options:

- find a single solution that satisfies all currently specified rules (constraints);
- find several solutions by specifying a limit for the maximal number of solutions or by limiting the amount of time during which solutions may be calculated;
- find a solution that minimizes (or maximizes) an optimization criteria defined by a user as an expression of the existing fact types.

In this manner, Rule Solver goes well beyond traditional inference rule engines by empowering business users with a new functionality without forcing them to specify rules for all possible situations.

4 Related Work and Future Development

The integrated use of business rules and constraint programming has been described in several works [12], [13], [15], [16]. In most cases, business rules are used to define a specific business problem and then CP is used to solve the problem. The early versions of Rule Solver [8] offered generic rule templates that allowed a user to directly use CP concepts represented through business rules. The closest approach to the one described in this paper was proposed in [14] where an automatically generated

CSP was used to validate the consistency of a stand-alone classification rules table. However, that previous approach did not validate the consistency of multiple decision tables and, more importantly, was not able to execute the rules. To the best of our knowledge there were no known software products that use a constraint solver as a truly declarative (not sequential) rule engine.

With the Decision Model gaining in popularity as a decision management methodology, several vendors extended their product offerings to enable the creation and management of decision models in accordance with [3]. Such products as SAPIENS [9], interGREAT [10], and RuleGuide [11] provide powerful graphical interfaces for the creation and validation of decision models and OpenRules 6.0.1 [8] released in March 2011 became the first business rules product that allows business users to define and execute their decision models.

The approach described in this paper has been implemented as an advanced Rule Solver component of the OpenRules BDMS [8]. It allows a user to check if custom decision models are compliant with the Decision Model principles [3]. In cases when these principles have been violated, Rule Solver shows a user how to improve their models. In addition to traditional rule engine functionality, Rule Solver can deal with practical situations where a custom decision model does not cover all possible combinations of fact types. Instead of simply failing to find a decision, Rule Solver can offer a user either a feasible or an optimal solution.

The proposed approach has not yet been tested on large industrial problems. It was also not possible to do a performance comparison with Rete-based rule engines since there are still no available Rete engines that implement The Decision Model. However, the automatically generated CSPs are simple from the CP perspective, they are highly constrained and do not require an optimal search for many practical situations. When we conducted performance tests using relatively small rule sets and the default search strategies of several open source CP solvers, the high performance results came as no surprise. CP solvers have proven records of solving much more complex constraint satisfaction problems to compare with ones that automatically generated from the decision models. However, we plan to conduct further tests using more complex rules with multiple inferential dependencies and data coming from real-world projects.

From a practical perspective, the performance should not be an issue as it is not an issue for most existing rule engines. What is especially important is the fact that the Decision Models can be executed "as is" without any conversion of the original Excel-based rule families (created by business users) and without additional coding. The creators of business rules, who usually have no idea about Rete or any other rule engine algorithm, do not have to know anything about CP either. They may continue to use only business terms to define their business logic and the system will communicate with them in the same terms. As a result, business users can test and maintain their decision models themselves without help from software developers. The same decision model can be used with Rule Solver to validate its consistency, but then a user may switch back to a conventional rule engine to execute the model.

OpenRules plans to extend Rule Solver by covering more types of business facts with more operators (and related constraints) defined on these facts. We also plan to add the ability to minimize rule violations in accordance with the approaches described in [17] and [18].

Since Rule Solver's implementation is based on the JSR-331 standard [19], it remains independent of the underlying CP solvers. It also allows any JSR-331 compliant CP solver to use Rule Solver as a front-end for integration with business rules products. At the same time, different BRMS vendors may use the proposed approach to extend their product offerings by adding constraint-based rule engines.

References

1. Worldwide Decision Management Software 2010-2014 Forecast: A Fast-Growing Opportunity to Drive the Intelligent Economy. IDC Report for December 2010 (2010), http://www.idc.com/getdoc.jsp?containerId=226244
2. Forgy, C.: Rete: A fast algorithm for the many pattern/many object pattern match problem. Artificial Intelligence 19, 17–37 (1982)
3. von Halle, B., Goldberg, L.: The Decision Model: A Business Logic Framework Linking Business and Technology. Auerbach Publications/Taylor & Francis Group, LLC (2009)
4. IBM WebSphere ILOG JRules, http://www-01.ibm.com/software/integration/business-rulemanagement/jrules/
5. FICO Blaze Advisor business rules management, http://www.fico.com
6. JESS, the Rule Engine for the Java platform, http://jessrules.com
7. Drools, The Business Logic Integration Platform, http://www.jboss.org/drools
8. OpenRules, Open Source Business Decision Management System, http://openrules.com
9. Sapiens International Corporation N.V, http://www.sapiens.com
10. inteGREAT Enterprise 2010, http://www.edevtech.com/index.html
11. RuleGuide, New Wisdom Software, http://www.newwisdomsoftware.com
12. Bousonville, T., Focacci, F., Le Pape, C., Nuijten, W., Paulin, F., Puget, J.F., Robert, A., Sadeghin, A.: Integration of rules and optimization in plant powerops. In: van Beek, P. (ed.) CP 2005. LNCS, vol. 3709, pp. 1–15. Springer, Heidelberg (2005)
13. Feldman, J., Korolov, A., Meshcheryakov, S., Shor, S.: Hybrid use of rule and constraint engines, Patent no: WO/2003/001322, World Intellectual Property Organization
14. Feldman, J., Korolov, A., Meshcheryakov, S., Shor, S.: Consistency validation for complex classification rules. Patent no: WO/2003/017060, World Intellectual Property Organization
15. Feldman, J., Freuder, E.: Integrating business rules and constraint programming technologies for EDM. In: The 11th International Business Rules Forum (2008)
16. van der Krogt, R., Feldman, J., Little, J., Stynes, D.: An Integrated Business Rules and Constraints Approach to Data Centre Capacity Management. In: Cohen, D. (ed.) CP 2010. LNCS, vol. 6308, pp. 568–582. Springer, Heidelberg (2010)
17. O'Sullivan, B., Feldman, J.: Using hard and soft rules to define and solve optimization problems. In: The 12th International Business Rules Forum (2009)
18. Feldman, J.: Rules Violations and Over-Constrained problems. October Rules Fest (2009)
19. Java Request Specification (JSR) 331: Constraint Programming API. Java Community Process, http://www.jcp.org/en/jsr/detail?id=331
20. Corticon, Business Rules Management System, http://corticon.com
21. Visual Rules, Business Rules Management System, http://visual-rules.com
22. Ross, R.G.: Decision Analysis Using Decision Tables and Business Rules, http://www.brsolutions.com/b_decision.php
23. ACP, Association for Constraint Programming System, http://www.4c.ucc.ie/a4cp

SWRL-Based Context Awareness for Application Servers Hosting Digital Services

Yves-Gaël Billet, Christophe Gravier, and Jacques Fayolle

Université de Lyon, F-42023, Saint-Etienne, France
Université de Saint-Etienne, Jean Monnet, F-42000, Saint-Etienne, France
Télécom Saint-Etienne, école associée de l'Institut Télécom, F-42000, Saint-Etienne, France
LAvoratoire Télécom Claude Chappe (LT2C), F-42000, Saint-Etienne, France
{yves-gael.billet,christophe.gravier,
jacques.fayolle}@telecom-st-etienne.fr

Abstract. As the number of context-aware applications increases in the real world, it can be quite difficult to deploy such applications in traditional application servers, which are context-agnostics systems. To address this challenge, we propose a novel approach for easing the deployment of context-aware applications into application serversContext is encoded within an OWL-driven knowledge base. We couple this knowledge base with SWRL rules to encode context-awareness thresholds. SWRL rules are not predefined in the application server. They are instead embedded inside the application bundle built by the developer, next to the business logic of the application. At the application deployment time, SWRL rules are extracted to the knowledge base in order to monitor the relevant context for the application to be deployed. At runtime, the context of each session of the application is monitored in the knowledge base. When a rule is triggered (a context-awareness threshold is reached), a broker inside the application server notifies the application so that it adapts its behavior by switching to a more relevant modality. We show how our approach eases the work of developers for building context-aware application by using our context-aware framework.

Keywords: Rules, SWRL, Semantic, context-awareness computing, middleware, digital services, application server.

1 Needs for a Semantic CAS

We want to provide context awareness for digital service. The idea is to provide a context-aware framework for software architects in order to implement context awareness in their digital services. These services usually run on Applications Servers (henceforth AS) and are consumed through a network using the client-server paradigm. In this situation, context is composed of information about the network and features of the terminal. Context is session specific since applications are hosted on an AS, context-awareness could be externalized as a framework on them.

The objective is to provide a system that supports sensing, perception and reasoning over context. In this way, software developers could only focus on the

F. Olken et al. (Eds.): RuleML 2011 - America, LNCS 7018, pp. 222–229, 2011.

business logic and adaptation behavior of their application. Behaviors are specific for each application. Software developers must describe and model adaptation behavior for their digital services and communicate it to the context-aware framework.

Semantic Web technologies allow describing context and are comprehensible by both humans and computers and offer a loosely-coupling with the programming language.

Ontologies are used to model domain by describing concepts of the domain and relationships between those concepts [12]. The Web Ontology Language (OWL) was developed to provide a way to represent knowledge understandable by machines using a semantic formalization, in order to facilite computers to interpret human knowledge.

The Semantic Web Rule Language (SWRL) allows us to encode context rules on Horn clauses and designed for OWL. As presented in [13] rules are of the form of an implication between an antecedent (body) and consequent (head). SWRL are logical expression encoded in Conjunctive Normal Forms. It used to classify individuals according conditions. As stated in [14], SPARQL can be used to interrogate an ontology but it is RDF centric so not efficient when using OWL. O'Connor et al. proposes a Semantic Query-enhanced Web Rule Language (SQWRL) based on SWRL.

We propose a semantic context-aware system using OWL, SWRL and SQWRL to describe context and model the adaptation behavior for applications.

2 Related Works

2.1 Context-Awareness

Among the existing context-aware definitions [1-3], we base our definition from [2]. It defines context as "any information that can be used to characterize the situation of an entity. An entity is a person, place, or object that is considered relevant to the interaction between a user and an application, including the user and applications themselves."

We apply this definition in the case of digital services: a context-aware multimedia application is an application (entity), which can use the elements of context (any information that can be used to characterize the situation) to adapt his behavior in order to provide the corresponding interaction to the terminal.

2.2 Architectures of Context-Aware Applications

J. Coutaz et al. present in [4] a global architecture for context-aware applications based on levels of abstraction for a general-purpose context-aware system. They define four levels:

- **Sensing layer** provides numeric observables.
- **Perception layer** provides symbolic observables, which are interpretations from the numeric observable (i.e. transform GPS information in location name).
- **Situation and context identification layer** identifies context and propose adaptation. It is the reasoning core.

- **Exploitation layer.** It is an adapter between the application and the context infrastructure.

 Baldauf et al. in [5] also use a similar layered architecture to compare middleware and frameworks for context-aware systems.

2.3 Existing Works on Context-Aware Systems

Current approaches in context-aware frameworks make a clear separation between context acquisition, context processing and use. Thus, to create a separation of concerns as proposed by Dey [2]. He proposes a conceptual framework for supporting context-aware applications. The implementation of this framework is known as the Context-Toolkit [2]. It aims to ease development and evolution of context-aware applications using an object-based approach. It must be seen as an API for context-aware application. Each object from the API, which can be use to construct an application, has a role (i.e.: collect, transform, aggregate and serve context). The API approach creates a tight coupling between context processing and application.

More recent works, such as CoBrA or SOCAM are infrastructure-based approach rather than API. Hong et al. point out advantages of infrastructure for providing context abstraction [6].

CoBrA project from Chen et al. [7] is agent-oriented. A central unit, so called, a context broker, maintains and manages context on behalf of agents. An agent could be an application running on mobile devices, a service provided by a room, a web service, etc). The broker collects information about context and shares it with agents. This design addresses the issue for providing context-awareness to resource-limited computing devices.

The Service-Oriented Context-Aware Middleware (SOCAM) project introduces by Gu et al. [8] exists as middleware. In SOCAM, different services working together acquire, process, reason and deliver context to agents. The main contribution of this work is the context model, which uses ontology through OWL. The use of ontology allows them to describe context in a semantic way that is independent of programming language.

In context-awareness, the usage is a key element. Works presented in this section are related to the physical world. The main use is to provide services fitted to users activity (e.g.: forward calls to voice mails when users is currently sleeping in the bedroom, switch off light if the room is empty, etc).

3 Rule Driven Context-Awareness

Our motivations to use a middleware are driven by the will to be unobtrusive (1) and to create an abstraction for context-awareness (2). It aims at deploying regular applications and context-aware applications (related to (1)) and evolving the middleware without impacting the already deployed applications (related to (2)).

We use rules for providing context-awareness thresholds in application through what we call a context signature. It contains rules that define behaviors according to context, for each application. In order to create these rules, the software engineer must define a set of situations. A situation propose a running state for a corresponding environment, as for example, to stream a video through a 4 Mbit/s connection to a terminal we must code the video in 480p.

Each situation is made of observations of the computing environment and a corresponding reaction. Observations describe the computing environment for an application; upon relevant characteristic chosen by the software engineer. Indeed, in our reference scenario, bandwidth is a relevant characteristic. An observation is formatted as a triple (key, comparison operator and value). Values are strings or numeric; in case of a numeric value, a default unit is used. Key is the name of the characteristic, basically, the name of the data gathered by the sensors (e.g.: screen height for an observation about the height of a screen). The operator fills the gap between key and value.

Observations can be as simple as the reference scenario or more complex with additional elements. For example, a situation can be based on observations on bandwidth and screen size. But there can be only one reaction. So, a situation is composed by at least one observable and exactly one consequence.

Each reaction must be a running mode implemented. Rules allow choosing the most appropriate running mode for an application. For each relevant using case of a multimedia application, there must be a situation expressed as a rule. These rules are used against the knowledge base. Once the developer provides the context-aware application as a package which contains the binary and the context signature, the middleware unpacks these elements as shown in Fig. 1.

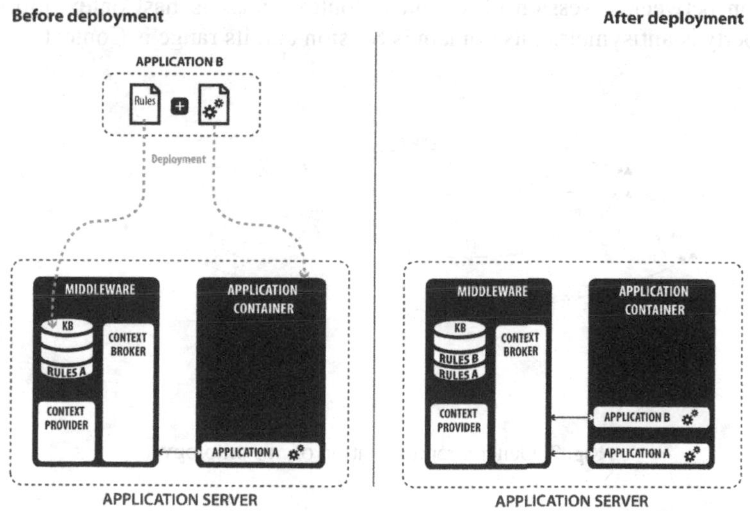

Fig. 1. Deployment of app in CAAS

The binary is deployed like a standard application and the signature is parsed in order to find rules. As stated before, a rule (situation) is composed with an antecedent (observation) and a consequence (reaction). Each one is then injected as knowledge in the KB. Rules are consider as knowledge because they present running modes and associated necessary conditions for using them, of the newly deployed application.

Context-logic signature defines requirements, in term of context information, for changing application's behavior. We define behavior as a business logic modulation. The main functionality does not change, but can be realized under different forms.

3.1 Storing Context in a Domain Ontology

A context aware application server (CAAS) hosts multiple digital services and provides context-awareness for them. Each application provides features under multiple running modes. A user is typified as a session, which consumes features offered by an application. Each session delivers its features through its environment called context. Sensors through context providers can grab it. Each one is able to gather only some kind of information (battery, screen size, localization, etc.) but not all data from the computing environment. In other words, a context-aware application relies on context providers to sense the environment, in order to choose the right business logic modality (or running mode) for a session.

These observations are the foundation for our resulting ontology. It uses two main classes (Context and Session) as shown in Fig. 2.

Context stores all necessary context information about the user computing environment. It is divided into subsets that represent a context provider.

Session represents all active connections to the CAAS. Each user, which consumes an application, is a member of the class session. Like the Session set, this class is divided into subclasses for representing applications.

Relation between a session class and a context class is hasContextInformation. This property is antisymetric, its domain is Session and its range is Context.

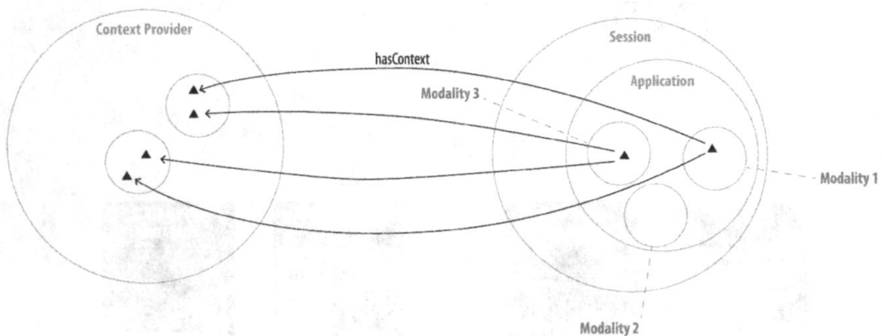

Fig. 2. General representation of our ontology

3.2 Reference Scenario

We will use as reference scenario, a video on demand (VOD) application. The digital service has 3 behaviors (i.e.: 480p, 720p or 1080p) for streaming a video to a user. The context information is the available bandwidth. The application changes the resolution of the video (behavior) according to the user's available bandwidth (context) as shown in Table 1. The context-signature provides semantic formalization of these context configurations that is a set of observations. A context signature maps each context configuration to a specific business logic behavior. This is a loose-coupling solution between business logic and context logic.

We run the above-mentioned ontology against our reference scenario. An application server with our middleware has a context provider called "User Terminal Context" that provide information's about the terminal like bandwidth, screen size and CPU load. The AS hosts a context aware digital service called "Adaptable Video-on-Demand", which provide adaptable video according user's bandwidth.

Table 1. Classes of the ontology under our reference scenario

Name	Parent	Description
Context Provider	Thing	All context providers
Session	Thing	All sessions using middleware
UserTerminalCtx	Context Provider	Context provider that gather information about bandwidth, screen size and CPU load
AdaptableVoD	Session	All sessions for the Adaptable Video-on-Demand digital service
C480p	AdaptableVoD	Sessions for AdaptableVoD using 480p resolution
C720p	AdaptableVoD	Sessions for AdaptableVoD using 720p resolution
C1080p	AdaptableVoD	Sessions for AdaptableVoD using 1080p resolution

The data gathered by the context provider are represented as datatype relations. In this scenario the context provider gather information about bandwidth, screen size and CPU.

Table 2. Relations in the ontology under our reference scenario

Name	Domain	Range	Description
hasContext	Session	Context	Link a session with a context provider
hasBandwidth	UserTerminalCtx	int	Available bandwidth gathered by context provider
hasScreenSize	UserTerminalCtx	string	Screen size gathered by context provider
hasCPULoad	UserTerminalCtx	float	CPU Load gathered by context provider

As stated before, individuals from the Session context are sorted according to rules, which are injected in the KB. We use SWRL to model the context logic dynamic using this feature. In our reference scenario, the Video-On-Demand service must adapt the video coding according to bandwith. From the OWL point of view, individuals from the set AdaptableVoD must be move either in the c480p, c720p or c1080p subset, each one represents a video coding (480p, 720p and 1080p). This behavior uses the following SWRL:

For more readability, the common part of equations is represents as (0)

$$AdaptableVoD(?s)\ \wedge hasContext(?s,?c)\ \wedge hasBandwidth(?c,?b) \tag{0}$$

$$(0)\ \wedge\ swrlb{:}greaterThanOrEqual(?b,3000)\ \wedge\ swrlb{:}lessThan(?b,6000) \rightarrow c480p(?s) \tag{1}$$

$$(0)\ \wedge\ swrlb{:}greaterThanOrEqual(?b,6000)\ \wedge\ swrlb{:}lessThan(?b,9000) \rightarrow c720p(?s) \tag{2}$$

$$(0)\ \wedge\ swrlb{:}greaterThanOrEqual(?b,9000) \rightarrow c1080p(?s) \tag{3}$$

In our model, the reasoner and KB, use OWL and SWRL to choose business logic modality according to context. Each time a new connection is setup, the middleware injects information about the session and the context in the KB. In order to switch modality, the application must be aware of the KB's classification. We use SQWRL to interrogate the ontology in order to notify applications about modality to use for each connection. A typical SQWRL query for this is: *Modality(?s) -> sqwrl:select(?s)*. In our reference scenario:

$$c480p(?s) \rightarrow sqwrl{:}select(?s) \tag{4}$$

$$c720p(?s) \rightarrow sqwrl{:}select(?s) \tag{5}$$

$$c1080p(?s) \rightarrow sqwrl{:}select(?s) \tag{6}$$

The first one provides all sessions that must use a 480p resolution, the second one for sessions use a 720p and the last one for session uses a 1080p.

4 Conclusion

We have proposed and implemented a novel architecture that makes AS taking into account the context-awareness of the digital service they host. The architecture employs domain ontology in order to monitor the applications' context. Moreover, when a new context-aware application is deployed on the application server, its context-logic (a set of SWRL rules which rely the domain ontology) is extracted from the application bundle. Each SWRL rule encodes a context-aware threshold for the application. When a rule is triggered at runtime, the application server notifies the application, so that the application change its service delivery modality, as the current context favors another service delivery modality different than the current one.

The primary goal is to help developer of context-aware applications to quickly encode context-aware thresholds. It helps them to develop the context logic of the application for it to adapt its behavior when a significant context change is detected. Developers can seamlessly encode those thresholds by writing the SWRL rules corresponding to the conditions under which the application follows each service delivery modality and then ship the SWRL file into their application bundle.

Previously, this task was not a service offered by the application server, unlike logging, database mapping, authentication, etc., but actually embedded in each application business logics as an ad hoc encoded algorithm. Therefore, this approach is also a framework, as developers of context-aware applications no longer have to write source code for handling context changes.

We are currently developing additional algorithms that will enhance the context assertions in the knowledge base. Especially, we will add to the context logic parameters for gathering context (e.g. context sampling frequency) as each application may have different temporal needs regarding context updates.

References

1. Zimmermann, A., Lorenz, A., Oppermann, R.: An operational definition of context. In: Kokinov, B., Richardson, D.C., Roth-Berghofer, T.R., Vieu, L. (eds.) CONTEXT 2007. LNCS (LNAI), vol. 4635, pp. 558–571. Springer, Heidelberg (2007)
2. Dey, A.: Understanding and using context, personal and ubiquitous computing, pp. 4–5 (2001)
3. Strassner, J., Liu, Y., Jiang, M., Zhang, J., van der Meer, S., Foghlú, M.Ó., Fahy, C., Donnelly, W.: Modelling Context for Autonomic Networking. In: 5th IEEE International Workshop on Management of Ubiquitous Communications and Services (MUCS), Brazil, April 11 (2008)
4. Coutaz, J., Crowley, J.L., Dobson, S., Garlan, D.: Context is key. Communication of the ACM 48, 49–53 (2005)
5. Baldauf, M., Dustdar, S., Rosenberg, F.: A survey on context-aware systems. International Journal of Ad Hoc and Ubiquitous Computing, 263–277 (2007)
6. Hong, J.I., Landay, J.A.: An infrastructure approach to context-aware computing. In: Human Computer-Interaction, vol. 16 (2001)
7. Chen, H.: An Intelligent Broker Architecture for Pervasive Context-Aware Systems. PhD thesis, University of Maryland, Baltimore County (2004)
8. Gu, T., Pung, H.K., Zhang, D.Q.: A middleware for building context-aware mobile services. In: Proceedings of IEEE Vehicular Technology Conference (VTC), Milan, Italy (2004)
9. Outtagarts, A., Martinot, O.: iSSEE: IMS Sensors Search Engine Enabler for Sensors Mashups Convergent Application. International Journal of Computer Science Issues, IJCSI 6, 1–7 (2009)
10. O'Connor, M.J., Das, A.K.: A Method for Representing and Querying Temporal Information in OWL. In: Fred, A., Filipe, J., Gamboa, H. (eds.) BIOSTEC 2010. CCIS, vol. 127, pp. 97–110. Springer, Heidelberg (2011)
11. ITU-T Recommendation, Y.2000-Y.2999, Next Generation Networks, Y-Series: Global Information Infrastructure, Internet Protocol aspects and Next-Generation Networks
12. Horridge, M., Knublauch, H., Rector, A., Stevens, R., Wroe, C.: A Practical Guide To Building OWL Ontologies Using Protege 4 and CO-ODE Tools Edition 1.2. Technical report, The University Of Manchester (March 2009)
13. Horrocks, I., Patel-Schneider, P.F., Boley, H., Tabet, S., Grosof, B., Dean, M.: SWRL: A semantic web rule language combiningOWL and RuleML (May 2004), `http://www.w3.org/Submission/2004/SUBM-SWRL-20040521/`
14. O'Connor, M.J., Das, A.K.: SQWRL: A query language for OWL. In: Hoekstra, R., Patel-Schneider, P.F. (eds.) OWLED. CEUR Workshop Proceedings, vol. 529, CEUR-WS.org (2008)

Cloud Computing: Combining Governance, Compliance, and Trust Standards with Declarative Rule-Based Frameworks

Said Tabet and Marlin Pohlman

EMC Corporation, Office of the CTO, Hopkinton, MA, USA
{said.tabet,marlin.pohlman}@emc.com

Abstract. Cloud computing has emerged as a major paradigm shift in information technology pushing corporations to redefine the way they conduct their business. While it promises many benefits, Cloud computing is also facing serious challenges. Those include legal and regulatory requirements, privacy and security needs, as well as other information and data related issues. To help address these concerns, a number of standards initiatives have been started. We believe that declarative rules can play an important role in standardizing legal and service level agreements and contracts by providing formalized languages that can enable intelligent compliance automation and trust. In the Cloud, automation is key and new architectures for service provider and service consumer dynamic interactions will need to be developed before organizations deploy their mission critical applications to the Cloud. In this paper, we will address these issues and provide a survey of existing standards and address the limitations of current efforts.

Keywords: Cloud Computing, Declarative rules, RuleML, SLA, Service level agreement, Cloud Compliance, GRC-XML, LegalRuleML, Ontologies, Taxonomies, Trust on the Cloud.

1 Introduction

Cloud computing has emerged as a new computing model that arrays multiple computers in both centralized and distributed data centers to deliver applications, application platforms, solutions and services via a utility model. Cloud computing relies on separating user applications from the underlying infrastructure using virtualization and information sharing through federation. While the idea of utility computing is not new, it has been given a new life and crucial developments with the major vendors playing an active role and providing virtual servers and storage on demand.

Although Cloud is an evolving paradigm, it is important to have a common definition. NIST provides a definition that is widely accepted in the industry. Cloud computing is defined as a model for enabling ubiquitous, convenient, on-demand network access to a shared pool of configurable computing resources (e.g., networks, servers, storage, applications, and services) that can be rapidly provisioned and released with minimal management effort or service provider interaction.

F. Olken et al. (Eds.): RuleML 2011 - America, LNCS 7018, pp. 230–236, 2011.

This cloud model promotes availability and is composed of five essential characteristics, three service models, and four deployment models [1].

One of the main challenges facing Cloud Computing is security. It is important that service providers deliver on key security components in order to provide necessary assurances for service consumers and develop a trusted relationship.

In order to establish a stable secure foundation, it is essential to make the virtual environment confidential and secure. To secure federation, cloud-based systems must implement mechanisms to ensure Quality of Service (QoS) and Service-Level Agreements (SLAs). There are two historical approaches: (1) remote API on the platform and (2) direct analysis of network packets flowing between components. They both fail when dealing with complex federated virtualized environments. An alternative approach is to use agents and semantic rule languages constructs to resolve the challenges of nested multi tier security. In this context, semantic agents are software components, which may be leveraged for resource management due to their autonomous, reactive, social, and self-learning properties. Semantic agents are a special kind of Cloud services that are used to implement and manage available Cloud services and resources.

Declarative rule languages will enable the dynamic interpretation of the contract between customers and service providers. Various performance metrics (e.g., uptime, throughput, and response time) may need to be guaranteed to Cloud users while privacy classification mechanisms are maintained, even through multi level security. This enables the resolution of multiple SLA's, QoS requirements and regulatory-imposed security levels, which can be implemented, based on data types or jurisdictions. Standards groups such as ISO/IEC and the UN-based ITU have acknowledged the need to resolve SLA's QoS requirements and trans-border jurisdictional mandates. We expect standards efforts in this area to start soon.

1.1 Background

In 1992, the MITRE Corporation implemented the Multilevel Secure Transactions (MUSET) database system. This project centered on heterogeneous database transaction management. Challenges MITRE addressed include concurrency control, recovery, and commit protocols for multi security level transactions. Multi security level transaction allows for concurrent operations at multiple security levels. In a multi security level system a sub-transaction at one site could operate at the unclassified level, whereas another sub-transaction at a different site could operate at the Secret level. MUSET assigned sensitivity and security levels to data, which utilized constraints and classification rules. Security constraints provided an effective classification approach. This ensured consistency of policy enforcement while at the same time minimized covert channels.

The Open Group Cloud Computing Work Group in its response to the European Commission's Cloud Computing Strategy DIGIT-IPM request for public consultation, highlighted the barriers to the use and provision of cloud computing. In his January 2011 address, Vice-President Kroes stated that there are a number of questions that need to be answered to make cloud computing happen in practice. These include legal, technical and commercial issues. In his address he highlighted three areas where advancement is required. Quoting Vice-President Kroes in his address:

First, the legal framework: This concerns data protection and privacy, including the international dimension. It also concerns laws and other rules that have a bearing on the deployment of cloud computing in public and private originations. And it concerns users' rights insofar as they are provided for by law.

Second, technical and commercial fundamentals: We want to extend our research support and focus on critical issues such as security and availability of cloud services. As a mediator, the Commission can also play a stronger role in the technical standardization of APIs and data formats, as well as in the development of template contracts and service level agreements.

Third, the market: We will support pilot projects aiming at cloud deployment. To really harness the power of public procurement we want to engage with our public sector partners on Member State and regional levels to work on common approaches to cloud computing.

1.2 Key Focus Areas

In their response, the Open Group suggested several key focus areas. The open group recommended the creation of a Consumer Bill of Rights. The response highlighted that users do not understand their rights from a Provider of Cloud Services. In answer to this need this paper presents RuleML as a framework to resolve this deficiency. RuleML may be used to provide enforcement standards for a consumer Bill of Rights. In the area of automated breach notification and service management RuleML can be used to automate process flows and assure supply chain members that service level agreements are being respected. RuleML may also be leveraged to create a more structured statement of regulatory expectations of providers. This could include automated delivery standards that Providers need to support. Using RuleML-driven policy engines, agents and semantic rule language constructs systems can execute explicit statements that Providers should provide to Buyers of Cloud Services. This may include details regarding the service location and provision, where tracking of usage and separation of services is done; how is security of data handled. RuleML enables the creation of semantic contracts in software and service licenses that involve multiple countries; Predicates defined by RuleML statements can adapt workflows to specific country requirements and may be executed in the context of local law where jurisdiction is concerned.

2 Multi-security and Cloud

In order to implement a multi security level ontology, the systems to be federated must share a common information model. Federated security systems must be transformed into the constructs of a common data model. This approach ensures that the policies enforced by the individual systems are maintained. Multiple schemas must be integrated to form a federated schema. Each component exports certain schema elements to the federation. These schemas are then integrated to form a federated policy. The challenge is to ensure that there is no security violation at the federation level. To address this challenge we must introduce the concept of semantic heterogeneity.

Semantic heterogeneity occurs when an entity is interpreted differently at different sites or different entities are interpreted to be the same object. Semantic heterogeneity is one of the major challenges for data integration as well as information interoperability. This challenge occurs not only in relational databases, but also in object databases and multimedia databases. Semantic heterogeneity permits context mediation, an approach for achieving semantic interoperability among sources and consumers of large-scale heterogeneous Cloud environments. The process of reconciling semantic heterogeneity involves two steps:

- In schema matching, Cloud implementers must find correspondences between sets of elements of the schemas that refer to the same concepts or legal mandates in the real world
- In the second phase, Cloud implementers must build on these correspondences to create the actual schema mapping expressions that reflect legal constrains.

RuleML presents itself as one such mechanism to express semantic heterogeneity and codify legal constraints imposed by jurisdiction and data type as declarative rules that are honored by the policy management infrastructure within the infrastructure of Cloud service providers.

3 Cloud Computing and RuleML

The RuleML Federation is an international non-profit organization formed in 2000 to provide a neutral platform for semantics-preserving interoperation of rules and rule-based web services across the Web between commercially important rule systems and to enable rule-based semantic web services. RuleML pioneered the XML representation of a modular family of webized rule sublanguages, catering to a variety of needs.

The RuleML language is an open semantic standard for rule modeling, modularization, serialization, webizing, interoperation, execution, and tooling. RuleML is a unifying family of XML-serialized rule languages spanning across all industrially relevant kinds of Web rules. It accommodates and extends other recent rule languages, building interoperation bridges between them. The specification of RuleML constitutes a modular family of Web sublanguages where each sublanguage has an XML Schema definition and a URI, which permits inheritance between sublanguage schemas and precise reference to the required expressiveness. The family structure provides an expressive inclusion hierarchy for the sublanguages, and their URIs are the subjects of (model-theoretic) semantic characterization.

The RuleML family's top-level distinction is deliberation rules (including derivation rules) vs. reaction rules (including production), which has been further refined in [8]. Complex event processing and legal rules are also being developed as part of the upcoming RuleML releases.

Having the choice between various types of rules using the RuleML modular framework, data centers automation can leverage various declarative formats for access control and security, compliance, policy and regulatory requirements, service level agreements and contracts, continuous control monitoring, business intelligence and semantic integration.

On the Cloud, there is a serious debate around legal issues such as regulatory requirements, agreements and contracts, jurisdictional challenges particularly for multinational corporations. Companies struggle to determine which regulations they need to comply with and where their data will reside and if the providers will be in compliance with the rules and policies of each relevant jurisdiction (country, territory, state, local, etc.)

Legal and policy documents can be represented as formalized statements in a declarative rule language, abstracted from the legal text and its multiple interpretations in any given country. LegalRuleML [9] has been started as a new effort from the RuleML community, which will lead to the development of a language that closes the gap between a legal text and the rule-based modeling of the norms it expresses in order to deliver an integrated and linked representation of legal documents on the Web. This will enable the creation of authoring and runtime tools for SLAs and contracts, enabling semantically rich data centers and supporting the realization of trust on the Cloud.

Using LegalRuleML, legal requirements can be implemented in a machine-readable syntax that can be fed into a business rule engine in order to continuously monitor the contract performance at runtime and automatically execute the corresponding business rules. Transparent assessment and reports can be made available to auditors and Cloud service consumers.

Within RuleML legal constraints can be expressed as predicates. Based on the context of the data in question, derivation rules may then be leveraged and generated from existing requirements. In complex multi-tenant environments, the RuleML framework offers the ability of rule chaining and reasoning over existing information and gathered facts, providing data center intelligence through agile services. In addition, it provides a declarative implementation of Trust on the Cloud using formal methods and the expressive power of the family of RuleML rule modules. To continuously apply and monitor information confidentiality and security and deploy effective and efficient controls, a rule-based approach is more appropriate than imperative and procedural solutions. This is the first step towards self-sustaining intelligent data centers on the Cloud where service providers can demonstrate on-demand to their end user organizations and consumers trust and offer interactive transparent audits. The Cloud Security Alliance, ISO and other standards bodies are all working on best practice and specification to help achieve these goals.

4 Policy-Based Multi-tenancy

Multi-tenancy is an architectural model used by cloud service providers to host multiple organizations (tenants) within a single server. There are many variations of this concept but overall they all have the same goal, which is to implement an efficient and cost-effective utilization of their resources. While it is a good solution for the providers, it forces tenants to share those resources, creating many operational and business risks. Large enterprise, before they can trust the providers with their sensitive data and services, they will need guarantees and assurances that internal controls are in place to provide security, confidentiality and privacy while at the same time deliver on performance and scalability on demand. Tenants need to have full audit and control, as they are ultimately responsible for compliance with relevant regulations within their jurisdictions. This is why automated and semantically rich data centers are needed. Declarative rule-based approaches can play a key role and now is the time to bring such solutions to the marketplace and to encourage research labs and universities to develop this field.

To implement resource and network segregation, an ontology can provide a classification that can be used for dynamic configuration and to enforce various levels of security policies. Reasoning over resources and automatically adjusting configurations will require the expressive power of rules beyond description logic to include complex events and modal logics (deontic and alethic operators).

Policy-based multi-tenancy requires rich semantics and real-time execution of rule sets (security, preferences, service configuration, etc.) based on network and resources as well as service consumer requirements. Standards developed by the Cloud Security Alliance are starting to gather momentum around industry best practice. Over the next few years, as these standards receive wide adoption, we will see new products that will support the required capability for larger enterprises to join the Cloud and trust the providers with their mission critical applications and sensitive information.

5 Conclusions

Cloud Computing is proving to be the next evolution of information technology and an enabler for advanced distributed web architectures. Investment in Cloud is growing worldwide with organizations adopting private clouds and exploring hybrid and public Cloud models. Semantic technology and languages such as RDF and OWL provide a taxonomic and description-logic modeling of resources on the Web. Semantic rules add another important layer for deductive reasoning. Applying these technologies to Cloud Computing is a key condition for the deployment of agile and intelligent data centers. The integration of ontologies and rules will enable the development of dynamic configuration of complex and heterogeneous physical and virtual resources and facilitate secure multi-tenant environments.

The use of declarative rules and ontologies will help Cloud service providers deal with rapidly changing requirements and newly discovered constraints such as new regulatory regimes and customer policies. It will also support the need for Cloud service consumers to audit the provider's internal controls and to implement an interactive information access and query in order to satisfy their own policy and regulatory compliance needs.

To realize the vision of the Cloud, linked data and semantic technologies need to be considered together with the current standards initiatives underway at ISO, CSA, W3C, OASIS, and OMG. Standards need to take the complex and dynamic nature of the Cloud into account and look beyond static descriptions of security vulnerabilities and procedural configurations of resources by exploring semantic knowledge representation as discussed in this paper.

References

1. Definition of Cloud Computing by NIST, http://csrc.nist.gov/publications/drafts/800-145/Draft-SP-800-145_cloud-definition.pdf
2. Cloud Security Alliance (CSA), https://cloudsecurityalliance.org
3. The RuleML Initiative, http://www.ruleml.org
4. Boley, H.: The RuleML Family of Web Rule Languages. RuleML.org
5. Palmirani, M., Contissa, G., Rubino, R.: Fill the Gap in the Legal Knowledge Modelling. In: Governatori, G., Hall, J., Paschke, A. (eds.) RuleML 2009. LNCS, vol. 5858, pp. 305–314. Springer, Heidelberg (2009)
6. Boley, H., Tabet, S., Wagner, G.: Design rationale for RuleML: A markup language for Semantic Web rules. In: Cruz, I.F., Decker, S., Euzenat, J., McGuinness, D.L. (eds.) Proc. SWWS 2001, The First Semantic Web Working Symposium, pp. 381–401 (2001)
7. Governatori, G., Rotolo, A.: Changing legal systems: Legal abrogations and annulments in defeasible logic. The Logic Journal of IGPL (2010)
8. Boley, H., Paschke, A., Shafiq, O.: RuleML 1.0: The overarching specification of web rules. In: Dean, M., Hall, J., Rotolo, A., Tabet, S. (eds.) RuleML 2010. LNCS, vol. 6403, pp. 162–178. Springer, Heidelberg (2010), http://www.cs.unb.ca/~boley/papers/RuleML-Overarching.pdf
9. The Object Management Group. Regulatory Compliance Domain Special Interest Group, http://www.omg.org
10. The Open Group Cloud Computing Work Group, http://www3.opengroup.org/getinvolved/workgroups/cloudcomputing

Role Assignment in Institutional Clouds for Rule-Based Enterprise Management

Jeremy Pitt[1], Julia Schaumeier[1], and Alexander Artikis[1,2]

[1] Department of Electrical & Electronic Engineering,
Imperial College London, SW7 2BT, UK
[2] Institute of Informatics & Telecommunications,
National Centre for Scientific Research "Demokritos",
Athens 15310, Greece

Abstract. In the context of engineering cloud computing applications for enterprise management, we want to represent a theory of institutions and role assignment in terms of a formal specification of rule-based action and agency. We consider how a tripartite distinction of institutional rules, as either constitutional-, collective- and operational-choice rules, can be mapped to a protocol stack for dynamic specifications. The mapping is illustrated with a specification and animation of changeable role assignment protocols, in which both institutional rules and institutional change are given a uniform and integrated specification in a formal action language. This shows how institutionalised principles of collective action can be transformed into runtime rule-based reasoning for self-organisation of 'institutional clouds' for enterprise management.

Keywords: Multi-Agent Systems, Institutions, Self-Organisation, Cloud Computing.

1 Introduction

We are interested in applications of multi-tenant cloud computing for enterprise management and business delivery, in particular the real-time on-demand provisioning of *-as-a-service (*aaS), where * = software, platform, data, infrastructure, etc. [4]. We consider the aggregation of a set of resources from the cloud to provision *aaS to a collection of clients or 'agents' [1]. To reduce the total cost of ownership, we want as many agents to use the resource aggregation without overloading it. From one perspective, this is a generalisation of well-studied optimisation problems such as channel allocation, service request brokering or job shop scheduling [7], except in our case the jobs are autonomous decision-makers and the number of jobs and machine availability changes over time.

Since each aggregation of resources can be considered as an open system, i.e. resource allocation requires decision-making between competing components with partial information and without centralised control, we propose to model these aggregations from the perspective of *institutions* for common pool resource management [10]. Specifically, we address the issue of *role assignment*, i.e. where one agent is appointed by the others to perform *access control* [13]. However, if

F. Olken et al. (Eds.): RuleML 2011 - America, LNCS 7018, pp. 237–251, 2011.

the access control regime is too strict, the number of agents using the resource is too few and the overall cost is prohibitive; if it is too lenient, the number of agents using the resource is too great and quality of service declines.

We propose to use rule-based role assignment to self-organise the cloud's client-base (the agents) into clusters, where each cluster uses an aggregation of resources to provide *aaS to a subset of the agents, and 'the cloud' is the totality of all the clusters. The agents in each cluster define and change a set of (institutional) rules to manage the *aaS themselves. Section 2 reviews the background to this work, including institutions for common pool resource management [10] and dynamic specifications for norm-governed systems [2]. Section 3 gives a formal model of institutional rules for role assignment, and Section 4 provides a dynamic specification of these rules in an action language. Section 5 reports on an experimental testbed which shows how a set of agents can self-organise the membership, role assignment and resource allocation in a way which increases overall 'satisfaction' (i.e. the trade-off between total cost of ownership and quality of service). Section 6 describes related and future work, and we conclude in Section 7 with some comments on the prospects for runtime rule-based reasoning for self-organisation of 'institutional clouds' and distributed energy resources.

2 Background

In this section, we relate the pre-formal socio-economic definition of 'institution' to a computational specification. We define an institution as a set of nested, changeable rules. To give a formal characterisation of these rules, we use norm-governed systems and the concept of institutionalised power [8]. The idea of dynamic specifications [2] is then used to formally represent the nesting and changing of the rules of an institution as a dynamic norm-governed system.

2.1 Institutional Rules

Ostrom [10] observed that common pool resource (CPR) management problems have often been resolved in human societies through the 'evolution' of institutions. Ostrom defined an institution as a "set of working rules that are used to determine who is eligible to make decisions in some arena, what actions are allowed or constrained, ... [and] contain prescriptions that forbid, permit or require some action or outcome" [10, p. 51]. She also maintained that the rule-sets were conventionally agreed (ideally by those affected by them); mutually understood, monitored and enforced; that they were nested; and that they were mutable.

Ostrom [10, p. 52] distinguished three levels of nested rules. These were, at the lowest level, *operational-choice* rules, which were concerned with processes of resource appropriation, provision, monitoring and enforcement. The middle level specified *collective-choice* rules, which were concerned with choosing the operational rules for managing the resource, as well as processes of policy-making, management and adjudication in disputes. At the highest level, the constitutional rules indirectly affected the operational rules by determining who is eligible to, and what rules are used to, define the set of collective-choice rules.

The nesting of rules was important for the process of *institutional change* for two reasons. Firstly, the changes which constrain action at a lower level occur in the context of a 'fixed' set of rules at a higher level. Secondly, lower level rules were easier and less 'costly' to change than the higher level rules, thus increasing the stability of strategies and expectations of those individuals having to interact according to a set of rules to achieve individual goals in a common setting.

2.2 Institutionalised Power

If the working sets of rules contain "prescriptions that forbid, permit or require some action or outcome", a formal representation can be given in terms of norm-governed systems [3]. A specification of a norm-governed system can be (partially) given by defining the permissions, prohibitions and obligations of the agents in the system, and the sanctions and enforcement policies that deal with the performance of prohibited actions and non-compliance with obligations.

To specify formally "who is eligible to make decisions", we also require the concepts of role, role assignment and *institutionalised power* [8]. The term institutionalised power refers to that characteristic feature of institutions, whereby designated agents, often acting in specific roles, are empowered to create or modify facts of special significance in that institution (*institutional facts*), through the performance of a designated action, e.g. by making a signal, or in certain cases, a speech act.

Therefore, it is generally not the specific agent that is eligible to make decisions, but the agent that occupies the role, that is empowered to make those decisions. It is necessary to define a role assignment protocol which appoints a specific agent to a specific role. It must also be possible to change which agent occupies that role, for example if the appointed agent leaves the system, performs badly or incorrectly, or lacks the resources to discharge the duties associated with the role. For this, we need dynamic norm-governed specifications.

2.3 Dynamic Specifications

Artikis [2] defined a framework that allowed agents to modify the rules or protocols of a norm-governed system at runtime. This framework assumed there were some object level protocols, and at any point during the execution of the object protocol the participants could start a meta-protocol in order to (try to) modify the object-level protocol.

The participants of the meta-protocol could initiate a meta-meta protocol to modify the rules of the meta-protocol, and so on. In general, in a k-level infrastructure, level 0 corresponds to the object-level protocol while a protocol at level n, $0 < n \leqslant k-1$ is used by the protocol participants to modify the protocol rules of level m, $0 \leqslant m \leqslant n-1$.

Apart from object and meta protocols, this framework for dynamic specifications includes 'transition' protocols. These protocols express, among other things, the conditions in which an agent may initiate a meta-protocol, who occupies what roles in the meta-protocol, and what elements (the *degrees of freedom*) of an object protocol can be modified as a result of the meta-protocol execution.

2.4 Institutional Rules as Dynamic Specifications

To summarise, we propose to characterise the institutional rules of Ostrom as norm-governed specifications using the concept of institutionalised power, represent the nesting of operational-choice rules within collective-choice rules within constitutional-choice rules as object, meta- and meta-meta-protocols, and handle *institutional change* within the framework of dynamic specifications. This proposal is illustrated in figure 1.

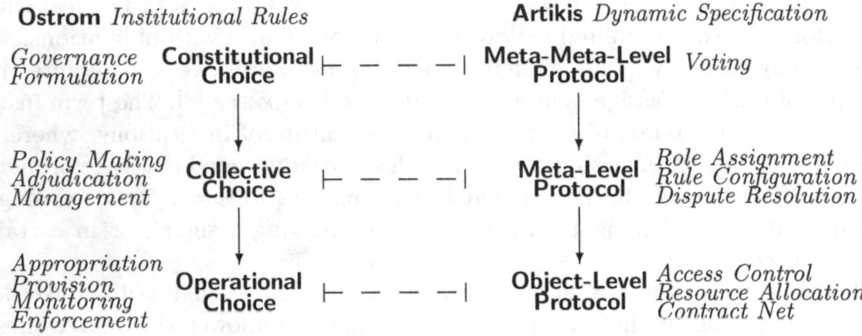

Fig. 1. Institutional rules and Dynamic specification

3 Institutional Rules for Role Assignment

In this section, we assume that a number of *aaS providers use the cloud computing paradigm to offer their services to an indeterminate number of possible clients. We define a cluster as an aggregation of resources providing the *aaS together with a collection of agents (clients or tenants) licensed to access the *aaS. An institution is a set of rules for runtime management of the *aaS capacity in a cluster. The ‘cloud’, from this abstract perspective, is the union of all the clusters. An *institutional cloud* $\mathcal{IC}$ is given by the distributed union of the institutions established for each of the clusters in the cloud.

We stipulate that one agent per cluster is appointed to the role *head* and one agent to the role *gatekeeper*. The *head* is responsible for managing the constitutional- and collective-choice rules, and in particular for evaluating the ‘performance’ of the agent in the *gatekeeper* role and the effectiveness of the cluster's access control method in balancing reduced cost vs. overcrowding. The *gatekeeper* is responsible for managing the operational-choice rule for admitting or denying access to the institution. Any other agent admitted to the institution is assigned to the role *member*.

Note that decision-making is endogenous: the *gatekeeper* decides which agent may join (occupy the role of *member*) or not; and collectively the *members* decide who gets to be the *gatekeeper*. We will define this reflexive relationship using a *hierarchical* specification of role assignment protocols as collective- and operational-choice rules.

Therefore let $\mathcal{I}_t$ be the institution for a given cluster defined at time t by:

$$\mathcal{I}_t = \langle \mathcal{M}, \epsilon, \mathcal{L} \rangle_t$$

and let $\mathcal{IC}_t$ be the institutional cloud at time t, consisting of n clusters:

$$\mathcal{IC}_t = \langle \mathcal{A}, \mathcal{I}_1, \ldots, \mathcal{I}_n \rangle_t$$

where (omitting the subscript t when obvious from context):

- $\mathcal{M}$ is the set of member agents and a subset of $\mathcal{A}$, the set of all agents in all clusters;
- ϵ is the environment, a pair $\langle Bf, If \rangle$ with Bf the set of 'brute' facts whose values are determined by the physical state, including the resource(s) to be allocated; and If the set of 'institutional' facts, whose values are determined by the conventional state, including the roles assigned to members of $\mathcal{M}$;
- $\mathcal{L}$, is the 'legislature', the set of rules by which the institution is managed.

Following Ostrom [10, pp. 52–53], the rules in $\mathcal{L}$ are divided into three levels, *OC*, *SC* and *CC*, where *OC* = *operational-choice* rules, *SC* = *(social) collective-choice* rules, and *CC* = *constitutional-choice* rules, as in Section 2.1.

We define two types of method, *wdMethod* and *acMethod*. The type of winner determination is *wdMethod*, e.g. plurality, runoff, instant runoff, borda or approval. The type of access control is *acMethod*, which can be attribute-based (if the applicant satisfies certain qualification criteria, it is automatically admitted), or discretionary (an applicant must satisfy the *gatekeeper*'s criteria, who is acting on behalf of the cluster in its appointed role). Note that the attribute-based access control is more 'lenient' and the discretionary method more 'stringent'.

The set $\mathcal{L}$ contains four nested rules for role assignment, see figure 2, with (in parentheses) the role responsible for its enactment and enforcement. $v_a(\cdot)$ denotes a set of expressed preferences on an issue by an agent $a \in \mathcal{M}$, and $k \in$ *wdMethod* is some 'fixed' winner determination method for the constitutional-choice. Note that k need not be fixed, but this treatment is in line with Ostrom's specification that a change of institutional rules (at a lower level) is conducted against a backdrop of 'fixed' rules (at a higher level). We will therefore assume that the role of *head* is 'fixed' although it too is mutable and the occupant selectable by a similar voting procedure.

In figure 2, the constitutional-choice rule $ccr \in CC$ maps a set of expressed preferences on a social collective-choice rule $scr_i \in SC$ to a winner determination method according to k. $scr_1 \in SC$ is the *gatekeeper* role assignment rule, and maps a set of expressed preferences to a designated member of $\mathcal{M}$, i.e. the *gatekeeper*, according to its winner determination method. $scr_2 \in SC$ maps a

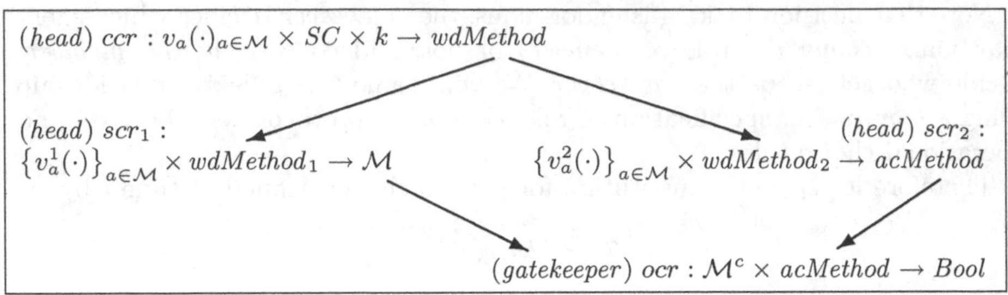

(head) ccr : $v_a(\cdot)_{a\in\mathcal{M}} \times SC \times k \to wdMethod$
(head) scr₁ :
$\{v_a^1(\cdot)\}_{a\in\mathcal{M}} \times wdMethod_1 \to \mathcal{M}$
(head) scr₂ :
$\{v_a^2(\cdot)\}_{a\in\mathcal{M}} \times wdMethod_2 \to acMethod$
(gatekeeper) ocr : $\mathcal{M}^c \times acMethod \to Bool$

Fig. 2. Nesting of *OC*, *SC* and *CC* rules for Role Assignment in $\mathcal{I}$

set of expressed preferences to an access control method according to its winner determination method; and an operational-choice rule $ocr \in OC$ maps an application from an agent not in $\mathcal{M}$ to a boolean outcome depending on the selected access control method. Thus, *ocr* is the *member* role assignment rule.

In the next section, we map these institutional rules onto a formal protocol specification in an action language. We specify the operational-choice rule as an object level protocol, and the social collective-choice rules as meta-level protocol for changing the degrees of freedom (i.e. the *gatekeeper* or the access control method) of the operational-choice rule.

4 Dynamic Specification of Role Assignment

In this section, we formalise the institutional rules of the previous section as a dynamic specification. For this, we will use the Event Calculus (EC) [9], the version used here is fully described in [2]. The EC is a logic formalism for representing and reasoning about actions or events and their effects. An *action description* in EC includes axioms that define: the action occurrences, using happensAt predicates; the effects of actions, using initiates and terminates predicates; and the values of the *fluents*, using initially and holdsAt predicates. A fluent is a property that is allowed to have different values at different points in time, the term $F = V$ denotes that fluent F has value V. Events initiate and terminate a period of time during which a fluent holds a value continuously.

4.1 Fluents (Institutional Facts)

Some of the institutional facts in *If*, represented as fluents $F = V$ in the EC, in whose values we are interested are shown in Table 1. These fluents record the roles that agents occupy; note that an agent can have only one role in a single institution. The multi-valued fluent *acMethod* determines which access control method the *gatekeeper* must use in determining *member* role assignment. There is one fluent for the winner determination method for each of the two (social) collective-choice rules. The final three fluents record the (institutionalised) powers, permissions and obligations of each agent.

Table 1. Fluents for EC role assignment protocols

Fluent (F)	**Range (V)**
$role\_of(A, member, I)$	$\{head, gatekeeper, member\}$
$acMethod(I)$	$\{attribute, discretionary\}$
$wdMethod(scr_1, I)$	$\{plurality, runoff, borda, \ldots\}$
$wdMethod(scr_2, I)$	$\{plurality, runoff, borda, \ldots\}$
$headcount(I)$	$integer$
$\mathbf{pow}(Agent, Action)$	$boolean$
$\mathbf{per}(Agent, Action)$	$boolean$
$\mathbf{obl}(Agent, Action)$	$boolean$

4.2 Expressed Preferences – Voting

A feature of all the operational-, collective- constitutional-choice rules is that they map a set of expressed preferences onto a specific outcome. Therefore we require a 'standard' protocol which enables an empowered agent to call for votes (*cfv*) on a particular issue in the context of institution I. The issues include:

$$\begin{aligned}
gatekeeper \text{ role: } & cfv(H, gatekeeper, I) \\
\text{access control method: } & cfv(H, acMethod, I) \\
\text{winner determination, } gatekeeper \text{ role: } & cfv(H, wdMethod(scr_1), I) \\
\text{winner determination, access control method: } & cfv(H, wdMethod(scr_2), I)
\end{aligned}$$

Such an action, by an empowered agent, initiates and initialises a ballot on the relevant issue. For example, to enact scr_2 the head agent H can call for a vote on which *acMethod* is to be used by the *gatekeeper* agent in its enforcement of the operational-choice rule:

$$\begin{aligned}
& cfv(H, acMethod, I) \;\; \mathsf{initiates} \;\; ballot(acMethod, I) = [\,] \;\; \mathsf{at} \;\; T \;\; \leftarrow \\
& \quad \mathbf{pow}(H, cfv(H, acMethod, I)) = true \;\; \mathsf{holdsAt} \;\; T \\
& \mathbf{pow}(H, cfv(H, acMethod, I)) = true \;\; \mathsf{holdsAt} \;\; T \;\; \leftarrow \\
& \quad role_of(H, I) = head \;\; \mathsf{holdsAt} \;\; T
\end{aligned}$$

Agents who are members of the institution can vote (once) on the issue:

$$\begin{aligned}
& vote(A, X, acMethod, I) \;\; \mathsf{initiates} \;\; ballot(acMethod, I) = [(X, A) \mid L] \;\; \mathsf{at} \;\; T \;\; \leftarrow \\
& \quad \mathbf{pow}(A, vote(A, X, acMethod, I)) = true \;\; \mathsf{holdsAt} \;\; T \;\; \wedge \\
& \quad ballot(acMethod, I) = L \;\; \mathsf{holdsAt} \;\; T \\
& \mathbf{pow}(A, vote(A, _, acMethod, I)) = true \;\; \mathsf{holdsAt} \;\; T \;\; \leftarrow \\
& \quad role_of(A, I) = member \;\; \mathsf{holdsAt} \;\; T \;\; \wedge \\
& \quad ballot(acMethod, I) = L \;\; \mathsf{holdsAt} \;\; T \;\; \wedge \\
& \quad \mathbf{not} \;\; on_list((_, A), L)
\end{aligned}$$

The appropriately empowered agent uses the votes cast (i.e. $\{v_a^2(\cdot)\}_{a\in\mathcal{M}}$) and the operative winner determination rule to create or change institutional facts, as shown in the next two sub-sections.

4.3 Operational-Choice Rule – Member Role Assignment

The dynamic specification of the operational-choice rule *ocr* is given by a role assignment protocol for membership. An agent can apply for membership to an institution I if it is not a *member* (or other role) in any other institution I', e.g.:

$$\begin{array}{l} \mathit{apply}(A,I) \;\; \textsf{initiates} \;\; \mathit{applied}(A,I) = \mathit{true} \;\; \textsf{at} \;\; T \;\; \leftarrow \\ \qquad \textbf{not} \;\; \mathit{role\_of}(A,I') = \mathit{member} \;\; \textsf{holdsAt} \;\; T \end{array}$$

The *gatekeeper* agent is empowered to admit the agent depending on the access control method. If the *acMethod* is *attribute*(-based), the *gatekeeper* is empowered to assign the role *member* provided the applicant satisfies certain (external) role conditions. We also place the *gatekeeper* under an obligation to make the member role assignment under these conditions. Otherwise if the *acMethod* is *discretionary*, the *gatekeeper* is simply empowered to assign the role (and whether it does so or not is the outcome of its own (internal) decision-making with respect to its knowledge of the environment):

$$\begin{array}{l} \mathit{assign}(G,A,\mathit{member},I) \;\; \textsf{initiates} \;\; \mathit{role\_of}(A,I) = \mathit{member} \;\; \textsf{at} \;\; T \;\; \leftarrow \\ \qquad \textbf{pow}(G,\mathit{assign}(G,A,\mathit{member},I)) = \mathit{true} \;\; \textsf{holdsAt} \;\; T \\ \mathit{assign}(G,A,\mathit{member},I) \;\; \textsf{initiates} \;\; \mathit{headcount}(I) = M1 \;\; \textsf{at} \;\; T \;\; \leftarrow \\ \qquad \textbf{pow}(G,\mathit{assign}(G,A,\mathit{member},I)) = \mathit{true} \;\; \textsf{holdsAt} \;\; T \;\; \wedge \\ \qquad \mathit{headcount}(I) = M \;\; \textsf{holdsAt} \;\; T \;\; \wedge \\ \qquad M1 = M + 1 \\ \textbf{pow}(G,\mathit{assign}(G,A,\mathit{member},I)) = \mathit{true} \;\; \textsf{holdsAt} \;\; T \;\; \leftarrow \\ \qquad \mathit{applied}(A,I) = \mathit{true} \;\; \textsf{holdsAt} \;\; T \;\; \wedge \\ \qquad \mathit{acMethod}(I) = \mathit{attribute} \;\; \textsf{holdsAt} \;\; T \;\; \wedge \\ \qquad \mathit{role\_of}(G,I) = \mathit{gatekeeper} \;\; \textsf{holdsAt} \;\; T \;\; \wedge \\ \qquad \mathit{role\_conditions}(\mathit{member},A,I) = \mathit{true} \;\; \textsf{holdsAt} \;\; T \\ \textbf{pow}(G,\mathit{assign}(G,A,\mathit{member},I)) = \mathit{true} \;\; \textsf{holdsAt} \;\; T \;\; \leftarrow \\ \qquad \mathit{applied}(A,I) = \mathit{true} \;\; \textsf{holdsAt} \;\; T \;\; \wedge \\ \qquad \mathit{acMethod}(I) = \mathit{discretionary} \;\; \textsf{holdsAt} \;\; T \;\; \wedge \\ \qquad \mathit{role\_of}(G,I) = \mathit{gatekeeper} \;\; \textsf{holdsAt} \;\; T \\ \textbf{obl}(G,\mathit{assign}(G,A,\mathit{member},I)) = \mathit{true} \;\; \textsf{holdsAt} \;\; T \;\; \leftarrow \\ \qquad \mathit{applied}(A,I) = \mathit{true} \;\; \textsf{holdsAt} \;\; T \;\; \wedge \\ \qquad \mathit{acMethod}(I) = \mathit{attribute} \;\; \textsf{holdsAt} \;\; T \;\; \wedge \\ \qquad \mathit{role\_of}(G,I) = \mathit{gatekeeper} \;\; \textsf{holdsAt} \;\; T \;\; \wedge \\ \qquad \mathit{role\_conditions}(\mathit{member},A,I) = \mathit{true} \;\; \textsf{holdsAt} \;\; T \end{array}$$

4.4 Collective-Choice Rule – Gatekeeper Role Assignment

Similarly, using the social collective-choice rule scr_1 to assign the role of *gatekeeper* to an agent is initiated by:

$$
\begin{aligned}
&\mathit{cfv}(H, \mathit{gatekeeper}, I) \;\; \textsf{initiates} \;\; \mathit{ballot}(\mathit{gatekeeper}, I) = [\,] \;\; \textsf{at} \;\; T \;\; \leftarrow \\
&\qquad \mathbf{pow}(H, \mathit{cfv}(H, \mathit{gatekeeper}, I)) = \mathit{true} \;\; \textsf{holdsAt} \;\; T \\
&\mathbf{pow}(H, \mathit{cfv}(H, \mathit{gatekeeper}, I)) = \mathit{true} \;\; \textsf{holdsAt} \;\; T \;\; \leftarrow \\
&\qquad \mathit{role\_of}(H, I) = \mathit{head} \;\; \textsf{holdsAt} \;\; T
\end{aligned}
$$

The agent empowered to call the vote is also the agent empowered to declare the result, and assign the *gatekeeper* role, although it may be that H is *empowered* to perform this action, it may not be *permitted* to do so, unless certain other conditions are satisfied (for example, unless 'enough' members, say two-thirds, have voted):

$$
\begin{aligned}
&\mathit{assign}(H, G, \mathit{gatekeeper}, I) \;\; \textsf{initiates} \;\; \mathit{role\_of}(G, I) = \mathit{gatekeeper} \;\; \textsf{at} \;\; T \;\; \leftarrow \\
&\qquad \mathbf{pow}(H, \mathit{assign}(H, G, \mathit{gatekeeper}, I)) = \mathit{true} \;\; \textsf{holdsAt} \;\; T \;\; \wedge \\
&\qquad \mathit{ballot}(\mathit{gatekeeper}, I) = L \;\; \textsf{holdsAt} \;\; T \;\; \wedge \\
&\qquad \mathit{wdMethod}(scr_1, I) = \mathit{WDM} \;\; \textsf{holdsAt} \;\; T \;\; \wedge \\
&\qquad \mathit{winner\_determination}(\mathit{WDM}, L, G) \\
&\mathbf{pow}(H, \mathit{assign}(H, G, \mathit{gatekeeper}, I)) = \mathit{true} \;\; \textsf{holdsAt} \;\; T \;\; \leftarrow \\
&\qquad \mathit{role\_of}(H, I) = \mathit{head} \;\; \textsf{holdsAt} \;\; T \\
&\mathbf{per}(H, \mathit{assign}(H, G, \mathit{gatekeeper}, I)) = \mathit{true} \;\; \textsf{holdsAt} \;\; T \;\; \leftarrow \\
&\qquad \mathit{role\_of}(H, I) = \mathit{head} \;\; \textsf{holdsAt} \;\; T \;\; \wedge \\
&\qquad \mathit{ballot}(\mathit{gatekeeper}, I) = L \;\; \textsf{holdsAt} \;\; T \;\; \wedge \\
&\qquad \mathit{headcount}(I) = M \;\; \textsf{holdsAt} \;\; T \;\; \wedge \\
&\qquad \mathit{length}(L) = \mathit{Len} \;\; \wedge \;\; \mathit{Len}/M > 0.66
\end{aligned}
$$

Note that the *winner_determination* is a polymorphic relation. Given votes on a binary choice it returns true or false; given votes on a list of candidates, it returns one of them; and so on.

5 Testbed and Evaluation

In this section, we present an experimental testbed for modelling the *institutional cloud* as defined in Section 3. We give the design and algorithm of the testbed, and present and discuss some experimental results.

The scenario is the delivery of a *aaS, with particular service instances provided by a set of clusters. A number of agents want to use each service instance, all of which are resource-constrained. The institutional rules associated with each cluster are then intended to trade off the number of agents using the service (i.e. the total cost of ownership) against the quality of service (which diminishes if there are too many agents using too few resources).

5.1 Testbed Specification and Algorithm Design

The UML diagram in figure 3 specifies the relationship between the classes of the testbed. The focus of this implementation is on the impact of role assignment by the *gatekeeper* to the role of *member* (scr_1), and by the *head* to the role of *gatekeeper* as decided by a vote of the members. The *head* is assumed to be present permanently and is empowered to perform the EC actions call for votes (*cfv*) and assign roles. It is also responsible for resource allocation, monitoring the performance of the selected access control method, and for evaluating the performance of the assigned *gatekeeper* in delivering the cluster's objectives.

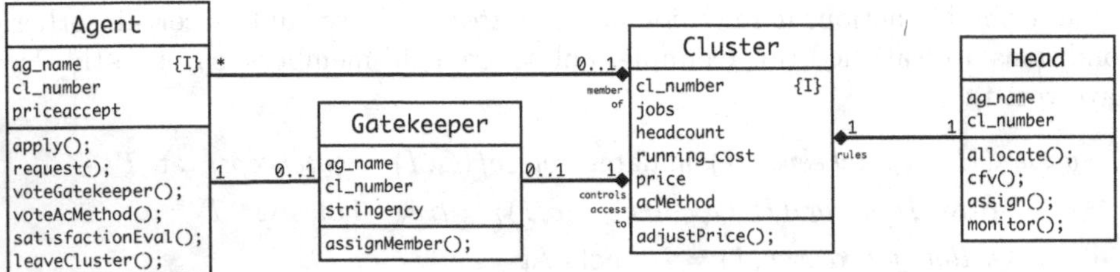

Fig. 3. Testbed class diagram

As per the definition in Section 3, a cluster, or institution, is composed of its members, encapsulates an environment (including its physical and institutional facts), and implements its operational- and collective-choice rules.

One of the members is assigned to the role of *gatekeeper*, see figure 4. Here, stringency is a measure of how 'strict' an individual agent is in applying the environmental factors to the *member* role assignment: some agents are much 'stricter' than others (and may be 'better' in the role under certain conditions).

The implementation of the UML specification defines a cloud $\mathcal{IC}$ as an aggregate of n institutional clusters $\{I_1, \ldots, I_n\}$ that each perform a number of requested services per time step. Furthermore, each cluster I_i ($i = 1, \ldots, n$) has M_i (headcount) members who regulate the allocation of resources (services/jobs) between themselves by appointment to the roles of *member* and *gatekeeper*.

The *gatekeeper* uses one of the access control methods *attribute* or *discretionary* to admit more or fewer new members into the cluster. This role assignment protocol implements the collective-choice rule (*ocr*) described in Section 4.3. Which of the methods, *attribute* or *discretionary*, is used, is determined by the members within the cluster by a vote (cf. Section 4.2). The *head* checks whether the *acMethod* is still applicable given the change of *environment* ϵ, or whether the *gatekeeper* performs as expected. The *head*'s main tasks are calling for a new vote (*cfv*) for either a new *gatekeeper* (scr_1) or a different *acMethod* (scr_2), as defined in Section 4.2. Furthermore, the *head* allocates the available services to requesting members. All members update their satisfaction depending on ϵ and decide to stay in or leave the cluster.

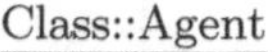

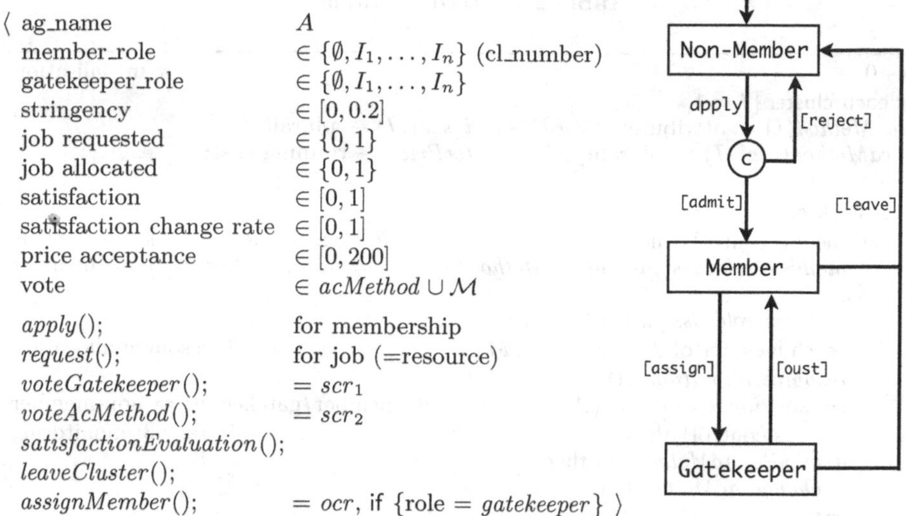

Fig. 4. Agent class description and Statechart

The testbed's control loop, see Table 2, has a global control variable, access control, allowing comparison between the effect of access control and monitoring, against having neither. After initialisation, each cluster is visited in turn. There are three main stages in processing each cluster: membership application and role assignment; resource allocation and satisfaction update; and monitoring, which may involve *gatekeeper* role assignment or change of access control method.

5.2 Experimental Results and Discussion

Figure 5 shows the average over 100 trials of two runs of an institutional cloud $\mathcal{IC}$ over 200 time steps. In total there are 150 agents, and 10 clusters with a running cost of 200 each. The solid lines are the results with access control and monitoring, the dotted or dashed lines are the results with no access control.

The first graph shows the sum of all the cluster members' satisfaction (= 150 at theoretical maximum). The second graph shows the number of agents that were members of a cluster in that timestep (top two lines) and the number of agents that left their cluster due to dissatisfaction (bottom two lines). In the third graph, the average price per populated cluster is shown (with 10 and 200 being the theoretical minimum and maximum, respectively).

We deduce from the graphs that, after an initial stabilisation phase, the run with assigned roles and access control leads to a considerably higher satisfaction than without access control. It leads to about the same amount of members but a much lower leaving rate and furthermore the price is considerably smaller.

For figure 5, this means in numbers over the total lifespan: a 34% increase in satisfaction by using access control and role assignment, a merely 3% decrease

Table 2. Testbed algorithm

```
t ← 0                                                        # initialisation
for each cluster {I = 1,...,n}
  acMethod(I) ← attribute;     wdMethod(scr_1, I) ← plurality;
  wdMethod(scr_2, I) ← plurality;     clusterPrice ← running_cost;
repeat
  for each cluster {I = 1,...,n}
    if {access control} then              # stage 1: member role assignment
      member_role_assignment (acMethod)     # non-member ⇒ (non-)member
    else
      member_role_assignment (none)
    for each member of I {A = 1,...,M}       # stage 2: resource allocation
      resource_allocation (A)
      satisfaction_evaluation (A)        # member/gatekeeper ⇒ non-member
    if {access control} then                         # stage 3: monitoring
      if monitorAcMethod (I) then
        change_acMethod (I)
      else
        if monitorGatekeeper (I) then
          gatekeeper_role_assignment (I)           # gatekeeper ⇔ member
    for each member of I {A = 1,...,M}      # members update preferences
      preferenceUpdate (A, I)
    sortPricelist (I)
  t ← t + 1                                                  # next state
until forever
```

in membership, a 71% decrease for leaving agents and a 20% decrease of the average cluster price when using the proposed scheme. The access control leads to a higher satisfaction, because the agents self-organise their distribution over the clusters, and as a result the total cost of ownership is averaged out and more agents are allocated resources.

One of the interesting features of these experiments is that using a rule-based system mitigates the vicious circle leading to a price war, i.e. the chain of actions "price increases (i.e. when there are too many members) → satisfaction decreases → members leave → members get into another cluster → price increases → ...". Ostrom's analysis of CPR systems without institutions often led to 'pumping races' of this sort, which ruined the common resource.

6 Related and Further Work

Since the job shop scheduling problem is known to be NP-complete and our formulation is a generalisation of that problem, it too is NP-complete. Given that this formulation is an accurate abstraction of *aaS provision, this explains why heuristic solutions have been adopted by SaaS and IaaS providers for run-time cloud management. In related work [1], a game theoretic approach is proposed, based on competing SaaS providers managing IaaS provider capacity.

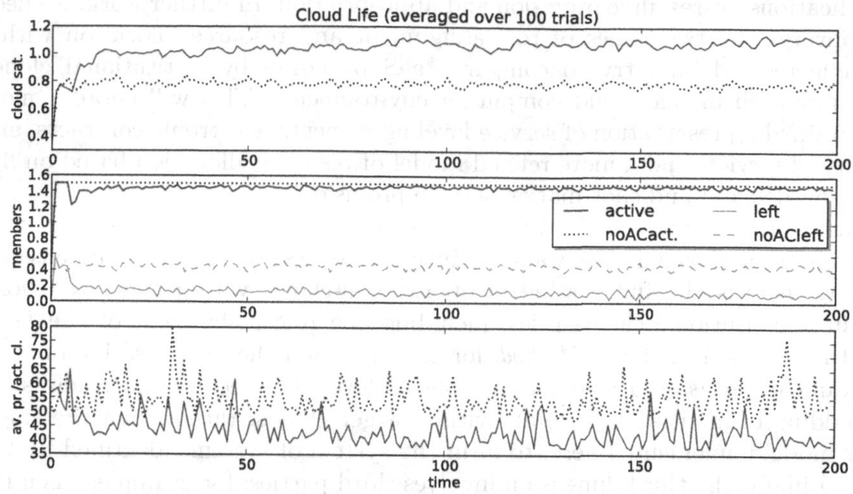

Fig. 5. Lifespan of $\mathcal{IC}$ with (solid) and without access control (dotted/dashed)

Ostrom [10] theorised that self-governing institutions offered a resolution to the 'tragedy of the commons' predicted by game theory, and we have suggested here an institutional approach to runtime cloud management by considering *aaS from the perspective of common pool resource management.

A second area of related research is role-based access control (RBAC) [14]. Currently, we have kept separate the issues of role assignment and access control, and implemented the role assignment via a norm-governed protocol and two (relatively) simple access control methods, i.e. attribute-based and discretionary. For full deployment of the proposed mechanisms for cloud management, it would be necessary to investigate how, for example, the NIST model of role-based access control, with its four levels of increasing functional capability (flat, hierarchical, constrained and symmetric), could be specified in the framework of Section 2.3. We can then use EC role assignment protocols to implement role-based access control, and use the testbed to investigate the effect of this richer model on self-organisation.

Much of the work on policies for cloud computing focuses on the issue of security and defining security policies [4,5]. Since role assignment is important for some aspects of security (i.e. access control), we believe this work complements that research. Furthermore, in real-world cloud computing environments there may be multiple access control policies and even multiple gatekeepers. The non-monotonic reasoning about institutional facts supported by the EC supports straightforward modelling of such situations. Moreover, alternative dispute resolution methods can be formalised in the same language and used to implement conflict resolution protocols.

We have also considered institutional rules and institutional change from the viewpoint of role assignment. In related work we analysed resource allocation within the institution [11], and how this can be formalised as dynamic specifications for resource provision and appropriation. In further work, we need to converge the two issues of role assignment and resource allocation within a single testbed, and try to compare *aaS provision by institutional clouds with provision in real cloud computing environments. This will entail a more fine-grained representation of service level agreements, electronic contracts, and quality of service; and a more refined model of resource allocation based on flat rates, on-demand and spot market service provision.

There are a number of further experiments on the notion of 'nesting' that need to be performed. We want to investigate nesting in three dimensions. Firstly, there is the full nesting of operational-choice within collective-choice within constitutional-choice rules, including the role assignment of the *head*, and the selection of the *wdMethod*, for example, and the formalisation of what Ostrom calls *decision arenas* for each nested level. The second dimension is the embedding of institutional clouds within larger clouds, rather than the single layer model implemented here, to form the system of systems identified by Ostrom. Finally, the third dimension involves third parties: for example, when the cloud provider is the third party, a brokerage for cloud services which acts as third party between the agents and the cloud service providers, or other more complex supply chains [6].

There are also aspects of Artikis' framework [2] which are currently underutilised. This includes the use of a topological space to express the 'distance' between two specification instances and its relationship to the 'cost model' of institutional change defined by Ostrom, and their joint impact on the role assignment protocol (i.e. some agents may be 'trusted' more than others to occupy a role). Furthermore, the testbed generates EC narratives from each of its stages. These can be checked by an EC engine to validate the sequence of actions. In the current testbed, agents do not violate their permissions and obligations, but in future work it will be interesting to investigate the effect of such violations on the performance of the system.

7 Summary and Conclusions

In summary, we have represented elements of a theory of institutions, institutional change, and institutional management of common pool resources in a framework for dynamic norm-governed systems. We showed how the nesting of constitutive-, collective- and operational-choice rules could be represented as dynamic protocols. The approach was illustrated with a role assignment protocol, and applied to a resource allocation rule for cloud computing service delivery. Our initial experiments showed how runtime rule-based reasoning could be used for self-organisation of 'institutional clouds'. This is demonstrating decentralised access control, in contrast to other rule-based access control schemes which tend to be centralised (e.g. [5]).

In conclusion, we have proposed an institution-based approach to the problem of dynamic load balancing in an open distributed system. Our experiments have shown that a collaborative process of institutional change can achieve improved performance through self-organisation, in what might otherwise be considered as an N-player non-cooperative game. However, there remain many open issues concerning deployment of this model in a real-world cloud computing environment, but also opportunities to apply this model to microgrids, virtual power plants, and the allocation of distributed energy resources [12]. These represent the real challenges ahead.

Acknowledgements. We would particularly like to thank the anonymous reviewers for their useful suggestions and feedback.

References

1. Ardagna, D., Panicucci, B., Passacantando, M.: A game theoretic formulation of the service provisioning problem in cloud systems. In: WWW 2011, pp. 177–186 (2011)
2. Artikis, A.: Dynamic protocols for open agent systems. In: Proc. AAMAS 2009, pp. 97–104. IFAAMAS (2009)
3. Artikis, A., Sergot, M., Pitt, J.: Specifying norm-governed computational societies. ACM Transactions on Computational Logic 10(1), 1–42 (2009)
4. Birman, K., Chockler, G., van Renesse, R.: Toward a cloud computing research agenda. SIGACT News 40(2), 68–80 (2009)
5. Carminati, B., Ferrari, E., Perego, A.: Enforcing access control in web-based social networks. ACM Trans. Inf. Syst. Secur. 13(1), 1–38 (2009)
6. Easwaran, A., Pitt, J.: Supply chain formation in open, market-based multi-agent systems. International Journal of Computational Intelligence and Applications 2(3), 349–363 (2002)
7. Garey, M., Johnson, D., Sethi, R.: The complexity of flowshop and jobshop scheduling. Mathematics of Operations Research 1(2), 117–129 (1976)
8. Jones, A., Sergot, M.: A formal characterisation of institutionalised power. Journal of the IGPL 4(3), 427–443 (1996)
9. Kowalski, R., Sergot, M.: A logic-based calculus of events. New Generation Computing 4, 67–95 (1986)
10. Ostrom, E.: Governing the Commons. CUP (1990)
11. Pitt, J., Schaumeier, J., Artikis, A.: The axiomatisation of socio-economic principles for self-organising systems. In: Proceedings SASO 2011 (2011)
12. Pudjianto, D., Ramsay, C., Strbac, G.: Microgrids and virtual power plants: concepts to support the integration of distributed energy resources. Proc. IMechE, A: J. of Power and Energy 222, 731–741 (2008)
13. Sadighi Firozabadi, B., Sergot, M.: Contractual access control. In: Christianson, B., Crispo, B., Malcolm, J.A., Roe, M. (eds.) Security Protocols 2002. LNCS, vol. 2845, pp. 96–103. Springer, Heidelberg (2004)
14. Sandhu, R., Ferraiolo, D., Kuhn, R.: The NIST model for role-based access control: Toward a unified standard. In: 5th ACM Workshop Role-Based Access Control, RBAC 2000, pp. 47–63 (2000)

Standards, Data Models, Ontologies, Rules: Prerequisites for Comprehensive Clinical Practice Guidelines

Emory Fry[1] and Davide Sottara[2]

[1] Department of Modeling and Simulation, Naval Health Research Center, 140 Sylvester Road San Diego, CA 92106, USA
eafry@gmx.com

[2] DEIS, University of Bologna, Viale Risorgimento, 2 40136 - Bologna, Italy
davide.sottara2@unibo.it

Abstract. General technical challenges in providing a standardized semantic, structural, and conceptual foundation for comprehensive Clinical Decision Support (CDS) are introduced. The prerequisite requirements for a) standard representations of domain data, b) standard vocabularies to unambiguously define and declare domain concepts, and c) an expressive description logic syntax with which to articulate and encode domain knowledge are examined with reference to the use of CDS in automating Clinical Practice Guidelines. Semantic web, uncertainty and other cognitive technologies are discussed in the context of improving the reliability and adaptability of clinical guidelines in real-world scenarios. Select opportunities for incorporating standards and technology capabilities available in non-medical communities are highlighted when appropriate.

1 Introduction

Clinical Decision Support (CDS) refers broadly to the application of information technology in support of medical cognitive processes. Since the advent of electronic medical systems, investigators have explored how rule and workflow management technologies might be leveraged to support healthcare requirements. Capabilities ranging from diagnostic guides, to provider order entry systems, to ambitious attempts at guideline management are maturing rapidly. Recent efforts at expanding the general availability of information technology and curb the exponential increases in healthcare costs are accelerating the time when medical infrastructure might realize the opportunities that CDS promises to deliver [32]. The attendant funding is fueling a CDS renaissance of sorts within the industry.

The following provides a cursory review of technical challenges in providing the semantic, structural, and conceptual foundation needed for comprehensive CDS. It is not meant to be an exhaustive or definitive analysis, but rather an introduction illustrating that the medical informatics community shares many of the same concerns as the larger business community.

F. Olken et al. (Eds.): RuleML 2011 - America, LNCS 7018, pp. 252–266, 2011.

2 Foundational Pillars

Effective knowledge representation and management mandate foundational support for a) standardized representations of domain data, b) standardized vocabularies to unambiguously define and declare domain concepts, and c) description logic syntax with which to encode domain knowledge. Clinical Decision Support is similarly constrained by these requirements [33]. While the structural integrity of each of these pillars is still uneven and not fully mature, considerable academic and organizational investment is being made to ensure they are appropriately addressed.

2.1 Decision Logic

Early efforts at clinical decision support used conventional programming approaches that by their nature mixed inference and control logic into discrete procedural steps [37]. Using this strategy, decision flow control is made explicit. Such declarative representations were readily developed using the technologies and programmer skill sets available at the time, and indeed, clinical decision support use cases that relied on decision trees, for example, were efficiently implemented.

Coupling control and inference logic, however, makes reusing and managing large collections of knowledge modules or procedures more difficult. A more comfortable paradigm in which to express medical declarative logic was found in the use of production rules that separate the if-then statements used to articulate domain knowledge from the control logic required by the application [34]. Cleanly separating inference and control concerns with production rules, using either forward chaining or backward chaining approaches, is arguably a more extensible approach to clinical decision support. Decision Tables, reflecting the natural expression of production rules, proved a popular and effective paradigm for expressing medical declarative logic. Encapsulation of inference logic inside a production rule managed by a dedicated engine also provided for the evolution of domain specific languages largely abstracted from implementation concerns [15].

An early clinical informatics standard, Arden Syntax, bridges procedural approaches to building CDS systems with production rule engines. Arden organizes domain knowledge into Medical Logic Modules (MLMs) having more than a cursory resemblance to procedural paradigms. They also incorporate the notion of an activation event used to direct module execution similar to concept of a trigger commonly found in production rules [18]. Unfortunately, Arden has a somewhat simplistic object model where the implementation specifics for the data used by a rule evaluation are under-specified. Commonly referred to within the community as the curly braces problem, the specific object model used by an Arden MLM are deferred to the implementer [20]. The lack of constraint on run-time bindings reduces Arden's potential for build sharable logic modules. It has also been suggested that its more technical procedural syntax for expressing declarative logic is hard to read and thus validate by domain experts [15].

As a result, Arden Syntax has engendered limited adoption within the healthcare vendor community.

Reflecting the ongoing debate within the business community, medical informatics has reached little consensus regarding a lingua franca for expressing clinical declarative logic. As a consequence, logic developed at one organization using the expressive syntax best matched to the local run-time infrastructure, cannot readily be shared or exchanged even with willing recipients. Content development is arguably the most expensive, labor-intensive, and knowledge dependent aspect of clinical decision support [13]. Our inability to cross-compile domain knowledge once encapsulated requires that a recipient commit significant effort and labor to re-validating and re-implementing shared rule or CDS artifact. This duplication of effort is an important economic obstacle to the widespread adoption of clinical decision support. The complexity and rapidly evolving nature of medical domain knowledge, the lack of a lingua franca, and the critical shortage of the medical informaticians [16] required to facilitate knowledge encapsulation is a priority that must be addressed.

2.2 Guideline Formalisms

Clinical Practice Guidelines (CPG) are a mainstay for consolidating expert opinion and communicating evidence-based best practice. A comprehensive and workflow driven CPG articulates not only discreet decision points, but also temporal constraints that should be respected when implementing the evidence-based care they recommend. While it is indeed possible to express time dependent guidelines using Arden, the standard is better suited for expressing discrete, stateless rule evaluations with only limited chaining[37].

Other approaches attempting to better reflect clinical guideline and medical workflow formalisms soon emerged. GELLO [39] is an ongoing effort to increase the workflow expressiveness of CDS artifacts. Based on OMG's Object Constraint Language, GELLO facilitates the retrieving of data models from HL7[1] Reference Information Model (RIM) compliant databases and then logically reasoning over the data. It is object-oriented, can leverage OCL compliant tooling, and was designed to provide a rich expression language for decision logic in guideline formalisms.

Nevertheless, guidelines imply stateful, long-lived processes for which GELLO's object constraint syntax is not ideal. Consequently, process oriented guideline projects merged to better support effective clinical decision support in the clinical work environment. ASBRU [36], PRODIGY [21], EON [40] and GLIF [5] are all notable examples of initial task oriented clinical guideline systems. These projects represent early definitional and semantic efforts to identify tasks, roles and responsibilities common to the medical domain. Later, systems such as GUIDE [10] and SAGE [41] led an evolution towards not only defining the conceptual and semantic landscape, but also prototyping the technical implementations to enact clinical decision support recommendations in their real-world environments .

[1] www.hl7.org

The work with Arden Syntax, GELLO, and automated guideline management have yet to capture the imagination of the vendor community. Medical workflow formalisms have been slow to incoporate business process management innovations such as Business Process Modeling Notation (BPMN2[2]) or OASIS Business Process Execution Language (WS-BPEL[3]). Such standards have reached significant conceptual maturity and run time engines capable of encoding complex business relationships and behaviors are readily available. As an example, work represented by the OASIS Web Services Human Task standard reflects sophisticated conceptual refinement regarding transfer versus delegation of responsibility. The standard's task state engine has significant implications for optimizing human and system behaviors that are critically important for innumerable medical workflows; the transfer of patient care between attendings, housestaff, nursing, or consultants can only be represented adequately if the distinction between transfer and delegation are formally recognized. Commercially available infrastructure supporting such concepts is available, but there has been comparatively little refinement in the medical community regarding how such products can be leveraged for clinical decision support.

The standardization efforts that are ongoing and accelerating at other layers of our infrastructure must be extended to the realm of declarative logic and workflow management if the commercial availability, affordability and sustainability of clinical decision support are to be realized.

2.3 Clinical Data Models

The second pillar of our hypothetical foundation for CDS is the data model used to instantiate clinical concepts, observations, and real-world facts. Data models play a crucial role in reliably and accurately communicating information within a run-time system, during an exchange with an external partner, and for ensuring conceptual relationships are preserved on storage to or retrieval from a persistence store. Medicine has at its disposal several languages for defining such data structures, including, but not limited to, Clinical Element Model [11], GALEN Representation and Integration Language [35], Archetype Definition Language [3], and more recently Web Ontology Language[4]. These languages are all capable of defining reproducible and conceptually consistent structures that rule and workflow implementations require for reliable execution. In the United States, Health Level 7 Reference Information Model (RIM) Version 3 is the predominant defacto standard.

As a conceptual model, RIM allows for numerous representations tailored to specific use cases through iterative constraints during implementation. The RIM can be instantiated in structured documents using HL7s Clinical Document Architecture (CDA), or as messages optimized for the real-time communication requirements of laboratory, order-entry, and other transactional business

[2] www.omg.org/spec/BPMN/2.0/
[3] docs.oasis-open.org/wsbpel/2.0/wsbpel-v2.0.html
[4] www.w3.org/2007/OWL

processes. HL7 Standards like CDA or V3 Messaging ensure consistency with the RIM, but they do not guarantee interoperability between systems that typically have concrete interface and class requirements. They do not ensure that the data bindings expected by a CDS are unambiguous and machine consumable. These standards are under-specified and must be further constrained by implementation specifications from organization such as Integrating the Healthcare Enterprise (IHE[5]) or Healthcare Information Technology Standards Panel (HITSP[6]) before true interoperability can be achieved.

The HL7 RIM Version 3 also provides the conceptual framework for building the run-time object models that middle tier components and services require. Unfortunately, HL7 does not yet provide object model specifications sufficient to avoid the curly braces problem and to support seamless sharing of rules between clinical decision support systems. Even if the rule could be loaded into a partners inference engine, object model discrepancies would preclude reliable execution. Consensus regarding object classes, attributes and required semantics has not been achieved, and implementation specificity is still left to interpretation by the engineer. As a consequence, clinical decision support systems, especially those that rely on concrete class structures to represent data relationships, cannot be expected to consume and process decision-support rules from non-self systems without significant analysis, mapping, and reimplementation.

There are many groups actively working to define to fully constrained detailed clinical models that satisfy particular domain conceptual requirements. The HL7 Clinical Decision Support Working Group[7] sponsors two initiatives, Detailed Clinical Models (DCM) and the Virtual Medical Record (vMR), that are of illustrative of these efforts. HL7 DCMs intend to provide unambiguous semantics and structural constraints on the RIM so that clinical information can be more readily instantiated as interoperable, standalone clinical "components reusable in a variety of EMR, warehousing, messaging or health information technology deployments [14]. vMR is a complimentary effort to identify further restrictions to HL7 models for defining a simplified subset of data representations specifically relevant for CDS. A principle goal of the vMR is the creation of a unified CDS data model that reduces structural and semantic discrepancies, simplifies CDS development, and ensures a consistent set of standardized data inputs and outputs for inference services [24].

While considerable progress has been made in facilitating the implementation of detailed clinical models, these efforts, as are the initiatives of many similar international efforts, remain incomplete. Our ability to build run-time artifacts with the structural and semantic consistency required for authoring rules sufficiently decoupled from local infrastructure to be sharable is limited. There is a vital need to establish a publically accessible canonical object model standard. Until this is accomplished, our ability to share artifacts, reduce content development costs, and encourage widespread CDS adoption will remain impeded.

---

[5] www.ihe.net

[6] www.hitsp.org

[7] www.hl7.org/Special/committees/dss/index.cfm

2.4 Semantics and Terminology Services

The final foundational pillar consists of the vocabularies and terminologies used to unambiguously define domain concepts. Here again healthcare enjoys a wealth of candidate vocabularies, developed initially within particular clinical communities with domain specific requirements. Available vocabularies include SNOMED, LOINC, CPT, ICD-9, and ICD-10. These terminologies are highly variable in both conceptual granularity and in their comprehensiveness. This discordance creates several challenges for Clinical Decision Support for is not uncommon to store data in one system using a vocabulary (e.g. diagnoses using ICD-9) for which there is no precise, corresponding concept in the vocabulary (e.g. SNOMED) used by another system encoding similar data. Such one-to-many mapping concerns can not easily be adjudicated without potentially affecting the conceptual analysis of the data [12]. When aggregated for the purpose of CDS analysis, data terminology differences must optimally be resolved (translated) before a single rule can reason over the collective. Similarly, when rules are used to analyze data of varying conceptual granularity, the system must determine the conceptual equivalence (subsumption) of the data to ensure all relevant evaluations are performed. A particularly difficult situation occurs when a rule employs one vocabulary, but is presented facts utilizing another. In such cases both translation and subsumption may be required.

CDS Terminology Services, therefore, play a crucial role in any comprehensive, real-world scenario where semantic discordance between local and/or distributed source systems is commonly encountered. Systems such as the National Library of Medicine Unified Medical Language System (UMLS) [28], or the proprietary 3M Health Data Dictionary [9], define concrete conceptual maps for translating between terminologies. While in the short term, such static mappings are feasible and even expedient for select CDS uses, the long-term maintainability and brittleness of such mappings is probably unsustainable. Medical terminologies are constantly evolving to accommodate exponential increases in domain knowledge; the level of effort required to sustain static translational mappings in such run-time environments are enormous and expensive.

An alternative approach, as of yet immature, relies on evolving current medical terminologies into ontologies. An ontology describes, using an appropriate Description Logic, the relevant concepts in a domain, the known individuals of that domain, and all the relationships between them including hierarchical membership and subsumption relations. A semantic reasoners (specialized type of inference engine) can leverage this expressiveness to match and even translate between concepts defined in one or more ontologies [29].

While an ontology approach holds greatest promise for supporting rich and flexible semantic infrastructures, in the near-term static-mapping approaches are more realistic. HL7 relies on over 100 distinct vocabularies and taxonomies to provide the conceptual definition required when constraining its reference information model. Harmonizing these vocabularies and their conceptual relationships into ontologies usable by Semantic Web technologies is undoubtedly a long term objective.

3 Towards Semantic Guidelines

There is tremendous interest within the medical informatics community regarding other ways semantic technologies can be utilized in the development of software applications, including (Clinical) Decision Support Systems. Semantic reasoners can deliver other capabilities including (i) inferring additional hierarchy relations implicitly present in the descriptions, but not explicitly asserted; (ii) deciding whether an individual is an instance of a class by virtue of its properties and the class definition; and (iii) creating concrete models which can be used for rule-based inference.

For example, while many medical terminologies lack the constraints used by full-fledged ontologies to help prevent semantic inconsistencies [8], combinations of higher-level ontologies and more simplistic vocabularies can enable complex "sentences" suitable for expressing clinical practice guidelines that can be shared between different organizations ([17]). The additional ontologic structure ensures that both parties can unambiguously understand the semantic content of what would otherwise be a simple syntactic construct. Such definition is a mandatory prerequisite for sharing guideline content between different organizations or performing translations into different languages (e.g. a non-standard, private representation internal to a company) while still preserving the original intended meaning.

While a semantic reasoner might process such "semantic" guidelines to potentially evaluate other components of a CPG (guideline inclusion criteria, decision logic, or recommended interventions), more dynamic evaluations, including the execution of actions, are instead better defined and executed using rules. This duality can pose integration problems, since semantic and rule-based reasoners, in general, do not share the same internal structures and inference capabilities. In particular, semantic reasoners are proactive and make Open World assumptions treating missing information as unknown and delaying any decision depending on that information. Rule-based reasoners are typically reactive, make Closed World assumptions, and consider missing information to be false. Furthermore, semantic reasoners are usually based on triples, while rule-based reasoner exploit frames or even proper objects [22].

Such architectural details make the interaction non-trivial, to the point that several more recent systems tend to prefer the exclusive use of a semantic reasoner over a rule based one. In KON [7], for example, all the inference is done using a semantic reasoner, while the actions are delegated to native code without even using a rule engine. Other systems (e.g. [22]) utilize rules written with the Semantic Web Rule Language (SWRL), which has the advantage of being for optimized for execution by a semantic reasoner. The language, however, is not as expressive as a full rule syntax might be; SWRL rules are also executed under Open World assumptions.

If required, hybrid systems capable of leveraging both types of reasoners can be implemented. As described in [23]: rules executed by a rule engine can be defined using concepts derived from an ontology, allowing part of the rule evaluation to be delegated to a semantic reasoner. In this approach both reasoners share the same fact and data model (some conversion might be needed depending on the internal representations used by each engine) facilitating the choice of the most appropriate reasoning style. The maximum level of integration would be achieved if a single hybrid engine was capable of performing both types of reasoning, thus eliminating the need to make calls between two separate components.

4 Uncertainty Enriched Systems

A semantically constrained guideline, processed by either rule-based or semantic reasoners, would help ensure that a it is applied and executed uniformly. Nevertheless, enriching the expressiveness of the languages, augmenting the complexity of the data models, and improving the computational capabilities of the inference engines might not be sufficient to capture all the nuances explicitly and implicitly present in a clinical guideline. CPG authors usually express their domain knowldge in natural language - these reference documents are prone to misinterpretation and erroneous implementation by non-clinical engineers.

A medical guideline is likely to be affected by various forms of imperfection [42] that cannot be encapsulated directly using the techniques discussed so far. We use the term imperfection in the sense of Smets [38], i.e. a condition of imprecision, uncertainty or vagueness which inherently pervades an accurate model of the real world. Ignoring this imperfection does not make a guideline more robust, and may even make it more difficult to apply in practice.

4.1 Vagueness

For example, clinical problems and their solutions are often imperfectly defined, even in clinical guidelines developed by consensus. Domain knowledge provided by subject matter experts might be inherently vague, for example, a Family Practice guideline for the diagnosis and treatment of jaundice in "young babies" that does not precisely define what "young babies" means or implies. For the intended audience, such terms are naturally constrained by the demographics of the patient populations they treat. For the CDS engineer attempting to encode the guidelines intent, these assumptions may not be recognized - they must be made explicit. In cases where disambiguation is not possible, fuzzy logic is an appropriate and effective modelling tool for decision making in ambiguous medical contexts [27], [42]. Fuzzy logic allows a guideline modeller to give quantitative definitions to vague, qualitative concepts (e.g. age - young, weight - fat, pressure - high) using membership functions. The use of fuzzy properties also avoids critical discontinuities that can result in different treatments for patients which have, in reality, the same condition. Consider for example the declarative statements "give Tylenol if fever is high" as opposed to "if greater than 38C". Using the first expression, a provider may or may not treat depending on their interpretation of "high". In the latter, the final decision is definitively directed even when a patient's body temperature is close to the threshold value.

4.2 Uncertainty

In contrast to vagueness which stems from inadequate definition, uncertainty results from missing or incomplete information and is another unavoidable characteristic of most clinical decision processes. Even under the best of conditions, diagnoses are often not 100% certain; a medication or a procedure is not guaranteed to have always the same (desired) effect; or the pathophysiology of a disease may be incompletely understood. Decisions made at various branching points within a guideline should take this uncertainty into account.

Several attempts at incorporating uncertainty into CDS have been made. An early approach relied on "certainty factors" [6] used to approximate a form of Bayesian inference. After the formal discovery of Bayesian Networks and related probabilistic reasoning and inference techniques, the management of uncertainty in CDS in general, and clinical guidelines in particular, has shifted to the use of two main approaches.

One strategy extends the native capabilities of logic and rule-based systems with uncertainty. The first category includes all systems based on certainty factors and evolutions thereof, including but not limited to belief functions (e.g.[25]). A second strategy focuses on probabilistic models that are given a logical interpretation - this approach includes systems based on neural networks and statistical methods (e.g. [1]). From a user perspective these differences in strategy are not always clear; the former class of systems uses a top down approach, building on top of expert knowledge; the latter use bottom-up approaches in which models are trained using raw data and thus are more suitable when explicit knowledge is not available [31].

Despite the apparent conveniences, only a few CDS using fuzzy logic have been developed [1], and most mainstream guideline modelling tools do not currently support uncertainty [26]. One possible reason is that such reasoning techniques typically require dedicated inference engines that common workflow / production rule engines do not usually support. Again, the complexity of managing multiple run-time engines is a major deterrent to applying the best inference strategy for the problem at hand. Cognitive support to the healthcare provider could be optimized if a single hybrid engine was capable of performing multiple types of reasoning. At the present time, if a guideline needs production rule, vagueness and/or uncertain support, this integration must be provided explicitly.

5 Runtime Adaptation

Even if guideline implementations are precise semantically, capable of managing vagueness and uncertainty, they are not guaranteed to be appropriate for a given run-time context. Clinical Practice Guidelines are consensus driven and thus make idealized assumptions regarding physician capabilities, patient characteristics, and clinical context. In practice there are countless exceptions to these assumptions. It would be impractical to accommodate all possible scenarios explicitly and a physician might still deliberately want to override the guideline workflow. When such situations are encountered, guideline execution needs be able to gracefully deviate from the original specification.

Several attempts at adapting clinical guideline execution have been reported. Some of these projects interpret process flow as plans in the AI sense where a sequence of actions aims to achieve a defined goal. In [30], case-based reasoning techniques are used to define a default plan suitable for a class of problems. This plan may then be refined using proper planning techniques [2] to match the identified context.

In the approach proposed in [4] the guideline plan is not modified dynamically to accommodate for exceptional situations. Instead, the CDS performs compliance checks to determine if the actions that were directed by the user are compatible with its original specifications. The criteria for determining such compatibility are explicitly defined as adjunct rule sets that evaluate whether alternative actions might be justified. Notice that the criteria to detect the anomalies and the logic to deal with them are not part of the guideline, but are defined in modules which can be composed as needed. Whenever the execution flow deviates from planned or expected behaviour, a violation is logged and then evaluated. If a violation can be justified, the user's actions are permitted and the system compensates for the perceived plan violation. If the action can not be justified, the conformance violation is reported and the system may optionally cancel the guidelines execution.

6 Distributed Decsion Support Services and Knowledge Management Respository

Naval Health Research Center, San Diego's Distributed Decsion Support Services and Knowledge Management Respository (DDSS-KMR) project is a standards-based engineering effort addressing many of the challenges described above. The project implements key concepts from a variety of initiatives, particularly SAGE, to implement a robust knowledge management infrastructure using available open source technologies.

DDSS-KMR provides standards-based object models that are based on the HL7 RIM, use V3 Messaging and CDA standards to define datatypes and attributes, and follow HITSP/IHE implementation specifications to constrain terminologies and structure. Clinical data, aggregated from local and distributed repositories, are mapped into this canonical fact model and stored in rule engine's working memory as a patient specific virtual medical record. This stateful in-memory vMR enables workflow, inference and predictive analytic technologies to provide high performance cognitive and process support.

A hybrid architecture provides commercially available engines to deliver these capabilities. Event Driven Architecture (EDA) components provide the temporal responsive required for effective Clinical Decision Support, triggering appropriate analytic processing in response to real-time events. Triggers can be messages, for example the HL7 transaction sets used to communicate laboratory results, healthcare summaries delivered dynamically from outside organizations, or patient monitor waveforms that require Complex Event Processing to be handled effectively. Upon receiving the data, the system transforms the information into the same canonical object structure as data retrieved from a persisted store.

A Production Rule engine, exposed as a Decision Support Agent using the Foundation for Intelligent and Physical Agents' Agent Communication Language (FIPA-ACL[8]). This architecture is utilized to a) capture and encode clinical domain expertise, b) ensure process validity with respect to declarative constraints, and c)provide flexible control over application/middle tier behavior. The system uses Drools (aka JBoss Rules[9]). While engines from other vendors can be substituted, the ability to manage both inference and workflow within the same instance of the engine simplifies service orchestration tremendously. A design principle unique to the DDSS-KMR approach is that rule and workflow processing can be executed within a patient-specific session, each being dynamically instantiated and provisioned with the patient's vMR and context-specific knowledge bases. This design, while resource intensive, ensures personalized, high-performance rule evaluations; scalability is ensured by a series of enhancements collectively called "Drools Grid" that is now available as an add-on that can be integrated with the core engine. While still experimental, Grid enables dynamic provisioning of rule sessions on any available machine.

Initiated workflows are enacted using Service Oriented Architecture (SOA) components, each service ensuring that core business logic is well-abstracted, reusable, and encapsulated behind standards-based interfaces. A WS-Human Task service manages the lifecycle of tasks assigned to human performers by the rule engine. The actual performance of those tasks is accomplished by a series of connectors packaged as a Task Library providing interfaces for sending email, booking appointments, placing orders, escalating messages, making phone calls, and sending SMS text messages.

Not all clinical decisions are best approached with declarative logic - some require alternative inference techniques. To expand the analytic capabilities available, we implemented a Predictive Model Markup Language (PMML[10]) infrastructure, the de facto standard used to represent predictive models, so that resource-capacity planning, risk-assessment, and diagnostic models could be plugged into the Clinical Decision Support architecture.

DDSS-KMR provides integrated knowledge management, analytic, and predictive modeling capabilities. As a standards-based Clinical Decision Support environment, it is well suited to deliver knowledge services that can be layered on a variety of health information networks. An additional goal is to contribute a reference architecture that can be leveraged by CDS researchers, either within their own labs for their own purposes, or as part of a more collaborative community effort. DDSS-KMR will be open sourced release as a community contribution to the Federal Health Architecture Group CONNECT [11] project in early 2012.

[8] www.fipa.org
[9] www.jboss.org/drools
[10] www.dmg.org/pmml-v4-0-1.html
[11] www.connectopensource.org

7 Conclusion

Despite the resurgent interest in Clinical Decision Support and the enormous capital investments currently underway, CDS as a fundamental infrastructure capability continues to struggle with typical implementation concerns. As with any early stage deployment of knowledge management infrastructure, numerous inter-dependent business processes remain poorly understood and incompletely implemented. Clinical processes, architectures, domain standards, and behaviors remain hotly contested as participants initially focus on requirements felt to be singularly important to preserve. Such turmoil hampers the implementation of CDS which benefits significantly from standardized, predictable processes and business requirements.

The future contribution of CDS to quality of care and patient outcomes remains uncertain and its near-term impact should be viewed with healthy skepticism. The practical effectiveness of existing CDS has been evaluated several times in recent years. While many researchers agree that CDS can result in significant changes in practitioner performance, the final effectiveness varies according to the specific application, with some (e.g. drug prescription) being more suitable candidates for decision support than others. The impact on patient outcomes is considerably less clear with fewer studies identifying positive benefits. [19] Such cautionary data underscores the need for a considered, iterative approach to CDS implementation. Medicine is a community poised for making large captial investments in health information technology; it should consider carefully whether it truly has the conceptual refinement, the organizational maturity, and the necessary standards to implement large scale CDS deployments without considerable risk. Given the social-polical-economic environment, healthcare has an unprecedent opportunity to redefine its technological foundation; it should remain cognizant that considerable organizational introspection and process reengineering is needed to implement any technology successfully.

Nevertheless, given the successful application of inference and workflow technology in other communities, there should be considerable optimism that this most complex of human endeavors can indeed be decomposed into more manageable and predictable system component and interfaces. It's also true that early and seemingly irreconcilable differences often prove less important once the reengineering effort matures. If the experiences, standards and technology capabilities that found success in business markets at large can be harmonized with healthcare concerns, the full integration of clinical decision support into the very fabric of our health care delivery system may be closer than one might otherwise expect.

References

1. Abbasi, M., Kashiyarndi, S.: Clinical Decision Support Systems: A Discussion on Different Methodologies Used in Health Care (2010)
2. Anselma, L., Montani, S.: Supporting and Optimizing Clinical Guidelines Execution. Citeseer (2008)

3. Beale, T.: The OpenEHR Archetype System. 1, 1–19 (2003)
4. Bottrighi, A., Chesani, F., Mello, P., Montali, M., Montani, S.: Conformance Checking of Executed Clinical Guidelines in Presence of Basic Medical Knowledge. Event (London), 1–12
5. Boxwala, A., Peleg, M., Tu, S., Ogunyemi, O., Zeng, Q., Wang, D., Patel, V., Greenes, R., Shortliffe, E.: GLIF3: a Representation Format for Sharable Computer-Interpretable Clinical Practice Guidelines. Journal of Biomedical Informatics 37(3), 147–161 (2004)
6. Buchanan, B.G., Shortliffe, E.H.: Rule-based Expert Systems: The MYCIN Experiments of the Stanford Heuristic Programming Project. Addison-Wesley, Reading (1984)
7. Ceccarelli, M., Stasio, A.D., Donatiello, A., Vitale, D.: A Guideline Engine For Knowledge Management in Clinical Decision Support Systems (CDSSs)
8. Ceusters, W., Smith, B., Flanagan, J.: Ontology and Medical Terminology: Why Description Logics Are Not Enough. Computing (2003)
9. Che, C., Monson, K., Poon, K.B., Shakib, S.C., Lau, L.M.: Managing Vocabulary Mapping Services. In: AMIA Annual Symposium Proceedings, vol. 2005, p. 916. American Medical Informatics Association (2005)
10. Ciccarese, P., Caffi, E., Quaglini, S., Stefanelli, M.: Architectures and Tools for Innovative Health Information Systems: The Guide Project. International Journal of Medical Informatics 74(7-8), 553–562 (2005)
11. Coyle, J., Mori, A., Huff, S.: Standards for Detailed Clinical Models as the Basis for Medical Data Exchange and Decision Support. International Journal Of Medical Informatics 69(2-3), 157–174 (2003)
12. Doerr, M.: Semantic Problems of Thesaurus Mapping. Journal of Digital Information 1(8), 1–27 (2001)
13. Eccles, M., Mason, J.: How to Develop Cost-Conscious Guidelines. Health Technology Assessment (Winchester, England) 5(16), 1–69 (2001)
14. Goossen, W., Goossen-Baremans, A., van der Zel, M.: Detailed Clinical Models: A Review. Healthcare Informatics Research 16(4), 201–214 (2010)
15. Greenes, R.A.: Clinical Decision Support: The Road Ahead. Academic Press (2006)
16. Hersh, W.: Health and Biomedical Informatics: Opportunities and Challenges for a Twenty-First Century Profession and Its Education. Yearb. Med. Inform., 157–164 (2008)
17. Hrabak, K.M., Campbell, J.R., Tu, S.W., McClure, R., Weida, R.T.: Creating Interoperable Guidelines: Requirements of Vocabulary Standards in Immunization Decision Support.. Studies In Health Technology And Informatics 129(Pt 2), 930–934 (January 2007)
18. Hripcsak, G., Clayton, P., Pryor, T.: The Arden Syntax for Medical Logic Modules. In: 14. Annual Symposium on Computer Applications in Medical Care, pp. 200–204 (1990)
19. Jaspers, M.W.M., Smeulers, M., Vermeulen, H., Peute, L.W.: Effects of Clinical Decision-Support Systems on Practitioner Performance and Patient Outcomes: A Synthesis of High-Quality Systematic Review Findings. Journal of the American Medical Informatics Association 18(3), 327–334 (2011)
20. Jenders, R.A., Sujansky, W., Broverman, C.A., Chadwick, M.: Towards Improved Knowledge Sharing: Assessment of the HL7 Reference Information Model to Support Medical Logic Module Queries. In: Proceedings of the AMIA Annual Fall Symposium, pp. 308–312 (January 1997)

21. Johnson, P.D., Tu, S., Booth, N., Sugden, B., Purves, I.N.: Using Scenarios in Chronic Disease Management Guidelines for Primary Care. In: Proceedings of the AMIA Annual Fall Symposium, pp. 389–393 (January 2000)
22. Jovic, A., Prcela, M., Gamberger, D.: Ontologies in Medical Knowledge Representation. In: 29th International Conference on Information Technology Interfaces, pp. 535–540 (June 2007)
23. Kashyap, V., Morales, A.: On Implementing Clinical Decision Support: Achieving Scalability and Maintainability by Combining Business Rules and Ontologies. In: AMIA Annual Symposium, vol. 40(C) (2006)
24. Kawamoto, K., Del Fiol, G., Strasberg, H., Hulse, N., Curtis, C., Cimino, J., Rocha, B., Maviglia, S., Fry, E., Scherpbier, H., et al.: Multi-National, Multi-Institutional Analysis of Clinical Decision Support Data Needs to Inform Development of the HL7 Virtual Medical Record Standard. In: AMIA Annual Symposium Proceedings, vol. 2010, p. 377. American Medical Informatics Association (2010)
25. Kong, G., Xu, D., Yang, J., Body, R., Mackway-Jones, K., Carley, S.: A Belief Rule-Based Decision Support System for Clinical Risk Assessment of Cardiac Chest Pain. pp. 1–31
26. Kong, G., Xu, D.L., Yang, J.B.: Clinical Decision Support Systems: a Review of Knowledge Representation and Inference Under Uncertainties. International Journal of Computational Intelligence Systems 1(2), 159 (2008)
27. Liu, J.C.S., Shiffinan, R.N.: Operationalization of Clinical Practice Guidelines Using Fuzzy Logic. Medical Informatics, 283–287
28. McCray, a.T., Nelson, S.J.: The Representation of Meaning in the UMLS. Methods of Information in Medicine 34(1-2), 193–201 (1995)
29. Mirhaji, P., Zhu, M., Vagnoni, M., Bernstam, E.V., Zhang, J., Smith, J.W.: Ontology Driven Integration Platform for Clinical and Translational Research. BMC Bioinformatics 10(suppl. 2), S2 (2009)
30. Montani, S.: Case-Based Reasoning for Managing Noncompliance with Clinical Guidelines. Computational Intelligence 25(3), 196–213 (2009)
31. Onisko, A., Lucas, P., Druzdzel, M.J.: Comparison of Rule-Based and Bayesian Network Approaches in Medical Diagnostic Systems
32. Osheroff, J.A., Teich, J.M., Middleton, B., Steen, E.B., Wright, A., Detmer, D.E.: A Roadmap for National Action on Clinical Decision Support. Journal of the American Medical Informatics Association 14(2), 141 (2007)
33. Parker, C.G., Rocha, R.A., Campbell, J.R., Tu, S.W., Huff, S.M.: Detailed Clinical Models for Sharable, Executable Guidelines. Studies in Health Technology and Informatics 107(Pt 1), 145–148 (2004)
34. Quinlan, J.R.: Generating Production Rules From Decision Trees.. In: Proceedings of the Tenth International Joint Conference on Artificial Intelligence, vol. 30107, pp. 304–307. Citeseer (1987)
35. Rector, A., Bechhofer, S., Goble, C., Horrocks, I., Nowlan, W., Solomon, W.: The GRAIL Concept Modelling Language for Medical Terminology. Artificial Intelligence in Medicine 9(2), 139–171 (1997)
36. Shahar, Y., Miksch, S., Johnson, P.: The Asgaard Project: A Task-Specific Framework for the Application and Critiquing of Time-Oriented Clinical Guidelines. Artificial Intelligence in Medicine 14(1-2), 29–51 (1998)
37. Sherman, E.H., Hripcsak, G., Starren, J., Jenders, R.A., Clayton, P.: Using Intermediate States to Improve the Ability of the Arden Syntax to Implement Care Plans and Reuse Knowledge.. In: Proceedings of the Annual Symposium on Computer Application in Medical Care, p. 238. American Medical Informatics Association (1995)

38. Smets, P.: Imperfect Information: Imprecision and Uncertainty, pp. 225–254 (1996)
39. Sordo, M., Boxwala, A.A., Ogunyemi, O., Greenes, R.A.: Description and Status Update on GELLO: A Proposed Standardized Object-Oriented Expression Language for Clinical Decision Support. Studies in Health Technology and Informatics 107(Pt 1), 164–168 (2004)
40. Tu, S.W., Musen, M.A.: The EON Model of Intervention Protocols and Guidelines. In: Proceedings of the AMIA Annual Fall Symposium, pp. 587–591 (January 1996)
41. Tu, S., Campbell, J., Glasgow, J., Nyman, M., McClure, R., McClay, J., Parker, C., Hrabak, K., Berg, D., Weida, T., et al.: The SAGE Guideline Model: Achievements and Overview. Journal of the American Medical Informatics Association 14(5), 589 (2007)
42. Warren, J., Beliakov, G., Zwaag, B.V.D.: Fuzzy Logic in Clinical Practice Decision Support Systems. Computing 00(c), 1–10 (2000)

Event Condition Expectation (ECE-) Rules for Monitoring Observable Systems

Stefano Bragaglia[1], Federico Chesani[1], Emory Fry[2], Paola Mello[1], Marco Montali[1], and Davide Sottara[1]

[1] DEIS, University of Bologna, Viale Risorgimento, 2
40136 - Bologna, Italy
{name.surname}@unibo.it

[2] Department of Modeling and Simulation, Naval Health Research Center
140 Sylvester Road, San Diego, CA 92126, USA
eafry@gmx.com

Abstract. The standardization and broad adoption of Service Oriented Architectures, Web Services, and Cloud Computing is raising the complexity of ICT systems. Hence, assuring correct system behavior with regard to established design and business constraints is of the utmost importance. Run-time monitoring, where the outcomes of an observed system are continuously checked against what is expected of it, is one possible approach to providing the required oversight.

In this paper, we discuss this notion of rule expectations, their violation and/or fulfillment, and use these concepts to define the concept of an Event-Condition-Expectation (ECE-) rule, a variation of the traditional Event-Condition-Action rule pattern. To demonstrate these concepts, we present extensions to the syntax used by the production rule engine, Drools, and describe their use in a medical case study. The clinical decision support system being developed monitors rule evaluations and expectations, detects constraint violations and is able to take recovery/compensation actions as appropriate.

1 Introduction

In the last ten years there has been a flourishing of models and technologies for developing, deploying, and maintaining ICT systems based on heterogeneous and distributed components. Paradigms such as Service Oriented Architectures (SOA), Web Services (WS), Cloud Computing, Business Process Management Systems and Workflows (BPMS) have been already largely adopted by the ICT industry. When focusing on the medical and healthcare context, automated clinical guidelines [4], care plans, and clinical decision support in general aim to ensure that care standards can be implemented reliably and effectively. These solutions allow for increasingly complex systems, while the adoption of standards pushes for the use of heterogeneous, third-party (software/hardware) components. Consequently, assuring the correct behaviour of such systems is becoming a harder task. Traditional debug techniques alone might not be enough, either

F. Olken et al. (Eds.): RuleML 2011 - America, LNCS 7018, pp. 267–281, 2011.

because of the complexity of the overall system, or because third-party components are often treated as black boxes and so it is not possible to use debugging tools. Run-time monitoring techniques could be of some help by checking if the system behaves correctly while it is *executing*. Typically, a system developer specifies in advance the correct outcomes for any/some possible input. By observing the inputs and the outputs of the system, a monitor automatically verifies that the outputs match with the expected outcomes. In case of a positive answer, the system is deemed to be *conformant*. Such approach is exploited also to verify the correctness of complex systems against some high-level constraints. For example, Quality of Service (QoS) criteria must be continuously monitored, and proper actions must be taken if such criteria are not met. Likewise, legal aspects and business constraints could be subjected to monitoring. A possible way for expressing the desired behaviour of a system is by means of *rules* (ECA Rules, logic-based rules, etc.), that define the *expectations*. Intuitively, we consider an expectation a "justified state of anticipation" about the state of a system, given that some *conditions* on the current system's state and its environment already hold. However, to the best of our knowledge, the notion of *expectation* is rarely used as a "first-class entity" and it is only partially supported. Instead, we strongly believe that it can greatly help in the task of specifying the desired behaviour of a system, since it is a natural, direct way for characterizing the desired behaviour of a system. In addition, we also propose to exploit the concepts of *fulfillment* and *violation* to model the actual outcome of an expectation. Taking inspiration from the ECA rule family, we propose the "Event Condition Expectation (ECE-) Rules". In such rules, the premise defines the facts and events required to trigger an expectation, while the conclusion contains the description of what is expected to be observed. In this paper, we present our idea of expectation and ECE-Rules, and discuss the features that should be supported by this new class of rules (Section 2). We present also a first, prototypical implementation of these concepts based on the Drools [12] Framework (Section 3). In particular, we provide a new language for ECE-Rules (Section 4), and show its application in a real scenario (Section 5).

2 Expectations, Their Fulfillment and Violation

2.1 Related Works

The notion of expectation has been a research subject in many different IT-related fields, where the need for monitoring systems at run-time found a possible solution in the idea of checking the *conformance* of the observed system against some expected behaviour.

The deontic concepts and operators useful to represent norms, obligations and similar concepts have been individuated and mapped to an abductive logic programming context in [2]. Although motivated by a different scope, it provides a background and starting point that is also valid for the semantics of our proposal. In the Multi-Agent Systems (MAS) field, social approaches specify the agents' allowed interactions as expected behaviours (externally observed), and define fulfillment/violation in terms of deviance from what is expected. The framework SCIFF [1], for example, is mainly focused on a logic-based notion of *expectations* and their fulfillment/violation. Commitments, as deeply investigated by authors such as Singh [17,5,20] or Colombetti and Fornara [7], are defined as promises arising from agents interaction: a debtor agent becomes committed towards a creditor (i.e., it is *expected*) to bring about a certain property, i.e. make it true. In the Business Process research field, van der Aalst and colleagues propose declarative languages that focus on the properties that the system should exhibit: in the DecSerFlow language [14] the users can specify which are the business activities that are (not) *expected* to be executed, as a consequence of previously (not) executed activities. Within the field of legal reasoning and normative systems, authors like Governatori and Rotolo [11,16,9,10,8] have proposed temporal logic frameworks and languages to represent legal contracts between parties: primarily focused on *compliance* issues, such tools simulate the possible course of actions of a system and evaluate if contract agreements are indeed respected.

In the following we introduce our vision about expectations, and discuss a (preliminary, not exhaustive) set of features that, from our viewpoint, should be strictly linked to the notion of expectation, and to the idea of ECE-Rules.

2.2 Desiderata for the Notion of Expectation

Expectations should be about events and/or properties. In the literature it is possible to find expectations about different possible outcome types. An expectation could be about the *happening of an event*, described in terms of the happening time instant and the event duration, or it could be about the reaching a certain state of affairs, or a *property becoming true*, such as in the case of commitments. In particular, it could be desirable that such property is true in a certain instant, or for a whole time interval, continuously [19]. Notice that, in any case, we need to deal with (at least) a description, an initial time instant (a *start*), and a time duration (or, equivalently, an *end*).

Expectations should support closed, as well as open interactions. In *closed-interaction* complex systems, the set of possible events is tipically known a-priori, and at any given time, only few events are supposed/allowed to happen: unexpected events are an evident violation, since anything not explicitly expected is implicitly forbidden. However, the ongoing challenges posed by the new Internet era require very "flexible" systems able to cope with unpredictable, changing and dynamic environments, where the autonomy of interacting entities and the possibility of exploiting new opportunities must be preserved as much as possible [21], or the expertise of workers must be exploited at best [15]. In this context, "closed approaches" show some drawbacks in this regard. *Open interactions* overcome such limits, since they focus on the (minimal) set of constraints that must be guaranteed to successfully interact. To this aim, a further step is required: expectations about what should *not* happen should be supported, thus involving some notion of *prohibition*.

Expectations should be about future, as well as past events. Expectations should allow the user to specify *when* a certain event is expected. It is very intuitive to define expectations about future events, but it is also mandatory to be able to treat past expectations. Within a monitoring setting, it is often assumed that at any time instant T the set of already happened events is fixed, i.e., that any newly observed event will happen at a time greater than T (with a possible approximation Δ). Determining if an expectation about a past event is satisfied or not amounts to look for a matching event in such fixed set. Differently, any reasoning on expectations about future events should be "suspended", as far as future events are unknown. W.r.t. the time axis, monitoring is usually *closed* towards the past, and *open* towards the future.

Expectations should support temporal deadlines. In general, without any temporal deadline, it would not be possible to determine if an expectation has been fulfilled or violated. The problem is somehow mitigated for expectations about past events due to the the semi-open nature of the monitoring task, while any conclusion would be indefinitely suspended by an ideal monitor for expectations about future events. To avoid such situations, some systems (e.g., [1]) envisage a special *closure* event, whose semantic is that no more events will ever happen, allowing the monitor to draw final conclusions.

2.3 Desiderata for a Framework Supporting Expectations

Support for one/many matching functions. When an event happens, it is necessary to decide if it has any relation with what is currently expected. This task is performed by a matching function, that decide if there is a compatibility between the two. A simple matching function could evaluate the syntactical equality of the events' descriptions. However, only more powerful matching functions based on, for example, regular expressions, fuzzy pattern matching, or Prolog-like unification, would be of practical interest. Ideally, a framework should allow for many different matching functions, and, possibly, also for custom-defined functions.

Support for fulfillment and violation. It should be always possible to know if an expectation has been satisfied (fulfilled) or not (violated). Note that, in case of open-interaction systems, such notions would apply differently to expectations and to prohibitions. Roughly speaking, in the former case an expectation could be considered fulfilled if at least a matching event happens, while in the latter the expectation about the non-happening is fulfilled if no matching event ever happened. A doubt might arise about the happening of multiple events matching the same expectation. A framework should support the user to define these characteristics of the fulfillment/violation process.

Support for the life-cycle of an expectation. The life cycle of an expectation should capture all its possible states within the system's life. In particular, we envisage at least three fundamental states: a *pending* one, indicating that an expectation is active but lacking information for deciding its fulfillment or violation, a *fulfilled* state and a *violated* one. Such states should be accessible as explicit meta-information, both about individual expectations and groups thereof, possibly using them to trigger new events and/or derived expectations.

Support for some notion of "global conformance". If the notions of fulfillment and violation are referred to a single expectation, a framework should support also some global notion of fulfillment (conformance of the whole monitored system). Such notion could be simply defined as a logical "and" of all expectations' fulfillments, or could be user-defined by means of some metrics, such as statistics, or by means of some other criteria like a fuzzy evaluation.

2.4 Desiderata for the ECE-Rules

Direct support for compensation and awarding mechanisms. In our view, ECE-Rules define the events the conditions that trigger an expectation, i.e. make it pending, and resolve it either by fulfillment or violation. Quite often, in the case of violations (res. fulfillments), compensation (resp. award) mechanisms are required: their preconditions can be easily expressed if the framework supports some reification (in terms of events) of the state transitions during an expectation's life cycle. However, such situation is so frequent that also we foresee the possibility of defining compensation/awarding mechanisms directly in the ECE-Rules. So, the rules would be single yet complete "knowledge items", containing the events and the conditions for expectations to become pending, as well as what to do in case the expectation is fulfilled or violated.

3 The Drools Rule Engine

Drools[1] is an open source *"knowledge modelling and business logic integration suite"* composed of several modules. Its core component is a reactive production rule engine, based on an object-oriented version of the RETE algorithm [6].

From a user perspective, the system offers a blackboard-like container, called *Working Memory* (WM), where the facts describing the "state of the world" can be `inserted`, `updated` or `retracted`. The rules, then, are *activated* accordingly whenever the WM is modified. A rule is an `IF-THEN` like construct, composed of a premise (Left Hand Side, LHS for short) and a consequence (Right Hand Side, RHS). The LHS part is composed by one or more *patterns*, which must be matched by one or more facts in the WM for the rule to become active. An active rule is then eligible to be fired, executing the actions defined in the RHS, which may either be logical actions on the WM or side effects. A pattern is a sequence of constraints that a fact must satisfy in order to *match* it. Since facts are objects in Drools, the first constraint is a *class* constraint and the following are boolean expressions involving one or more object's *fields*. The constraints of a pattern are evaluated in chain, acting as a series of increasingly fine-grained filters that progressively retain less and less objects until only the ones matching

[1] `http://www.jboss.org/drools`

```
declare Message @role(event) end
rule "CEP Rule Example"
when
  $m: Message( $s: sender, $r: receiver, content == "HELO" )
      not Message( sender == $r, receiver == $s,
                   content == "+ACK", this after[0,5s] $m  )
then
  log("Acknowledgement expected, not received in 5 seconds");
end
```

Fig. 1. A simple Drools Fusion theory catching the violations of a simple protocol

the pattern are left. Such operation is optimized by the RETE algorithm, which allows to share common sequences of constraints between rules.

The additional modules that Drools provides tackle specific needs such as workflow management, rule authoring and planning: in particular, the module dedicated to *complex event processing* (*CEP*) [13] is called Drools Fusion. In this context, an event is *"a significant state change in an observed system, taking place at a specific point in time"*. Drools Fusion allows to annotate fact classes with metadata: the engine will then consider their instances as event payloads, managing any related temporal information autonomously. Such information may be drawn directly from the objects' fields, or automatically added by the engine, wrapping the instances using appropriate decorators. Drools Fusion adheres to the well-established semantics of temporal intervals proposed by Allen [3]. The engine is not only able to evaluate temporal constraints, but also to delay and schedule activations, and to perform temporal truth maintenance by retracting events irrelevant to the computation. To this aim, the engine has an explicit notion of time maintained by a pluggable clock, which allows to determine the events that fall in a given time interval. The provided default implementations, *pseudo-clock* and *real-time clock*, can be used to control the flow of time during simulations or to build online reactive systems.

As an example, consider the code snippet presented in Fig. 1, which shows how Drools Fusion handles `Message` events to notify the violation of a simple protocol. This protocol requires a server to send back an acknowledge notification within 5 seconds from the moment it receives an hand-shake request from a client. In practice, each time a client sends a `"HELO"` message to a server and no `"+ACK"` message is returned in time, a notification of the violation is logged.

4 The "expect" Extension to the Drools Language

In our vision, we would like to exploit a CEP engine to model and solve online monitoring and conformance verification problems. This task would be dramatically simplified if the target system supports the concept of expected behaviour natively. To the best of our knowledge, however, no existing CEP engine provides high-level primitives to handle expectations as discussed in Section 2.

⟨*rhs content*⟩ ::= 'then', { ⟨*expectation block*⟩ }, { ⟨*java statement*⟩ };
⟨*expectation block*⟩ ::= ⟨*expectation list*⟩, { 'or', ⟨*expectation list*⟩ };
⟨*expectation list*⟩ ::= ⟨*expectation*⟩, { 'and', ⟨*expectation*⟩ };
⟨*expectation*⟩ ::= [⟨*id*⟩, ':'], 'expect', ['not' | ['one'], ⟨*id*⟩, ':'], ⟨*pattern*⟩, ⟨*follow-up*⟩;
⟨*follow-up*⟩ ::= ['on', 'fulfillment', ⟨*fulfillment block*⟩], ['on', 'violation', ⟨*violation block*⟩];
⟨*fulfillment block*⟩ ::= '{', { ⟨*repair*⟩ }, ⟨*rhs content*⟩, '}';
⟨*violation block*⟩ ::= '{', { ⟨*repair*⟩ }, ⟨*rhs content*⟩, '}';
⟨*repair*⟩ ::= 'repair', ⟨*id*⟩, ';';

Fig. 2. The ECE sub-grammar, in EBNF form

To this end, we have created an extension to Drools Fusion that enriches the expressiveness of its language with ECE concepts. Such extension is in charge of managing expectations and autonomously executing the proper actions in case of fulfillment, violation or compensation, according to the policies encoded in the rules. Thus the system is no more limited to the traditional Drools' logical operations (`insert`, `retract`, `update`) or free-form side effects, but includes the explicit declaration of expectations.

In our proposed extension, expectations can be nested, so that complex norms may be atomically expressed within a single rule. A nested (conditional) expectation is an expectation generated as a consequence of a previous expectation's fulfillment or violation, and possibly it may depend on the facts or events which triggered the parent expectation.

The ECE rules also automatically generate standard events which reify an expectation and its life cycle, allowing the user to predicate on them using other rules. Although not required in general – and indeed not even recommended is some cases (such as for hard-time constrained CEP), the reification allows the rules to target those concepts directly, possibly even combining them with domain events. An organization that certifies the compliance of some domain's objects to a given regulation, for example, may want to keep track of the amount of violations over the number of activations of a specific expectation, to determine whether some norms need a clearer explanation. Although enabled by default, this feature is actually optional and can be disabled, providing a more slender but slightly less expressive tool.

4.1 The ECE Language

To support ECE-Rules, we have extended the standard Drools parser, allowing the engine to recognize and process the new concepts. Normal rules are handled as usual, while ECE statements are intercepted and redirected to a separate sub-parser and compiler for further interpretation and rewriting. Fig. 2, in particular, contains the extension proposal for ECE-Rules to the Drools language, expressed in EBNF syntax. This grammar shows how to change the consequent of a Drools' rule to include (possibly nested) complex formulas involving

```
rule "ECE-Rule Example"
when
  $m: Message($s: sender, $r: receiver, content == "HELO")
then
  $e1: expect one Message( sender == $r, receiver == $s,
                           content == "+ACK", this after[0, 10s] $m )
    on fulfillment {
      insert(new Message($s, $r, "MAIL")); }
    on violation {
      $e2: expect Message( sender == $r, receiver == $s,
                           content == "+RDY", this after[0, 2m] $m )
        on fulfillment {
           repair $e1;
           insert(new Message($s, $r, "MAIL")); }
        on violation {
           insert(new Message($s, $r, "STOP")); }    }
end
```

Fig. 3. An example of an ECE-Rule

expectations. Any individual expectation has two optional blocks, namely a fulfillment and a violation block, where it is possible to generate new expectations as well as applying consequences. Notice that the ⟨*rhs content*⟩ grammar rule overrides the original one, adding the expectation block; ⟨*java statement*⟩, ⟨*id*⟩ and ⟨*pattern*⟩ are imported directly from the Drools grammar.

Moreover, it is possible to explicitly compensate any previously violated expectation. We have deliberately introduced this feature to allow the recovery of a violation by means of a `repair` statement. This action can be executed as a consequence either of a fulfillment or a violation of an expectation. The only constraint is that the repaired expectation must be defined within the same rule.

To fully understand the scope of our proposal, let us consider the example presented in Fig. 3, which shows the compensation of the violation of a simple protocol, involving a single ECE-Rule. This theory uses the same `Message` class introduced before (not present here for lack of space), but defines a sightly more complex mail protocol[2]. The interaction is again started by a `"HELO"` message *$m*, and a `"+ACK"` messege is expected in 10 seconds: such expectation is labeled as *$e1*. In case of success, the interaction continues with a `"MAIL"` from the client, requesting the list of new mails to the mail server. In case of violation, we proceed instead to the evaluation of the nested expectation: if busy for some reason, the server may still issue a `"+RDY"` message within 2 minutes from *$m*. The rule states that *$e1* may be considered repaired on fulfillment of *$e2*, meaning that it is no more treated as a violation when validating the protocol. In case of a second violation, the client simply closes the interaction with a `"STOP"` message. Notice that the declaration of *$e1* includes the keyword `one`, meaning that, for each message matching *$m*, the fulfillment (violation) branch is only evaluated once after the first `"+ACK"` message is (not) received in time.

[2] In our toy example, any exchange of messages between the client and the mail server (and vice-versa) is accomplished by the insertion of a proper instance of `Message` into the WM.

4.2 The Expectation Meta-Model

To allow the engine to process the grammar defined in section 4.1 and manage the expectations and their life-cycle, we have defined a theory composed by a set of general rules and a set of declared fact classes, whose instances can be manipulated within the WM as appropriate.

Those rules translate any ECE statements into common rules and, optionally, instances of the classes mentioned below, both decorating the starting theory. These rules (not provided for lack of space) permit complex expectations to be spanned over several rules, retaining conceptual dependencies and other relations between expectations, and allow the natural triggering of expectations within other expectations. The straightforward conversion of ECE statements into instances of a few coded class types is often referred as "*reification*": it is not mandatory for the approach, but it allows Drools (that natively works on objects) to declaratively predicate on them. Thus, despite being not the only possible strategy to encode the knowledge, it is very simple and sound, and grants additional expressiveness to the framework. This process is also transparent (the conversion is done autonomously) and optional (it can be disabled to trade some expressiveness for a speedup).

Specifically, the `Expectation` is an abstraction where the (temporal) constraints to be satisfyed are held. The temporal constraints may refer either to the past and the future and have a duration, autonomously handled using Drools Fusion, that starts from the moment they are generated and lasts until the moment they are first fulfilled or violated. `Expectations` are also identified by a `Label` whose purpose is to group together expectations that refer to the same object tuple, since an `Expectation` can be generated several times, as different object tuples `Activate` the rule at different times, in different `Contexts`. A `Context` is usually the initial activation of an ECE-Rule or, in case of nested expectations, the activation of another parent expectation. When an `Expectation` is generated, it is considered `Pending` until it is either `Fulfilled` by an object matching the pattern defined by the expectation, `Violated`, or `Closed`. By aggregating all the `Expectations` generated within the same `Context`, it is possible to define if the activation of an ECE-Rule has been a `Success` or a `Failure` given the monitoring constraints. For more details on pending expectations and possible outcomes of an expectation see the proper paragraphs in Section 4.3. Eventually, violated `Expectations` may be `Compensated` by other events. Notice that all the class types introduced here are considered by our system as instant events with the only exception of `Expectations` whose duration equals their life-time.

4.3 Rule Generation

In addition to the initial, user-provided theory, we preprocess the ECE-Rules and rewrite each one into one or more traditional rules, thus allowing the use of the standard Drools Fusion engine to execute them. Consider an ECE-Rule R such as the one in Fig. 3, having a standard Drools' LHS and an extended RHS with nested expectations. After parsing the rule, we obtain an *Abstract Syntax Tree* (*AST*) with a regular and recursive structure, derived from the grammar in Fig. 2. Any node i of the AST obtained from an expectation block's expression is the child of a pattern P^i and the ancestor of an and/or subtree whose leafes are $n(i) \geq 0$ expectations $E^i_{j:1..n(i)}$. Each leaf expectation E^i_j defines an expectation pattern P^i_j and up to two expectation blocks, corresponding to the optional fulfillment and violation branches. Moreover, an expectation block also has a sequence of actions A_i. According to the natural semantics of the language, actions A_i should be executed only when the pattern P^i has been matched. Notice that, in case of nested expectations, any pattern associated to a more external block must have been likewise already matched. In addition, when and only when P^i has been matched, any expectation E^i_j should be generated so that, according to the presence or absence of a fact/event matching its pattern P^i_j, that expectation E^i_j can be considered pending until fulfilled or violated. For every ECE-Rule, the AST thus obtained is visited several times, to create various derived rules which manage the expectations' life cycle.

(Re)action rules. The goal of these derived rules is the execution of the actions A_i when the appropriate conditions apply. One rule is created when visiting the AST for each action block A_i, starting from its root node and using a recursively built LHS L_i, after being initialized with the LHS of the original ECE-Rule R. The first rule is simply `when` L_0 `then` A_0 and corresponds to the rule R *without* the extended expectation block. The action rules are derived only from the simple expectations, so the visitor ignores any `and/or` node to process only the expectations E^i_j. When an expectation node with children `on fulfill` or `on violation` branches is encountered, the local positive and negative LHS, L^{i+}_j and L^{i-}_j, are respectively built from the current LHS L_i and the local expectation pattern P^i_j. In particular, the pattern is added in positive form when visiting `on fulfill` children branches, and in negative form, using the negated existential quantifier `not`, when visiting `on violation` branches, i.e. $L^{i+}_j = L_i \cup P_j$ and $L^{i-}_j = L_i \cup \neg P_j$. The resulting rules, up to two for every expectation, are traditional Drools/Fusion rules with no notion of expectation or any other related fact. While generated using a more declarative language, they correspond to the rules which would have been written using a naive, hard-coded approach. The main advantage is that they do not incur in any overhead from the meta-level framework, but still capture the behaviour defined by the business author.

Fulfillment/Violation rules. In addition to executing the business logic, we also want to provide an explicit and automatic management of the expectations' lifecycle, as motivated in paragraph 2.3. To this end, we again visit the AST and generate up to three different rules. The first rule, created visiting a pattern node P_i is used to generate the actual `Expectation` in the working memory. The premise of this rule coincides with the local LHS L_i created recursively during the visit to generate the business rules, while the consequence generates an `Expectation` instance for each expectation node E^i_j defined in the expectation block of P_i. At runtime, when the premise L_i is matched by a tuple T, one or more expectations will be inserted within the working memory: their context will be associated to the initial activation of the ECE-Rule which triggered the sequence of expectations, but T will be the actual trigger tuple for all the expectations. As soon as an `Expectation` is inserted in the working memory, a `Pending` fact is also generated to trace the fact that the expectation has not been resolved.

In order to close an expectation E_j^i, two additional rules are written. Since the expectations are defined in terms of a pattern P_j^i, which needs to be captured to determine the expectation outcome, the LHS of these rules is simply derived from L_j^+ and L_j^-, adding a pattern matching the appropriate unresolved expectation (i.e. with an existing joint `Pending` fact). The join is performed on the expectation label (known at compile time), the context, and using the bindings on the patterns in L_i to recreate the parent tuple which generated the expectation and use it as a constraint. Notice that, since the LHS of these conformance rules extends the LHS of a corresponding business rule, the RETE will eventually merge them again, eliminating any redundancy introduced at this level. These latter rules are then simply used to instantiate the `Fulfillment` and, respectively, `Violation` events, collecting the required information from the rule activation records, and inserting them in the working memory.

With this pattern-based approach, it is possible that more than one object's pattern P_j^i matches an expectation E_j^i and fulfills it. In fact, expectations remain pending until explicitly retracted or *closured* (if no temporal constraint is imposed). On the other hand, the same fact/event can match different expectations at the same time. If the user wants an expectation to be fulfilled only once (using the `expect one` syntax), the fulfillment rule will be slightly modified to retract the `Pending` fact associated to the expectation, preventing further fulfillments.

Repair rules. ECE-Rules support the "repairing" of violated expectations: for every `repair` statement, a rule is created with the same LHS as its enclosing expectation block. This rule inserts a `Compensation` fact which is joined to its matching `Violation` by a general rule: the `Violation`, then, is marked as compensated.

Success/Failure rules. While fulfillments and violations are handled at the level of each single expectation, we also provide an overall evaluation of the system behaviour in the context of each activation of an ECE-Rule r, as discussed in paragraph 2.3. We provide support for "global" conformance at the level of activations, by expressing and evaluating possibly complex and/or formulas involving expectations. In particular, we define the notion of `Success` and `Failure` from the `Fulfillment` and `Violation` of individual expectations. For complex expectations, the definition is as follows:

$$Succ(E_1 \wedge E_2) = Succ(E_1) \wedge Succ(E_2) \qquad Succ(E_1 \vee E_2) = Succ(E_1) \vee Succ(E_2)$$
$$Fail(E_1 \wedge E_2) = Fail(E_1) \vee Fail(E_2) \qquad Fail(E_1 \vee E_2) = Fail(E_1) \wedge Fail(E_2)$$

When defining success and failure for individual expectations, instead, one must consider any nested sub-expectation, if present, so $Succ(E)$ (resp. $Fail(E)$) is not trivially $Fulf(E)$ (resp. $Viol(E)$). Expectations defined in `on fulfill` (resp. `on` violation) blocks will be generated only when the parent expectation is fulfilled (resp. violated), but they must be taken in consideration when present. Notice that, since violations can be repaired, even expectations generated by violations are still relevant for the final evaluation.

The Success of an Expectation E is then determined by its fulfillment and either (i) the success of any on fulfill expectation block (if E was fulfilled) or (ii) the success of any on violation expectation block (if E was violated and then repaired). Likewise, the failure of a parent expectation may be due to its violation, the failure of its fulfillment block or the failure of its violation block (assuming it was violated and then repaired). Notice also that a repaired violation is equivalent to a fulfillment during the evaluation of the overall success/failure, while a non-repaired violation corresponds to the negated form of a fulfillment. Those definitions, then, can be further simplified and expressed as follows by adopting an compact EBNF-like notation:

$$\begin{aligned}
Succ(E) &= Fulf(E)\Big[\wedge\Big((Fulf(E) \wedge Succ(E_F))\Big|(Viol^\star(E) \wedge Fulf(E_V))\Big)\Big] \\
&= Fulf(E)\Big[\wedge\Big(Succ(E_F)\Big|Fulf(E_V)\Big)\Big] \\
Fail(E) &= Viol(E)\Big[\vee\Big((Fulf(E) \wedge Fail(E_F))\Big|(Viol^\star(E) \wedge Fail(E_V))\Big)\Big] \\
&= Viol(E)\Big[\vee\Big(Viol(E_F)\Big|Fail(E_V)\Big)\Big]
\end{aligned}$$

Such definitions can be applied directly to the AST tree, generating two conformance rules for each ECE-Rule R that lead to either a Success or a Failure events for each activation (or nothing if some expectations are still pending). While not *global* per se, such events ease the creation of conformance rules by providing more complex events than fulfillments and violations.

Closure. As outlined in Section 2.2, we regard the expectations as closed toward the past and open toward the future. This choice may lead to some issues when dealing with the expectations that are still pending. The open expectations, in fact, are not caught –and hence not reported– by the monitoring framework (i.e. when halting the system). The procedure of identification and notification of the pending expectations with respect to the open time horizon is called "*closure*" and it is directly managed by our implementation within the general theory. To this aim, a dedicated special fact is inserted into the WM, making a rule to react by joining that fact with any open expectation. As a result, the expectation is closed (its Closed field is changed) by flagging a Violation (for positive expectations) or a Fulfillment (for negative ones). Notice that the clipping of the pending expectations forces the generation of a Success/Failure event. Our implementation also supports a finer "*targeted closure*": only open expectations whose label matches a specific value are closed.

5 A Use Case in the Medical Field

The Knowledge Management Research (KMR) team at Naval Health Research Center, San Diego has been particularly interested in developing the functional

```
rule "Risk factor evaluation"
when
    $pat : Patient( ... ) $prov : Provider( ... )
    // model result: risk factor and confidence degree
    $risk : HasRisk( $pat, $disease, $factor, $conf )
then
    expect HasRisk( this == $risk, confidence > C_THOLD )
    on fulfillment {          // prediction is reliable
       expect HasRisk( this == $risk, factor < R_THOLD )
         on fulfillment { log( $pat + " safe" ); }
         on violation { /* manage high risk patient */ } }
    on violation {          //request info from patient
        insert( new Message($prov, $pat, "quest" ) ); }
end
rule "Fill Questionnaire Request Protocol"
when
    $m : Message( $prov, $pat, "quest" )
then
    $e : expect Message( $pat, $prov, $answers ; this after[0,T] $m )
        on fulfillment{ insert($answers); }
        on violation {
            // T2 > T, giving additional time to $pat
            expect Message( $pat, $prov, $answers ; this after[0,T2] $m )
               on fulfillment { repair $e; insert($answers); }
               on violation { alert( ... ); }
            insert( new SMS($prov, $pat, "quest") ); }
end
```

Fig. 4. PTSD Risk Factor (abstract) Use Case

ontology and semantics required to define "operational constraints" to the execution of a rule. Operational constraints are supervisory (meta) rules that establish expectations for the clinical context a given rule was designed for – they help ensure that the resultant events or behaviors are appropriate for the setting. For example, they might modulate the recommendation for a blood transfusion in a trauma case when the patient "context" is that of a Jehovah's Witness.

Separating the logic of a discreet medical decision from that used by operational rules used to manage clinical context has important implications. Decision support rules should be authored with a focused clinical perspective and that the final result is dependent on other clearly defined orthogonal perspectives that the knowledge management system must orchestrate. It implies that rule execution is not necessarily an all-or-none event, but rather a cascade of constraint evaluations that in aggregate ensure the system's end behavior is individualized and nuanced. This separation of concerns helps clarify what is evidence-based best clinical practice and what are non-medical restrictions imposed on the delivery of that care by the realities of the real-world and the individual patient. As an example use case, consider the following scenario. After returning from a yearlong deployment, a United States Marine is seen by his physician. The doctor's Clinical Decision Support System (CDSS) collects all relevant information about him and feeds it into a Post Traumatic Stress Disorder (PTSD) predictive model that estimates he has a 35% risk of developing PTSD within the next three years. Recognizing, however, that several important historical facts about his past medical history are missing, the patient is asked to take an online survey at home. When he forgets to complete the survey, the system automatically sends a reminder SMS text prompting the Marine to complete the requested task. When he does so, the system then automatically recalculates the risk score. This time the risk is 80% and the confidence acceptably narrow, so an alert is instantly generated.

Fig. 4 represents an abstract (due to space limitations) version of the rules which could be written to model the desired outcome for the use case. The first rule manages the results of the PTSD predictive model evaluation (see [18]), first checking that confidence in the output result is sufficient and then validating that the risk assessment itself is low enough for the patient not to require further evaluation. If either expectation is violated, appropriate actions are taken; either a new workflow to solicit additional information from the patient is started, and/or the patient is scheduled for additional testing. Notice that the same policies could have been written using standard rules, but the proposed syntax makes the definition more compact (1 rule instead of 4) and, most of all, ensures that the results of the constraint checks are recorded formally. Likewise, the second rule monitors the interaction between the patient and the provider, using the same pattern shown in section 4.1.

6 Conclusions

We have extended a production rule language to support the concept of expectations, the fulfillment or violation of which result in different consequences or behaviors. These syntactical additions enable a rule author to easily define and apply conformance criteria to the execution of the default rule logic. Rule expectations, if need be, can be cleanly deactivated and meta-reasoning disabled, thereby restoring more traditional rule behavior. The language extensions have been integrated into our reference run-time implementation, Drools, where it can exploits the engine's native complex event processing capabilities to better support temporal reasoning. Our next objective will be to research "fuzzy expectations" introducing uncertainty to the absolute fulfillment or violation of a constraint. Expectations that cope with the ambiguities of the real-world promise to provide important support for graded degrees of conformance testing.

Acknowledgements. We wish to thank the U.S. Navy KMR-II Project, the Health Sciences and Technologies - Interdepartmental Center for Industrial Research (HST-ICIR) - University of Bologna and the DEIS DEPICT Project which co-sponsored this research. The opinions of the authors do not necessarily state or reflect those of their respective employers, the United States Navy, the Department of Defense, or the United States Government, and shall not be used for advertising or product endorsement purposes.

References

1. Alberti, M., Chesani, F., Gavanelli, M., Lamma, E., Mello, P., Torroni, P.: Verifiable agent interaction in abductive logic programming: The SCIFF framework. ACM Trans. Comput. Logic 9(4), 1–43 (2008)

2. Alberti, M., Gavanelli, M., Lamma, E., Mello, P., Torroni, P., Sartor, G.: Mapping deontic operators to abductive expectations. CMOT 12(2-3), 205–225 (2006)
3. Allen, J.F.: Maintaining knowledge about temporal intervals. Commun. ACM 26(11), 832–843 (1983)
4. Damiani, G., Pinnarelli, L., Colosimo, S., Almiento, R., Sicuro, L., Galasso, R., Sommella, L., Ricciardi, W.: The effectiveness of computerized clinical guidelines in the process of care: a systematic review. BMC-HSR 10(1), 2 (2010), `http://www.biomedcentral.com/1472-6963/10/2`
5. Desai, N., Chopra, A.K., Singh, M.P.: Representing and reasoning about commitments in business processes. In: AAAI, pp. 1328–1333. AAAI Press (2007)
6. Forgy, C.: Rete: A fast algorithm for the many patterns/many objects match problem. Artif. Intell. 19(1), 17–37 (1982)
7. Fornara, N., Colombetti, M.: A commitment-based approach to agent communication. Applied Artificial Intelligence 18(9-10), 853–866 (2004)
8. Governatori, G.: Representing business contracts in *ruleml*. Int. J. Cooperative Inf. Syst. 14(2-3), 181–216 (2005)
9. Governatori, G., Hulstijn, J., Riveret, R., Rotolo, A.: Characterising Deadlines in Temporal Modal Defeasible Logic. In: Orgun, M.A., Thornton, J. (eds.) AI 2007. LNCS (LNAI), vol. 4830, pp. 486–496. Springer, Heidelberg (2007)
10. Governatori, G., Rotolo, A.: Norm Compliance in Business Process Modeling. In: Dean, M., Hall, J., Rotolo, A., Tabet, S. (eds.) RuleML 2010. LNCS, vol. 6403, pp. 194–209. Springer, Heidelberg (2010)
11. Governatori, G., Rotolo, A., Sartor, G.: Temporalised normative positions in defeasible logic. In: ICAIL, pp. 25–34. ACM (2005)
12. JBoss: JBoss Drools 5.2 - Business Logic Integration Platform (2011), `www.jboss.org/drools`
13. Luckham, D.: The Power of Events: An Introduction to Complex Event Processing in Distributed Enterprise Systems. Addison-Wesley Longman, Amsterdam (2002)
14. Montali, M., Pesic, M., van der Aalst, W.M.P., Chesani, F., Mello, P., Storari, S.: Declarative specification and verification of service choreographiess. TWEB 4(1) (2010)
15. Pesic, M., van der Aalst, W.M.P.: A declarative approach for flexible business processes management. In: Eder, J., Dustdar, S. (eds.) BPM Workshops 2006. LNCS, vol. 4103, pp. 169–180. Springer, Heidelberg (2006)
16. Sadiq, S.W., Governatori, G., Namiri, K.: Modeling control objectives for business process compliance. In: Alonso, G., Dadam, P., Rosemann, M. (eds.) BPM 2007. LNCS, vol. 4714, pp. 149–164. Springer, Heidelberg (2007)
17. Singh, M.P., Chopra, A.K., Desai, N.: Commitment-based service-oriented architecture. IEEE Computer 42(11), 72–79 (2009)
18. Sottara, D., Mello, P., Sartori, C., Fry, E.: Enhancing a production rule engine with predictive models using pmml. In: KDD 2011 (to appear, 2011)
19. Torroni, P., Chesani, F., Mello, P., Montali, M.: Social commitments in time: Satisfied or compensated. In: Baldoni, M., Bentahar, J., van Riemsdijk, M.B., Lloyd, J. (eds.) DALT 2009. LNCS, vol. 5948, pp. 228–243. Springer, Heidelberg (2010)
20. Torroni, P., Chesani, F., Yolum, P., Gavanelli, M., Singh, M.P., Lamma, E., Alberti, M., Mello, P.: Modelling Interactions via Commitments and Expectations. IGI Global (2009)
21. Yolum, P., Singh, M.P.: Flexible protocol specification and execution: applying event calculus planning using commitments. In: AAMAS, pp. 527–534. ACM (2002)

Designing for Compliance: Norms and Goals

Guido Governatori[2], Francesco Olivieri[2,1,3],
Simone Scannapieco[2,1,3], and Matteo Cristani[1]

[1] Department of Computer Science, University of Verona, Italy
[2] NICTA, Queensland Research Laboratory, Australia
[3] Institute for Integrated and Intelligent Systems, Griffith University, Australia

Abstract. We address the problem of define a modal defeasible theory able to capture intuitions as "being compliant" with a set of *norms* and a set of *goals*. We will treat norms and goals as modalised literals. From the definition of this new kind of logic, two main issues arises whether a theory is compliant or not: (a) how to revise a non compliant theory to obtain a new compliant one; (b) in case the theory is compliant how to create an entirely new process starting from the theory, i.e., from the fully declarative description of the specifications for a process and the norms.

1 Introduction

Business process modelling technology (BPM) emerged as a strong paradigm for the modelling, analysis, improvement, and automation of the day-to-day activities of organisations. The field is now a mature research field with a widespread adoption in industry. BPM covers a wide variety of methodologies; from graphical modelling languages to ease the understanding of the stakeholders (e.g., EPC, BPMN) to fully precise mathematical formalisms (e.g., Petri Nets, π-calculus) for formal analysis of the properties and automated verification of the processes.

Most of the existing approaches in the field are *procedural*: they point out step by step what to do in many different scenarios. If from one side this procedural nature is their strength, it is also their main drawback. In fact, they suffer two main limitations: such a paradigm is not suitable to capture flexible business processes (BPs), i.e., processes whose internal structure and relationships among the various tasks is dynamic and with a large degree of variations. Secondly, it is hard to obtain precise information about the order of the actions to be performed from the business requirements.

To obviate these problems, the trend of modelling processes by *declarative specifications* gained momentum. Instead of specifying a process step by step, the focus in this approach is on defining relationships among the tasks to be executed to achieve a goal. Examples are temporal relationships between tasks (e.g., before, after), co-occurrence/absence, dependency and so on. For a seminal work in this area see [1]. Thus, in this paradigm there is a switch from *how* (procedural) to *what* (declarative).

Another crucial aspect in the recent investigation on BPM is on regulatory compliance, again an area where the focus is on *what* a BP does. Compliance is the study of the *norm* regulating the organisational environment. Norms from a regulative source represent the perfect example of declarative specifications [2], and the related topic of

F. Olken et al. (Eds.): RuleML 2011 - America, LNCS 7018, pp. 282–297, 2011.

norm compliance has consequently become a crucial issue in BP design and verification. Nowadays, the study of compliance focused only on norms, defining formalisms to express them, and conditions under which a system described with such formalisms can be considered *compliant* with the norms. Thus, to the best of our knowledge, there is a lack of formalisms describing systems to be compliant with a set of *goals*, even if this topic appears to be of main interest[1].

The issue is to extend the existing formalisms to the new concept of *goal compliance*: the motivation is that, given a system, it is easy to give criteria to be compliant with a set of norms but such that they do not allow to get the final goals of the enterprise.

Let us consider the following example. We have to manage the BP of a library. A norm could state that each book must be returned to the library before a fixed deadline. One of the (non-plausible) policy to be compliant with this (plausible) norm is not to lend books anymore (in clear contrast with the final aim of a library).

The aim of this work is to formally define a framework that integrates norm compliance with goal compliance, in such a way that declarative specifications of a BP could satisfy at the same time the goals of the organisation, and the norms governing the business. The contribution of the paper is twofold: First of all, we explicitly introduce the notion of goal compliance. Additionally, we work with fully declarative specifications of the capabilities of an organisation, its goals and the norms regulating the underlying business. Accordingly, we have to depart from the algorithms devised to determine whether a procedural BP is compliant, and we have to introduce the notion of violation. Given that we model the various notions in modal defeasible logic, we show how to extend the proof mechanisms of the logic to identify non-compliant situations.

The layout of the paper is as follows. In Section 2 we formalise the framework adopted, based on a particular type of Modal Defeasible Logic. Such a formalism is the tool exploited in Section 3 to integrate the concepts of norm and goal in a business process. The main core of this work is Section 4 where we present theoretical properties and definitions of *norm and goal compliance*. In there, we also outline possible future research developments.

2 Logics

In this section we are going to introduce the logic we use to model processes, their organisational goals, and the norms governing them. The logic is an extension of Defeasible Logic (DL) [3]. In particular, it extends and combines the deontic DL of violations [4] for modelling contracts and then used for regulatory compliance of processes [5,6], and the defeasible BIO (Belief-Intention-Obligation) logic for modelling agents [7].

2.1 Language of Modal Defeasible Logic

The main aim of this subsection is to build an inference process to compute factual knowledge (through belief rules), goals and obligations from existing facts, primitive

[1] In here we follow the classical definitions of norm and goal as give in the literature for agents where a norm is an external constraint while a goal is a internal one.

goals and unconditional obligations. As a first step, we build a defeasible theory whose basic elements are (1) a set of *facts* or indisputable statements, (2) three sets of rules: for beliefs, goals, and obligations, (3) a superiority relation to determine the relative strength of conflicting rules. Thus, a defeasible theory T is a structure $(F,R,>)$, where F is the set of facts, R is the set of rules, and $>$ is a binary relation over R.

Belief rules are used to relate the factual knowledge of an enterprise, composed by

- the set of *actions* (or *tasks*) an organisation can do;
- the *pre-conditions* under which tasks can be executed;
- the *effects* derived by the execution of these tasks (also called *post-conditions*).

Specifically, belief rules describe the logical relationship between pre-conditions and tasks, tasks and their effects, relationships between tasks, relationships between states. As such, provability for beliefs does not generate modalised literals. *Obligation rules* determine when and which obligations are in force. The conclusions generated by obligation rules are modalised with obligation. Finally, *goal rules* establish the goals of an organisation depending on the particular context. Accordingly, similar to obligation rules, the conclusions of this type of rules take the goal modality.

Following ideas given in [8], rules can gain more expressiveness when a *preference operator* $\odot$ is used, whose meaning will be clearer in the remainder. Intuitively, an expression like $A \odot B$ means that if A is possible, then A is the first choice, and B is the second one; if $\neg A$ holds, then the first choice is not attainable and B is the actual choice.

We now introduce the language adopted in the rest of the paper to make precise the above mentioned ideas. Let PROP be a set of propositional atoms, $\mathrm{MOD} = \{\mathrm{B},\mathrm{G},\mathrm{O}\}$ the set of modal operators, Lab be a set of arbitrary labels, and $\mathrm{Act} = \{t_1,\dots,t_n\} \subseteq \mathrm{PROP}$ be a set of basic actions (or tasks). The set $\mathrm{Lit} = \mathrm{PROP} \cup \{\neg p | p \in \mathrm{PROP}\}$ denotes the set of *literals*. The *complementary* of a literal q is denoted by $\sim q$; if q is a positive literal p, then $\sim q$ is $\neg p$, and if q is a negative literal $\neg p$ then $\sim q$ is p. The set of modal literals is $\mathrm{ModLit} = \{Xl, \neg Xl | l \in \mathrm{Lit}, X \in \{\mathrm{G},\mathrm{O}\}\}$[2]. We introduce two preference operators, $\otimes$ for obligations and $\oplus$ for goals, and we will use $\odot$ when we refer to one of them generically. These operators are used to build chains of preferences, called $\odot$-expressions. The formation rules for $\odot$-expressions are: (a) every literal is an $\odot$-expression, (b) if A is an $\odot$-expression and b is a literal then $A \odot b$ is an $\odot$-expression. In addition we stipulate that $\otimes$ and $\oplus$ obey the following properties: (1) $a \odot (b \odot c) = (a \odot b) \odot c$ (associativity); (2) $\bigodot_{i=1}^{n} a_i = (\bigodot_{i=1}^{k-1} a_i) \odot (\bigodot_{i=k+1}^{n} a_i)$ where exists j such that $a_j = a_k$ and $j < k$ (duplication and contraction on the right). Such $\odot$-expressions can be given both by the process designer, and can be obtained through *construction rules* based on the particular logic adopted REF.

We adopt the classical definitions of *strict rules*, *defeasible rules*, and *defeaters* in DL [9]. However, for the sake of simplicity, and to better focus on the non-monotonic aspects that DL offers, in the remainder we use only defeasible rules. In addition we have to take the modal operators into account. A defeasible rule is an expression $r : a_1,\dots,a_n \Rightarrow_X c$, where

[2] For the belief modal operator B, we assume that the "X" modal operator is the empty modal operator, thus essentially a modal literal Bl is equivalent to the unmodalised literal l.

1. $r \in \text{Lab}$ is the name of the rule;
2. $a_1, \ldots, a_n$, the *antecedent* of the rule, is the set of the premises of the rule (alternatively, it can be understood as the conjunction of all the literals in it). Each a_i is either a literal or a modal literal;
3. $X \in \text{MOD}$ represents the type of modality introduced by the rule itself (from now on, we omit the subscript B in rules for beliefs, i.e., $a_1, \ldots, a_n \Rightarrow c$ will be used as a shortcut for $a_1, \ldots, a_n \Rightarrow_{\text{B}} c$);
4. C is the *consequent* (or *head*) of the rule, which is an $\otimes$-expression involving literals in rules for obligations, an $\oplus$-expression involving literals in rules for goals, and a single literal in rules for beliefs[3].

Several obvious abbreviations on sets of rules can be used. For example, R^X ($R^X[q]$) denotes all rules introducing modality X (with consequent q), and $R[q] = \bigcup_{X \in \text{MOD}} R^X[q]$. With $R[c_i = q]$ we denote the set of rules whose head is $\otimes_{j=1}^n c_j$ for obligation rules and $\oplus_{j=1}^n c_j$ for goal rules where for some i, $1 \leq i \leq n$, $c_i = q$.

The meaning of $\odot$-expressions as consequent of rules is the following:

For obligations, a rule $a_1, \ldots, a_n \Rightarrow_{\text{O}} o_1 \otimes o_2 \otimes \ldots \otimes o_l$ means that if conditions $a_1, \ldots, a_n$ hold, then the obligation in force is o_1, but if $\neg o_1$ is the case, then the new obligation in force is o_2, and so on. Then, obeying obligation o_l represents the last chance to obtain a still acceptable situation with respect to the regulative system in force, but it is not possible to recover from its violation. In deontic logic, this type of expressions, namely the activation of certain obligations in case of other obligations being violated, is referred to as *contrary-to-duty* (abbreviated CTD) obligations, or *reparation obligations* [2].

For goals, a rule $a_1, \ldots, a_n \Rightarrow_{\text{G}} g_1 \oplus g_2 \oplus \ldots \oplus g_m$ means that if conditions $a_1, \ldots, a_n$ hold, then we have to reach the goal g_1, but if it is not possible, then the goal to achieve is g_2, and so on. A chain for goals can be seen as a mean to express a preferential list of organisational objectives such that every goal is more restrictive than all other successive goals in the chain. As such, g_m is the last acceptable outcome we expect to obtain from the business process with respect to this particular chain.

The terminology defined so far is mostly taken from [7], where an extension of DL with modal operators is introduced to differentiate modal and factual rules. However, labelling the rules of DL produces nothing more but a simple treatment of the modalities, thus two interaction strategies between modal operators are analysed:

1. *rule conversions:* using rules for a modality X as they were for another modality Y, i.e., the possibility to convert one type of conclusions into a different one. For example, if 'a car industry has the purpose of assembling perfectly working cars' and 'it is known that in every working car there is a working engine', then 'a

[3] It is worth noting that modalised literals can occur only in the antecedent of rules: the reason is that the rules are used to derive modalised conclusions and we do not conceptually need to iterate modalities. The motivation of a single literal as a consequent for belief rules is dictated by the intended reading of the belief rules, where these rules are used to describe the environment.

car industry has also the purpose of assembling working engines in every car produced'. Formally, we define a binary relation Convert $\subseteq$ MOD $\times$ MOD such that Convert(X,Y) means 'a rule of type X can be used also to produce conclusions of type Y'. This intuitively corresponds to the following logical schema:

$$\frac{Ya_1,\ldots,Ya_n \quad a_1,\ldots,a_n \Rightarrow_X b}{Yb}\ \text{Convert}(X,Y)$$

2. *conflict-detection* and *conflict-resolution:* it is crucial to identify criteria for detecting and solving conflicts between different modalities. For example, if 'a tyre industry wants to produce cheaper tyres with a pollutant emission greater than *pe*', and 'by law the pollutant emission must be lower than threshold *pe*', then the tyre industry can not economise the production if she wants to obey the law. Formally, we define an asymmetric binary relation Conflict $\subseteq$ MOD $\times$ MOD such that Conflict(X,Y) means 'rule types X and Y are in conflict and modality X prevails over Y'. Consider the following theory:

$$a \Rightarrow_X c$$
$$b \Rightarrow_Y \neg c$$

   If both a and b are derivable and Conflict(X,Y) holds, then we derive Xc.

As beliefs represent the factual knowledge of the organisation, belief rules can be used to derive both obligations and goals. Thus, the following formulation of Convert arises:

$$\text{Convert} = \{(\text{B},\text{G}),(\text{B},\text{O})\}$$

Furthermore, as our main purpose is to build a new process which is compliant with a set of given norms, it seems reasonable that rules for obligations take precedence over rules for goals (i.e., an organisation tries to achieve its purposes not violating the norms). Hence, the following definition of Conflict (reflecting the behaviour of a *social agent* as described in [7]) will be used in our analysis:

$$\text{Conflict} = \{(\text{B},\text{O}),(\text{O},\text{G}),(\text{B},\text{G})\}$$

The construction of the *superiority relation* combines two components: the first $>^{sm}$ considers pairs of rules of the same modality. This component is usually given by the designer of the theory and capture the meaning of the single rules, and thus encodes the domain knowledge of the designer of the theory. The second component, $>^{\text{Conflict}}$, is obtained from the rules in a theory and depends on the meaning of the modalities. Formally, the superiority relation $>$ is such that $> = >^{sm} \cup >^{\text{Conflict}}$, where

- $>^{sm} \subseteq R^X \times R^X$ such that if $r > s$, then if $r \in \text{R}^X[p]$ then $s \in \text{R}^X[\sim p]$ and $>$ is acyclic;
- $>^{\text{Conflict}}$ is such that $\forall r \in \text{R}^X[p], \forall s \in \text{R}^Y[\sim p]$, if Conflict$(X,Y)$, then $r >^{\text{Conflict}} s$.

2.2 Inference in Modal Defeasible Logic

Proofs in a modal defeasible theory T are linear derivations, i.e., sequences of *tagged literals* of the form $+\partial_X q$ and $-\partial_X q$. Given $X \in$ MOD, $+\partial_X q$ means that q is defeasibly provable in T with modality X, and $-\partial_X q$ means that q is defeasibly refuted with modality X. Similarly, $\pm\partial q$ will be used as a shortcut of $\pm\partial_{\mathrm{B}} q$. The initial part of length i of a proof P is denoted by $P(1..i)$.

We now define when a rule is applicable or discarded. A rule for a belief is applicable if all the literals in the antecedent of the rule are provable with the appropriate modalities, while the rule is discarded if at least one of the literals in the antecedent is not provable. For the other types of rules we have to take the relation Convert into account.

Definition 1. *Let* Convert *be the conversion relation between elements in* MOD.

- *A rule r in R^{B} is* applicable *iff $\forall a \in A(r)$, $+\partial a \in P(1..n)$ and $\forall Xa \in A(r)$, where $X \in$ MOD, $+\partial_X a \in P(1..n)$.*
- *A rule $r \in R[c_i = q]$ is* applicable *in the condition for $\pm\partial_X$ iff*
  1. *$r \in R^X$, $\forall a \in A(r)$, $+\partial a \in P(1..n)$ and $\forall Ya \in A(r)$ $+\partial_Y a \in P(1..n)$, or*
  2. *$r \in R^Y$,* Convert(Y,X)*, $A(r) \neq \emptyset$, and $\forall a \in A(r)$, $+\partial_X a \in P(1..n)$.*
- *A rule r is* discarded *if we prove either $-\partial a$ or $-\partial_X a$ for some $a \in A(r)$.*

The proof conditions for $\pm\partial_X$ are thus as follows:

$+\partial_X$: If $P(n+1) = +\partial_X q$ then
(1) $\exists r \in R[c_i = q]$ such that r is applicable, and $\forall i' < i$, $-\partial c_{i'} \in P(1..n)$; and
(2) $\forall s \in R[c_j = {\sim}q]$, either s is discarded, or $\exists j' < j$ such that $+\partial_X c_{j'} \in P(1..n)$, or
  (2.1) $\exists t \in R[c_k = q]$ such that t is applicable and
  $\forall k' < k$, $-\partial c_{k'} \in P(1..n)$ and $t > s$

$-\partial_X$: If $P(n+1) = -\partial_X q$ then
(1) $\forall r \in R[c_i = q]$, either r is discarded or $\exists i' < i$ such that $+\partial c_{i'} \in P(1..n)$, or
(2) $\exists s \in R[c_j = {\sim}q]$, such that s is applicable and $\forall j' < j$, $-\partial_X c_{j'} \in P(1..n)$ and
  (2.1) $\forall t \in R[c_k = q]$ either t is discarded, or
  $\exists k' < k$ such that $+\partial c_{k'} \in P(1..n)$ or $t \not> s$

Notice that the condition of provability of a literal q in a chain for obligations (or goals) implies that all antecedents of the rule are provable in the theory, and that we have proved that every element p prior to q in the chain is not defeasibly proved (i.e., we have $-\partial p$). This means that the theory (process) fails to fulfil an obligation or achieving the goal corresponding to p. Given an obligation or goal rule

$$a_1, \ldots, a_m \Rightarrow_X c_1 \odot \cdots \odot c_n$$

if the rule is applicable, then the obligation (and possible ways to recover from its violation) is in force (for an obligation rule) and that an organisation commits to a series of progressively less stringent alternative goals (for a goal rule). In both interpretations c_n is the last chance to be compliant with the rule. In case of obligation, c_n is the last thing we can obey to to result in a situation that is still deemed as legal (though not an ideal situation); in case of a goal, c_m is the least of the acceptable outcomes of a process.

We are going to formally capture this intuition. To this end we introduce the literal $\bot$ whose interpretation is a non-compliant situation, and at the same time we provide proof conditions to (defeasibly) derive it. Thus, to derive a non-compliant situation ($+\partial\bot$) there is an applicable rule such that all the elements of the head are violated (for obligations) or not achieved (for goals). Conversely, to be compliant ($-\partial\bot$) for every applicable rule, at least one obligation has been complied with, or goal achieved.

More formally, for $X \in \{O, G\}$:

$+\partial_X \bot$: If $P(n+1) = +\partial_X \bot$ then
(1) $\exists r \in R$ such that r is applicable, and
(2) $\forall c_i \in C(r) \ -\partial c_i \in P(1..n)$.

$-\partial_X \bot$: If $P(n+1) = -\partial_X \bot$ then
(1) $\forall r \in R$ either r is discarded or
(2) $\exists c_i \in C(r)$ such that if $-\partial c_j \in P(1..n)$ for $\forall j \leq i$, then $+\partial c_i \in P(1..n)$.

3 Norm and Goal Compliance

Informally, a *business process* is a collection of related activities (or *tasks*) to be performed to achieve one or more organisational *goals*. Many years of thorough analysis in the field of BPM led to the definition of several techniques apt to model and reason about BPs, from the early stages like graphical modelling (e.g., BPMN) up to the definition of running process instances starting from graphical models (e.g., BPEL).

In fact, the classical definition of BP as reported above does not take into account many factors that deeply affect the phase of process definition and maintenance. For example, when an organisation is seen as an entity embedded in an environment regulated by norms, the concept of *compliance* comes into play. In this scenario, an organisation has to take care both of the achievement of the goals it aims at (*goal compliance*), and the norms in force in the environment (*norm compliance*).

The research field resulting from the interaction of BPM approach with legal reasoning, i.e. *business process compliance*, addresses all problems regarding the alignment of the formal specifications of a (set of) BP(s), and the formal specifications of a set of norms governing the surrounding environment. Most of the research in this field regards the analysis of conditions and methodologies to check if a given (set of) BP(s) is compliant with a set of given norms. An extensive survey about the topic is given in [2], where the authors define a framework to suitably represent (1) BPs (through process graphs, e.g., in BPMN), (2) norms (using Formal Contract Logic, shortly FCL, a combination of classical DL [9] and a deontic logic of violations), and (3) the concept of norm compliance. Without entering too much into details, BP models are extended with *annotated tasks*, where annotations specifies: (1) the artefacts or *effects* of executing a task, and (2) the rules describing the norms relevant for the process.

The main result given in this work is the definition of an algorithm that:

1. traverses the graph describing the BP and identifies the sets of effects (sets of literals) for all the tasks (nodes) and propagates the effects in the process according to the execution semantics specified (token-passing mechanism as in Petri Nets [10]).
2. for each task, uses the set of effects for that particular task to determine the normative positions triggered by the execution of the task. Thus, effects of the task are used as a set of facts, and the conclusions of the defeasible theory resulting from the effects and the FCL rules annotating the task are computed. In the same way effects are accumulated, the algorithm accumulates (undischarged) obligations from one task in the process to the task following it in the process.

3. for each task, compares the effects of the tasks and the obligations accumulated up to the task. If an obligation is fulfilled by a task, the algorithm discharges the obligation, otherwise if the obligation is violated, a violation is signalled. Finally, if an obligation is not fulfilled nor violated, the obligation is kept in the stack of obligations and propagated to the successive tasks.

In this framework, the concept of goal compliance is not mentioned, but it can be trivially treated: BPs are given as an input of the compliance checking phase; as such, it seems reasonable to assume that they already achieve the goals they were built for.

Based on the same ideas about conditions a system must satisfy to be compliant with a set of norms, we are now ready to give an informal definition about what we intend for a process to be *goal compliant*. Roughly speaking, given conditions describing states of the environment we act in, we are able to perform some actions which lead us in a state of the world where all the goals we aim for are achieved. For example, if we want to go to the airport and not to be hungry, the actions of catching the train from our place to the airport, and stopping in a fast food to buy an hamburger, result in a state of the world where all our desires are fulfilled.

According to the motivations proposed in Subsection 2.1, we take in consideration norms compensating other norms, we use the same intuition also for goals: we will consider goals 'compensating' other goals, i.e., a system which fails to achieve a primary goal A, but succeeds in reaching goal B such that B is less preferred than A but still acceptable, is a system that reaches a desirable state of the world.

In other terms, where contrary-to-duty chains were meant to be norms repairing the failure of the system to be adherent to previous norms, 'contrary-to-duty chains' for goals can be seen as *preference chains* [11,12]. Let us assume to have the CTD of goals $\Rightarrow_{\mathrm{G}} A \oplus B$. Its meaning is that we would prefer A but, if A is not the case, then our second preference is for B and, if also B is not the case, then we have no further preferences ('we give up'). De facto, such chains form a preference partial order among elements of our theory[4]. In a situation like the previous one, while A represents the most preferable goal, B is not just the less preferable goal but it embodies the last chance for the system to be compliant with such a chain. B can be seen as an element of the set containing all the minimal goals (the last elements in every chain for goals) to be achieved.

More formally, given a theory T describing our world, with *Goals* representing the set of objectives, and *Norms* representing the set of obligations in force, a system is *norm* and *goal compliant* if

1. *norm compliant*: each norm is not violated, or if so, it is compensated (i.e., there no exists derivation in T leading to an opposite of an element in *Norms* that has no further compensation);
2. *goal compliant*: the process ends having reached at least all the minimal objectives. In other words, a business process is goal compliant if there exists at least one possible way to execute it, and the execution satisfies at least one of the goal in each active goal chains.

---

[4] For example, we can express the fact that we have no preference between two elements, A and B, by both $A \oplus B$ and $B \oplus A$.

We now propose an example to better explain the new concepts introduced in this section; in Section 4 where we will formalise it in our logic (Example 3).

Example 1. PeoplEyes is an eyeglasses manufacturer. Naturally, its final goal is to produce cool and perfectly assembled eyeglasses. The final steps of the production process are to shape the lenses to glasses, and mount them on the frames. To shape the lenses, *PeoplEyes* uses a very innovative and expensive laser machinery, while for the final mounting phase two different machineries can be used. Although both machineries work well, the first and newer one is more precise and faster than the other, so *PeoplEyes* prefers the usage of the first machinery as much as possible. Unfortunately, a new norm comes in force stating that no laser technology can be used, unless human staff wears laser-protective goggles.

If *PeoplEyes* has both human resources and raw material, and the three machineries are fully working, but it has not yet bought any laser-protective goggles, all its goals would be achieved but it would fail to comply with the regulatory, since the norm for the no-usage of laser technology is violated and not compensated.

If *PeoplEyes* buys the laser-protective goggles, its entire production process also becomes norm compliant. If, at some time, the more precise mounting machinery breaks, but the second one is still working, *PeoplEyes* still remains goal compliant since also the usage of the second machinery leads to a state of the world where the goal of mounting the glasses on the frames is reached. In this last scenario, *PeoplEyes* reaches the 'minimal set' of goals. Again, if *PeoplEyes* has no protective laser goggles and both the mounting machineries are out of order, *PeoplEyes* production process is neither norm nor goal compliant.

4 Designing for Compliance

We formalised in Section 2 the logic to use, while in Section 3 we informally described what we intend for a process to be *norm compliant* and *goal compliant*.

Briefly recalling those ideas, a process adheres to the sets of goals and norms when, during its execution, there is no violation of the ruling norms (or when a violation occurs, the process compensates that), and once the process ends up, all the goals are achieved (or at least a minimal set of them). Thus, to describe our processes we need

- A library of tasks: $t_1, \dots, t_n$. Tasks correspond to actions that can be performed by the system.
- Belief rules for the activation of a task t, and to obtain a specific condition c:
  - $c_1, \dots, c_m, t_1, \dots, t_n \Rightarrow t$;
  - $c_1, \dots, c_m, t_1, \dots, t_n \Rightarrow c$.[5]

[5] Here we assume that a pre-condition for a task to begin its execution can include both logical expressions and the previous execution of other tasks (*task dependency*), for example "We buy an ice cream if the sun is shining and we go to downtown". Notice that the study of dependencies among tasks is out of the scope of this work; anyway, we refer to [13] for an initial study of how to capture control flow patterns in Modal DL.

- Rules for relationships between tasks: $t_i \Rightarrow_O t_1, \ldots, t_i \Rightarrow_O t_n$, meaning that if task t_i is performed, then tasks from t_1 to t_n must be executed as well.
- Rules describing obligations: $c_1, \ldots, c_m \Rightarrow_O \bigotimes_{i=1}^{n} a_i$, where the consequent is a reparative chain of obligations.
- Rules describing goals: $c_1, \ldots, c_m \Rightarrow_G \bigoplus_{i=1}^{n} a_i$, where the consequent is a preferential chain of goals.

In the following, when possible, we will use the subscripted literal t to denote a task, and the subscripted literal c to denote a condition. Given a modal defeasible theory $T = (F, R, >)$, the set of facts F contains:

- literals for conditions that are to be considered true at the beginning of an instance of a BP;
- literals for tasks that can be performed with no other conditions but the ones in F (or without any condition at all);

We impose that no modalised literals for norms or goals are facts, since we do not want in this preliminary analysis to consider *primitive intentions* and *unconditional obligations*. Thus, primary norms and goals are translated in our framework as the corresponding modalised rules without antecedents.

Let us consider the following example to show how a theory can fail to be compliant with respect to a modalised operator.

Example 2. Let T be the theory with only the following rule:

$$r_1 : \Rightarrow_X a \odot b$$

This modal rule is obviously applicable, as its antecedent is empty. Furthermore, no rule whose consequent is $\neg a$ is in the theory. By definition, we obtain $+\partial_X a$. Since there are no belief rules for a (nor for b), the theory derives, in cascade: $-\partial a$, $+\partial_X b$, $-\partial b$ and $+\partial_X \bot$. Hence, T is not compliant with respect to modality X. If we add b as a fact, or we introduce a rule like $\Rightarrow b$, then T becomes compliant since we can derive $+\partial b$ (as a compensation of a) which leads us to derive $-\partial_X \bot$.

The ideas enlightened by the previous example underpin the conceptual bases of this work: the obligation to do a thing does not imply at all that such a thing should eventually be executed by the system. The same reasoning is valid also for goals: aiming at a goal does not result in possessing the means to reach it. Moreover, if such an obligation (goal) has no further compensation, then we definitely obtain a derivation for $\bot$ with respect to this particular chain.

The above reasoning allows us to give a formal definition of a theory to be norm compliant and goal compliant based only on the modalised derivations of $\bot$.

Definition 2 (Norm and Goal Compliance). *Let T be a modal defeasible theory. T is* norm compliant *if $T \vdash -\partial_O \bot$ and it is* goal compliant *if $T \vdash -\partial_G \bot$.*

Example 3. We now extend Example 1 formalising it in our logic.

$$
\begin{array}{ll}
F = \{Lenses, Frames\} & \\
R = \{r_0 :\Rightarrow_G EyeGlasses & r_5 : MountingMach1 \Rightarrow \neg MountingMach2 \\
\quad r_1 :\Rightarrow Laser & r_6 : Glasses, MountingMach1 \Rightarrow EyeGlasses \\
\quad r_2 : Lenses, Laser \Rightarrow Glasses & r_7 : Glasses, MountingMach2 \Rightarrow Eyeglasses \\
\quad r_3 :\Rightarrow MountingMach1 & r_8 :\Rightarrow_O \neg Laser \otimes WearGoggles \\
\quad r_4 :\Rightarrow MountingMach2 & r_9 :\Rightarrow_G MountingMach1 \oplus MountingMach2\} \\
>^{sm} = \{r_4 > r_3\} &
\end{array}
$$

Since there no exists rule for goggles, the theory is goal compliant, but not norm compliant. If we add

$$r_{10} :\Rightarrow WearGoggles$$

to R we are both norm and goal compliant, and also if we add

$$r_{11} : OutOfOrderMountingMach1 \Rightarrow \neg MountingMach1$$

and *OutOfOrderMountingMach1* as a fact.

4.1 Revision in Case of Non Compliance

Norm and goal compliance give rise to non-trivial questions: what should we do when a BP is not norm compliant or goal compliant, or even both? Are there (efficient) ways to make a BP norm compliant once a violation of a norm occurs without affecting goal compliance? And from the other point of view, how to make a BP goal compliant once some of its goals are not achieved without affecting norm compliance? Answering these questions attains the area of *business process revision*, which has received great attention in recent years given its crucial influence on organisation practices.

Roughly speaking, all the efforts spent in this research area subscribe to two general approaches. *The first approach* relies on modelling notations defining the structural aspects of BPs, which are extended with other formalisms apt to represent the behavioural aspects. As an example, BPMN enriched with semantic annotations is able to describe the effects implied by the execution of a particular task [2]. On the same grounds, several translations from modelling notations into other formalisms have been proposed, e.g., semantic nets [14] and BP graphs [15]. *The second approach* instead is completely based on pure logical formalisms, where revising a BP means revising the logical theory describing the BP itself. The underlying theory formally represents at the same time the structure and the behaviour of the BP [13].

Describing pros and cons of both approaches is out of the scope of this paper and will be matter of future work. However, it is worth taking both into account, as they capture different (and interesting) aspects of revision. The first aims at revising a BP at an higher level, in terms of removal, addition, swapping and substitutions of tasks in the BP. On the other hand, the second one abstracts from the concepts of task and conditions that trigger (or are caused by) a task: they are all denoted by literals in the same theory, and the main focus is on how they work together to derive other literals. We suggest below one representative example of each approach, and we briefly report some hints on how the proposed ideas could be exploited for our purposes.

Reusable modules. The first idea, given in [16] and developed in [17], relies on the ever more emerging trend of designing BPs as related collections of *reusable* modules, i.e., set of standardised actions to be performed to achieve the goals modules have been built for (thus giving goal compliance), and that can be used with slight or no modifications also in other BPs. Modules are further augmented with built-in statements assuring that the usage of a particular module in a BP implies the norm compliance with respect to the statements specified in the module. This approach can be theoretically applicable both when a norm uncompliant process is given, or must be built from scratch and we have to assure its norm and goal compliance at design time. For the first case, we recall that the algorithm given in [2] allows to know the *exact* point in a BP where a violation of an obligation occurs. Thus, we can substitute the uncompliant part of the BP with a module that reaches the same goals and compensates the previous violation(s). In the second case, we try to build the process starting from a given repository of modules, based on goals we want to achieve and norms we have to comply with.

Theory change via proof tags analysis. We have already afforded the problem of revising defeasible theories by only changing the superiority relation between rules [18]. The major result is the identification of three relevant cases, named *canonical*, where a revision operator could apply only changing the relative strength between pairs of rules. More specifically, the revision operator could act on a defeasibly proved literal p and makes it not provable anymore, i.e., from $+\partial p$ to $-\partial p$ (*first case*); or could act on a defeasibly proved literal p and makes its opposite defeasibly proved, i.e., from $+\partial p$ to $+\partial{\sim}p$ (*second case*); or more, could act on a not defeasibly proved literal p and makes it defeasibly proved, i.e., from $-\partial p$ to $+\partial p$ (*third case*). Additional proof tags other than strict ($\pm\Delta$) and defeasible proof ($\pm\partial$) for a literal are used to better study the cases. Some preliminary work suggests that proof tags analysis could represent a valid mean to categorise all possible situation an hypothetical revision operator has to cope with. Indeed, by definition of $+\partial_X\bot$, there exists at least one rule r for goals or obligations such that (1) r is applicable, and (2) each element p in the chain is not defeasibly provable as a belief, i.e., $-\partial p$ holds. Thus, it seems reasonable that there are two ways to regain compliance with respect to the corresponding modality: we can focus on the consequent of r, making at least one element p on the chain defeasibly provable (and falling in the third canonical case, that is from $-\partial p$ to $+\partial p$); or we can focus on the antecedent of r, making the rule discarded in the sense of Definition 1 (that is, making at least an antecedent p not defeasibly provable with respect to its modality X). This is represented by a modalised variant of the first canonical case, i.e., from $+\partial_X p$ to $-\partial_X p$.

4.2 Compliance by Design

The idea of *Compliance by Design* is to create an entirely new process starting from a fully declarative description of the specifications for a process and the norms. These specifications are encoded in a modal defeasible theory. This theory describes the capabilities, resources of a company, and the environment the enterprise acts in; it also contains the norms governing the business and the goals the enterprise wants to achieve. We also assume such a theory to be norm and goal compliant. Thus, after the building process ends up, there is no need of checking compliance again, since the process will be compliant with norms and goals by design. Thus, from the fact that the theory we work with has been proved to be compliant, it follows that a compliant process exists. The issue is now to study methodologies to extract the graph of the process from the initial theory. Our intuition is that a derivation of a task literal corresponds to a plan leading to the achievement of the task. In this perspective the problem reduces to how to assemble together from the many derivations of the goals the corresponding plans to obtain a single business process graph.

In the current literature, two approaches appear promising for realising compliance by design. The first approach, based on the *process mining* [19,20], consists in applying the same techniques devised to induce a process graph starting from *workflow logs*, to the many derivations from the theory leading to goals and norms. In the second method, we start from the set of goals we want to achieve, and we iteratively construct the graph, rule by rule, following the structure of the theory and using its extension.

Process Mining Approach. [19,20] define techniques and algorithms for discovering workflow models starting from "workflow logs". A workflow log contains informations about the workflow as it is actually being executed: all the traces in a workflow log are representative and a sufficiently large subset of the possible behaviours of systems modeled in the workflows themselves. Through process mining, authors start from linear sequences of tasks to obtain complex structures capturing parallelism and choices.

We can apply the same methodologies in our case. The statement is motivated by the following reasoning. Given a reachable goal, a derivation for it is a linear sequence of (proved) literals in the theory. Thus, such a derivation can be understood as a log trace. Even if, to obtain a literal, the derivation rule has a set of premises that contains more than a single element, there exist procedures to automatically obtain derivations. For example, given the theory with the only rule $r : p, q \Rightarrow t$, where p and q are facts, we obtain as derivations $p \rightarrow q \rightarrow t$ and $q \rightarrow p \rightarrow t$. Being the theory compliant, the issue is to extract all the traces from such derivations, and combine them together to get a single business process graph.

Backward Graph Approach. BPs consist of separate activities. An activity is an action that is a semantical unit at some level. In addition, an activity can be thought of as a function that modifies the state of the process, making true some conditions, false some others, and letting some tasks to start their execution. BPs are modelled as graphs with individual activities as nodes. The edges on the graph represent the potential flow of control from one activity to another.

The modal defeasible theory we start with is rich of informations: there are literals describing tasks and conditions, rules describing the activations of tasks and their effects, reparation chains both for norms and goals. Moreover, the superiority relation states conditions under which a rule is activated (preferred) instead of another and, finally, patterns on the rules allow to identify parallel and (exclusive) choice structures.

We want to exploit all these informations to build the BP. The idea is to start from the extension of the theory (i.e., the literals that have been defeasible proved) and from the set of reachable goals, and to create a node for each goal that is a task. For each of them, we find out every rule proving it whose antecedents are all in the extension of the theory, and we store them. For every such antecedent that is also a task literal, we create a new node (if it does not exist yet) and we link it with a directed edge from it to the corresponding goal node. For every new node, we iterate the process. The procedure terminates when we reach literals for facts.

Notice that in the process described above, we never add nodes for conditions. This follows from the fact that all the conditions needed for being norm and goal compliant are already satisfied (since the initial theory is compliant). Thus, there is no need to consider literals for conditions: we must only establish which antecedents generate such literals and propagate these informations.

Since, nowadays, there is yet no algorithm computing this procedure, an empirical proof of the termination does not exist. Anyway, the compliance of the theory implies that every goal and norm is derived or compensated, and so the derivation process ends in a finite number of steps. Since the above procedure represents a "backward mirroring" of the derivation process, it also must come to an end.

5 Conclusions

The first contribution of this paper is the introduction of the notion of "goal compliance" and we have argued that to check whether a BP achieves the goals of an organisation can be dealt with the same methodology as "norm compliance". This provides a further motivation to subscribe to the declarative way to specify processes.

While the idea behind this work looks very natural and at the core of BPs and glimpses of it can be found in closely related areas (e.g., process verification [10] and automated planning [21]), to the best of our knowledge, this is the first work that explicitly addresses the two types of compliance from a fully declarative point of view, and proposes a formal framework for modelling and reasoning with them. The paper identifies further areas of research –in the *compliance by design* space– stemming from the work presented here, namely: process compliance resolution (how to revise a non-compliant theory) and process derivation (how to extract a business process from compliant declarative specifications for it). We have outlined some possible developments inspired by automated planning [21] and process mining [20].

The closest work to our approach is [22] proposing LTL (Linear Temporal Logic) to describe compliance rules, to use automated reasoning techniques to generate LTL models of processes and then using process mining techniques to extract business processes. The main limitations of this work is that, while LTL is suitable to represents the temporal relationships involving the tasks, alone is not suitable to faithfully represent the normative (nor business) requirements.

Defeasible Logics are a very powerful tool to describe an environment, and in the years scholars extended the primitive formalism to deal with many different kinds of situations. [23] introduces a temporalised DL, while [13] describes many types of obligations, and shows how control flows (and other relationships among process tasks) are modelled using the various types of obligations. It seems very likely that the formalism introduced in this work can be further extended to handle both temporal constraints, and different types of obligations either when determining if a Modal DL theory is compliant with sets of norms and goals, revising it, or creating a business process starting from its compliance. It seems also of great interest to incorporate idea from [24] to model resources and complex events in our logical framework.

Acknowledgements. NICTA is funded by the Australian Government as represented by the Department of Broadband, Communications and the Digital Economy, the Australian Research Council through the ICT Centre of Excellence program and the Queensland Government.

References

1. van der Aalst, W.M.P., Pesic, M., Schonenberg, H.: Declarative workflows: Balancing between flexibility and support. Computer Science - R&D 23, 99–113 (2009)
2. Governatori, G., Sadiq, S.: The journey to business process compliance. In: Handbook of Research on BPM, pp. 426–454 (2008)
3. Antoniou, G., Billington, D., Governatori, G., Maher, M.J.: Representation results for defeasible logic. ACM Transactions on Computational Logic 2, 255–287 (2001)
4. Governatori, G.: Representing business contracts in RuleML. International Journal of Cooperative Information Systems 14, 181–216 (2005)
5. Governatori, G., Milosevic, Z., Sadiq, S.: Compliance checking between business processes and business contracts. In: Hung, P.C.K. (ed.) 10th International Enterprise Distributed Object Computing Conference (EDOC 2006), pp. 221–232. IEEE Computing Society (2006)
6. Sadiq, S., Governatori, G., Naimiri, K.: Modelling of control objectives for business process compliance. In: Alonso, G., Dadam, P., Rosemann, M. (eds.) BPM 2007. LNCS, vol. 4714, pp. 149–164. Springer, Heidelberg (2007)
7. Governatori, G., Rotolo, A.: Bio logical agents: Norms, beliefs, intentions in defeasible logic. Journal of Autonomous Agents and Multi Agent Systems 17, 36–69 (2008)
8. Governatori, G., Rotolo, A.: Logic of violations: A gentzen system for reasoning with contrary-to-duty obligations. Australasian Journal of Logic 4, 193–215 (2006)
9. Antoniou, G., Billington, D., Governatori, G., Maher, M.J.: Representation results for defeasible logic. ACM Trans. Comput. Logic 2, 255–287 (2001)
10. van der Aalst, W.M.P.: The application of petri nets to workflow management. Journal of Circuits, Systems, and Computers 8, 21–66 (1998)
11. Dastani, M., Governatori, G., Rotolo, A., van der Torre, L.: Programming cognitive agents in defeasible logic. In: Sutcliffe, G., Voronkov, A. (eds.) LPAR 2005. LNCS (LNAI), vol. 3835, pp. 621–636. Springer, Heidelberg (2005)
12. Dastani, M., Governatori, G., Rotolo, A., van der Torre, L.: Preferences of agents in defeasible logic. In: Zhang, S., Jarvis, R.A. (eds.) AI 2005. LNCS (LNAI), vol. 3809, pp. 695–704. Springer, Heidelberg (2005)
13. Governatori, G., Rotolo, A.: Norm compliance in business process modeling. In: [25], pp. 194–209
14. Ghose, A., Koliadis, G.: Auditing Business Process Compliance. In: Krämer, B.J., Lin, K.-J., Narasimhan, P. (eds.) ICSOC 2007. LNCS, vol. 4749, pp. 169–180. Springer, Heidelberg (2007)
15. Dijkman, R.M., Dumas, M., van Dongen, B.F., Käärik, R., Mendling, J.: Similarity of business process models: Metrics and evaluation. Inf. Syst. 36, 498–516 (2011)
16. Schumm, D., Leymann, F., Ma, Z., Scheibler, T., Strauch, S.: Integrating Compliance into Business Processes Process Fragments as Reusable Compliance Controls. Universitätsverlag Göttingen, 2125–2137 (2010)

17. Schumm, D., Türetken, O., Kokash, N., Elgammal, A., Leymann, F., van den Heuvel, W.J.: Business Process Compliance Through Reusable Units of Compliant Processes. In: Daniel, F., Facca, F.M. (eds.) ICWE 2010. LNCS, vol. 6385, pp. 325–337. Springer, Heidelberg (2010)
18. Governatori, G., Olivieri, F., Scannapieco, S., Cristani, M.: Superiority based revision of defeasible theories. In: [25], pp. 104–118
19. Agrawal, R., Gunopulos, D., Leymann, F.: Mining process models from workflow logs. In: Schek, H.-J., Saltor, F., Ramos, I., Alonso, G. (eds.) EDBT 1998. LNCS, vol. 1377, pp. 469–483. Springer, Heidelberg (1998)
20. van der Aalst, W.M.P., Weijters, T., Maruster, L.: Workflow mining: Discovering process models from event logs. IEEE Trans. Knowl. Data Eng. 16, 1128–1142 (2004)
21. Ghallab, M., Nau, D.S., Traverso, P.: Automated Planning: Theory and Practice. Morgan Kaufmann (2004)
22. Awad, A., Goré, R., Thomson, J., Weidlich, M.: An Iterative Approach for Business Process Template Synthesis from Compliance Rules. In: Mouratidis, H., Rolland, C. (eds.) CAiSE 2011. LNCS, vol. 6741, pp. 406–421. Springer, Heidelberg (2011)
23. Governatori, G., Rotolo, A., Sartor, G.: Temporalised normative positions in defeasible logic. In: ICAIL 2005, pp. 25–34. ACM Press (2005)
24. Governatori, G., Rotolo, A., Sadiq, S.: A model of dynamic resource allocation in workflow systems. In: ADC 2004, pp. 197–206. ACS (2004)
25. Dean, M., Hall, J., Rotolo, A., Tabet, S. (eds.): RuleML 2010. LNCS, vol. 6403. Springer, Heidelberg (2010)

LegalRuleML: XML-Based Rules and Norms

Monica Palmirani[1], Guido Governatori[2], Antonino Rotolo[1], Said Tabet[3], Harold Boley[4], and Adrian Paschke[5]

[1] CIRSFID, University of Bologna, Italy
{monica.palmirani,antonino.rotolo}@unibo.it
[2] NICTA, Brisbane, Australia
guido.governatori@nicta.com.au
[3] EMC Corporation, Office of the CTO, Hopkinton, MA, USA
said.tabet@emc.com
[4] Institute for Information Technology, National Research Council Canada
Fredericton, NB, Canada
harold.boley@nrc.gc.ca
[5] Computer Science Department, Freie Universitaet Berlin, Germany
paschke@inf.fu-berlin.de

Abstract. Legal texts are the foundational resource where to discover rules and norms that feed into different concrete (often XML-based) Web applications. Legislative documents provide general norms and specific procedural rules for eGovernment and eCommerce environments, while contracts specify the conditions of services and business rules (e.g. service level agreements for cloud computing), and judgments provide information about the legal argumentation and interpretation of norms to concrete case-law. Such legal knowledge is an important source that should be detected, properly modeled and expressively represented in order to capture all the domain particularities. This paper provides an extension of RuleML called LegalRuleML for fostering the characteristics of legal knowledge and to permit its full usage in legal reasoning and in the business rule domain. LegalRuleML encourages the effective exchange and sharing of such semantic information between legal documents, business rules, and software applications.

Keywords: Legal Rules, Legal XML Standards, Semantic Web, Legal Reasoning, LegalRuleML.

1 Rationale

The AI & Law community dedicated a good part of the last twenty years to model legal norms using different logics and formalisms [30]. The methodology used starts with a re-interpretation of a legal text by a Legal Knowledge Engineer who extracts the norms, applies models and a theory within a logical framework, and finally represents the norms using a particular formalism. In the last decade, several Legal XML standards were proposed to describe and represent legal texts [23; 35; 4] with XML based rules (RuleML, SWRL, RIF, LKIF, etc.) [12; 7]. In the meantime, the Semantic Web, in particular Legal Ontology research combined with semantic norm

F. Olken et al. (Eds.): RuleML 2011 - America, LNCS 7018, pp. 298–312, 2011.

extraction based on Natural Language Processing (NLP) [10; 8; 25; 24], gave a great impulse to the modeling of legal concepts [7]. In this paramount scenario, there is urgent need to find a robust and expressive XML annotation, compliant with the Semantic Web technologies, able to meet all the unique particular aspects rising from the legal domain and in the same time close the gap between legal text descriptions, using XML techniques, and norms modeling, in order to realize an integrated and self-contained representation of legal resources available on the Web [26; 22]. This integration is fundamental for fostering Semantic Web advantages applied to legal norms like: NLP, IR, graph representation, Web ontologies and rules, etc.

The second requirement is to capture the processes description embedded into the norms for extracting the business rules and for passing them to other important applications like workflow or business rule engines. There is a gap currently between the norms modeling and business rules, even if the latter are strongly influenced by the former. This knowledge is an important input for several applications in Cloud computing, eGovernment, eCommerce [20; 14; 31], eHealth, etc. Of particular importance in such scenario, the requirement for compliance checking [32; 16; 18; 19] theory and applications.

The third aspect is to permit an agile annotation of all the instruments necessary to capture the legal norms [11] that usually the normal rule XML standard doesn't include. Our goal is to have an expressive XML standard for modeling normative rules that will satisfy the legal domain requirements. This will enable a legal reasoning level on top of the ontological layer, following the Tim Berners-Lee semantic web stack[1]. Finally, particular attention is paid to the Linked Open Data [3] approach to modeling, regarding not only the semantics of raw data (act, contracts, court files, judgments, etc.), but also of rules in conjunction with their functionality and usage. Without rules or axioms, legal concepts represent nothing more than a taxonomy [35].

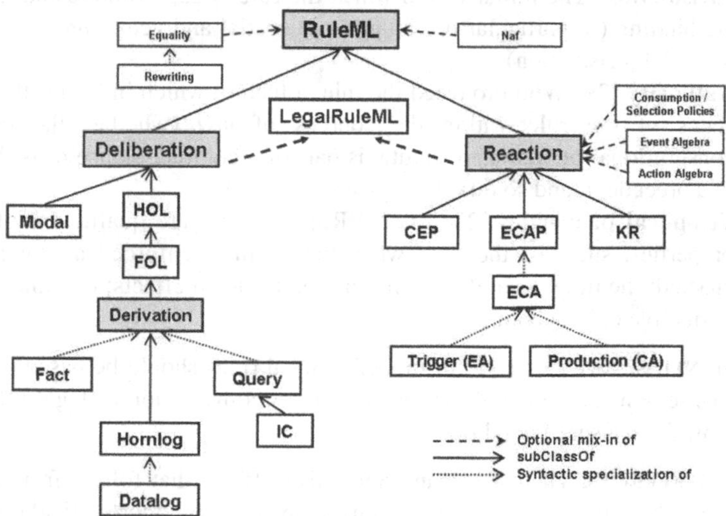

Fig. 1. LegalRuleML position in the current RuleML architecture (adapted from [5])

[1] http://www.w3.org/2007/Talks/0130-sb-W3CTechSemWeb/#%2824%29

In this scenario we have extended RuleML [5; 6; 38; 34] to include, in orthogonal way (see Fig. 1), a new dialect capturing all those requirements, not fully incorporated in the original version of RuleML. We call this new dialect LegalRuleML. It is positioned between the Deliberation rules and the Reaction Rules facilitating the modeling of either norms or business rules. This approach provides support for the implementation of reasoning engines combining both norms and business rules.

2 Characteristics of Legal Norms

RuleML provides a good framework to start working towards the above-mentioned goals. We define the main characteristics needed for modeling norms and the essential features needed to apply legal reasoning in effective and computable way. We can divide the characteristics in three main groups: semantic features, logic features, and legal process features.

2.1 Semantic Features

ISOMORPHISM [1] To ease validation and maintenance, there should be a one-to-one correspondence between the rules in the formal model and the units of natural language text which express the rules in the original legal sources, such as sections of legislation. This entails, for example, that a general rule and separately stated exceptions, in different sections of a statute, should not be converged into a single rule in the formal model.

REIFICATION [13] Rules are objects with properties, such as:

- **Jurisdiction**. The limits within which the rule is authoritative and its effects are binding (of particular importance are spatial and geographical references to model jurisdiction).
- **Authority** [29] Who produced the rule, a feature which indicates the ranking status of the rule within the sources of law (whether the rule is a constitutional provision, a statute, is part of a contract clause or is the ruling of a precedent, and so on).
- **Temporal properties** [28, 15, 27] Rules usually are qualified by temporal properties, such as: the time when the norm is enforced and/or has been enacted; the time when the norm can produce legal effects; the time when the normative effects hold.

RULE SEMANTICS. Any language for modeling legal rules should be based on precise and rigorous semantics, which allow for the correct computation of legal effects that should follow from a set of legal rules.

NORMATIVE EFFECTS. There are many normative effects that follow from applying rules, such as obligations, permissions, prohibitions and also more articulated effects such as those introduced, e.g., by Hohfeld (see [36]). Below is a rather comprehensive list of normative effects [33]:

- **Evaluative** indicates that something is good or bad, is a value to be optimized or an evil to be minimized. For example, "Human dignity is valuable", "Participation ought to be promoted";
- **Qualificatory** describes a legal quality to a person or an object. For example, "Joe is a citizen";
- **Definitional** specifies the meaning of a term. For example, "Tolling agreement means any agreement to put a specified amount of raw material per period through a particular processing facility";
- **Deontic** typically imposes the obligation or confers the permission to do a certain action. For example, "x has the obligation to do A";
- **Potestative** assigns powers. For example, "A worker has the power to terminate his work contract";
- **Evidentiary** establishes the conclusion to be drawn from certain evidence. For example, "It is presumed that dismissal was discriminatory";
- **Existential** indicates the beginning or the termination of the existence of a legal entity. For example, "The company ceases to exist";
- **Norm-concerning effects** states modifications of norms such as abrogation, repeal, substitution, and so on.

VALUES [2]. Usually, some values are promoted by legal rules. The modeling of rules sometimes needs to support the representation of values and value preferences, which can also play the role of meta-criteria for solving rule conflicts (given two conflicting rules r1 and r2, value v1, promoted by r1, is preferred to value v2, promoted by r2, and so r1 overrides r2).

2.2 Logic Features

DEFEASIBILITY [13; 29; 37]. When the antecedent of a rule is satisfied by the facts of a case (or via other rules), the conclusion of the rule presumably holds, but is not necessarily true. The defeasibility of legal rules breaks down into the following issues:

- **Conflicts** [29]. Rules can conflict, namely, they may lead to incompatible legal effects. Conceptually, conflicts can be of different types whether two conflicting rules: i) are such that one is an exception of the other (i.e., one is more specific than the other); ii) have a different ranking status; iii) have been enacted at different times.
- **Exclusionary rules** [13; 29; 37]. Some rules provide one way to explicitly undercut other rules, namely, to make them inapplicable.

CONTRAPOSITION [29]. Rules do not counterpose. If the conclusion of a rule is not true, the rule does not sanction any inferences about the truth of its premises.

CONTRIBUTORY REASONS OR FACTORS [37]. It is not always possible to formulate precise rules, even defeasible ones, for aggregating the factors relevant for resolving a legal issue. For example: "The educational value of a work needs to be taken into consideration when evaluating whether the work is covered by the copyright doctrine of fair use."

RULE VALIDITY [17]. Rules can be invalid or become invalid. Deleting invalid rules is not an option when it is necessary to reason retroactively with rules, which were valid at various times over a course of events. For instance: The annulment of a norm is usually seen as a kind of repeal, which invalidates the norm and removes it from the legal system as if it had never been enacted. The effect of an annulment applies *ex tunc*: annulled norms are prevented from producing any legal effects, also for past events. An abrogation on the other hand operates *ex nunc*: The rule continues to apply for events that occurred before the rule was abrogated.

2.3 Legal Process Features

LEGAL PROCEDURES. Rules not only regulate the procedures resolving legal conflicts (see above), but also are used for arguing or reasoning about whether or not some action or state complies with other, substantive rules. In particular, rules are required for procedures which regulate methods detecting violations of the law; determine the normative effects triggered by norm violations, such as reparative obligations, namely, which are meant to repair or compensate violations. Note that these constructions can give rise to very complex rule dependencies, because the violation of a single rule can activate other (reparative) rules, which in turn, in case of their violation, refer to other rules, and so forth.

PERSISTENCE OF NORMATIVE EFFECTS [15]. Some normative effects persist over time unless some other and subsequent event terminates them. For example: "If one causes damage, one has to provide compensation." Other effects hold on the condition and only while the antecedent conditions of the rules hold. For example: "If one is in a public office, one is forbidden to smoke".

An interesting question is whether rule interchange languages for the legal domain should be expressive enough to fully model all the features listed above, or whether some of these requirements can be met at the reasoning level, at the level responsible for structuring, evaluating and comparing legal arguments constructed from rules and other sources.

3 LegalRuleML

To extend RuleML into LegalRuleML, we have defined two more XML-schemas: LegalMeta.xsd module and Legal_operators.xsd module (see Fig.2). Legal_meta.xsd is devoted to model all the legal metadata concerning the legal rules. Legal_operators.xsd defines the legal operators: deontic operators and behaviours. It is also necessary to have a module to connect derivation rules with reaction rules, in order to foster the potentiality of the reaction rules. This paper is a preliminary proposal for testing the rational presented in the § 1 and 2, so in the future we intend to modularize better the schemas in order to improve scalability and maintenance over the time. This proposal aims to open a debate, not to fix a solution, and make possible the mark-up of some pilot cases in order to evaluate the correctness of the solution in the RuleML community.

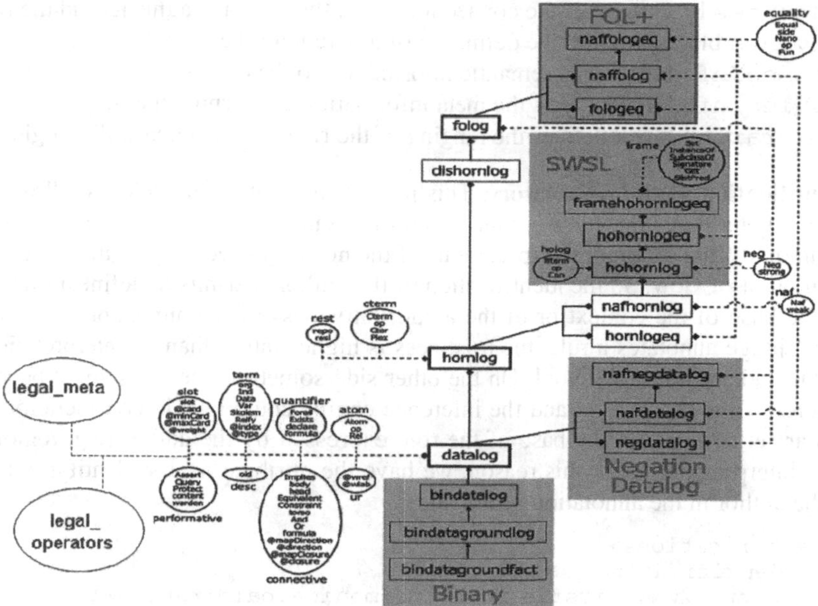

Fig. 2. Legal_metadata module included in the `datalog` component (adapted from [34])

3.1 Legal Meta Data

The root tag of Legal_metadata.xsd is `metaInfo` that includes the following optional metadata:

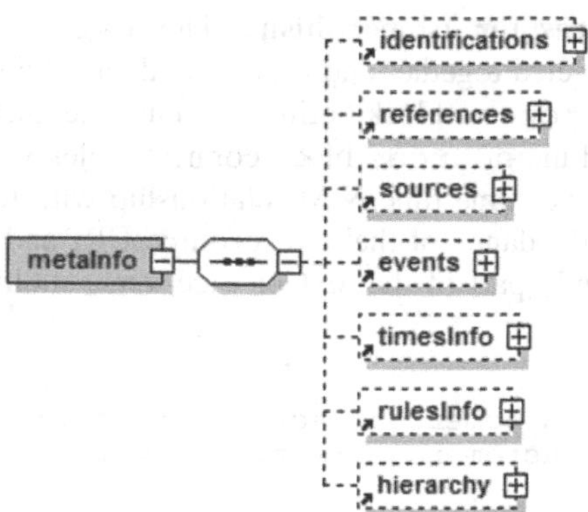

Fig. 3. MetaInfo module organization

- `identification` block provides information on the authors of the rules;
- `references` block provides identification of the textual fragments involved in the rules modeled;

– `sources` block models the connections with the textual fragments and the rules;
– `events` block provides the definition of any temporal event;
– `timesInfo` block adds semantic information to the events;
– `rulesInfo` block models the meta information concerning the rules;
– `hierarchy` block defines the ranging of the rules in the defeasibility logic.

Identification of the Annotators. This part of metadata is modeled to allow a multiple annotation of the rules coming from different authors. In the legal domain it is common to find different interpretations of the norms and equally legitimate under the legal point of view. So the identification of the authors permits to define a trust policy on the base of the context or of the authoritativeness of the annotator. If a constitutional judge annotates a rule, the trustiness is higher rather than an interpretation of a Ph.D. student of a law school. On the other side sometime the rules could be slightly different from the context and the inference engine could take in consideration a particular set of rules on the base of the role expressed by the author (e.g. regional vs. state interpretation). For this reason, we have the attribute `as` for identifying the role of the author in the annotation of the rule.

```
<identifications>
   <identification id="aut1"
uri="http://www.cirsfid.unibo.it/monica.palmirani.owl"
as="author"/>
   <identification id="aut2"
uri="http://www.nicta.com.au/guido.governatori.owl"
as="editor"/>
</identifications>
```

In this section two authors (`aut1`, `aut2`) are defined and connected with their ontology and role (`aut1` is the author of the rule, `aut2` is the editor of the rule). The same could be applied to the authorities, institutions, legal entities, juridical persons.

Sources and References for Isomorphism. The `references` and `sources` blocks are strictly connected together and they provide a solution to the isomorphism requirement. The `references` block defines the entire textual fragment involved in the rules modeling, and the `sources` block connects rules with the appropriate references. Because we have some time N:M relationship with text and rules, this mechanism permits the redundancy of the text resource URI and in the meantime connects one rule to multiple part of the text or vice versa multiple rules to the same fragment of text.

```
<references>
   <reference id="customerContract" uri="http://text1#art1"/>
   <reference id="customerContract2" uri="http://text1#art2"/>
</references>

<sources>
   <source element="#rule1" refersTo="#customerContract"/>
   <source element="#rule1" refersTo="#customerContract2"/>
   <source element="#rule2" refersTo="#customerContract2"/>
</sources>
```

This is particularly true in case of penalty-reparation rule. Usually the definition of the penalty is expressed in one clause and the conditions of reparation in another clause, but together they determine the body and the header of a unique normative rule. In the following fragment we have two citations (clauses 8 and 5) that constitute the body of the rule and the header is in the clause 10.

> *Clause 10, point 1, letter c)*
>
> *If Google does not meet the Google Apps SLA (clause 8), and if Customer meets its obligations under this Google Apps SLA (clause 5), Customer will be eligible to receive the Service Credits of X days.*

This rule is modeled in such way:

```
<references>
   <reference id="GoogleSLA" uri="http://text1#clouse8"/>
   <reference id="GoogleSLA" uri="http://text1#clouse5"/>
   <reference id="GoogleSLA" uri="http://text1#clouse10"/>
</references>
```

```
<sources>
   <source element="# rule1_body " refersTo="#GoogleSLA8"/>
   <source element="#rule1_body" refersTo="#GoogleSLA5"/>
   <source element="#rule1_header" refersTo="#GoogleSLA10"/>
</sources>
```

Events and Temporal Parameters. The `events` block detects the events related to a set of norms, in neutral way, without any semantic interpretation. The `timesInfo` block assigns the legal semantic to each group of events. In this way we could connect each atom, body, header, rule with the appropriate `timesInfo` block without any redundancy of data, preserving a compact annotation and high expressiveness. Next, we use attributes not elements in order to avoid both temporal predicates and arbitrary nomenclature to the functions.

Consider now the following clause coming from a SLA contract:

> *A customer is "Premium" if their spending has been min 5000 dollars in the previous year*

We have at least four temporal events in this provision: a) the time when the text creates rights, duties and obligations (e.g. time of *enter into force*, after the signature of the contract); b) the time when the provision is *effective* (e.g. the time when the service starts, 1 Jan 2012); c) the time when the provision is *applicable* (e.g. after at least one year from the efficacy time); d) the temporal conditions included in the provision that is a dynamic dimension (e.g. "previous year"). A new question arise concerning the continuity of the temporal condition: i) the customer have to spend at least one order min 5000 dollars (only one event is sufficient); ii) the customer could aggregate several spending for min 5000 dollars (set of events create the condition); iii) the customer have to maintain their orders min 500 dollars (continuity of condition). For this reason we have introduced an attribute (`perdurant`) with several parameters: and (true for all t_i of an interval), or (true if at least one t_i satisfies the condition), xor (true if only one t_i satisfies the condition) , agg (true if the aggregation of a set of t_i satisfies the condition).

We can model those events as follow:

```
<events>
   <event id="e1" value="2011-08-25T01:01:00.0Z"/>
   <event id="e2" value="2012-01-25T01:01:00.0Z"/>
   <event id="e3" value="2013-01-25T01:01:00.0Z"/>
</events>

<timesInfo>
   <times id="t1">
     <time start="#e1" timeType="efficacy"/>
     <time start="#e1" timeType="inforce"/>
     <time start="#e3" timeType="application"/>
   </times>
   <times id="t2">
     <time duration="-P01Y" timeType="internal" timeType
="application" perdurant="agg"/>
   </times>
</timesInfo>
```

Note the time of application "previous year" is modeled as internal event of the norm and represented using the negative period of duration (-P1Y, following the standard syntax of xsd).

The mechanism presented for modeling the temporal parameters connects times to norms and rules and it fosters effective legal reasoning algorithm about facts occurred in the past, or that happen in the future, with uncertain events and with complex conditionals.

Hierarchy and Type of Norms. The non-monotonic legal reasoning needs to manage the hierarchy of rules [see § 2]. The hierarchy block defines the superiority relationship between two rules: it is a binary operator that creates a meta-rule among existing rules.

Because the superiority relationship depends to some conditions we have several attributes that anchor the association to specific parameters: author and time. It is so possible to have the same rule with different superiority relationship, made in a different time, by a different author.

```
<hierarchy>
   <range id="rng1" function="superior" from="#rule1"
to="#rule2" timesBlock="#t1" author="#aut2"/>
</hierarchy>
```

Semantic Qualification of Rules. In the `rulesInfo` block, we define some properties of the rule like the `ruleType` (e.g. defeasible, defeater, strict, metaRule), the `author` and qualification using the attribute `refersTo`. Fostering the `referesTo` attributes we could connect any external legal concept defined with a given ontology.

```
<rulesInfo>
   <ruleInfo source="#rule1" ruleType="defeasible" refersTo
="/ontology/usaJurisdiction.owl" author="#aut2"/>
```

```
  <ruleInfo source="#rule1" ruleType="strict" refers-
To="/ontology/definition.owl" author="#aut2"/>
</rulesInfo>
```

Let us come back to our example:

A customer is "Premium" if their spending has been min 5000 dollars in the previous year.

The above is modeled as follow in enriched way, ready for legal reasoning base don defeasible logic.

```
<Assert mapClosure="universal">
   <Implies timesBlock="#t2" ruleType="defeasible" id="rule1">
     <then timesBlock="#t1">
       <Atom id="atm1">
         <Rel>premium</Rel>
         <Var>customer</Var>
       </Atom>
     </then>
     <if timesBlock="#t1">
        <Atom id="atm2" timesBlock="#t3">
           <Rel>previous year spending</Rel>
           <Var>customer</Var>
           <Var>x</Var>
           <Data>= 5000$ </Data>
        </Atom>
     </if>
   </Implies>
</Assert>
```

3.2 Legal Operators

In the module Legal_operators.xsd we have defined all the operators needed for managing deontic logic and behaviors like violation and reparation.

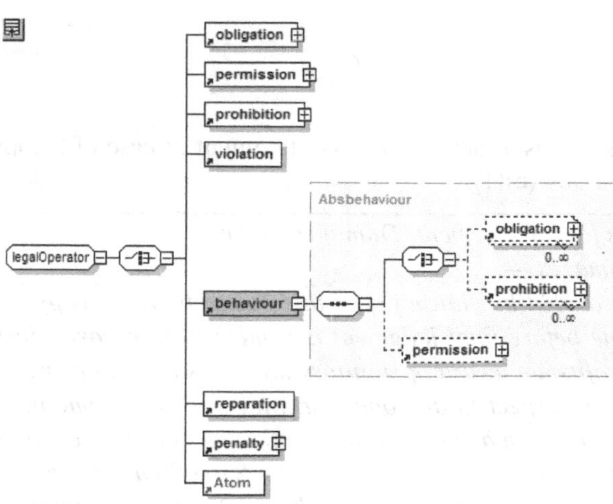

Fig. 4. Legal_operators.xsd elements

Behavior represents a particular sequence of deontic operators that starts with an obligation or a prohibition and ends with a permission.

The `violation` is a unary relationship that refers to the obligation/prohibition subject of the violation. The `reparation` is a unary relationship providing a link to the relevant penalty.

For a better understanding of their usage, we describe an example coming from the US Code related to the infringement of the copyright, Title 18, Chapter 6:

> *§ 602 (b) In a case where the making of the copies or phonorecords would have constituted an infringement of copyright if this title had been applicable, their importation is prohibited.*

To model this example, we first start with the rule 602b where we find in the conclusion a prohibition to import material that infringes the copyright law:

```
<Implies id="rule602b">
   <then>
      <prohibition>
         <Atom id="rule602b-prh1-atm1">
            <Rel>importation is prohibited</Rel>
            <Var>z</Var>
         </Atom>
      </prohibition>
   </then>
   <if>
      <And>
         <Atom id="rule602-if-atm1">
            <Rel>copies or phonorecords</Rel>
            <Var>z</Var>
         </Atom>
         <Atom id="impl602-1-if-atm2">
            <Rel>without the authority of the owner of copyright
</Rel>
            <Var>x</Var>
         </Atom>
      </And>
   </if>
</Implies>
```

After that, we assume as a fact the penalty statement in case of a copyright infringement following the 504 (c)(1):

> *§ 504. Remedies for infringement: Damages and profits*
> *(c) Statutory Damages.—*
> *(1) Except as provided by clause (2) of this subsection, the copyright owner may elect, at any time before final judgment is rendered, to recover, instead of actual damages and profits, an award of statutory damages for all infringements involved in the action, with respect to any one work, for which any one infringer is liable individually, or for which any two or more infringers are liable jointly and severally, in a sum of not less than $750 or more than $30,000 as the court considers just. For the purposes of this subsection, all the parts of a compilation or derivative work constitute one work.*

```
<Atom id="atm504">
        <penalty id="atm504-pnl1">
           <obligation id="obl2" subject="z" beneficiary="y"
timesBlock="#t2">
              <Atom id="atm504-pnl1-atm1">
                 <Rel>award of statutory damages to</Rel>
                 <Var>z</Var>
                 <Data>min $750 </Data>
                 <Data>max $30,000  </Data>
              </Atom>
           </obligation>
        </penalty>
  </Atom>
```

Finally we define a new rule that connects the `reparation` with the violation of the rule602b, and the reparation with the penalty (see the `penalty="#atm504-pnl1"` attribute). We have reparation only if the subject violated the rule602 and has paid the award of statutory damages to the copyright owner.

```
<Implies id="rule602b-rep">
   <then>
      <reparation id="rule602b-rep1" penalty="#atm504-pnl1"/>
   </then>
   <if>
      <violation source="#rule602b"/>
   </if>
  </Implies>
```

3.3 Semantic Qualification of Negation

One of the main problems in legal reasoning is to qualify the negation. To solve this problem, we have customized the module neg_module.xsd and naf_module.xsd in order to include a link to the semantic meaning. The attribute `refersTo` permits to link the markup to specific concept ontology.

```
  <xs:attributeGroup name="Neg.attlist">
   <xs:attributeGroup ref="refersTo"/>
  </xs:attributeGroup>

  <xs:attributeGroup name="Naf.attlist">
   <xs:attributeGroup ref="refersTo"/>
  </xs:attributeGroup>
```

3.3 Extension of the RuleML Modules

To support the application of that metadata, we have extended several modules, like atom_module.xsd that could host the time parameters and the id attribute:

```
<xs:attributeGroup name="Atom.attlist">
      <xs:attributeGroup ref="closure.attrib"/>
      <xs:attributeGroup ref="timesBlock"/>
      <xs:attributeGroup ref="idReq"/>
</xs:attributeGroup>
```

The `connective_module.xsd` is extended in order to define, apart from the time parameters and the id, the type of rule, following the defeasible classification: strict, defeasible, defeater, metaRule.

```
<xs:attributeGroup name="Implies.attlist">
      <xs:attributeGroup ref="closure.attrib"/>
      <xs:attributeGroup ref="direction.attrib"/>
      <xs:attributeGroup ref="material.attrib"/>
      <xs:attributeGroup ref="timesBlock"/>
      <xs:attributeGroup ref="idReq"/>
      <xs:attributeGroup ref="ruleTypeDef"/>
</xs:attributeGroup>
```

In legal_metadata.xsd we define the list of values:

```
<xs:simpleType name="ruleTypeValue">
      <xs:restriction base="xs:token">
         <xs:enumeration value="strict"/>
         <xs:enumeration value="defeasible"/>
         <xs:enumeration value="defeater"/>
         <xs:enumeration value="metaRule"/>
      </xs:restriction>
  </xs:simpleType>
```

4 Conclusion

This paper presents an extension of RuleML customized to support legal requirements. The goal is to have a clear and expressive XML language integrated as part of the RuleML family capable to support the modeling and the representation of legal norms and rules. In this first step we have implemented the following features:

Table 1. List of LegalRuleML features and the extended modules

Features	LegalRuleML	RuleML extension
Isomorphism	sources and references	legal_meta.xsd
Jurisdiction	refersTo	legal_meta.xsd
Authority	author	legal_meta.xsd
Temporal parameters	event and timesInfo	legal_meta.xsd connective_module.xsd atom_module.xsd
Qualification/Definitional/ Valuable	refersTo	legal_meta.xsd
Semantic of Negation	refersTo	Neg_module.xsd Naf_module.xsd
Deontic operators	legalOperator	legal_operators.xsd connective_module.xsd atom_module.xsd
Defeasible logic	hierarchy and typeRules	legal_meta.xsd
Behaviors	legalOperator	legal_operators.xsd connective_module.xsd atom_module.xsd

LegalRuleML language aims to interoperate with Reaction RuleML modules. Our next steps include a better modularization of the main features from a syntactical point of view, extend the modularization to all the modules of the Declarative Rules and Reactive Rules, and develop a proof of concept implementing a sample set of acts and contracts. The LegalRuleML Initiative has been working with OASIS, especially the LegalXML Technical Committee, on organizing future efforts.

References

1. Bench-Capon, T., Coenen, F.: Isomorphism and legal knowledge based systems. Artificial Intelligence and Law 1(1), 65–86 (1992)
2. Bench-Capon, T.: The missing link revisited: The role of teleology in representing legal argument. Artificial Intelligence and Law 10(1-3), 79–94 (2002)
3. Berners-Lee, T.: Long Live the Web: A Call for Continued Open Standards and Neutrality. Scientific America (2010)
4. Boer, A., Radboud, W., Vitali, F.: MetaLex XML and the Legal Knowledge Interchange Format. In: Casanovas, P., Sartor, G., Casellas, N., Rubino, R. (eds.) Computable Models of the Law. LNCS (LNAI), vol. 4884, pp. 21–41. Springer, Heidelberg (2008)
5. Boley, H., Paschke, A., Shafiq, O.: RuleML 1.0: The Overarching Specification of Web Rules. In: Dean, M., Hall, J., Rotolo, A., Tabet, S. (eds.) RuleML 2010. LNCS, vol. 6403, pp. 162–178. Springer, Heidelberg (2010)
6. Boley, H., Tabet, S., Wagner, G.: Design rationale for RuleML: A markup language for Semantic Web rules. In: Cruz, I.F., Decker, S., Euzenat, J., McGuinness, D.L. (eds.) Proc. SWWS 2001, The First Semantic Web Working Symposium, pp. 381–401 (2001)
7. Breuker, J., Boer, A., Hoekstra, R., Van Den Berg, C.: Developing Content for LKIF: Ontologies and Framework for Legal Reasoning. In: Legal Knowledge and Information Systems, JURIX 2006, pp. 41–50. ISO Press, Amsterdam (2006)
8. De Maat, E., Winkels, R.: Automated Classification of Norms, in Sources of Law. In: Francesconi, E., Montemagni, S., Peters, W., Tiscornia, D. (eds.) Semantic Processing of Legal Texts. LNCS, vol. 6036, pp. 170–191. Springer, Heidelberg (2010)
9. Francesconi, E., Passerini, A.: Automatic Classification of Provisions in Legislative Texts. In: ICAIL 2007, vol. 15, pp. 1–17. ACM (2007)
10. Francesconi, E., Montemagni, S., Peters, W., Tiscornia, D.: Semantic Processing of Legal Texts: Where the Language of Law Meets the Law of Language. Springer, Heidelberg (2010)
11. Gordon, T.F., Governatori, G., Rotolo, A.: Rules and Norms: Requirements for Rule Interchange Languages in the Legal Domain. In: Governatori, G., Hall, J., Paschke, A. (eds.) RuleML 2009. LNCS, vol. 5858, pp. 282–296. Springer, Heidelberg (2009)
12. Gordon, T.F.: Constructing Legal Arguments with Rules in the Legal Knowledge Interchange Format (LKIF). In: Computable Models of the Law, Languages, Dialogues, Games, Ontologies 2008, pp. 162–184. Springer, Heidelberg (2008)
13. Gordon, T.F.: The Pleadings Game; An Artificial Intelligence Model of Procedural Justice. Springer, New York (1995); Book version of 1993 Ph.D. Thesis; University of Darmstadt (1993)
14. Governatori, G., Pham, D.H.: Dr-contract: An architecture for e-contracts in defeasible logic. International Journal of Business Process Integration and Management 5(4) (2009)
15. Governatori, G., Rotolo, A.: Changing legal systems: Legal abrogations and annulments in defeasible logic. The Logic Journal of IGPL (2010)
16. Governatori, G., Milosevic, Z., Sadiq, S.: Compliance checking between business processes and business contracts. In: Proc. EDOC 2006, pp. 221–232. IEEE (2006)

17. Governatori, G., Rotolo, A., Sartor, G.: Temporalised normative positions in defeasible logic. In: Proc. ICAIL 2005, pp. 25–34. ACM Press (2005)
18. Governatori, G., Rotolo, A.: Norm Compliance in Business Process Modeling. In: Dean, M., Hall, J., Rotolo, A., Tabet, S. (eds.) RuleML 2010. LNCS, vol. 6403, pp. 194–209. Springer, Heidelberg (2010)
19. Governatori, G.: Representing business contracts in RuleML. International Journal of Cooperative Information Systems 14(2-3), 181–216 (2005)
20. Grosof, B.: Representing e-commerce rules via situated courteous logic programs in RuleML. Electronic Commerce Research and Applications 3(1), 2–20 (2004)
21. Hage, J.C.: Reasoning with Rules – An Essay on Legal Reasoning and its Underlying Logic. Kluwer Academic Publishers, Dordrecht (1997)
22. Hu, Y.-J., Boley, H.: SemPIF: A Semantic Meta-policy Interchange Format for Multiple Web Policies. In: Web Intelligence 2010, pp. 302–307 (2010)
23. Lupo, C., Vitali, F., Francesconi, E., Palmirani, M., Winkels, R., de Maat, E., Boer, A., Mascellani, P.: General xml format(s) for legal sources - Estrella European Project IST-2004-027655. Deliverable 3.1, Faculty of Law. University of Amsterdam, Amsterdam, The Netherlands (2007)
24. Mazzei, A., Radicioni, D.P., Brighi, R.: NLP-Based Extraction of Modificatory Provisions Semantics. In: ICAIL 2009, pp. 50–57. ACM Press, New York (2009)
25. Palmirani, M., Brighi, R.: Model Regularity of Legal Language in Active Modifications. In: Casanovas, P., Pagallo, U., Sartor, G., Ajani, G. (eds.) AICOL-II/JURIX 2009. LNCS, vol. 6237, pp. 54–73. Springer, Heidelberg (2010)
26. Palmirani, M., Contissa, G., Rubino, R.: Fill the Gap in the Legal Knowledge Modelling. In: Governatori, G., Hall, J., Paschke, A. (eds.) RuleML 2009. LNCS, vol. 5858, pp. 305–314. Springer, Heidelberg (2009)
27. Palmirani, M., Governatori, G., Contissa, G.: Modelling temporal legal rules. In: ICAIL 2011 Proceedings. ACM (2011)
28. Palmirani, M.: Time Model in Normative Information Systems. In: Proceedings of the Workshop The Role of Legal Knowledge in eGovernment, ICAIL 2005 (2005)
29. Prakken, H., Sartor, G.: A dialectical model of assessing conflicting argument in legalreasoning. Artificial Intelligence and Law 4(3-4), 331–368 (1996)
30. Proceeding of the 13th International Conference on Artificial Intelligence and Law, Pittsburgh, June 6-10. ACM, NY (2011)
31. Rotolo, A., Sartor, G., Smith, C.: Good faith in contract negotiation and performance. International Journal of Business Process Integration and Management 5(4) (2009)
32. Rotolo, A.: Rule-based agents, compliance, and intention reconsideration in defeasible logic. In: Pasche, A. (ed.) RuleML 2011 - Europe. LNCS, vol. 6826, pp. 67–82. Springer, Heidelberg (2011)
33. Rubino, R., Rotolo, A., Sartor, G.: An OWL Ontology of Fundamental Legal Concepts. In: JURIX 2006, pp. 101–110. IOS (2006)
34. RuleML. The Rule Markup Initiative, `http://www.ruleml.org` (August 20, 2009)
35. Sartor, G., Palmirani, M., Francesconi, E., Biasiotti, M.: Legislative XML on Semantic web. Springer, Heidelberg (2011)
36. Sartor, G.: Legal concepts as inferential nodes and ontological categories. Artif. Intell. Law 17(3), 217–251 (2009)
37. Sartor, G.: Legal Reasoning: A Cognitive Approach to the Law. In: Pattaro, E., Rottleuthner, H., Shiner, R., Peczenik, A., Sartor, G. (eds.) A Treatise of Legal Philosophy and General Jurisprudence, vol. 5. Springer, Heidelberg (2005)
38. Wagner, G., Antoniou, G., Tabet, S., Boley, H.: The abstract syntax of RuleML – towards a general web rule language framework. In: Proc. Web Intelligence 2004, pp. 628–631. IEEE Computer Society (2004)

Author Index

Author Index